FREE THINKER

Also by Kimberly A. Hamlin

*From Eve to Evolution: Darwin, Science, and Women's
Rights in Gilded Age America*

Helen Hamilton Gardener, 1913, just as she found her calling as the suffragists' "Diplomatic Corps" in Washington, D.C.

FREE THINKER

SEX, SUFFRAGE, AND THE

EXTRAORDINARY LIFE

of

HELEN HAMILTON GARDENER

KIMBERLY A. HAMLIN

W. W. NORTON & COMPANY
Independent Publishers Since 1923

For information about permission to reproduce selections from this book, write to
Permissions, W. W. Norton & Company, Inc., 500 Fifth Avenue, New York, NY 10110

For information about special discounts for bulk purchases, please contact
W. W. Norton Special Sales at specialsales@wwnorton.com or 800-233-4830

Manufacturing by Lake Book Manufacturing
Book design by Brooke Keven
Production manager: Julia Druskin

ISBN 978-1-324-00497-4

W. W. Norton & Company, Inc., 500 Fifth Avenue, New York, N.Y. 10110
www.wwnorton.com

W. W. Norton & Company Ltd., 15 Carlisle Street, London W1D 3BS

1 2 3 4 5 6 7 8 9 0

To Ruby and Elias

Contents

PART III: TWO CALLING CARDS, 1901–1925

Preface

O N JUNE 4, 1919, the U.S. Senate followed the House in passing the Susan B. Anthony Amendment. After three generations of activism, this amendment removed "sex" as a legal basis for denying citizens the right to vote. One triumphant woman rushed to attend the signing ceremony. And why not? She had planned it—down to purchasing the fancy gold pen the vice president and the Speaker of the House would use to endorse the amendment before sending it off to the states for ratification. She took her deserved place beside both men as they signed. Flash bulbs captured her standing proud, and her image graced the front pages of newspapers across the nation. Days later, she arranged for the Smithsonian Institution to display the first-ever exhibition on the long history of the suffrage movement. Within the year, she had become the highest-ranking and highest-paid woman in federal government: the personification of what it meant, finally, for women to be full citizens. Her name—at the time—was Helen Hamilton Gardener, and she was famous.

She was also transgressive and bold and a very unlikely woman to become the public face of female citizenship. Though hardly anyone knew it—certainly not her suffrage colleagues—Gardener was a "fallen woman." In her early twenties, when she was working as a school principal in Sandusky, Ohio, she had an affair with a prominent elected official who also happened to be a married father of two. As a result, she lost her hard-earned job and her reputation. Rather than accept her fate as a fallen woman and recede quietly into the shadows, she determined to figure out why chastity was considered a woman's most valuable asset and why men were held to such different standards when it came to sex. Then she turned her findings into a lifetime of feminist reform.

Born when most women dared not speak in public and when few had a voice in public or private decisions, Gardener pioneered an independent life for herself. After her affair, she moved to a new city and changed her name from Mary Alice Chenoweth to Helen Hamilton Gardener. She did not marry until she was almost fifty. And, significantly, she was neither a mother nor a spinster. Vivacious and charismatic, Gardener loved to entertain but hated to cook. Though she lacked a steady income until her late sixties, she prided herself on her stylish clothes and elegant tastes. She tolerated the two men she lived with as husbands, endured their many foibles, and reserved her strongest emotional attachments for her female friends, especially Elizabeth Cady Stanton.

Gardener's early sex scandal and ongoing romantic struggles opened her eyes to the links between women's sexual, financial, and political autonomy. Her life's goal was to secure all three. To convince her peers that women were "self-respecting, self-directing human units with brains and bodies sacredly their own," she realized that she had to challenge the foundational stories about women inscribed in the Bible, science, fiction, and the law.[1] So she rewrote those, too. She became one of the most sought-after speakers on the nineteenth-century lecture circuit, published seven books and countless essays, supported herself, hobnobbed with the most interesting thinkers of her era, visited twenty-two countries, and was celebrated for her audacious ideas and keen wit. News reports often commented on the contrast between her tiny stature—she was barely 5 feet tall and weighed less than 100 pounds—and her big ideas.

After charting an independent and unconventional life throughout the United States and abroad, Gardener settled in Washington, D.C., and joined the suffrage movement. In the 1910s, many suffragists deftly lobbied in Washington, but only one lived next door to the

Speaker of the House of Representatives and only one became a welcome daily presence at the White House. Gardener's many successes in
D.C. demonstrate that not only is the personal political, but so, too, is
the political personal. Upon Gardener's death in 1925, suffrage leader
Maud Wood Park described her friend as "the most potent factor" in
securing congressional passage of the Nineteenth Amendment.[2] And
Carrie Chapman Catt, the former president of the National American
Woman Suffrage Association, lauded Gardener as "one of the most
courageous of our time."[3]

In her eulogy, Catt also referred to Gardener as a "great White soul,"
revealing the extent to which Gardener's story, and the larger story of
the women's suffrage movement, is about race and, more to the point,
whiteness. Even though she took great pride in her Virginia family's
bold stance against slavery and intrepid service in the Union army,
Gardener devoted the penultimate chapter of her life to securing the
vote for white women, all the while knowing that black women in the
South, along with other women of color, would not be enfranchised.
For all her intellectual bravery and iconoclasm, she could not see her
way through racism. Her life sheds new light on the racial—and racist—
dynamics underscoring the women's suffrage movement and why it was
not until the passage of the 1965 Voting Rights Act that the Nineteenth
Amendment became a reality for all women.

Gardener's dying wish was that the "George Washington, Thomas
Jefferson, and Alexander Hamiltons" of the women's rights movement
would be studied by schoolchildren, commemorated in museums,
and have their graves tended by citizens paying tribute to the women
who devoted their lives to what she called the "greatest bloodless revolution."[4] In a curious twist, her brain remains on display at Cornell
University, but hardly anyone has ever heard of Helen Hamilton Gardener or the countless other women who endured decades of scorn and
unimaginable obstacles in their long campaign to attain the right to live
as autonomous people.

A quintessentially American story of self-making, Gardener's life
provides a window into another America—a nation that women helped

to make and the nation that women imagined America might become. This book is an invitation, an entreaty, to look for more Helen Hamilton Gardeners—of all backgrounds, races, and ethnicities—to learn from the worlds they hoped to create; to revise our national stories to celebrate their experiences and contributions; and to become familiar with their complexities, failures, and triumphs so that we might better understand our own.

PART ONE

Mary Alice Chenoweth

1853–1883

1

A Chenoweth of Virginia

I have good reason to think well of my ancestors. They have
made it easier for me to be fearless in telling the truth.

—HELEN HAMILTON GARDENER, 1895

I N 1884, Helen Hamilton Gardener made her national debut by delivering a speech entitled "Men, Women, and Gods." Poised behind a
music stand at New York City's Chickering Hall, she told a rapt audience that the biblical creation story had been written by fallible men,
not enacted by an omniscient creator, and that this bogus tale had
resulted in the degradation of women for centuries. As a woman who
entered public life by denouncing the Adam and Eve myth, Gardener
understood the importance of origin stories. She had at least two herself: one for Mary "Alice" Chenoweth, her birth name, and one for
Helen Hamilton Gardener, the name she chose for herself in 1884.

Not much is known about the actual birth of Alice, as she preferred to
be called, the youngest child of Rev. Alfred and Catherine (Peale) Chenoweth of Virginia. She always listed her birth as occurring on January
21, 1853, but Virginia did not yet require birth certificates, so none exists
for Alice. Within a few months of baby Alice's arrival, the Chenoweths
departed Virginia for good, leaving few traces. Even though she lived

in the state for only the first few months of her seventy-two years of life, Alice always prided herself on being a Chenoweth of Virginia.

Alice did not receive much money or property from her Chenoweth ancestors, but she did inherit a strong family lore and the confidence that she was descended from people of significance. For centuries, the Chenoweths had been stalwart landowners, town settlers, and Westward expanders. In their native England and, later, in the New World, the Chenoweths bought and cleared land, built homes and established families, planted crops, and created communities across their holdings. Over hundreds of years, the Chenoweth characteristics of tenacity and property ownership became inscribed in their understanding of themselves and their place on this earth.

The first Chenoweths to leave England for the American colonies were John and Mary, who arrived in 1715. Believing themselves descended from Lord Baltimore, John and Mary settled in Baltimore County to claim 7,200 acres of land near the Chesapeake Bay that Maryland colonial officials had taken over from the Susquehannock people. From there, John and Mary's descendants went on to settle towns, villages, and farms from Maryland to Virginia to Ohio and Indiana, all the way to Kentucky and Missouri. Alice's great-grandfather, a Revolutionary War veteran also named John, eventually settled in Berkeley County, Virginia (now West Virginia).[1]

In between John Chenoweth's homestead in West Virginia and the graves of Alice's parents in Greencastle, Indiana, lie nearly a dozen towns, streets, and squares named Chenoweth. As founding families of many white communities, the Chenoweths tended to marry well, aligning themselves with other prominent landowners and civic leaders. Later generations became ministers and inventors, craftsmen and builders, doctors and statesmen.

But Alice's family stories contrasted starkly with the realities of her life as a white woman in mid-nineteenth-century America, a woman who would lose her name in marriage, who was not allowed by law to own property, to participate in politics, or to lead any communities herself. Her life's trajectory testifies to the outrage she felt at the chasm between her birthright as a Chenoweth of Virginia and the legal and cultural constraints placed upon her as a woman.

⎯⎯⎯

THE OUTLINES OF Alice Chenoweth's life began to take shape four decades before she was born, with the birth of her beloved father in February of 1809. Alfred Griffith Chenoweth grew up surrounded by propertied white elites and the privileges accorded to landowning patriarchs in Virginia. His grandfather, John Sr., owned more land than nearly anyone else in Berkeley County, Virginia, and his father, John Jr., inherited much of it. John Sr. owned between five and eight slaves; John Jr. owned two, Jerry and Mariah.[2] Alfred and his brothers grew up in a home with a library and tutors, in "an atmosphere of scholarly investigation and calm," understanding that they were destined to succeed their father as county squires.

Early on, Alfred learned that with land and slave ownership came exalted status within the community and within the Episcopal Church of his birth. Alice later recalled that the tethering of wealth, enslavement, and church membership in antebellum Virginia did not sit well with her father. "The easy-going, gentle Episcopalianism of [Alfred's] home-training, with its morning and evening, perfunctory, family prayers, its 'table grace' and its Sunday service, where all the leading families of the county were to be seen, and where the Rector read with so much finish and the choir sang so divinely, the same old hymns, week after week, had so far been as much a part of his life," Alice wrote, "and were accepted as mechanically,—as were the daily meals, the unpaid negro labor, and the fact this his father, the old 'Squire,' sat in the best pew, because he had built and endowed the finest church in the State."[3] Rather than the privilege of sitting in the finest pew, young Alfred craved a more authentic connection with his God and with his fellow man.

By the late 1820s, Alfred began expressing serious doubts about his family's religion and its tacit, sometimes explicit, endorsement of slavery. All around him he heard of upstart faiths, preached by men freed from tradition and even from churches; men who rode across the countryside on their horses, sharing the good news of Christ's salvation with hundreds of people gathered in makeshift tents. These new "circuit riding" ministers and the personal, urgent beliefs they professed resonated with Alfred. Like thousands of other Americans, Alfred was born again in Christ during the Second Great Awakening.

Between the 1820s and the 1850s, Christians such as Alice's father sought to revitalize both society and themselves. Their motto was "Make thyself perfect as God in heaven is perfect." Prompted by a millennialist conviction that the "cosmos was crumbling," Americans inaugurated a host of reforms—from abolition to temperance to vegetarianism—and new religious movements to promote them.[4] Unlike the Great Awakening of the 1740s, the goal of the Second Great Awakening was not to revive individual churches but to make American society itself sacred. Rapid industrialization and urbanization had given rise to numerous social problems—the entrenchment of slavery, intergenerational poverty, prostitution, crime, public drunkenness—that reformers hoped to eradicate through good works and active prayer.

Abolition was by far the most popular movement of the era, with temperance a distant second. Women and men alike were caught up in the reformist zeal, and by the 1840s, some white women began to understand their own second-class status as linked to that of enslaved people. In 1838, Sarah Grimké, an abolitionist from a slave-owning family in South Carolina, published "Letters on the Equality of the Sexes," in which she argued that women should be allowed to speak in public, as she had been chastised for doing, and that women were inherently equal to men. Religious denominations split over whether or not to oppose slavery, and abolitionists splintered over whether or not women should be allowed to speak in public.

Objecting to slavery but ambivalent about the role of women, Alfred Chenoweth was drawn to Methodism. On his nineteenth birthday, in 1828, Alfred was baptized in Virginia's Opequon Creek, disowned by his father, and welcomed as a circuit riding preacher by the Methodists. For the next six years, Alfred traveled all over Virginia and Pennsylvania telling the good news of Christ's salvation. He composed his sermons while riding on his faithful horse Selim, singing hymns to himself along the way.[5] By 1836, Alfred had reconciled with his father and been admitted as a minister and a deacon in the Methodist Church.[6]

While crisscrossing the state of Virginia, Alfred rode along the Spotswood Trail (Route 33), a major East-West thoroughfare. He likely frequented the churches and homes near Peales Crossroads, at the corner of the Spotswood Trail and Route 276, a North-South artery, 5 miles from Harrisonburg, Virginia.[7] For generations, and even today, Peales Crossroads has greeted travelers arriving from all four directions.

Peales Crossroads came into existence in 1811 when Bernard Peale bought 101 acres near the Spotswood Trail and built a log cabin for his family, including his daughter Catherine Ann, who was born in 1812.[8] Bernard Peale owned several slaves, and in 1816, he was tried and acquitted of whipping an enslaved woman named Rachel to death.[9]

Two years later, Bernard Peale died. His daughter Catherine Ann was just six years old. To what extent the death of Rachel or the death of her father affected Ann, as she was called, we will never know. Like nearly all women of her time, Ann left behind no diaries or letters (and most of the Rockingham County, Virginia, records were burned during the Civil War). Ann grew up on the homestead at Peales Crossroads, attending the Presbyterian Church across Spotswood Trail with her mother and siblings. Her eldest brother, Jonathan, took over the family lands, leaving Ann to help supervise the household, meals, and childcare.

In 1838, at the relatively advanced age of twenty-six, Ann Peale married the circuit riding minister Alfred Griffith Chenoweth, whom she probably met as he rode through Peales Crossroads.[10] Ann's marriage to the near-penniless itinerant minister was surely not what the Peale family had hoped for their first-born daughter. A few years after Ann's marriage, her brother Jonathan razed the original Peale log cabin and built a Greek Revival mansion in its place. Ann's younger sister Amanda married George Keezell II, son of the founder of Keezletown and an esteemed Virginia patriarch, a much more suitable match for a daughter of Peales Crossroads.

Ann and Alfred Chenoweth, on the other hand, owned no home and moved to a new town each year as the Methodist Church demanded. If Alfred had resented the connection between a parishioner's wealth and that parishioner's standing in the Episcopal Church, he certainly went to the opposite extreme in joining the ranks of itinerant Methodist preachers.

Upon their marriage, Ann brought along her inherited slaves, and her father-in-law insisted that the young couple also take Jerry, the enslaved man who had helped to raise Alfred, and his family with them as well. Alfred had already realized that he opposed slavery, but he tried to draw a moral distinction between inheriting slaves and buying people outright. Together with the enslaved people they had inherited, Alfred and Ann continued his itinerant preacher lifestyle throughout the 1840s and into the 1850s. By 1853, they had seven children, each born in a different house in a different Virginia town.

The youngest of the seven Chenoweth children, Alice, was born in January 1853, near Winchester, Virginia. Just three years later and less than 30 miles south of Peales Crossroads, Woodrow Wilson was born in Staunton, Virginia, to another minister and his wife. As a boy born to a family of privilege, however, Wilson's life would not mirror Alice's in any meaningful way until the two Virginians reconnected in the 1910s, in the White House, and realized that their shared Virginia heritage bound them together.

AFTER THE Compromise of 1850 strengthened the Fugitive Slave Act, abolitionist sentiment grew in fervor. Reverend Alfred Chenoweth could no longer quietly abide his complicity in this humanitarian crisis. He determined to raise his children without the taint of slavery and to emancipate the men and women that his family had held in bondage. But how? Because Virginia was a slave state, Alfred prepared manumission papers and moved everyone to Washington, D.C., in 1854, when Alice was just one year old.

In Washington, Alfred was appointed pastor at Ebenezer United Methodist Church, at the corner of 4th and D Streets, SE, one of the first churches founded by African Americans during slavery.[11] He hoped that his post at Ebenezer would help Jerry, Mariah, and the other people formerly enslaved by his family to acclimate to their new lives as freedmen and freedwomen. But Alfred worried whether these men and women, especially the older ones, would be able to find work in the District and what freedom would mean for them in this precarious context.[12]

Meanwhile, Alfred's former neighbors condemned his "damned foolishness" because it threatened the social order of their society. The Chenoweths were cast out by their Virginia relatives and friends, who fretted that Alfred's action would upset the balance of power on their own farms and plantations. Alice's mother Ann bore the brunt of her husband's decision, a decision in which she neither had a say nor agreed with fully but had to defend just the same.[13] Ann never returned to Peales Crossroads and would raise her seven children in a series of unfamiliar places.

Even though Alice was just one when her family left Virginia, this move shaped her understanding of her country, her upbringing, and herself. Indeed, it was one of the defining moments of her life. Alfred's courageous decision also cast him as Alice's lifelong hero. As she would later recall, "To those whose traditions of ancestry all center about one locality, it costs a fearful struggle to tear up root and branch and strike out into unknown fields among people of a different type and class; with dissimilar ideas and standards of action and belief. To such it is almost like the threat or presence of death in the household." Her father's decision required "a heroism, a fidelity to conscience and, withal, a confidence in one's own judgement and beliefs that surpass the normal limit." He made this change "in pursuance of a moral conviction," knowing it would "surely result in financial loss and material discomfort," something no one should expect from anyone who was "less than heroic."[14]

Alice was just an adolescent when she abandoned her belief in the biblical origins story that she had descended from a woman who dared eat fruit from the Tree of Knowledge, but she held tenaciously to Chenoweth family lore and the memory of her father's bravery. She was equally, if paradoxically, drawn to the stature of the Chenoweth name and to her father's decision to refuse his birthright, even though neither was supposed to pertain to a young woman. Alice learned early on that bucking social customs, family ties, and conventional wisdom in support of one's moral convictions came with steep personal and financial costs. But in the tradition of her iconoclastic father, she would choose this same path in her own life, time and time again.

RIGHTLY PREDICTING that the sectional conflict over slavery would soon turn violent and that much of the fight would take place in Virginia, Alice's extended Chenoweth family had begun buying land in Indiana in the 1840s. First her uncle John, Alfred's older brother, moved to Putnam County; a few years later, his aging parents joined him. And finally, in 1855, Alfred and his family, plus baby Alice's black nurse Aunt Judy (a former slave), moved to Greencastle, Indiana, where Alfred had secured an appointment as a Methodist minister.

In Greencastle, the Chenoweths lived in the upscale neighborhood known as the Eastern Enlargement, where their neighbors included the pharmaceutical pioneer Eli Lilly, the architect Elisha Braman, and faculty members from Indiana Asbury University, the new Methodist college (now known as DePauw University).[15] This would be the first home that Alice was old enough to remember and the first home that the Chenoweths lived in for longer than one year.

Greencastle had been settled as the county seat of Putnam County in the 1820s and boasted nearly 3,000 residents by the time the Chenoweths arrived in the 1850s. The town converged on a two-story, brick Greek Revival courthouse, ringed by restaurants and shops, including

Alice Chenoweth, age two, with her older sister Julia, living in Greencastle, Indiana.

Eli Lilly's first drug store, which opened in 1861. The spiritual and community center of Greencastle, however, was Indiana Asbury University, which began enrolling male students in 1837. In 1852, the railroad came to town, bringing increased growth and commerce and also, most likely, the Reverend Chenoweth and his family. With fertile farmlands, thriving local industry, and a prestigious new college, Greencastle prospered throughout the nineteenth century and attracted many settlers from the East and South.[16]

To the former county squires of Virginia, however, Greencastle seemed a provincial boondocks. As recently as 1836, the county clerk had paid residents $2 for each wolf they killed.[17] One early resident lamented that it seemed as if the townspeople had "expended their entire stock of enterprise and public spirit upon the one object of founding the university, and have nothing left for further improvement."[18] Another observer recalled that in 1854, Greencastle was "celebrated for the unprogressive spirit and rusticity of its inhabitants, its miserable dwellings and filthy hotels."[19]

Even with new railroads, commerce, and colleges, Indiana lacked the gravitas of Virginia: no founding fathers or presidents hailed from Indiana (President William Henry Harrison served as governor of the Indiana Territories, but he was born in Virginia), and it had only been a state since 1816. Even the famed arboreal beauty of Putnam County was no match for the grand vistas of the Shenandoah Mountains. The Chenoweths missed the stature that being a Chenoweth in Virginia and a Virginian in America had conferred.

Shortly after the Chenoweths arrived, Alice's two oldest brothers, Bernard and William, began taking classes at Indiana Asbury (girls were not yet allowed to enroll); Alice and her younger siblings were taught by private tutors.[20] In public school or with a private tutor, the books most commonly assigned to young students in the Midwest were *McGuffey's Eclectic Readers*, the best-selling school books and, by the 1870s, the second-most-read books in America, behind only the King James Bible. The *Readers* contained stories, poems, and history lessons in increasing levels of difficulty. Through stories such as "Do Not Meddle," "Boy on a Farm," and "Respect for the Sabbath Rewarded," children learned about gender and racial norms as well as the industriousness and Christian virtues of the ideal American.[21]

Alice later recalled chafing against this rote style of learning, with its emphasis on memorization and its clear delineation between right and wrong. She remembered one grammar lesson that required students to use their dictionaries to complete the sentence "I like to ___ in the garden." Eager to please the teacher and show off her erudition, one not-so-bright girl wrote in "ferment" because the dictionary told her it was a synonym for work. This impressed upon Alice that it might be misguided "to teach young people to have that absolutely blind faith in dictionary definitions and synonyms." "Shades of meaning" are lost "by this blind adherence to authority."[22] Alice's lifelong aversion to unquestioned authority seemed innate.

Alice's greatest teachers, however, were her family and her house full of books. Reverend Chenoweth was admired for being "affable, courteous, and companionable" as well as "sound in theology, unremitting in labor, and faithful to duty."[23] His youngest daughter imbibed these character lessons along with the warmth of his good reputation. From her father, Alice also learned biblical stories and the Methodist commitment to putting "faith and love into action."

In addition to her father's regular Sunday sermons, Alice and her siblings were expected to attend annual revivals. Each year, the local churches joined together to sponsor these week-long events. As one such week dragged on, Alice and her friend Isabel felt panicked that they were the only two "eager sinners" in their Sunday school class who had not yet been saved. As the two girls stood worrying in the revival tent, "a tall, thin, dark, and terrible looking" clergyman came toward them, clasped their hands, and demanded: "Do you want to go to Hell?"

The minister's "explosive voice" made Alice "jump out of her small boots, while Isabel fell to weeping bitterly." The minister brought the girls to the mourner's bench, where they continued to cry until they fell asleep. Hours later, the clergyman found them still there, sleeping, and pronounced them saved. All the townspeople rejoiced and congratulated them. The following day, Alice and Isabel admitted to each other that they felt no different, despite their purported salvation. The next Sunday they were "taken in on probation" at church. Six months later the girls were confirmed as full members of the Methodist Church.[24] Later in life, Alice credited the "extreme conservatism of this early training" with influencing her "radical views on questions of religion."[25]

Rather than seeking inspiration from her father's Bible, Alice was drawn to the books of her eldest and favorite brother, Bernard Peale Chenoweth. Seventeen years her senior, Bernard was like a second father to Alice. In Greencastle, Bernard earned a reputation as being "very well educated, for he was a youth who got at the insides of books, character, and life."[26] She also befriended his classmates, including Greencastle's most famous son, John Clark Ridpath, who would go on to become a prominent historian and writer and, eventually, a colleague to Alice. Her older brothers nicknamed her Robin because her eyes and mouth were always wide open and she "saw and heard everything."[27]

Like his father had done a generation earlier, young Bernard revolted against the religion of his parents. He began by reading the works of Thomas Paine, one of the most revered yet controversial contributors to American intellectual history. Credited with stirring up popular passion in support of the American Revolution through his best-selling pamphlet "Common Sense," Paine nevertheless had become anathema to mainstream Americans by the early 1800s. In fact, Paine nearly rotted to death from an infected ulcer in a French prison because the American representative in France so opposed his blasphemous writings that he refused to intervene on Paine's behalf. It took the election of Paine's old friend Thomas Jefferson as president to bring him back to America in 1802. But even Jefferson's blessing could not soften the fallout resulting from the publication of *The Age of Reason*.[28]

In *The Age of Reason*, Paine critiqued the hypocrisy, material greed, and lust for power that he believed characterized the Christian Church, and he proclaimed that he did not accept any Bible stories that contravened the laws of science and reason. In other words, he rejected virgin births, earth-cleansing floods, water turned to wine, and the spontaneous generation of loaves and fishes. In place of these fables, Paine praised the God who created nature and rational minds. Bernard Chenoweth sided with Paine. In the fervently religious Chenoweth household, Alice recalled that Bernard had to buy two copies of *The Age of Reason* because their mother burned the first one.[29]

INTELLECTUAL SKIRMISHES ASIDE, Alice's family adjusted well to life in Putnam County. In 1858, the Methodist Church promoted Alfred to presiding elder over the Northwest District, and by 1860, he had amassed over $15,000 worth of property.[30] To purchase this land, however, Alfred borrowed heavily from his father John. Alfred Chenoweth owned many acres of land, but his family remained cash poor.

One Christmas, Alice later recounted to a friend, she wanted to buy her mother a sewing machine and her father a gold pencil. Having no understanding of money or that her family had little of it, she went to the general store at Courthouse Square. The proprietor told Alice's mother Ann about her visit, and Ann managed to convince Alice that all her parents desired for Christmas were pink and white gum drops. Alice had always supposed that if her family didn't have something it was simply because they did not want it, so her mother's explanation made perfect sense. Growing up, she "had never heard and did not know the meaning of 'we cannot afford it.'"[31]

Even as the Chenoweths adjusted to their new life, Indiana would never be home. After all, they had not so much moved to Putnam County as they had moved away from Virginia in the hopes of avoiding war. But they soon learned that even in Greencastle, they would not be able to escape the coming national crisis.

Indiana was a free state dominated by the Republican Party. But Putnam County had been settled by Southerners, and Democrats represented its citizens in Congress and in the mayor's office. A vocal minority of Putnam County residents sympathized with slave ownership, in part because many, like the Chenoweths, had relatives in the South.[32] With Greencastle so close to the National Road and on two railroad lines, many prominent politicians and thinkers passed through town. Alice and her siblings were privy to increasingly heated debates about slavery and secession.

Eldest son Bernard—who had been named for his maternal grandfather, Bernard Peale, the man acquitted in 1816 for whipping his slave Rachel to death—felt the call to action. At age twenty-two, Bernard left college and traveled throughout the South, searching for a place where he could make a meaningful stand against slavery. The most pressing slavery-related question had to do with whether Kansas would be admitted to the Union as a slave state or as a free state. In 1859, Bernard moved to St. Joseph, Missouri, a border town at the epicenter of this controversy, and invested $1,500 in a Free Soil newspaper called the *Free Democrat*. Together with his partners, Bernard "set the border aflame" with his outspoken opposition to slavery.[33]

On March 4, 1861, Abraham Lincoln was sworn in as the sixteenth president of the United States, prompting the escalation of hostilities with the seceding Southern states. The *Free Democrat* published its last edition on April 13. "At the firing of the first shot," Bernard enlisted in the Union army.[34] Days later, Alice's second-eldest brother, William Erasmus, was among the first to join the 16th Indiana Infantry Regiment. Alice followed along on their adventures through letters. Even when separated, "Robin" was watching and learning.

Alice recalled that her mother "felt faint and sick when she realized that two of her boys had gone to fight against her people. She knew that her own brothers and nephews would all be on the other side, and that [Alfred's] were there too."[35] Alice's uncle Jonathan Peale, Ann's oldest brother, had inherited the family's land at Peales Crossroads, and by 1860, he owned more than a dozen slaves. Jonathan leveraged his privilege in full support of the Confederacy. During the Shenandoah Valley Campaign of 1862, the Peales hosted Stonewall Jackson and sixty of his troops at their magnificent home. General Jackson even used the house, with its second-floor porches facing in both directions, as his headquarters during the Battle of Cross Keys and, later, as a hospital.[36] Alice's aunt Amanda Peale and her husband George Keezell also supported the Confederacy. Together they had one son, George Bernard Keezell, who assisted Confederate troops in the mundane tasks assigned to boys too young to take up arms.[37] The Civil War splintered Alice's family.

THROUGHOUT THE FALL OF 1861, Bernard remained on the western front, while William's regiment was sent back to the Winchester, Virginia, region of Alice's birth. On October 21, William's unit was dispatched on a routine reconnaissance mission across the Potomac River, near Ball's Bluff. This mission ended in a humiliating defeat for the Union army and, among other things, revealed to the Confederates that Union leaders did not know their way around Virginia.

Following the Union trouncing at Ball's Bluff, Indiana governor Oliver Morton, a passionate supporter of Lincoln, implored Reverend Chenoweth to volunteer his services as a Union scout in Virginia. Who could know Virginia backroads and valleys better than a circuit riding minister who had once traversed them on foot and on horseback? "It is my old State," Alfred protested. "I love it and my people. I have done enough for my country. I have done my share. I have given my property, my friends, my home, and now my boys—all, all I have given for my conscience and my country's sake. Surely I have done my whole duty. I will not betray my State." But Governor Morton forwarded his name to President Lincoln. The president summoned Alfred to the White House and beseeched him "to make [Union generals] as familiar with [Virginia] as you are yourself."[38] With son William's life in danger, Alfred reluctantly agreed.

This decision left Alice's mother at home alone with their four youngest children, ranging in age from eight to seventeen (son John had died years earlier). Alfred spent three months mapping the land of his youth and showing Union commanders its "real topography," as Lincoln had commanded.[39] His Methodist colleagues recalled that Reverend Chenoweth led "the marshaled hosts of freedom through the mountain gaps and defiles, which in earlier years he had traversed as an itinerant preacher, to decisive and cheering victories."[40]

Shortly after the Union victory at the Battle of Shiloh in April 1862, Alfred returned home to Greencastle. The Chenoweth family briefly rejoiced before learning, in June, that Bernard had become ill with typhoid fever and what he described as "temporary insanity."[41] After returning to active duty, Bernard became a protégé of General Ulysses S. Grant and was dispatched to New Orleans, where he met seventeen-year-old Caroline Van Deusen, a wealthy debutante. He returned to Greencastle to marry her in March 1863.[42] Bernard's visit cheered the Chenoweths, who waited for news from William, who eventually became captain of the 16th Indiana Infantry. Just days after Bernard's wedding, sixteen-year-old Alfred, Alice's youngest brother, shocked the family by secretly enlisting in the Union army. That July, he contracted "epidemic opthalmia," for which the Army surgeon repeatedly "burnt his eyes with blue stone" (copper sulfide). Alfred continued to fight with his regiment, even as his eyesight deteriorated.[43]

During these long months of war, Alice and her two sisters helped their mother around the house and tried to distract themselves from thoughts of their brothers in uniform. To them, the war meant stoic silences, anxious nights, and feelings of uselessness. "Silent, patient, inactive anxiety! The part of war the women bear is by far the harder part," Alice would later recall.[44] For the rest of her life, she was haunted by memories of the Civil War. Years later she attended a Decoration Day parade in New York City where aged and infirm Civil War veterans paraded with their tattered flags. More than the men themselves, the sight of these decrepit flags, so lovingly crafted by bereft wives, sisters, and mothers, devastated her. "Poor, tattered silken wrecks! What memories they arouse! What tears they start!" she wrote. Upon realizing that no one cheered for "these pathetic symbols of glory and of death," she found herself "with pictures of unutterable sorrow in my heart and tears on my cheeks."[45]

Ten-year-old Alice interpreted these wartime feelings of uselessness and angst differently than did her older sisters, who were already contemplating marriage. Alice felt that she had more in common with her brothers. In the autobiographical novel she later wrote about her family's Civil War experiences, she gave herself no sisters. Alice wrote as if she had been the only Chenoweth daughter, a young girl whose three doting brothers sent news from the front lines filling her imagination with brave sacrifices and battles, intellectual and martial. She later declared that readers of this novel, *An Unofficial Patriot* (1894), "will know all about me and mine."[46]

EAGERLY ANTICIPATING a visit from newlyweds Bernard and Caroline, Reverend Chenoweth delivered a particularly inspired sermon on Sunday, April 24, 1864, focusing on his happy religious experiences, and then served communion to congregants in Indianapolis.[47] Inclement weather prevented him from traveling home, so he spent the night at a friend's house. The next morning he died of a massive heart attack. He was 55.

Alfred's death shattered Alice, age eleven, who would later describe her father as "the soul of my home" and attribute his untimely death to the strain of the war.[48] Within a few months, Alice's paternal grandparents, John and Mary Chenoweth, followed their son to the grave. By the end of the summer, all three of her brothers—Bernard, William, and Alfred—had sustained devastating war wounds. In addition to Bernard's typhoid and Alfred's eye injuries, William's leg was crushed by a horse, leaving him in constant pain and unable to do sustained work for the rest of his life.[49]

Alfred's sudden death left Ann with three single daughters, ages eleven to twenty, a farm, a homestead, and several hundred acres of land to manage in and around Greencastle. When her own father had died, Ann's mother relied on her oldest son to run things. Because of the war, Ann had no such option. As a widowed woman in 1864, Ann had few options at all.

Throughout much of the nineteenth century, a married woman's legal identity was subsumed under that of her husband in the legal tradition known as "coverture." Married women could control no property—including their own earnings or inheritance—and they had few, if any, legal rights to the children born from their own bodies. Beginning in the 1820s, freethinking lecturer Frances "Fanny" Wright and a few other intrepid women had urged legal reforms for married women. This movement gained ground after abolitionist women, including Sarah and Angelina Grimké, began lobbying for women's rights. In the 1840s and 1850s, some states revised married women's property laws. Male legislators were often compelled to action not by concerns about women's autonomy but rather by paternal fears of dissolute sons-in-law. If a wealthy man had no sons and thus had to leave property to his daughter, who could say whether or not his son-in-law would take good care of it? Better to pass laws allowing daughters to retain their inherited lands. Husbands drawn to risky business ventures also favored these statutes as a way of preserving their assets from creditors.[50]

By the 1860s, pioneering women's rights activists, such as Elizabeth Cady Stanton, who decades later would become Alice's close friend, had attained minimal rights for married women, but these varied widely by state. Reformers suspended their efforts during the Civil War so that they could fully support the Union, only to see many of their hard-won legal gains overturned. As Ann struggled to navigate the byzantine probate proceedings required of widows, she likely had no idea that women had begun organizing to change the laws to make them more favorable to women like herself.

Even though Indiana had among the more progressive laws regarding married women's rights, the Putnam County Probate Court did not appoint Ann to administrate Alfred's will, and she had to petition the court to be appointed legal guardian of her own minor children. Nor could she dispense with the family's property or money as she saw fit—she had to first get the probate court's permission each and every time she wanted to sell a parcel of land. Compounding matters, Alfred Chenoweth had died in debt. He had repeatedly borrowed money from his father John, leaving Alfred's estate indebted to his father's.

Within months of Alfred's passing, Ann received court approval to sell the family house and land. With this cash in hand, Ann was able to repay most, but not all, of the estate's debts, leaving a total of $625.52 for each child, from which Ann paid herself for feeding and housing them.[51]

The stress of Alfred's death and of settling his estate overwhelmed Ann. With one son already dead and three sons on active duty, Ann entrusted her youngest child Alice to her own devices and steered her other two daughters to early marriage. After his discharge in the summer of 1864, Bernard moved with his wife Caroline to St. Charles County, Missouri, near the town of Dardenne, to try his hand at farming. The rest of the family soon joined him there in the hopes of starting over once again.

In moving from Virginia to Indiana to Missouri, the Chenoweths followed a familiar path for members of the Virginia gentry. One of the most prominent families in Dardenne were the Hatchers, descended from John Hatcher, a Revolutionary War veteran and Virginia state legislator, whose son Henry had helped settled the town.[52] Seizing her best opportunity for advancement, in 1866 Alice's sister Julia, then seventeen, married thirty-seven year old Frederick Hatcher, a Union veteran and son of town founder Henry.[53] The following year, Alice's brother William married Parmela Hatcher, Frederick's younger sister. Alice and her mother moved in with William and Parmela and soon their three children under the age of four.

Ann still had to travel back to Indiana several times a year to appear before the Putnam County Probate Court to provide receipts for her expenditures and report on her children, including her oldest daughter Kate, who had married a farmer and returned to Indiana. On October 29, 1867, Ann trekked to Greencastle to request that the court remove her as Alice's legal guardian. She affirmed that Alice was living with William and that he should be her legal guardian; the court agreed.[54]

There is no way to tell what fourteen-year-old Alice thought about this arrangement. Even if she and her mother remained in the same house, Alice must have known that her mother had revoked an official legal tie with her. She also might have wondered, rightly, what was to become of her. For a family whose ancestral pride was grounded in land ownership, this branch of Chenoweths now owned scarcely an acre. The family homestead gone, Alice shuffled between the farms of her older siblings. The stories she had grown up hearing about the Chenoweths and Peales of Virginia seemed a far cry from the reality of the Chenoweths of Dardenne, Missouri.

The Chenoweths arrived in Dardenne a few years before the advent of electricity and mechanization. For them, farm life meant backbreaking labor and constant uncertainty. The vast majority of white farmers in St. Charles County raised wheat and corn as well as cattle and swine. Prior to the Civil War, the owners of large plantations relied on the labor of enslaved people to clear and harvest the crops. As yeoman farmers after the war, the Chenoweth-Hatchers may have employed a few black sharecroppers or freedmen, but if so, no such records exist. Most likely, they worked the land themselves. As a teenager, Alice's life revolved around preparing meals, tending crops and animals, and helping care for a growing brood of nieces and nephews. The Hatchers were founding members of the Dardenne Presbyterian Church, and "nearly everybody within reach of the church attended the services."[55] Alice was likely conscripted into church attendance whether she wanted to go or not. One bright spot to farm life: young Alice developed a lifelong love of horseback riding.

Neither did farm life suit Alice's brother Bernard. His lingering typhoid made it difficult for him to work the long farm hours, and he lacked the capital necessary to get a successful farm up and running. A

Alice Chenoweth, age sixteen, hoping for a life beyond her siblings' farms in Dardenne, Missouri.

Civil War friend encouraged him to apply for a job as superintendent of schools of Worchester, Massachusetts. A glowing letter of recommendation from Ulysses S. Grant guaranteed the post, and Bernard moved his family across the country. Alice never saw her favorite brother again.

Bernard's failing health made it impossible for him to stay in Massachusetts. His doctor advised him to seek a warmer climate, so within a year, Bernard returned to Virginia, this time to Richmond. Bernard purchased three cows and sold milk to his neighbors. Even though he was a valiant soldier, a trusted officer, and a good man, Bernard made "no money during the war and has made none since."[56]

Grant's election as president in 1868 gave Bernard hope. It seemed his fortunes might rebound when Grant nominated him to be the U.S. consul in China. This post and its $4,000 annual salary provided welcome news for Bernard, who by then was "living on pawned watches and rings . . . but painfully short of money for dinners for himself, wife, and two children." Bernard eagerly accepted the post, but his typhoid was too far advanced for him to enjoy it. He served in China for just six months before dying in the summer of 1870.[57] He was thirty-four years old. His widow ably fulfilled his duties and petitioned to be made the U.S. consul herself. Caroline was not formally appointed, but some histories of the Foreign Service include her as an early female diplomat.[58]

Alice was devastated by Bernard's early death. Bernard had been a passionate abolitionist, doting brother, and "a kind son and a good man" who had "shielded his widowed mother from every hardship." But because Bernard was also an "unbeliever," their mother Ann fretted over his destination in the afterlife. "As [Ann] sat and gazed at his dear face in a transport of grief," Alice wrote in her first published essay several years later, "the door opened and her preacher came in to bring her the comfort of religion." But to Alice, the minister's words seemed cruel. He told this grieving mother that because Bernard had "not accepted what was freely given" he was damned to hell. The minister told Ann that she would never be reunited with Bernard and that she should instead focus on loving her youngest living son, Alfred, a churchgoing man who had recently become a doctor, settling with his wife, Ella Crume, in nearby Olney, Missouri.[59]

Alice's mother decided to follow Alfred to Olney, limiting her youngest daughter's options. Brother William planned to move his family to Cowley County, Kansas, well over 400 miles away, where his prospects looked better. Should Alice make the trek with William's family to an even more remote part of the country? Move in with her pious brother Alfred the doctor, as her mother had done? Remain on sister Julia's farm in Dardenne?[60] Or should she marry young, as both sisters had done, and start her own family?

None of these alternatives appealed. No doubt Alice also knew that some colleges admitted women, but even if she could gain admission, who would pay her tuition and board? Even as a relatively privileged white female from a landowning family, Alice's options were very limited. She knew that there were few ways for her to sustain herself financially, most of them distasteful and really only one respectable. Inspired by the daring examples of her cherished father and eldest brother and with little left to lose, Alice chose to make her own way in the world as a teacher.

2

The Best and Cheapest Teachers

The past education of woman gave her an outlook which
simply embraced a husband or nothing at all, which was often
only a choice between two of a kind.
                              —HELEN HAMILTON GARDENER, 1885

B Y THE SUMMER OF 1872, nineteen-year-old Alice Chenoweth had packed up her meager belongings and traveled the 380 miles from Dardenne, Missouri, to Cincinnati, Ohio.[1] During the eight years since her father's sudden death, Alice had come of age watching her nation and her family teeter on the brink of destruction.

Alice had witnessed her sisters and sisters-in-law bear and bury babies and her brothers suffer from gruesome wartime wounds, both visible and invisible. She had watched her mother struggle to remain financially solvent and to navigate the various legal and societal barriers erected to keep women dependent on men. Growing up on tales of her father's bravery and forced to sit on the sidelines awaiting her brothers' news from the front, Alice had imagined a different life from that on a farm in Dardenne. In later years, she would never mention having lived in Missouri.

To a farm girl in Missouri, Cincinnati appealed as a big city, easily accessible by steamboat or direct train from St. Louis. By 1870, Cincinnati was the sixth-most populous city in America and one of the nation's most densely populated urban centers. Cincinnati boasted 45 miles of streetcar tracks, 170 miles of gas mains, 5,290 public lamps, and 151 firemen who ably protected every district. In 1869, the Cincinnati Red Stockings inaugurated professional baseball, and by the end of the decade, Cincinnati opened its world-class Music Hall and Zoo.[2] In the 1870s, the "Queen City" was the place to be.

When Alice stepped off the train, she would have smelled the barley and hops from one of the city's legendary breweries as well as the scent of fresh-cut lumber from one of the nearby lumber yards. She would also have smelled the slaughterhouses—Cincinnati earned its nickname "Porkopolis" by leading the nation in the production of pork. As a bustling manufacturing city, coal powered life in Cincinnati, creating dark thick smoke that obscured Alice's view even on perfectly sunny days. What a thrill to witness, smog and all, the growth of industry and the making of an American metropolis.

As she traversed the few blocks from the train station to her boarding house on West 8th Street, Alice passed Joseph Brothers Scrap Iron Yard, various livery stables, a Presbyterian church, a German Protestant church, Baptist churches, three public markets selling produce and flowers, and several schools. She could also glimpse the largest suspension bridge in the world, built by John Roebling, who later designed the Brooklyn Bridge.

Alice's neighborhood, now known as the West End, had borne intimate witness to the coming of the Civil War and its aftermath. For generations, freedom seekers had crossed the Ohio River from Kentucky into Cincinnati, from slavery into freedom, and many settled in neighborhoods like the West End, not far from the river. The children in Cincinnati's public schools did not model the diversity in the West End neighborhood, though, because black students attended segregated schools.

This multiracial industrial neighborhood was not the only legacy of the Civil War visible to Alice. On her walks, she would have also passed by two of the nation's leading manufacturers of prosthetic limbs, James A. Foster's Union Patent Artificial Limbs and Dr. Bly's Patent Artificial Limbs, and maybe even nodded to veterans on their way to and from selecting new arms and legs.[3] Alice had not yet been alive for twenty years, but so far, the Civil War had shaped nearly every aspect of her life and every decision she had made, including her move to Cincinnati as a single woman living on her own.

BACK IN DARDENNE, Alice, an attractive young woman from a respected family, no doubt entertained suitors and listened to her mother's entreaties about the importance of early marriage. Both of her sisters had already married, and for women, the average age for marriage was twenty. For Alice, then nineteen, marriage provided the path of least resistance and the most obvious route out of her sister Julia's farmhouse. But having spent her teens tending to her nieces and nephews on the farm, Alice was not interested in a traditional marriage buttressed by the domestic servitude of wives. She would later write that "the past education of woman gave her an outlook which simply embraced a husband or nothing at all, which was often only a choice between two of a kind."[4]

Rather than opt for a husband or nothing at all, Alice ventured to Cincinnati to seek an education and start a new life as a teacher. In this, she typified the experiences of a growing number of young women in the decades immediately following the Civil War. The women of Alice's generation—those born in the 1850s and 1860s—represented a turning point for single women, or "spinsters" as they were then called. A record 7 percent of women in Alice's generation remained single, and among women born between 1855 and 1900, over 10 percent never married.[5] For some, the decision to remain single wasn't really a decision at all. The Civil War took the lives of at least 620,000 men (2 percent of the total population) and maimed untold thousands more.[6] In the 1870s and 1880s, there simply were not enough eligible men to go around.

A young woman's decision to remain single also reflected a small but significant expansion of opportunities for women in education and in the labor market. Throughout the nineteenth and early twentieth centuries, domestic service employed more women than any other field, but Civil War necessity had turned nursing, clerical work, and teaching into acceptable professions for women. Thus, for the first time in American history, young women had the potential to support themselves, albeit tenuously. Alice aimed to be one of these self-supporting women.

Alice's path as a teacher was paved by reformer Catharine Beecher, sister of Harriet Beecher Stowe, who began arguing for the importance of female education and female teachers in the 1820s. To Beecher's mind, women were naturally suited for teaching because it afforded them an expanded stage on which to perform the instructional work they were already doing at home. Beecher first put her ideas into motion with the Hartford (Connecticut) Female Seminary, which she founded in 1823. Later, she created another school for women in Cincinnati and continued to lobby for teaching as a profession, really *the* profession, for women. As she explained to members of Congress in the 1850s, not only were women better than men at dealing with children, but women "can afford to teach for one-half, or even less, the salary which men would ask."[7] Women, she promised, would be the best and cheapest teachers.

Beecher's arguments coincided with a huge increase in public schools and a pressing demand for teachers. The common school movement, an outgrowth of the Second Great Awakening and widespread concerns about a virtuous citizenry, took hold across America by the 1850s. For the first time, many states in the North and West required free primary school for children, at least up to age fourteen. The literacy gap between men and women closed, and nearly all white Americans could read and write.[8] Who better to teach all these new pupils than the thousands of young women left single after the Civil War? Beecher's arguments proved decisive, and young women took up teaching in earnest.

As an intellectually curious young woman looking to leave the farm and postpone marriage, if not avoid it all together, Alice Chenoweth regarded teaching as an ideal and expedient way out of Dardenne.

***

UPON ARRIVING in Cincinnati, Alice rented a room at 335 West 8th Street, where she could easily walk the two blocks to the new Cincinnati Normal School.[9] Cincinnati sustained several dozen schools and institutes in the 1870s, but the Cincinnati Normal School, founded in 1868, was recognized as the biggest and best teacher training school west of the Allegheny Mountains. Its mission was to provide skilled teachers for Cincinnati's growing number of public primary schools. By the time Alice arrived, Cincinnati's school system boasted that it was second in excellence and enrollment only to Boston, which everyone knew to be the most educated city in America.[10]

Along with Alice Chenoweth, forty-one young women, mostly locals, entered the class of 1873. For young women (all the students were female) who had graduated from Cincinnati schools, tuition was free as long as they promised to teach in Cincinnati public schools after graduation. Students not from Cincinnati had to pass an entrance exam and pay $60 in annual tuition. Graduates of the normal school were guaranteed the first crack at jobs within the district as well as a starting salary of $500 per year, $100 more than the norm. Because of the bump in pay afforded to graduates of the normal school, some veteran teachers enrolled in order to earn the certificate. But, like Alice, most of the students were in their late teens.[11]

Normal school leaders prided themselves on the new "natural" teaching method, as opposed to the old "empirical" method. A hallmark of the normal school's curriculum were the many hours teachers-in-training spent in the classroom with students. All student teachers were under the constant supervision of "critic teachers" who evaluated their efforts in the classroom according to "punctuality, promptness, personal bearing, neatness (in person and work), correct use of language, improvement of time, ability to control, ability to construct, ability to criticize and ability to profit by criticism."[12]

To earn a certificate, Alice had to master mental and practical arithmetic, English grammar, geography, United States history and general history, reading, spelling, natural philosophy, anatomy and physiology, music, drawing, and penmanship.[13] School administrators stressed that the most important lessons taught at the normal school were how to teach and how—not what—to think. As Principal Delia Lathrop outlined in her 1873 annual report, normal school graduates did not memorize facts, they learned how to think for themselves. Real thinking "assorts and arranges; it inquires into relations; it looks for causes; it uses authorities but does not accept them unquestionably; it doubts that it may know what it believes. The reason for accepted opinions, the significance of processes, the appropriateness of terms, the causes of the conflict of authorities, are the proper objects of its activity."[14]

This invitation to intellectual freedom starkly contrasted with the traditional morals and memorization emphasized by the *McGuffey Readers* and church teachings of Alice's childhood. Alice had already acquired a love of reading and an appreciation for history from her older brothers and religious instruction from her parents; penmanship, as a glance at her diaries reveals, not so much. But questioning authority, tracing processes, trusting nothing without examination, this sort of thinking appealed to a young woman who had already seen her world turned upside down before, during, and after the Civil War. Even as she went about her daily routine, these questions—why, how, and says who?—obsessed Alice as she sought to make sense of her life.

From afar, Alice may also have been following the women's rights movement, which had several high-profile events in the early 1870s. Since their mutual inception in the 1830s, the abolition movement and the women's rights movement had functioned as two branches of the same tree, working toward a shared goal of "universal suffrage." Believing that black people and white women had been unfairly omitted from the promises of the Declaration of Independence, many reformers, including Susan B. Anthony and Elizabeth Cady Stanton, hoped that the Civil War would both outlaw slavery and enfranchise all people—black and white, male and female—previously barred from voting. But these reformers had their hopes dashed.

The debates surrounding the Fourteenth and Fifteenth Amendments, ratified in 1868 and 1870, respectively, made clear that women would not be enfranchised after the Civil War. To the contrary, the Fourteenth Amendment inserted the word "male" into the Constitution for the first time. The Fifteenth Amendment guaranteed that voting rights could not be "denied or abridged" on the basis of "race, color, or previous condition of servitude." Significantly, it also granted the federal government, not individual states, the power of enforcement. Republican leaders and many abolitionists argued that enfranchising women together with black men would be too radical; they insisted instead on one reform at a time. Stanton and Anthony had thrown themselves into supporting the Union cause and were devastated by what they felt was a betrayal. They refused to support the Fifteenth Amendment, prompting a rift in the movement (the reformers who did support the Fifteenth Amendment soon formed the American Woman Suffrage Association). Dismissing the arguments of black women—including Sojourner Truth and Frances Ellen Watkins Harper—who pointed out that it was impossible to separate sex from race and who urged the movement to keep its focus on universal suffrage, Stanton and Anthony severed ties with many of their reformist friends, started their own group called the National Woman Suffrage Association (NWSA), vowed to work no more with men and, in 1869, began working toward a federal amendment to enfranchise women.[15]

At the same time, several women's rights activists began to argue that women had, in fact, been enfranchised by the Fourteenth and Fifteenth Amendments because they, too, were "citizens" and because they interpreted the Constitution as conferring voting rights on all citizens. They referred to this legal strategy, championed by Victoria Woodhull in 1871 when she became the first woman to testify before a House committee, as "the New Departure." To test the theory that citizenship inherently included voting rights, women across the country—including Anthony and a group of her female friends in Rochester, New York—registered and voted in the 1872 election. For this offense, Anthony was arrested. She fought the charges in court and refused for the rest of her life to pay the fine. Meanwhile, in Missouri, a woman named Virginia Minor approached the local registrar with a similar question. If she was a citizen, why couldn't she vote? Minor, along with her husband Francis, developed the constitutional argument for the New Departure and took her case testing the limits of national citizenship all the way to the Supreme Court. In 1875, the court ruled that the Constitution did not "confer the right of suffrage upon any one."[16]

After the defeat of both the universal suffrage and national citizenship arguments, Stanton and Anthony redoubled their efforts for a Fifteenth Amendment for women—a law that would prohibit sex discrimination in conferring voting rights (but remain mute on other forms of discrimination) and that would be enforced by the federal government. So Stanton drafted the text of a proposed Sixteenth Amendment, modeled word for word on the Fifteenth, substituting "sex" for "race." This amendment was first introduced in Congress in 1878. As a young woman, Alice lived through these debates and maybe even read about them in the news coverage of women's rights and especially the New Departure. But she could never have predicted that debates about the Fourteenth and Fifteenth Amendments would later consume her life.

ON A TYPICAL DAY, Alice woke at dawn in her small room. She then walked a few blocks to the 8th District School. She spent the rest of the day, five or six days a week, inside its small, dark, overcrowded classrooms. Street lamps lit her walk home, but inside she supped and read by candlelight. For a special treat, she could have ridden Cincinnati's first funicular railway, the Main Street Incline built in 1872, to the top of Mt. Auburn and enjoyed a snack at the Lookout House while surveying the panoramic views of the city and the Ohio River that had until just recently separated slavery from freedom.

After growing up in a house dominated by her father and older brothers, in a world consumed with the business of men—the ministry, war, politics—Alice must have enjoyed discussing ideas with other smart women. She befriended the other students and admired the normal school's esteemed principal, Delia Lathrop, who was just a few years older than her charges. Shortly after Alice graduated, Lathrop announced her retirement so that she could enter into her true calling: marriage. Her colleagues threw her a bittersweet retirement party and showered her with gifts. Friends celebrated that Miss Lathrop left her post to, as the *Cincinnati Enquirer* put it, "enter upon a consummation that is, no doubt, wished upon by other school-marms."[17]

Teaching allowed women to provide for themselves and better their marital prospects in the years between coming of age and finding an acceptable mate. Ideally, this period was to last but a short time. Testifying to the brief tenure of the ideal teaching career, teacher salaries topped out after seven years and laws barred married women from working altogether.[18]

For Alice, teaching was a means to an end, but unlike her principal and most of her classmates, her end goal was not marriage. Having witnessed the many pitfalls of women's dependence on men, she sought out alternative domestic arrangements.

JUST AS HER SECOND SEMESTER of normal school began, Alice's sister Julia died, most likely as a result of childbirth. Julia was twenty-four. She left behind no living children, no obituary was published to mark her life, no diaries or letters remain to illuminate her thoughts and experiences. Separated by just three and a half years, Julia and Alice had gone through life together side by side in church pews, in wagon seats, at family meals, and probably in a shared bed. Their sister Kate was five years older than Julia and nearly nine years older than Alice; she had been more of a minder to them, less a compatriot. Alice's perspective on life may have grown to differ from Julia's, but their bodies had always been in close, familial contact. After Julia died on the Hatcher family farm, Alice likely experienced intense grief mixed with relief: Julia's fate would not be her own.

Within months, Alice's older brother William (still her legal guardian), his wife Parmela, and their children left Dardenne, Missouri, for Cowley County, Kansas. Alice never saw her brother again. Shortly after the birth of her seventh child, Parmela died, leaving William, who still suffered from his Civil War leg injury, struggling to keep the family together. William remarried shortly after the death of Parmela, only to die a few months later himself. He was not yet forty.[19]

The single life Alice had embarked on was a risky, new path for women, but she knew all too well that for women, married life came with its own limitations and hazards. The best-selling women's magazines and books, including *The American Woman's Home* (1869) by Harriet Beecher Stowe and her sister Catharine, extolled the blessings of marriage and motherhood, creating a nationwide "cult of domesticity." Writers like the Beechers promised women that true happiness could be found only in well-appointed homes with a bushel of children, dotingly attended to by Christian mothers. But such teachings must have rung hollow to Alice, whose main observations of home thus far had involved loss, abandonment, endless drudgery, downward mobility, and death. The cascading traumas Alice experienced in her adolescence surely shaped her conception of home and family. For much of her adult life, she would be drawn to the familiarity of chaos even as she craved security and belonging.

Besides marriage, other types of romantic encounters presented themselves to Alice and the other teachers-in-training, many of whom were living on their own in the big city for the first time. The *Cincinnati Enquirer* published numerous stories warning of "woman's weakness" and the "naughty conduct of a truly good man." The good man in this instance was the son of a pastor and a teacher at another normal school who had recently been run out of town for attempting to register a hotel room for himself and a "Miss H" to whom he was not married.[20]

Cautionary tales such as this one detailed courtship gone awry when young, unmarried women got swept up by passion upon meeting older, more experienced men. Alice would have read such stories in the local newspaper, as well as in novels, an entire genre that, by some accounts, centered on the trope of the "fallen woman."[21]

For much of the nineteenth century, parents had regulated the courtship of their children. Most young people had remained at home until marriage, so parents could easily control, monitor, and in some cases arrange the marriages of their children. But after the Civil War, when industrial and economic need drew thousands of young women and men away from their homes to new urban centers, there was no telling who young women would meet or be seduced by. The prospect of virile, unmarried young people living on their own terrified parents, clergy, and community leaders who proposed various solutions—from single-sex residential centers, such as the Young Men's Christian Association (YMCA), to sex-segregated public amusements, to censorship—in the hopes of curbing premarital sex. Such checks were not enough to safeguard young women from more experienced men or from exploring their own natural sexual urges, as Alice Chenoweth would soon find out.

3

A Very Bad Beecher Case

A man is valued of men for many things, least of which is
his chastity. A woman is valued of men for few things, chief
of which is her chastity. This double code can by no sane or
reasonable person be claimed as woman made.

—HELEN HAMILTON GARDENER, 1890

ALICE CHENOWETH graduated from the Cincinnati Normal
School on June 21, 1873, the first day of summer and a day sym-
bolic of new beginnings. Because travel was expensive, it is unlikely that
her mother or her surviving siblings attended the commencement ceremony. With crops to tend and small mouths to feed, the Chenoweths
of Missouri could not make twenty-year-old Alice the priority. Most
likely, Alice marked her accomplishment in the same way that she had
achieved it: alone.

Alice began the 1873 school year with a classroom of her own in Sandusky, Ohio, 230 miles north of Cincinnati, where she had been offered
a promising position in a growing school district and her first regular
paycheck.[1] For the second summer in a row, Alice placed her belongings in her trunk and headed for the train station. Sandusky's leading
citizen, Oran Follett, had helped create several of the city's new railroad

lines, including the Sandusky-Columbus-Cincinnati track that would have ferried Alice to her new home in one day's time. This was the farthest north Alice had yet traveled, and besides her stay in Cincinnati, it was her first experience living in a community not dominated by white transplants from Virginia.

Sandusky was settled by residents of Connecticut in the early 1800s and had the look and feel of a New England town. Located on the shores of Lake Erie, blue water as far as the eye could see, Sandusky had long served as a hub on the Underground Railroad. From Sandusky, freedom seekers crossed over into Canada or took the train to Detroit or Chicago to join long-standing communities of freed people. The Civil War was also marked on Sandusky's landscape and psyche by the presence of Johnson's Island in Sandusky Bay, which had imprisoned more than 15,000 Confederate soldiers and officers during the war.

When Alice arrived in Sandusky, less than ten years after the sectional peace, the city was remaking itself into a transport and recreation hub. Louis Zistel had built the ships used to transport Confederate prisoners to Johnson's Island. After the war, he repurposed them to carry tourists to nearby Cedar Point, the "Queen of American Watering Places." Tourists and residents could also avail themselves of several popular steamboat excursions to the islands of Lake Erie, known collectively as "vacationland."[2] Compared with Cincinnati's telltale odors and coal-choked vistas, Sandusky's charms appealed.

Alice's lodging situation also improved in Sandusky, where she rented a room at Catherine Melville's house.[3] In 1861, Mrs. Melville's husband, a railroad executive and business leader, died suddenly at the age of forty-one, leaving her to support eight children, the youngest just two weeks old. The Widow Melville began taking in boarders. Of "quiet and domestic tastes," Mrs. Melville was an ideal "Christian mother whose faith was as strong as her purpose."[4] Her stately home, located at 319 Lawrence Street, just a few blocks from the high school and from Lake Erie, housed many prominent visitors over the years and is now listed on the National Register of Historic Places.

Alice boarded at the Melville home along with the newlyweds John and Alice Mack, the brother and sister-in-law of Isaac Mack, editor of the *Sandusky Daily Register*. Just a few years older than Alice, the Macks had met as students at Oberlin College, the first college to enroll both white women and African Americans. John helped his brother Isaac run the newspaper, and the two Alices became good friends. As a boarder, Alice would have eaten her breakfast and dinner with the Melville family and the Macks, sharing news of the day and plans for the future. The trade-off for such sociability, as Alice would soon learn, was lack of privacy.

DURING HER FIRST YEAR in the classroom, Alice distinguished herself among her peers. On May 9, 1874, her students passed Superintendent Ulysses T. Curran's phonics quiz at the fortnightly teachers meeting and excelled in division. The *Sandusky Daily Register* raved about "Miss C's" classroom presence, noting that she "possesses the happy, and may we add essential, faculty of presenting the lesson, and by a natural ingeniousness, procures the attention of her scholars, which she retains throughout the entire lesson."[5] The next month, Miss Chenoweth's students were singled out as having the finest penmanship in the district.[6]

After her standout performance at the end-of-year events, Superintendent Curran selected Alice, just twenty-one, to be the principal of Sandusky's brand new teacher training school. From her office in the new school, Alice supervised the training of five novice teachers, each posted at a different primary school. Administrators and education experts agreed that the Sandusky teacher training school provided a "very excellent arrangement."[7] By the school's second year, Alice had sixteen aspiring teachers in her class.[8] For the rest of her life, she took great pride in having been the youngest school principal in Ohio history, prominently including this achievement in all her profiles.

Parents and school visitors could have been forgiven for mistaking this young principal for a student herself. In addition to her youth, Alice stood just over 5 feet tall and weighed 90 pounds. Even as an old woman, new acquaintances regularly assumed that she was twenty or more years younger. Her dark, inquisitive eyes enhanced her aura of youthfulness and charmed students and peers alike.

Alice's high-profile post as principal also elevated her status in the Sandusky community. With her annual salary of $800, she could afford to buy tickets to the town's weekly lectures and concerts.[9] She also befriended the leading citizens of Sandusky. Mrs. Melville's husband and in-laws had helped run the Mad River and Lake Erie Railroad, the first chartered railroad west of the Allegheny Mountains. And as newspaper publishers, her fellow boarders, the Macks, knew everyone in town.

After spending eight years in a small farm town, Alice eagerly engaged in the social and intellectual life of Sandusky. She had grown up hearing about Virginia society but had not previously had the opportunity to participate in "society" events. As with school teaching, Alice

Alice Chenoweth as a teacher, soon to become the youngest school principal in Ohio and a fixture in the state's newspapers.

was a natural. On New Year's Day 1875, she helped host a party at the four-story mansion owned by the Folletts, who were railroad investors, philanthropists, and civic leaders.[10] And she always remembered the life-changing revelation she experienced when she invited herself—the youngest person and only woman allowed—into a prominent judge's home for a heated discussion of a controversial article entitled "The Relations of Women to Crime," recently published in *Popular Science Monthly*. The author, Ely Van de Warker, shocked readers by arguing that woman "must be regarded as one in whom the passions burn with as intense heat as in the other sex."[11] Now that was an argument Alice had surely not encountered at the Cincinnati Normal School, in her brother Bernard's books, or at her father's revivals, and it was a truth that Sandusky leaders most certainly were not ready to contend with among their own teachers.

BY THE SPRING OF 1876, after nearly three years in the city, Alice had fallen out of favor with Sandusky leaders. On April 28, Isaac Mack, brother of Alice's housemate and the editor of the local paper, published an editorial demanding an end to taxpayer funding of Alice's $800 salary.[12] Mack charged that Alice had "coaxed the [school] board into the scheme" of funding the teacher training school and then "induced" them to hire her an assistant. An assistant was then "imported from Cincinnati" at the rate of $600 per year. Mack approached a member of the school board and demanded to know just what Miss Chenoweth did to justify her $800 salary ($17,000 today). "Nothing," responded the board member. "And now we ask in behalf of the burdened tax payer," Mack pressed, "how much longer $1,400 of public money is to be squandered to keep two young women busy doing nothing." Later that evening, Alice Chenoweth tendered her resignation on account of ill health.[13]

But it was not Alice's $800 salary that piqued Mack and the school board (her salary was well within the normal range). That was a dissimulation. What Alice had done was violate the public's trust. Her noteworthy appointment as the state's youngest principal, together with her feminine good looks, had brought her to the attention of Charles Selden Smart, the Ohio commissioner of common schools and a married father of two.

Born in Virginia, Charles Smart grew up in Ohio and attended Ohio University. Upon graduating in 1859, he became a teacher and soon announced plans to open his own school. The former president of Cincinnati's Wesleyan Female College endorsed Smart as "a young man of excellent abilities, and of superior scholarship, and of good moral character."[14] In 1861, Smart married Lovenia "Love" Cating, but the Civil War derailed their plans to start a school (the hall they hoped to use was requisitioned as a hospital).[15]

By 1867, Charles and "Love" Smart operated a classical and English school in Jackson, Ohio. Charles taught mathematics and languages, while Love instructed the younger students.[16] Smart served as superintendent of Union schools in Jackson before accepting the post of superintendent in Circleville, Ohio, 50 miles away. In 1872, Smart came just a few votes shy of securing the Democratic nomination for Ohio commissioner of schools.[17] During the next election cycle, Smart's friends recognized him as "every way fitted for a more enlarged sphere of duty" and unanimously nominated him for state school commissioner once again. This time the handsome and outgoing Smart secured the nomination on the first ballot and was elected to the post in October 1874.[18]

As commissioner of common schools, Smart traveled around Ohio meeting with teachers, principals, and school board members and in general ensuring that the public schools were performing well. He also attended teacher conferences, observed teachers in the classroom, and gave talks advancing his views on pedagogy. Newspapers covered his occasional visits home to see his wife and their two daughters, Cora and Iva, but Smart spent most of his time on the road.

Commissioner Smart's travels increasingly brought him to Sandusky, which raised eyebrows because Sandusky did not rank among Ohio's biggest or most important cities. Alice's friends and neighbors grew concerned that Smart had been visiting Sandusky altogether too frequently and for inappropriate reasons. For months, rumors circulated that the commissioner had been coming to Sandusky not to survey the schools but to see the young school principal.

Locals reported that "his visits to us were manifestly not in the line of his duty as a public officer." For example, he often arrived on Friday evenings and left on Monday mornings—a period of time when no schools were in session. Furthermore, during these weekends, Smart made no visits to the superintendent or the Board of Education. Instead, he called on the young teacher who boarded at the Widow Melville's. When "accused of improper intimacy with this innocent young lady teacher," Smart told people in Sandusky that he and his wife had agreed to separate two years before and that he intended to divorce her so that he could marry the teacher.

The "young lady's friends" found this excuse "very thin." When he broke the story in the *Sandusky Daily Register*, Isaac Mack reported: "We do not believe Smart ever intended to procure a divorce from his wife and we have the best information that his wife knows nothing of his conduct, much less of his professed intention to get rid of her. . . . We do know, however, that his conduct in this city has been a disgrace to him and to his office, and to the lady with whom he has been so intimate." Smart's conduct had "destroyed the reputation of an estimable young lady."[19] Mack did not identify who constituted "we" nor who comprised the young lady's "friends," but no doubt he procured his insider information from his brother and sister-in-law, Alice's housemates.

Rumors about the affair likely accounted for Alice's hasty resignation in April 1876, but the affair was not made public until that summer. On July 17, 1876, Mack printed a blunt but vague condemnation of Commissioner Smart in the *Daily Register*: "If half the stories told of State School Commissioner Smart are true, he is a disgrace to the State and to his office."[20] At first, Mack did not elaborate. Just what were these "stories," the *Springfield Republic* demanded? Mack replied in an extended editorial on July 21: "One of these stories is easily told. Commissioner Smart is a married man."[21]

Something must have transpired between April and July to compel Mack to write about an affair that had already resulted in Alice's resignation. Mack's initial accusations ran in the paper just a few days after Smart returned from representing Ohio at the 1876 Centennial Exposition in Philadelphia, the first world's fair to be held in the United States.[22] In a very high-profile assignment, Smart had been selected to lead Ohio's Educational Centennial Committee and develop the state's display.[23]

Because of the timing of Mack's first editorial, the probable scenario is that Alice accompanied Smart—on the state of Ohio's dime—to Philadelphia. Alice never wrote directly about having attended the World's Fair, but her first published essay includes an anecdote about a young woman who attended the centennial celebration and saw many things "new and beautiful."[24] She may have even encountered Elizabeth Cady Stanton and Susan B. Anthony, who set up elaborate protests to demonstrate "that the women of 1876 know and feel their political degradation no less than did the men of 1776" and to advocate for the Sixteenth Amendment.[25] If word had spread around Sandusky that Alice and Smart traveled together to Philadelphia, in a flagrant violation of both sacred vows and public trust, that would explain the timing of Mack's editorial.

ALICE NEVER acknowledged her affair with Charles Smart, but it fundamentally altered her life and put her on a path to radicalism and reform. There are many clues in her later writings, especially in her fiction, which she confided to friends was often autobiographical, about the allure of the charismatic, 6-foot-2 school commissioner and the seismic shift that the affair triggered in her life.[26] Unmoored by the Civil War, several moves, and the deaths of so many of her close family members, Alice was attracted to the tall, college-educated, thirty-seven-year-old Smart (the same age that her brother Bernard would have been) as a source of stability. Even more appealing, Smart was a rising star in the Democratic Party.

Alice also seemed drawn to Smart in the intense way so characteristic of first love, which may have been why, decades later, she still remembered the heated discussion about the *Popular Science Monthly* article that naturalized female desire.[27] Throughout her life, she alluded to their strong attraction to one another, an attraction that had few— if any—acceptable outlets for a young woman in Victorian America. Masturbation was considered a mortal sin for men and especially for women. And a new disease had recently been designated to pathologize women who suffered from persistent sexual urges: nymphomania.[28] While women who openly sought sexual release were diagnosed with nymphomania, women whose arousal found no outlet were diagnosed with hysteria, a disease that reached epidemic proportions in late nineteenth-century America.[29]

To the extent that Alice had read or heard about female sexual desire, it would have been in derogatory, pathological, or criminal terms. There was very little room in public or medical discourse for a woman in the 1870s to be understood as having healthy sexual urges, though of course many women experienced them in private. As the historian Linda Gordon asserted in her study of birth control, in the nineteenth century "normal" sex meant "a form of intercourse dictated primarily by male desires and typified by the mutually dependent institutions of marriage and prostitution."[30] Marriage was for procreative sex; prostitution for pleasurable sex, at least for the customers, leaving aside altogether female pleasure. Once considered essential for fertilization, by the nineteenth century the female orgasm (and even the clitoris itself) had dropped out of medical and anatomical guides entirely.[31] While Alice may have intuitively understood what she felt for the strapping and charming Smart, she would have found no reference to her sensations in books or women's magazines.

Just after Alice left Dardenne for Cincinnati, reformers concerned about extramarital sex scored a signature victory: the passage of the Comstock Laws, named after anti-vice crusader Anthony Comstock.

Passed along with 117 other bills in a hurried session on the eve of the second inauguration of President Ulysses S. Grant, in 1873, the Comstock Laws banned the publishing, selling, distributing, giving away, exhibiting, or just plain possessing of "any obscene book, pamphlet, paper, writing, advertisement, circular, print, picture, drawing or other representation, figure . . . on or of paper or other material." The text of the law was so wide-ranging that it defined as "obscene" nearly everything related to sex—from outright pornography to educational descriptions of anatomy.[32] One practical effect, then, was to bar women from accessing information about their reproductive health, including contraception and sexually transmitted disease.

Nineteenth-century periodicals often contained advertisements for quack medicines promising to cure all sorts of female ailments, including blocked menstrual flow, but safe, effective contraceptives were largely out of reach for middle- and lower-class women, especially after the passage of the Comstock Laws. Wealthy women living in urban centers could obtain barrier methods such as pessaries (early diaphragms) or perhaps even condoms, though getting a man to wear one would have been another struggle altogether because "unnatural devices" were closely associated with prostitutes. Most women, even women's rights activists, remained opposed to birth control because they feared that accessible contraceptives would further encourage husbands to pay for sex outside of marriage.[33]

To avoid pregnancy, Alice and Smart likely practiced the birth control methods deemed "natural" and at least somewhat acceptable: the rhythm method or coitus interruptus.[34] Smart's later medical history suggests that the pair may have suffered from infertility, a blessing and a curse given their illicit affair, possibly related to syphilis or gonorrhea, which were among the most prevalent infectious diseases of the nineteenth century.

Beyond a dearth of knowledge about sex, Alice also lacked people in whom she could confide such things. During the heated first months of her affair and then, soon after, when it became public knowledge, to whom and where could Alice have turned for advice and solace?

Surely not the Sandusky socialites like Mrs. Follett, whose 1875 New Year's Day tea she had helped host, or the Widow Melville, the ideal Christian mother in whose home she boarded. Alice's teacher friends also made for unlikely confidants. School teachers, by definition, were supposed to be passionless. Part of Catharine Beecher's mission in making teaching an acceptable profession for young single women was to create the institution in such a way as to obviate the possibility that these young single women, nestled into schools far from home, would sleep with the married men of the community. Through her affair, then, Alice not only lost her livelihood and good reputation, but also upset the tacit compromise that allowed single women to work as teachers in the first place.

This lack of female confidantes further tethered Alice to Smart and their shared secret, long after it ceased to be a secret in Ohio. Throughout the summer and fall of 1876, Smart traveled regularly, including frequent visits home to his wife and children, and thus could not have squeezed in many visits to Alice. If he wrote her any letters, they have not survived.

WHETHER OR NOT he wrote to Alice, Smart penned several public letters to defend himself. From his hotel room in Columbus, he denounced the *Sandusky Daily Register*'s charges as "utterly false." Smart's former hometown paper, the *Jackson Standard*, urged a full investigation in court. Smart had lived among the people of the county as their school superintendent and been their friend. The editors criticized Smart's associates in the Democratic Party who, as soon as the allegations surfaced, declared they knew he was guilty and that they "never had any confidence in him and always knew him to be a d___ed fool."[35]

Smart told another reporter that the false rumors stemmed from his opposition to a nefarious "school-book ring."[36] Isaac Mack denied this, noting that he had no knowledge of such a ring and that the existence of a book ring could not possibly explain the persistent "street gossip" in Sandusky. Mack proposed that Smart, as an act of repentance, come forward to expose the ring: "He may be forgiven his love making to interesting young school teachers, if he can expose a ring."[37]

Next, Smart blamed "the malicious intent" of Mack. Party politics no doubt played a role, as Smart was an elected Democrat and Mack a staunch Republican during one of the most intense election cycles in American history. Even though he denounced Smart "as slippery as Sam Tilden, his fellow Democrat," Mack denied ever having met Smart or having any feelings about him one way or another (though Mack most certainly did know Alice Chenoweth).[38]

By August 17, even Smart's hometown paper started to turn against him. The editors of the *Jackson Standard* admitted that they had met Smart several times and been impressed with him as a teacher and as a scholar. But they had also met Isaac Mack, who ran for lieutenant governor the previous year, and knew that "he is a man of ability" whose word should be taken seriously. The *Standard* then reprinted the two most recent Sandusky editorials about Smart and demanded, "Is Mr. Smart, by his silence going to admit that these damaging charges are true?"[39] With pressure mounting, Smart printed a flyer proclaiming his innocence. Even this did not assuage his critics or the newspaper editors who opined that "the card is a very tame affair and will not go very far in convincing the people of his innocence."[40]

Compounding Smart's problems, Lillian Durst, editor of the *Circleville Herald* (Circleville is where the Smart family had recently lived), reported that Smart had told a dentist in a nearby town that he was a widower. Durst had known Love Smart for many years, but she had a hard time convincing the dentist that Charles Smart was lying, so persuasive was the school commissioner. Smart traveled in person to Circleville to proclaim his innocence to Durst. Finding her out of the office, he left a note: "I never told a dentist or anyone else I am or was a widower. I never caused injury to any lady or woman in Sandusky or anywhere else."[41]

Charles Smart's affair with the young principal also called to mind another prominent scandal of the 1870s: the Beecher-Tilton affair. In its coverage of the Smart-Chenoweth scandal, the *Jackson Standard* described it as "a very bad Beecher case."[42] In 1872, the Reverend Henry Ward Beecher, "the most famous man in America" and the brother of Catharine and Harriet Beecher, had chastised the free love ideals of feminist Victoria Woodhull, who had championed the "New Departure" strategy and who was then running for president, the first woman to seek the office.

Woodhull was outraged. How dare Beecher criticize her relationships when she knew full well that the married Beecher had long been carrying on an affair with his parishioner Elizabeth Tilton, who also happened to be the wife of his close friend. To protest this obvious hypocrisy, Woodhull published an account of Beecher's transgressions in her newspaper, *Woodhull and Claflin's Weekly*. Woodhull wanted to defend herself as well as call attention to the sexual double standard for men and women.

In daring to write about Beecher's affair, however, Woodhull alone was punished. Beecher was ultimately acquitted of the affair in a civil trial brought by Elizabeth Tilton's husband and in the court of public opinion, but Woodhull was arrested for violating the Comstock Laws simply for writing about it. She spent the 1872 election night in a New York jail.[43]

The Beecher-Tilton affair, known to every literate American, provided a script through which people interpreted extramarital affairs. Men, married or otherwise, could do as they pleased, with little or no consequence. Women, on the other hand, routinely had their lives ruined—in a seemingly endless variety of ways—for having sex outside of marriage.

Despite Smart's protestations of innocence, the *Sandusky Daily Register* stood by their charges, promised to produce additional proof if necessary, and revealed that "through Smart's conduct the lady [teacher] was forced to resign and leave the city."[44] Who was the lady teacher? Everyone in Sandusky already knew, and in October, the *Jackson Standard* published her name: "Miss Chinoweth."[45]

ALICE CHENOWETH left Sandusky in the summer of 1876 and never returned to teaching. Meanwhile, Charles Smart completed his term as school commissioner and submitted a thoroughgoing report on the state's public schools. His reputation suffered as a result of the affair, but he did not lose his livelihood or his home over it. "A man is valued of men for many things, least of which is his chastity. A woman is valued of men for few things, chief of which is her chastity," Alice caustically observed years later. "This double code can by no sane or reasonable person be claimed as woman made." Of all the injustices and illogical practices Alice had witnessed in her twenty-three years, this humiliation stung the most. Men were encouraged to "sow their wild oats"; yet, for women, the premarital loss of virginity generally amounted to "social, moral, and physical death."[46] The aftermath of her affair set her on a lifelong course to understand why women were evaluated, publicly and privately, in terms of their sexual relationships with men—as virgins, wives, fallen women, or spinsters—and why women had no voice in the laws governing relationships between the sexes.

In her first novel, written fifteen years after the start of her affair, Alice detailed the condition of "fallen women," the term for women who had succumbed to premarital sex. It was "conventional opinion that it was the duty of a young girl to form and maintain, not only her own character and basis of action, but that she must hold her lover to a given line of conduct, failing which he was privileged to take advantage of her love and confidence with no shame whatever to himself." No matter how the relationship progressed, only the woman would be blamed. "If he were not a gentleman," Alice observed, "it was her fault. If he took advantage of her tenderness and confidence in him, it was her fault. If he swore to her by all that was holy, and she believed him, and acted upon his word, and the results were disastrous, it was her fault."[47] Everyone knew as much, and few thought to question this supposedly natural and eternal state of affairs.

Alice later learned that Smart had been untruthful in other dealings, so it is likely that he did lie to her about his wife—telling her, as her Sandusky neighbors reported, that he and Love were separated and that he would seek a divorce so that he could marry Alice. If she found out that this was a lie after they had had sex, what recourse did she, a "fallen woman," have? Smart's deception may have enticed Alice into the affair, and, once consummated, her best option seemed to continue with him down the illicit path. Her passion for Smart overtook her reason—the trait she most valued in others and in herself—and precipitated the affair that changed her life.

From a distance of several years and many states, Alice repeatedly asserted that she had married Smart in 1875, the year their affair began. All of the biographical entries about her in encyclopedias and "who's who" books repeat this information; their 1875 marriage date is even recorded as fact in the 1900 census. Everyone she later knew and everyone who knew of her accepted this as true, without question. The physical consummation of their affair may have seemed like a type of marriage to Alice, but the couple never legally married.[48] Until now, Alice's affair has never been part of her public biography. Perhaps Alice hoped she might marry Smart one day, but it is more likely that she deliberately chose the freedom of a fake marriage as the first step in her self-creation. Bound to no man, she would make her own rules.

4

Purgatory and Rebirth

*Every fallen woman is a perpetual monument to the infamy
of a religion and a social custom that narrow her life to the
possibilities of but one function, and provide her no escape—
a system that trains her to depend wholly on one physical
characteristic of her being, and to neglect all else.*

—HELEN HAMILTON GARDENER, 1884

A S THE NATION celebrated the American centennial, Alice Chenoweth left Sandusky, Ohio, in disgrace sometime between May
and September of 1876. The historical record does not reveal precisely
when she left town or where she went. In fact, she does not appear again
definitively until 1884. There are hints and occasional glimpses of her
during this exile, but her day-to-day comings and goings are open to
interpretation. One thing is certain: Alice spent these eight years using
her habits of "real thinking," honed at the Cincinnati Normal School,
to mull over her life experiences. When she reemerged, in 1884, Alice
had metamorphosed into a new person with a new name and a radical
new worldview.

Because she had inherited very little money from her father's estate and was now without a paycheck, Alice most likely packed her trunk and traveled the 590 miles from Sandusky back to Olney, Missouri, to live with her brother Alfred and their mother Ann. In spite of deteriorating eyesight resulting from his Civil War illness, Alfred had attained his medical license, married, and had three children, with a fourth on the way.

On her way to Olney, 80 miles from St. Louis, Alice's train would have stopped in Cincinnati. Perhaps she took the opportunity to visit friends from the normal school or to take in some of the summer activities in the Queen City, possibly including the speeches and hoopla surrounding the Republican National Convention, which would prove to be one of the most consequential political conventions in American history. Through her late brother Bernard, Alice would have known the names of the Republican power brokers in attendance and maybe even secured an invitation.

The question in the minds of Republicans that summer was the extent to which the next administration would continue federal Reconstruction in the South. Ohio governor Rutherford B. Hayes vied to succeed President Ulysses S. Grant. Another front-runner was James Blaine of Maine, the former Speaker of the House of Representatives. On the night of June 14, Republican leaders selected the Civil War veteran, railroad lawyer, and freethinker (agnostic) Robert Ingersoll, of Peoria, Illinois, to introduce Blaine at the following day's session. Even with just a few hours' notice, the speech Ingersoll delivered in Cincinnati on the afternoon of June 15, 1876, changed his life, Alice Chenoweth's life, and nearly the course of American history.

Widely considered one of the best political speeches of the nineteenth century, Ingersoll's "Plumed Knight" address, as it came to be known, almost earned Blaine the Republican nomination. After listening to Ingersoll, the crowd was riled up into such a frenzy that had the primary election been held right then, several observers commented, no doubt Blaine would have won. But Ingersoll's speech did not conclude until 5:15 p.m., so the chairman adjourned the convention.[1] The next day, cooler heads nominated Rutherford B. Hayes on the seventh ballot. That fall, Hayes narrowly lost the popular vote to Democrat Samuel Tilden but was elevated to the presidency through the compromise of 1877, which heralded the end of Reconstruction and ushered in Jim Crow segregation, racist voter discrimination, and unprecedented violence against African Americans.

Even though his candidate did not prevail, Ingersoll's personal stock skyrocketed after news of his talents as an orator spread throughout the nation. The *Chicago Evening Journal* reported that "never in the history of politics was there such a demand for any one speaker as there is . . . for Robert Ingersoll."[2] If Alice Chenoweth was not in Cincinnati that June evening to hear Ingersoll's speech in person, she likely read about it in the days and weeks that followed. Alice determined to learn more about this fascinating man who shared her agnosticism and whose powerful oratory catapulted him from Illinois lawyer to national celebrity.

BUOYED BY THE SUCCESS of the "Plumed Knight" speech, Ingersoll embarked upon his first national lecture tour, beginning in Missouri in April 1877, where Alice may have had occasion to see him. Women often outnumbered men at Ingersoll's lectures and tickets cost 50 cents, so Alice could easily have attended one or more of his lectures during the 1877 and 1878 seasons, events that regularly drew crowds by the thousands. And she surely followed his tour in the papers, which often provided front-page coverage and printed long excerpts from his talks.[3]

Ingersoll had become famous for his convention speech, but Americans did not buy tickets to hear him talk politics. Men and women flocked to hear Ingersoll describe his secular worldview, which offered listeners a new way to understand the world and their place in it. As a Union soldier, Ingersoll had become transfixed by the omnipresence of death and convinced that the only thing that mattered was the here and now. Ingersoll's signature saying was: "Happiness is the only good. The time to be happy is now. The place to be happy is here. The way to be happy is to make others happy." To mothers, fathers, siblings, and widows who lost loved ones in the Civil War and who found diminishing comfort in the prospect of reuniting with them in the afterlife, Ingersoll gave permission to reframe grief into the joy of living. His most sought-after talks criticized Christian orthodoxy, earning him the nickname "the Great Agnostic."

Ingersoll's thoughtful countenance, quick wit, and congenial manner warmed audiences, but Alice sensed a deeper connection to the Great Agnostic, himself the son of a minister. Ingersoll's most popular address during his 1877–1878 lecture tour was "The Liberty of Man, Woman, and Child." In this two-hour-long barnstormer, he critiqued slavery and tyranny of all sorts, especially anything that prohibited independent thought. This speech also contained a section called "The Liberty of Woman." Here, Ingersoll proclaimed his belief in the equality of women and the importance of egalitarian marriage. He decried stingy husbands, grumpy husbands, and husbands who acted as if they were the "boss" of their wives. Ingersoll also ventured to suggest that husbands got these pernicious ideas about marriage from an old book that taught that women were an afterthought of creation, taken from a man's rib to be his helper. "As long as woman regards the Bible as the charter of her rights," Ingersoll thundered, "she will be the slave of man."[4]

As Alice sat in torpid exile, ruminating on her fate and what had befallen her in Sandusky, Ingersoll's words offered a beacon. The free-thought movement appealed to her because it was here that she found people rationally discussing the restrictions of patriarchal marriage and the sexual double standard, putting words to inchoate feelings she had about her experiences. Indeed, freethinkers were more or less the only people openly talking and writing about marriage and sex in the late 1870s, so if Alice looked for reading material to help her understand her plight, she would have found her way to freethought publications, including *The Truth Seeker*, *Freethinkers Magazine*, and *Lucifer the Light-Bearer*.

MEANWHILE, Charles Smart continued on in his official duties as Ohio Commissioner of Common Schools, in spite of increasing calls for his resignation. In July 1877, newspapers reported on Smart's appearance at the state teachers' convention, where he delivered his report on Ohio's contributions to the 1876 centennial celebration in Philadelphia. More than 1,000 teachers were in attendance, but according to news reports, "the commencing of Smart's paper was followed by a general exodus of the audience," leaving just "forty-six persons, including the presiding officer, six reporters, a boy, and the speaker remaining." Smart "exhibited considerable vexation, and remarked that it would have been better for the association if he had stayed away."[5] His colleagues agreed.

Later that month, Smart narrowly lost the Democratic Party nomination for school commissioner to a Confederate veteran named J. J. Burns. Apparently, being a secessionist was better than being an adulterer.[6] Earlier that year, Smart had also been removed from the Ohio Centennial Commission and denied his salary for having served on it.[7] In January of 1878, Smart approached the Ohio State Legislature to demand $3,000 in back pay. Outraged by Smart's temerity, Isaac Mack editorialized that if the state granted this stipend, the taxpayers should revolt because "Smart did not devote half his time to the duties of his office, and whatever extra work he claims to have done could have been done by himself while he was playing sweetness to pretty school mistresses."[8] Smart never received his money.

Smart later recalled that he would not undergo the "persecution and annoyance" he suffered as school commissioner "for the best salary in America." For what he attributed to his controversial views about high school reform, he "was mocked, assailed in the press, among the people, among public officials, lied about, almost worried out of my life. If I hadn't been a great big fellow, with lots of animal life and fight in me, I'd have gone crazy."[9]

Rather than attempt to refurbish his reputation, Smart left Ohio altogether. He announced that he had accepted a job as Michigan State Agent for the Equitable Life Assurance Society.[10] No doubt, this position had been arranged for him by one of his prominent friends in the Democratic Party; a man with connections, even a disgraced one, always had options. A man had "open to him many avenues of happiness, many paths to honorable employment," Alice would later write. "If he fails in one there is still hope. If he misses supreme happiness in marriage he has still left ambition, labor, study, family." But for women, church teachings and social customs allowed but one option. As long as the church "made [woman] believe that she could bring to this world nothing of value but her capacity to minister to the lower animal wants of man, so long did it force upon her that single alternative—or starvation."[11] Smart may have been humiliated, but he did not starve.

Newspapers reported that Smart's family would accompany him to Detroit, but Love and their two daughters remained in Ohio. The 1878 Detroit City Directory listed him as "Colonel C. S. Smart, Manager of the Equitable Life Assurance Society of the U.S."[12] While there is no evidence that Smart served in the Civil War (or that he was a colonel in anything), Civil War service was an important marker in postbellum business and politics, much like service in the Second World War was in the twentieth century. For the rest of his life, Smart went by Colonel Smart, C. S. Smart, or C. Selden Smart. Such a subtle change allowed him to distance himself from the disgraced Commissioner Charles Smart of Ohio.

ANOTHER ASPECT of Smart's fresh start in Detroit involved ramping up his relationship with Alice Chenoweth. The couple appear to have begun living together in Detroit and telling people that they were married (Michigan friends later recalled meeting Alice during this period). There is no listing for Alice in the 1880 census or in the Detroit City

Directory, but family records from that time reference "Mrs. Alice Smart of Detroit."[13] The 1880 federal census enumerated Smart living with his family in a boarding house in Gallipolis, Ohio, though he appears to have just been passing through because his job remained in Detroit. Alice may not have known it, but Smart occasionally visited his family in Ohio and in Florida, where his wife brought their daughters in hope of curing Iva's sciatic neuralgia.[14]

Since her family believed her to be married to Smart, it is unlikely that Alice asked them for money. The couple most likely lived together in Detroit on Smart's salary, though he must also have sent funds home to Ohio for at least as long as he continued to visit. Alice may have earned additional money as a tutor or writer.[15] As an unmarried woman, she had more freedoms and more legal rights than a married woman. She had no legal obligation to obey a husband, and if she earned any money, she could keep it.

Alice later assailed the idea that a man who had seduced a woman under false pretenses could subsequently "make an honest woman of her" through marriage. "Why sustain the fiction," she demanded, "that a woman can be elevated by making her the permanent victim of one who has already abused her confidence and now holds himself— because of his own perfidy—as in a position to confer honor on his victim?" Alice described such thinking as "vicious" and concluded, "What fiction of fiction (and alas of law) could be more degrading to womanhood—and hence to humanity—than the thought here pre- sented?"[16] Rather than be "saved" by Smart through marriage, Alice endeavored to save herself.

She began to narrow in on intellectual and financial freedom as her life goals. The church had taught woman, she would soon write, that "her mind is to be of slight use to her; that her hands may not learn the cunning of a trade nor her brain the bearings of a profession; that men- tally she is nothing; and that physically she is worse than nothing only in so far as she may minister to one appetite."[17] In spite of, or perhaps because of, the tremendous loss and humiliation she had endured for her affair, Alice rejected such teachings outright. What women needed were the rights to think for themselves and support themselves. Free from husband and children, Alice began to chart an independent life, even as she lived with Smart.

But Alice's romantic situation remained precarious, no matter how she may have rationalized it to herself. If people in Detroit learned that she was not really Smart's wife, the couple's prospects would have been ruined in Michigan, too. If Smart returned to his wife, Alice would have been without a home once again. And if word of her unorthodox relationship with Smart resurfaced, who would marry or hire her, a woman with a tarnished reputation who had doubled down on her extramarital affair rather than repent? Moreover, what toll did this fake marriage, a lie first uttered as an act of self-preservation by a woman with no safety net and few options, exact on Alice's inner life?

THE BIG LIE ASIDE, Alice and Charles Smart appear to have led a full life in Detroit. Smart approached his post at Equitable Life with zeal, taking out regular advertisements in the *Detroit Free Press* and in the Detroit City Directory. He offered new customers deep discounts on insurance policies and was praised in the local paper for always giving "detailed information when asked in relation to the business at his office" in Detroit's bustling downtown.[18] As a "gentleman of recognized ability in the science of life insurance," he was promoted to General Inspector of Agencies for Equitable Life in November 1881. And in 1882, Equitable Life Assurance reported that it had issued more insurance policies than had "ever before been written in a single year by any company in America or abroad."[19]

In the late 1870s and 1880s, Detroit was a good place to explore new ideas and reinvent oneself. Not yet the Motor City, it was nevertheless a city on the move. Electric lights and telephones came to the city in the late 1870s, thrilling citizens with the new opportunities made possible by recent advancements in science and technology.

After the 1873 depression and massive labor strikes of 1877, business and commerce rebounded. By 1880, Detroit's population surpassed 116,000 and the city boasted a vibrant intellectual and cultural life. The opera house regularly hosted national speakers and world-class musical events. One history of Detroit refers to the 1880s as "the elegant eighties" because the city's streets were "wide and beautiful," supporting "many mansions with fine stables of superior horses." The people of Detroit "love entertainment and parties," and the city was "fat and content and purring to itself, a sleek cat drowsing in the sun."[20]

For the next phase of her education, Alice could have picked few places better than the new and expanded Detroit Public Library. Opened in 1877, by 1886 this stunning five-story library had doubled its holdings to 70,000 books. Within its elegant walls, she could read history, philosophy, science, and literature in sunny rooms overlooking the construction of a modern city.

She could even see the Detroit Public Library from the posh Griswold Hotel, where, by 1882, the not-exactly-married Smarts boarded. Located just one block from both the library and Smart's office on West Congress Street, the Griswold Hotel provided an ideal temporary home for two people in the process of reinvention. The hotel boasted a refrigerated buffet with several beers on tap and 160 guest rooms.[21] Off of the main lobby, several smaller lounges and cafes provided guests ample room for privacy and anonymity—including, for example, the opportunity to live with your lover and avoid scrutiny.

ALICE'S REINVENTION during these years in Detroit was also propelled by changes within the Chenoweth family. While she appears to have remained in contact with her mother and brother Alfred throughout the 1870s, perhaps even living with them between late 1876 and 1880, Alice's remaining family ties would soon be strained.

In 1874, when Alice was working in Sandusky, her mother Ann

drafted her will and listed Alice as the executor and sole beneficiary of her estate, which by then included 39 acres of land in St. Charles County, Missouri. Her brother Bernard and sister Julia had died, and Alice's three surviving siblings were married and settled. Only Alice, the youngest, remained single with an uncertain future. Her mother must have intended to provide for her most vulnerable daughter, perhaps feeling guilty for having legally severed ties with her in 1867.

Then, in February of 1881, Ann contracted pneumonia and died at Alfred's house. As a physician, Alfred cared for his mother during her final illness but resented the toll it took on him. That his youngest sister Alice stood to inherit their mother's estate must not have seemed fair, emotionally or financially, to Alfred.

Shortly after Ann's will was approved by the probate court, Alfred got himself appointed administrator of the estate, despite the fact that the will clearly named Alice as executor. Then, in July, Alfred and his sister Kate sued Ann's estate, listing Alice as codefendant. According to court documents, Mrs. Alice Smart of Detroit was summoned to appear before the Lincoln County Probate Court. But Alice did not contest her siblings' suit or show up for the hearings.[22] Perhaps she did not want to invite legal scrutiny of her marital status. Nevertheless, Alfred's treachery stung.

The court invalidated Ann's will and ruled that her estate had to be evenly divided among the living Chenoweth children, with additional shares going to the descendants of the deceased siblings. Part of Alfred's claim rested on the fact that Ann had lived with him, and he charged her estate for her room, board, and medical care. Ultimately, each sibling received $237 and their pick of Ann's belongings. Of the dozens of items listed in the three-page estate inventory—from books and family Bibles to linens and silverware—Alice claimed just one thing: a pair of gold spectacles, valued at $2.

A few years later, in her first public lectures, Alice spoke of a devout Sunday School superintendent she knew, a man much like Alfred, who "refused his mother her dying wish." The following Sunday, this man atoned for his "unhuman act by singing with the usual unction, 'how gentle God's commands,' and reading with devout fervor, 'the Lord is my shepherd I shall not want.'" Yet, this devout man's mother, who "had the same shepherd, had wanted for much." His mother "even wanted for a stone to mark her grave, because the money she had left for that purpose her holy son thought best to use, vicariously, upon himself." Reflecting on this man's acts, Alice concluded: "He is willing to take his heavenly home through the blood of Christ, and his earthly one out of the pockets of a dead mother."[23]

After Alfred and Kate prevailed in probate court, Alice went from being the sole beneficiary of her mother's will to being written out of it almost entirely. Her pious siblings had singled out Alice's inheritance as unfair, but she may have felt that they also singled out her—a young woman who always related more to her brothers than to her sisters, who inherited their father's iconoclasm and brother Bernard's agnosticism, and who had insisted on striking out on her own. Among the Chenoweth's immediate and more far-flung relatives stood women shaped by traditional Southern standards of feminine comportment. Alice's ambition and independence marked her as decidedly different.

WHILE THE FREETHOUGHT MOVEMENT had long appealed to Alice intellectually, she was also drawn to it by what she considered the hypocrisies of Christianity and, more to the point, the hypocrisies of the Christians in her own family. In part because she lacked a husband and a family to tell her not to, Alice read widely during her exile and determined that the barriers and degradations experienced by women could all be traced to the Bible and the churches that promulgated its messages. As a child, she had appreciated her brother's contraband copy of Paine's *The Age of Reason*. At normal school, she thrived in an environment that prized "real thinking," not rote learning. In Detroit, she had the opportunity to follow her intellectual passions wherever they logically led her, most likely in the voluminous stacks of the public library.

Alice's quest for knowledge coincided with the publication of a surge of books contextualizing and critiquing the Bible and providing revolutionary ways to think about the origins and development of human civilization and patriarchy. In place of biblical origin stories, the new anthropological and evolutionary accounts of human history appealed to Alice. The essays she would soon write contain detailed references to these landmark publications—John Stuart Mill's "The Subjection of Women"; W. E. H. Lecky's *History of European Morals*; Herbert Spencer's *Principles of Sociology*; and Henry T. Buckle's *History of Civilization*.

After the death of her mother, Alice began writing down her reading notes and her ideas about sex differences and gender roles, looking for answers to her predicament and by extension the challenges facing all women. In an early victory for her considerable personal charm, she shared one of these drafts with Robert Ingersoll, perhaps when he lectured at the Detroit Opera House on November 8, 1882.[24] Throughout her life, Alice would gain entry into elite circles by writing charming letters of introduction, often referencing—vaguely or by name—mutual friends. This is surely the tactic she employed to meet Ingersoll, a man famous for welcoming all callers. Once introduced, her vivacious personality and witty intellect cemented the connection.

Ingersoll liked what he read, and he urged Alice to keep at it.[25] The encouragement of the Great Agnostic provided Alice with much needed confidence and affirmation. Perhaps her years in purgatory would serve a larger purpose. Maybe all the suffering she had endured—the frequent moves, the loss of parents and siblings, and the public shaming resulting from her affair with Smart—had served a larger purpose, too. Perhaps she could join her father and her brother Bernard as a person who made brave sacrifices for a greater cause.

By the early 1880s, Alice had determined that her cause would be women's rights. She would fight for women, like her mother, who had subscribed to magazines such as *The Ladies' Repository* and learned from an early age that it was women's lot in life to clean and tidy the world of men.[26] She would speak for women like herself, who had been told they could be teachers, but only if they earned half as much as men, lived a circumscribed life, remained pleasant no matter what befell them, and retired upon marriage. She would voice the fears of young women taught to look pretty to attract a suitor, but not so pretty as to incite a man's lust, lest their own reputations be ruined. And she would preach to women who had been taught that the sins of the world rested on their shoulders—sins in which they had no say and for which they were cursed with pain in childbirth and perpetual servitude to men—that these sins were not their fault.

Each of Alice's advancements—her independent moves to Cincinnati and Sandusky and the unchartered path she negotiated with Smart—required new ways of relating to authority, the development of new skills, and mastering modes of life for which she had few, if any, female examples. This next move would be her boldest yet. If Ingersoll could attract crowds of 10,000 by subjecting biblical teachings to reason, why couldn't she? But first Alice Chenoweth needed a platform, a new home, and a new name.

PART TWO

Helen Hamilton Gardener

1884–1901

"Ingersoll in Soprano": Gardener, age thirty-two, as she appeared in her first book Men, Women, and Gods *(1885).*

5

Ingersoll in Soprano

There are a great many women to-day who think that orthodoxy is as great nonsense as I do, but who are afraid to say so. They whisper it to each other. They are afraid of the slander of the Church. I want to help make it so that they will dare to speak.

—HELEN HAMILTON GARDENER, 1884

ON A COLD, CLEAR EVENING in January 1884, the portentous first Sunday of the year, 800 people, mostly men, paid 75 cents to hear a young woman deliver a lecture in New York City's famed Chickering Hall, at Fifth Avenue and 18th Street, the very spot from which Alexander Graham Bell had placed the first interstate telephone call.[1] This particular night, the audience had not paid to witness a technological marvel but rather an intellectual one. It was rare indeed to pay good money to hear a woman speak, much less a woman no one had ever heard of before. Until just a few days earlier, this young woman had been known as Alice Chenoweth, a woman who had published no articles, championed no causes, and been involved in no reform efforts. That night in Chickering Hall, Alice Chenoweth became Helen Hamilton Gardener.

By the fall of 1883, Alice and Charles Smart had moved to New

67

York City, where they continued to live a public lie together as husband and wife. Equitable Life Assurance transferred Smart from the Detroit office to the company's flagship headquarters at 120 Broadway, the nation's first modern office building.[2] The couple attempted an equally modern life together as a reformist woman whose career was buttressed by a doting husband.

Alice later claimed that when she began extolling her radical ideas, she changed her name so as to not call attention to her Chenoweth heritage. But what she really did not want to draw attention to were the published reports of her sex scandal back in Ohio. Since "Mrs. Charles S. Smart" was already another woman's legal name, Alice came up with a brand new one that nevertheless signaled her fidelity to her lover. While she never gave a reason for her particular choice of names, genealogical research reveals that Hamilton and Gardener were the maiden names of Smart's two grandmothers (the former claimed to have descended from Alexander Hamilton).[3] Her last names were historical; her chosen first name was aspirational. In Greek, Helen means "bright one" or "shining light." Helen Hamilton Gardener would shine light on the injustices against women.

Upon arriving in New York, Gardener contacted Robert Ingersoll, who maintained a law office in the city, to let him know she had been working, as promised, on her freethought essays. He assured her that she "had written something valuable" and "at once declared it must be read in public." Gardener remained forever grateful to Ingersoll because he "placed my foot upon the first rung of the ladder as a writer and speaker." She had "come of a Southern line of ancestry whose women had never done any public thing," and she "trembled and feared from without lest I be wrong—lest my ability to do was purely imaginary." Ingersoll's encouragement was like a "Rock of Gibraltar" to Gardener at a time when she "boiled and seethed within with the need for self-expression and self-development." Ingersoll instructed Gardener to find her "own soul and then to stand erect and not to doubt and fear."[4] It was a directive she would ably follow for the next forty years.

But Ingersoll did more than offer crucial moral support to Gardener.

He used his "commanding position" to open doors for her and even traveled from his home in Washington, D.C., to Manhattan to introduce her inaugural lecture, guaranteeing crowds and publicity few first-time speakers could attract. Though Ingersoll encouraged the careers of many artists, he had never before—and never would again—take on a protégé. For the rest of his life, he lovingly referred to Gardener as "Heathen Helen" and treated her like a daughter.[5]

Just a few days before Gardener's debut, small advertisements in the New York papers promoted her lecture, promising that it would be "most interesting and characteristic of an educated and liberal-minded woman" and that Ingersoll himself would be there to "preside during the lecture." Tickets for her talk went on sale at Chickering Hall and Brentanos Bookstore at 9 a.m. Friday morning.[6]

Designed to house a music store, warehouse, and 1,450-seat concert hall, the four-story Chickering Hall, in the vibrant Union Square entertainment district, was considered an architectural masterpiece of brick, trimmed with gray marble and brownstone. It had recently hosted lectures by the poet Oscar Wilde and the famous naturalist Thomas Huxley, as well as numerous concerts utilizing its state-of-the-art $15,000 organ.[7] Attending lectures was a popular nineteenth-century leisure activity, and audiences expected talks to last two hours or more. But the vast majority of speakers were male.

After the Civil War, hundreds of thousands of women began tentatively entering American public life by joining one of the countless new women's clubs—from civic garden clubs to neighborhood groups to temperance organizations—that flourished from coast to coast. White and black women alike joined women's clubs, though the organizations were generally segregated. Unlike Gardener, however, these women generally engaged in activism because they believed that it was a Christian woman's duty to extend her sphere of influence beyond the home so that she might better protect her home. Such women generally spoke to women in public and male officials in private.

Gardener's inaugural lecture promised quite a different take on women's relationship to Christianity and public life.

PROTESTERS FLANKED the entrance to Chickering Hall on the night of Gardener's debut. Men and women representing the Salvation Army stood sentinel at the door and offered to buy back, at a profit, any tickets purchased for Gardener's talk. Her manager, Edward Bloom, tried to reason with the protesters by downplaying the content of her speech, a tactic to which Gardener vehemently objected. "Mrs. Gardener," he instructed, "I wish you would do the lecturing and let me do the lying."[8]

Shortly after 8 p.m., Gardener and Ingersoll took the stage together. The petite Gardener and the towering Ingersoll made a strange pair, with Ingersoll more than double Gardener's weight and over a foot taller. After enjoying several minutes of warm applause, Ingersoll quieted the crowd and, uncharacteristically, focused the attention on his stage mate. "Nothing gives me more pleasure, nothing gives greater promise for the future," proclaimed the Great Agnostic, "than the fact that woman is achieving intellectual and physical liberty." All men and especially women should heed this new voice, advised Ingersoll. "No human being can answer her arguments."[9]

Dressed in "plain black, with lace frilling on her throat and wrists," Gardener gathered her long brown hair "in a coil on the top of her shapely head, and in front were the customary bangs which believers and unbelievers among womankind seem to have in common." Despite her fashionable dress and bangs, Gardener looked much younger than her thirty years. One newspaper reported definitively that she was twenty-three.[10] The audience in Chickering Hall may well have doubted Ingersoll's grandiose claims about what this tiny young woman had to say.

After a brief, expectant applause, Gardener placed her printed lecture, "Men, Women, and Gods," on a small black music stand in the middle of the vast stage, empty save for Ingersoll, who looked on from the comfort of a plush armchair. "It is thought strange and particularly shocking by some persons for a woman to question the absolute correctness of the Bible," she ventured. "She is supposed to be able to

Robert Ingersoll, the "Great Agnostic," Gardener's close friend and champion.

go through this world with her eyes shut, and her mouth open wide enough to swallow Jonah and the Garden of Eden without making a wry face. It is usually recounted as one of her most beautiful traits of character that she has faith sufficient to float the Ark without inspecting its animals." But Gardener was not like these other women. "I claim that I have a right to offer my objections to the Bible," she announced.

At first, her voice waivered and she "comported herself like a young lady on commencement day," one newspaper reported, but by the second half of her two-hour address, Gardener, with a "clear and pleasant voice," hit her stride as a speaker worthy of Ingersoll's endorsement.[11] Her years of capturing and retaining her students' attention in the classroom translated well to the stage. The *Chicago Tribune* reported that Gardener delivered her address "like a little man."[12]

Although she did not mention her affair in Sandusky or her observations about her mother's and sisters' lives, these experiences informed her analysis of women's place in the world. Beginning with Eve eating fruit from the Tree of Knowledge, Gardener declared "every injustice that has ever been fastened upon women in a Christian country has been 'authorized by the Bible' and riveted and perpetrated by the pulpit." For example, the Bible taught that "a father may sell his daughter for a slave, that he may sacrifice her purity to a mob, and that he may murder her, and still be a good father and a holy man." Though Gardener hesitated to "soil my lips [or] your ears" with the details about what the Bible taught regarding women, she summarized several biblical stories to make her point that the Bible authorized and naturalized women's degradation.

In spite of these foundational edicts about female inferiority, women sat, week after week, in church pews, supporting the church with their money, their time, and their unpaid labor. The relationship between women and Christianity, then, was two-pronged: the Bible mandated women's second-class status while the church required her vigilant efforts to maintain it. By the 1880s, the notion that Christianity uplifted women and that women upheld the churches had become both sacrosanct and common knowledge. Nonsense, said Gardener. "Of all human beings a woman should spurn the Bible first." Women "above all others, should try to destroy its influence; and I mean to do what I can in that direction."[13]

Laws and social customs, based on the purported authority of the Bible, enforced female subservience to men in myriad ways. Husbands demanded purity upon marriage and fidelity after marriage; most wives could expect neither. Husbands could sue wives for divorce for any infraction; wives could not seek divorce for even the most grievous crimes, and if they dared to leave, mothers in the majority of states would lose custody of their children. Few women questioned the Bible or its lessons reiterated in law. Those who did were typically dismissed as insane, unfeminine, or sexually wanton. It was bad enough when men like Ingersoll attacked the Bible, one reviewer wrote scathingly, "but when a woman opens her mouth against the inspiration of The Book, it not only disgusts but terrifies one."[14]

Within days, reports of Gardener's remarkable speech spread from coast to coast. A headline in the *Detroit Free Press* declared "Christianity Crushed" by "Bullets from Bob Ingersoll's Mature Rosebud."[15] Newspapers proclaimed the existence of "A Petticoated Infidel," "A Fair Infidel," and "The Female Scoffer." Ultimately, the name "Ingersoll in Soprano," bestowed by the *New York Sun*, stuck.[16] Proud to be linked to Ingersoll in such a personal way, Gardener embraced this new moniker and the thousands of potential listeners it afforded.

INGERSOLL'S FAME as a speaker brought increased public attention to the causes he championed. The freethought movement reached the height of popularity in the United States in the late 1870s and 1880s. At the 1876 Centennial Exposition in Philadelphia, freethinkers established the National Liberal League to advocate for a truly secular nation—including the repeal of Sunday closing laws and Comstock Laws, the removal of the Bible from public schools, and universal suffrage.[17] This group, together with many state and local affiliates, sponsored numerous conventions, meetings, and publications each year, ensuring audiences and invitations for Gardener.

Freethought particularly appealed to Gardener because it addressed the root causes of women's oppression. She could not pinpoint one or two reforms that would have eased her mother's probate and guardianship struggles, nor could one law have prevented the public shaming she suffered in Sandusky. Such changes could only come from revolutionizing how Americans thought about the essential differences between men and women. She saw her unorthodox lectures as a step in that direction.

If Gardener's words shocked, that only added to the draw of her lecture tour. In the months to come, she went on to deliver "Men, Women, and Gods" in marquee venues throughout New York State, stopping in Syracuse, Rochester, and Buffalo, and on to Chicago.[18] Ingersoll was so impressed with Gardener that he continued as her mentor, encouraging her in subtle and overt ways as her career developed.

The novelty of Gardener's lecture tour made national news, but most reviews focused on her looks, sometimes to the complete exclusion of her remarks. The *Chicago Tribune*, for example, provided extensive coverage of her hair before concluding, "It is unnecessary to give a synopsis of her lecture."[19]

The persistence of such superficial reviews prompted Gardener to pen a spoof entitled "Lecture by the New Male Star," written "in the present style of reporting on women's lectures." Published in *The Truth Seeker*, the leading freethought publication and the only one with a national reach, the essay described in detail how a young male star looked and how he spoke, but included hardly anything about what he said.[20] "He is a small man, with large luminous brown eyes, and fair complexion," Gardener satirized. "He wore his hair cut short and parted on the left side, about an eighth of an inch from the middle." He styled his linen collar "close about a shapely throat" and from underneath his trousers "peeped the daintiest of feet, encased in patent leather shoes." The review concluded ceremoniously, "his necktie buckled in the back."[21] At the outset of her career, Gardener had found that humor was an effective way to combat sexism, a tactic she would employ time and again.

THROUGHOUT THE SUMMER OF 1884, freethought papers advertised Gardener as one of the movement's leading speakers and promised that she would headline the upcoming annual conference of the National Liberal League, held in conjunction with the New York State Freethinkers Association, at Cassadaga Lake, in New York, that September.[22]

Despite a grueling fourteen-hour train trip, Gardener expertly delivered "Men, Women, and Gods" at the Cassadaga meeting, convincing reviewers that she "deserves the success she has found in the lecture field."[23] During the business portion of the convention, the National Liberal League members changed the group's name to the American Secular Union (ASU) and elected Robert Ingersoll their president and Gardener to a prominent committee. Nine months from the day of her debut, Gardener had become among the most influential and well-known women in the burgeoning freethought movement.[24]

Even though freethinkers promoted universal suffrage, critiqued patriarchal marriage, and welcomed female voices and even female officeholders, the movement was nevertheless led by men who generally shared their era's views of women. Emboldened by Ingersoll's endorsement, Gardener felt secure enough in her status to take on the movement's male leaders. Just a few weeks after the close of the September 1884 convention at Cassadaga Lake, Gardener wrote a critical review of freethought leader Samuel P. Putnam's new book, *Waifs and Wanderings*. She grumbled that Putnam's otherwise promising book "dealt with woman too much upon the conventional theory that she is a convenient target at which to shoot sharp little sayings about peevishness, extravagance, and all the other frailties commonly enjoyed by vulgar humanity but usually denominated feminine."[25]

Putnam, a long-standing ASU official, popular speaker, and regular contributor to *The Truth Seeker*, did not take kindly to being criticized in the very paper that he helped to edit, especially not by a young woman whom he and the other male leaders had graciously welcomed into their ranks. He wrote Gardener a private letter asking her to expound on her thoughts about women's mental traits, though he hoped his inquiry would not "drown her in tears." Gardener published her reply in *The Truth Seeker*, clarifying that no tears had been shed by her on this or any other matter because "tears are not much in my line."

Above all, Gardener took issue with Putnam's mansplaining, noting that his letter was "delivered with that large confidence and breezy good nature characteristic of your sex." She also rejected his assertion

that men were inherently governed by reason. It was men, she countered, who were governed by superstition. Even the so-called liberal
ones encouraged their wives and daughters to go to church, Gardener
pointed out. Fathers denied their daughters the right to study science,
politics, and business and then complained that women were unreason-
able. Men "never think of training their boys to a future of idle dependence and emotional trust and faith that the Lord (or some other male
bird) will feed and clothe them." Yet, girls were "taught this hourly."

It was precisely because of such absurd teachings that Gardener
"publicly took the field." Countless people spoke against the Bible for
other good reasons, she declared, but *"I do it for women."* Men were
beginning to acknowledge that the Bible may not have been the best
reference on subjects like geology, but most still maintained that it was
right in its estimation of women. According to Gardener, nine-tenths of
liberal men argued, in theory, for the equality of women but "in act and
in ordinary life . . . their daughters are trained just as other girls are, to
go to Sunday-school and church, and never know their own disgrace in
so doing."[26]

BUT BEING INGERSOLL'S FAVORITE had its costs. Ingersoll's mentorship,
in particular, had begun to rankle some of her colleagues. While women
often spoke at small freethought meetings, none had taken the rostrum
at a venue comparable to Chickering Hall, much less been championed
by the Great Agnostic himself. By the spring of 1885, whispers of sour
grapes made their way into the freethought press. After all, there were
many women "whose writings are superior to Miss Helen H. Gardener's," Elmina Slenker asserted. Why had Ingersoll chosen to promote
Gardener above all others?[27] Over the next few years, similar critiques
appeared in *The Truth Seeker.* E. A. Stevens complained that Gardener's "particular claim for distinction consists of having been introduced

by Colonel Ingersoll as a Lecturer."[28] Another observed that Gardener's debut had "roiled the good disposition" of a "few of the old dames who had starred the country for seventy-five years."[29]

Gardener penned a public letter in her defense against Elmina Slenker's criticism, conceding that there were women who were superior writers and that she never claimed to be the best.[30] Lucy Colman, of Syracuse, a grand dame of the movement, chided Gardener's detractors, scolding "cannot one be glad for another that she may have had that advantage, even though she may be alone in the honor?"[31]

But neither Gardener nor her defenders answered the underlying question surely on everyone's mind: was she sleeping with Ingersoll? Probably not. Christian moralizers regularly tried to discredit freethinkers as debauched sexual deviants. In response, Ingersoll carefully crafted a persona as the nation's consummate husband and father—and, by all accounts, he was.

Many freethinkers, including Ingersoll, critiqued traditional marriage as stifling for women. Some even went so far as to call marriage "legalized prostitution" because, with few other avenues to support themselves, women essentially sold themselves to husbands in exchange for housing, food, and other necessities. But most stopped short of advocating free love—a fringe movement that promoted various iterations of an individual's right to natural sexual expression.[32] Nevertheless, the two "free" causes—free love and freethought—were linked by some common adherents and by their shared opposition to the Comstock Laws, under which both were regularly prosecuted. As passionately as he lobbied for secularism, Ingersoll decried free love and he most certainly did not want to be associated with free lovers.[33]

For her part, Gardener praised Ingersoll's devotion to his family throughout her life.[34] She even dedicated her first book to Mrs. Eva Ingersoll, "the brave, happy wife of America's greatest orator and woman's truest friend."[35] And she continued to spend time with the family at their Dobb's Ferry, New York, estate decades after Ingersoll's death.[36] Gardener publicly denounced free love in 1886, even as she was still engaging in it with Smart. She wrote: "We must all admit that love, to be love at all, must be 'free' to choose its object. But . . . I do not believe in any form of polygamy which has yet been tried . . . I believe in but one marital love in one life; but I am aware that some very good people differ from me wholly on this point. As to the promiscuity usually called 'free love,' it seems an utter abomination to me."[37] Privately, Gardener had felt the constraints of the "but one marital love" edict, but proclaiming a person's right to more than one marital love, much less a woman's right to passion, was out of bounds, even for "Heathen Helen."

DESPITE GARDENER'S successful 1884 lecture tour and meteoric rise within freethought circles, she returned to Missouri and made St. Louis her home base following the September meeting at Cassadaga Lake. One letter revealed that she went to Missouri to recover from her "present illness."[38] Since her time in Sandusky, she had regularly experienced periods of ill health. Most likely, she suffered from the nineteenth-century epidemic of neurasthenia, what today would loosely be understood as depression, perhaps triggered by the strain of living an increasingly public lie.

Her trip back to Missouri may also have been to help her lone surviving brother Alfred through a difficult time. Though they had been estranged since Alfred had her written out of their mother's will, Alfred's wife and children were in dire straits by 1884. Alfred's eye troubles made it impossible for him to carry on his work as a physician. So, in 1881, his family moved 21 miles from Olney to Troy, Missouri, where Alfred opened up a pharmacy. By 1884, he was blind and could no longer run the pharmacy.[39] His wife Ella bore their sixth and seventh children in Troy, one in 1882 and one in 1885, but neither child survived infancy. Gardener may have returned to Missouri to help run the pharmacy and care for the older children.

From the fall of 1884 until the spring of 1886, Gardener listed St.

Louis as her home, though she traveled as far away as Philadelphia and New York to lecture. Charles Smart moved to St. Louis with her and tried, unsuccessfully, to drum up business for the Equitable Life Assurance Society.[40] During this time, Gardener forged a close connection with Alfred's oldest daughter Minnie, then fourteen, who would one day name her own daughter Helen Gardener as a tribute to her favorite aunt.

Even though living in Missouri took Gardener out of the pulse center of reform circles, she made St. Louis a "grand battleground for freedom."[41] She sent letters to St. Louis papers in protest of clergymen's refusal to debate her colleague Charlie Watts. Clergy, she exclaimed, regularly pilloried "infidels" from their podiums, so why not debate one in person?[42] Local papers refused to publish her letters, so she sent them to *The Truth Seeker*. A few months later, she wrote to *The Truth Seeker* to complain of "library vandals" who defaced, with impunity, "liberal books." When her complaints got no attention from library staff, she alerted them that theological books had been mutilated. This prompted a thorough response.[43]

Gardener increasingly turned her attention to publishing her own book, a compilation of three of her lectures. Advertisements for the book began to run in September 1885, just as Gardener headlined the New York State Freethinkers Convention, held in Albany.[44] Gardener delivered her address, "Historical Facts and Theological Fictions," to a packed room at Leland's Opera House on Sunday, September 13, in a premier time slot just before Ingersoll.

Church teachings, Gardener proclaimed, denied that women were people with "absolute rights of persons," including the right to control their own bodies, "crushing [a woman's] self-respect and destroying her sense of personal responsibility as to her own acts in the matter of chastity." From Bible verses and Sunday sermons, a woman learned that she "must subordinate her own sense of right and her own judgment to the dictates of someone else—anyone else of the opposite sex."[45] The Bible offered no logical way to puzzle through the complexities women encountered in life and instead clouded women's thinking with stories about blessed virgins and the evils of women who craved knowledge.

Referencing the pagan Roman philosopher murdered by a Christian mob, one of the group's 2,600 members described Gardener as the "modern Hypatia, 'no less admired for her beauty than her wit.' When she discourses about 'men, women, and gods' all three listen."[46] Another attendee recalled his embarrassment at rudely dismissing Gardener, who stood out as "a bright-eyed, petite and extremely amiable young lady trying to get people acquainted and make everyone feel comfortable." He thought she seemed "silly" and gave her dirty looks only to realize later that she was the keynote speaker.[47]

Weeks after the convention, Gardener's *Men, Women, and Gods* proved an immediate success. Even the middle-brow *Chicago Times* praised the book.[48] Navy Secretary W. M. Chandler proclaimed that "a more readable, brave, sparkling and at the same time more true, original, and logical little volume was never written."[49] Antoinette Brown Blackwell, the first ordained female minister and the first woman to publish a feminist interpretation of evolution, also favorably reviewed Gardener's book. Blackwell declared that Gardener was "not only an able attorney for her sex, but a brave one too." Like Gardener, Blackwell saw hope in science's potential to nullify the Adam and Eve creation story which "has had the terrible effect of putting dishonor and privation upon the female sex for centuries of years."[50]

Dozens of people wrote to *The Truth Seeker* in praise of Gardener's book or to request a copy for 50 cents. Several writers suggested that every woman read *Men, Women, and Gods*. The book was even cited in a Cass County, Minnesota, divorce case. A young bride felt that her older husband, a wealthy doctor, had married her under false pretenses because he had claimed to be a Christian. When he gave her a copy of *Men, Women, and Gods*, she demanded that the court allow her to leave her husband. She lost.[51]

While most reviews were positive, reviewers could not resist including comments about Gardener's appearance, gender, and age. One reader noted, as a compliment, that the book was "forcible enough to be masculine, yet delicate and modest enough to be womanly in the truest sense of the word."[52] A reviewer in *The Sociologist* observed that "It is indeed progress that a young, refined, handsome woman should dare to mount the rostrum and address large audiences in behalf of her sex and to impeach before the bar of reason the false teachings which have been so effectual in keeping women in their position of industrial, political, and social dependence."[53]

Gardener herself was deluged with mail, but she became annoyed by the many clergymen who requested to meet with her privately so that they might convince her of the error of her ways. Who were these men to assume that she did not know her own mind or that they could change it through some unimpeachable force of their presence? To such correspondents, she said no thanks. When clergy would agree to publicly answer her points about Christianity, then and only then would she agree to meet them in private.[54] In a more measured reply written a few years later, Gardener shared that she saw her work "in the same line" as the clergymen who wrote her. She, too, was a preacher of sorts. But as an agnostic, she refused to concede that charity was inherently best practiced by Christians. To the contrary, she claimed to have "met it in its most exalted form among the 'heathen.'"[55]

THE SUCCESS OF *Men, Women, and Gods*—published years before better-known feminist critiques of Christianity, such as Matilda Josyln Gage's *Woman, Church, and State* (1893), Elizabeth Cady Stanton's *The Woman's Bible* (1895, 1898), and Charlotte Perkins Gilman's *Women and Economics* (1898)—elevated Gardener's status within and beyond the freethought movement. She began seeking wider, more mainstream venues in which to place her articles, and she contemplated her next move.

In March 1886, Gardener announced plans to settle permanently in New York City.[56] The Ingersolls had recently moved from Washington, D.C., to a mansion on Fifth Avenue, and Charles Smart's prospects appeared more certain tied to the home office of Equitable Life Assurance.

Gardener continued to struggle with ill health but went "back into the field" as a lecturer that summer, probably to finance her move. Many of the reformers she encountered had fortunes against which to buffer their unconventional ideas. Gardener had no such bulwarks, so she continued to brainstorm ways to make ends meet. Settling in Manhattan at the height of the Gilded Age and in the midst of national economic turmoil, however, would reveal to Gardener additional layers of women's degradation and the precariousness of her existence as a freethinking reformer cohabitating with a man to whom she was not legally married.

6

The Cultured Poor

*For the rich, the world is a playground. For the very poor, it is
a workshop, or a treadmill, or an almshouse. For the great and
steadily increasing middle class of cultured poor, it furnishes
neither pleasure, nor work, nor alms.*

—HELEN HAMILTON GARDENER, 1889

WHEN HELEN HAMILTON GARDENER arrived in Manhattan in
the spring of 1886, the city seemed tailor-made to greet her.
In the two years since her debut at Chickering Hall, she had traveled
around the East Coast and as far west as Chicago, but no city appealed
to her as much as New York. When health and family struggles had
compelled her back to Missouri, Gardener chafed against the small-
mindedness of St. Louis. She also resented the lingering influence of
her orthodox brother Alfred. In New York City, she could be herself.

It was in New York that she had become "Helen Hamilton Gardener," and by 1886, she moved there permanently so that she could
inhabit the new world that being Helen Hamilton Gardener had
opened up—a world of big ideas and of social events attended by the
most prominent thinkers, writers, artists, and politicians of the day. Gardener embraced her new cosmopolitan life with gusto, the only imped-

iments being her tenuous foothold on financial security and her erratic, often sick paramour Charles Smart, whom she claimed as her husband, truth be damned.

From the couple's new apartment at 44 East 21st Street, near Gramercy Park, Gardener contacted anyone and everyone she could think of who might be able to help her gain her foothold as a writer, not just a freethought writer, but a real writer. She began listing "writer" as her profession and eventually joined the Woman's Press Club of New York City, founded in 1889. She expanded her reach beyond freethought periodicals, publishing "Rome or Reason" in the November 1886 issue of the *North American Review*, the prestigious literary magazine once edited by Charles Eliot Norton and Henry Adams. She was in elite company. This particular issue included articles by Walt Whitman, Jefferson Davis, and Generals Ulysses Grant and William T. Sherman.[1]

Penning charming letters of introduction to powerful men remained a vital tool in Gardener's march to becoming a nationally known writer. "I am a Chenoweth of Virginia," she began her appeal to Edward Eggleston. Eggleston had served as a Methodist minister in Indiana with her father and was, by 1886, a novelist living in New York. Gardener had lived less than one year of her life in Virginia, but her Chenoweth ancestry provided entry into otherwise closed circles. She asked Eggleston if she and her husband could call on him and signed off as "Mrs. Alice Chenoweth Smart," making no mention of Helen Hamilton Gardener.[2]

Her most influential contact, in New York or elsewhere, remained Robert Ingersoll. Ingersoll quickly became a dominant presence in New York social and reform circles. He earned hundreds of thousands of dollars each year from his speaking engagements and legal work, and he lavishly spent every cent. His Fifth Avenue home, the first of four increasingly posh Manhattan mansions he would rent over the next decade, boasted a piano on all three floors. His final mansion, at 220 Madison Avenue, included a roof-top theater that could seat 200 people.[3]

Ingersoll loved to entertain and welcomed anyone who came to his door, especially on Sunday evenings, when he hosted weekly "at homes" that often lasted until dawn. The *New York Daily Graphic* heralded these gatherings as the social "events of the season." On any given Sunday, guests could expect to encounter industrial magnates like Andrew Carnegie, one of Ingersoll's most ardent admirers; politicians such as Speaker of the House Thomas Bracket Reed; the military hero General Sherman; famous reformers, including Elizabeth Cady Stanton and Henry George; writers, painters, and especially actors and musicians, Ingersoll's favorite guests. Visitors devoured feasts set on enormous banquet tables, danced, listened to legends, such as the Italian contralto Sofia Scalchi, and took turns playing Ingersoll's pianos.[4]

One correspondent described the Sunday at-homes as "a company of the most interesting men and women in New York" where everyone felt "exactly as though they had known each other all their lives" thanks to the Ingersolls' unpretentious "home folk ways." Describing Gardener's presence at these soirees, the reporter observed that "she is a pretty, petite, girlish-looking lady, whom nobody would suspect of holding opinions so ponderous, and launching them so courageously at the public." She "writes books worthy of the biggest-brained man and the most radical in America, but she doesn't look it."[5]

For nearly twenty years, Gardener was a regular at these parties.[6] She later reflected that Ingersoll "radiated love and confidence and happiness in his home," where it was her "privilege to spend many happy and instructive hours under his hospitable roof." On Sunday evenings "one met there the great men and women of the world, for men of all creeds and of none admired and loved the Great Agnostic. . . . It was a liberal education to know him and his friends."[7] Ingersoll's at-homes, as much as anything else, catapulted Gardener from obscurity into the world of letters.

GARDENER BEGAN most every week at the Ingersolls, and she often ended the week with a visit to the Manhattan Liberal Club, which gathered Friday nights at 8 p.m. at the German Masonic Lodge at 220 East 15th Street, in Union Square. Led by charismatic freethinkers, including Samuel Putnam (whose subtle misogyny she had critiqued in *The Truth Seeker*) and the radical abolitionist and anarchist Stephen Pearl Andrews (confidante of the feminist, free love advocate Victoria Woodhull), the Liberal Club welcomed both male and female speakers on "all sorts of social, political, scientific, or religious subjects." According to the New York *Sun*, "no topic is forbidden and the talk is very free."[8]

Each Friday the club hosted a different speaker and then debated the speaker's main points. In 1887 alone, the Liberal Club took up ideas as far-ranging as anarchism, free love, Marxism, temperance, and cooperative housekeeping. In addition to its weekly gatherings, the club also hosted secular, solstice-themed Christmas parties and celebrations of the birthday of Thomas Paine, still the lodestar of American secularism. From 1868 to the early 1910s (when the group splintered after officers refused to allow anarchist Emma Goldman and African American intellectual W. E. B. DuBois to speak), the Liberal Club provided the social and intellectual hub for New York's left-leaning literati.[9]

One night, as the Liberal Club discussed whether or not the death penalty should apply to women, Gardener made an especially noteworthy impression. She refused to abide the group's long-standing admission policy, which was to charge everyone 5 cents—except for Presbyterians and women, who were admitted for free. She told the group's secretary that "it was bad enough for women to be denied the right to vote or to be hanged, and to be robbed of other legal prerogatives, without being classed with Presbyterians as deadheads."[10] As she had done within freethought organizations, wherever Gardener went she sought not only to express her views but also to change institutions and structures to accord with them, often through humor.

In between the excitement of Ingersoll's Sunday at-homes and Friday evenings at the Liberal Club, Gardener wrote and worked, generally from the offices of *The Truth Seeker.* Percy Carrington, a young freethinker from Dillon, Montana, recalled his thrill upon stopping by the *Truth Seeker* offices at 33 Clinton Place only to find Gardener there. She even accompanied the boy and his family on a picnic and drive through Central Park. "We all like her ever so much," effused young Carrington.[11] By April 1887, *The Truth Seeker* reported that whenever Gardener went out in New York, "reporters throw themselves at her feet."[12] Another freethought paper, *Common Sense,* proposed that Ingersoll and Gardener run together for president and vice president in the 1888 election.[13]

FOR MOST OF THEIR TIME in New York, Gardener and Smart leased a two-bedroom apartment at 165 West 82nd Street in the neighborhood now called the Upper West Side.[14] Her apartment featured beautiful wood floors, high ceilings, tile fireplaces, spacious sitting areas for entertaining, and large floor-to-ceiling windows she could gaze out as she drafted her many essays. From her corner building, Gardener was midway between Central Park and Riverside Drive, bordering the Hudson River, and just a few blocks from the American Museum of Natural History. From this central perch, Gardener could enjoy Sunday strolls through Riverside Park and catch the nearby elevated train at the 81st Street station and be downtown in a matter of minutes.[15]

Gardener greeted the city's diverse residents with open curiosity. When they could afford it, she and Smart employed Japanese servants, not the more typical Irish girls.[16] She especially liked meeting people with different religious backgrounds because they provided her with fodder to contradict the prevailing American wisdom that Anglo Christians were the most moral people on the planet.[17] Gardener embraced the "melting pot" image of America that took hold in the late nineteenth century as immigration skyrocketed, an era memorialized with the dedication of the Statue of Liberty in 1886. In the summer of 1887, she attended a Decoration Day parade to honor Civil War dead. A British friend commented on how strange it was that so many of the city's municipal firemen and policemen did not appear to be native-born. Gardener countered that it was this very mix that made the forces so effective.[18]

But even as she embraced diversity in theory, her own existence in the Upper West Side had been made possible by the forceful removal of others. In the 1880s, city leaders extended rail lines and neighborhoods, improved infrastructure, installed underground electric and telegraph lines, built new parks, and erected the historic monuments that have come to symbolize the city—the Statue of Liberty, Grant's Tomb, and the Washington Square Arch. Gardener arrived just in time to witness New York City become the global metropolis that it remains to this day. But until the early 1880s, city planners' lofty aspirations for the West Side contrasted sharply with the reality of thousands of squatters residing in the neighborhood. After construction began on Central Park and especially after the economic Panic of 1873, thousands of homeless people lived on the West Side. By 1880, there were an estimated 10,000 squatters in several ethnically distinct shanty towns. After the extension of the el to Tenth Avenue, the shanty towns were destroyed.[19] Gardener moved in shortly thereafter.

This disturbing contrast between haves and have-nots became a telltale sign of city life in the 1880s and informed Gardener's thinking about wealth in America. Though she longed to recapture the status of her Chenoweth ancestors, who themselves came to Maryland thanks to a land grant extracted from Native Americans, she also disdained the modern corporation for creating huge economic disparities. She supported the reformer Henry George in his candidacy for mayor of New York in 1886 (he came in second but ahead of the third-place candidate, Theodore Roosevelt). In his best-selling book *Progress and Poverty* (1879), George proposed a "land value tax" on all private property, the vast majority of which was held by corporations, so that corporate profits would be reinvested in the public good.

In an essay entitled "The Cultured Poor," Gardener illustrated the plight of people like herself and Charles Smart—the sons and daughters of "merchants, lawyers, clergymen, book-keepers" who had grown up to be members of "that large class, the most pathetic of all the victims of our present social system who have the culture, tastes, and habits of the rich, combined with a purse not to be envied by the sturdy laundress." Gardener asserted that there were few jobs for educated middle-class people, much less women, yet no one would dream of offering them "cast-off clothes" or extending them alms.[20] While Gardener was willfully blind to other aspects of her privilege—she and Smart were far from the most pathetic victims of the era's economic policies—she movingly evoked the economic anxieties of the era.

Gardener was particularly concerned about poverty's impact on women. Around this time, she wrote a short story featuring a young woman who could not find a job and attempted to kill herself rather than turn to prostitution, the only path to survival open to her. The narrator declared that "her story was that of thousands of helpless girls who face the unknown dangers of a great city with the confidence of youth, and that ill training and ignorance of the world which is supposed to be a part of the charm of young womanhood."[21]

She published another story depicting a reform meeting, not unlike those she attended each Friday at the Liberal Club. In the story, a man named Roland Barker stops by the meeting to address a crowd of workingmen on "The Realities of Life" before venturing on to an elegant dinner party. He confidently declares that "poverty and toil are not, after all, the worst that can befall a man, and that the most acute misery dwells in palaces and is robed in purple."[22] Barker intimates that he is miserable in his marriage but stuck in it due to retrograde marriage laws, a far worse fate, he suggests, than to be poor but happily married.

Barker's speech is interrupted by a shy, haggard woman standing at the back of the crowded room. She raises her hand to counter that Barker "does not know what real suffering is. He cannot. No rich man can." Barker had argued that money without love does not bring happiness, but the woman contends that "the keenest agony that mortals ever bore" is the combination of love plus poverty. The woman asserts that when you love a husband or a child, yet do not have the money to properly care for them when they are ill, knowing that effective treatments exist just beyond your reach, that is the hardest of all life's struggles.[23]

Barker is deeply shaken by what the woman says and immediately understands it to be true. He later visits the woman in her ramshackle home and finds that she is caring, round the clock, for an invalid, mentally ill, and occasionally violent husband. Rather than watch him further degenerate without the possibility of an affordable cure, the woman poisons her husband and then herself. Barker and his doctor friend find the couple and conclude that the cause of death was "natural," a result of "the brutality and selfishness of man."[24]

In her depiction of the outspoken woman at the mostly male liberal meeting, Gardener was presenting a version of herself. In the few years since she had joined the freethought movement, Gardener had borne witness to no limit of bloviating by rich men on various topics at the Liberal Club, at reform meetings, and at the Ingersolls' Sunday gatherings. Gardener infiltrated these circles through her charm, wit, and elegant self-presentation, but underneath her one or two nice dresses, she remained an outsider with few resources.

Gardener trenchantly observed the connection between wealth and radicalism—it was easy to be a radical if you were rich, easier still if you also happened to be a white man. Commenting on the people who had hosted her 1886 lecture in Waynesburg, Pennsylvania, she described H. Clay Luse as a man who enjoyed not only a "free brain" but also "the happy combination of independent social and financial standing, which enables [him] to do justice to his brains without fear of doing injustice to his appetite."[25] This was a freedom that Helen Gardener would never know. Gardener's intellect would soon become legendary, but she would never enjoy the safety net conferred by a family fortune, a dependable career, or a wealthy husband.

Gardener in 1890, on the cusp of becoming a self-supporting writer and reformer in Manhattan.

GARDENER ALSO EXPERIENCED the economic struggles wrought by the rapid expansion of post–Civil War capitalism in her very own apartment, where Charles Smart returned each day to vent about his struggles at the Equitable Life Assurance Society.

The world headquarters of the Equitable Life Assurance Society, erected in 1870 at 120 Broadway, was one of Manhattan's architectural marvels. The building was the precursor to the modern skyscraper and the first to boast an elevator. Within a few years of its inception, Equitable had become the second largest insurance company in America. Its formidable founder, Henry Hyde, believed that the company needed a headquarters that visually represented its dominance. Hyde selected the design of Arthur Gilman and Edward Kendall among a field of top competitors. According to an architectural historian, the design was chosen "for its superior logic as well as its artistic bravura." As a place of work, the Equitable Building did not merely "accommodate corporate activity, it celebrated corporate enterprise."[26]

The actual benefits that the Equitable Building bestowed to workers and customers, however, were dubious and in some cases downright dangerous. Company letterhead boasted that the safety deposit vaults in the Equitable Building were the "most secure in the world." But internal memos tell a more nuanced story. A New York manager wrote to President Hyde in 1883 to report changes he had made to the reading room adjacent to the safe deposit area because the upholstered furniture was "of very little use excepting for chronic loungers." Each day several men spent hours sleeping in the lounge's comfortable chairs. As a result, the furniture was "alive with lice and a few bedbugs." These men also availed themselves of the adjacent basin, where rather than simply wash their hands, some stripped down and took baths. In response, the manager replaced the upholstered furniture with wood and removed the wash basin.[27] Just before Smart arrived in 1883, the building also witnessed its first fatality after a man was crushed to death under a descending elevator car.[28]

Located nearly 6 miles from his apartment in the Upper West Side, it was to this flagship building that Smart ventured each day in the hopes of turning a profit. But Smart, born in the 1830s and trained as a one-room schoolteacher, struggled to adapt to the fast-paced, modern mode of business. While he had once proved adept at selling himself within Ohio political circles, self-promotion for the sake of corporate profit was a different skill altogether.

Smart must have expressed reservations to Gardener about the ethics of the insurance industry because in July 1887, she published an article entitled "Lawsuit or Legacy" in *Popular Science Monthly* lambasting the insurance industry for scamming families out of money after their insured loved ones died. She objected to company policies that refused to pay claims on the grounds that the deceased had lived an "immoral" life. "Nowhere else in the history of large business organizations," charged Gardener, "has the debtor regulated his obligation by the morals of his creditor." By way of example, she clarified that if A owed B $50 and B was a murderer that did not mean that A did not have to pay the debt.[29]

Elsewhere, Gardener critiqued the gender bias of the insurance business, the very industry that pioneered the science of actuarial tables and pinpointed the monetary value of each human life according to age, race, and sex.[30] Insurance "estimates of longevity, desirability of risk, etc.," she claimed, were all "based upon male standards." Furthermore, insurance executives often used actuarial tables in contradictory ways to either deny women coverage or charge them more. Gardener told of a woman who was informed that she would have to pay significantly more for insurance than her brother, since women—as a result of childbirth—were "subject to more dangers of death than men." Later, her elderly mother went to the same insurance agent to invest in an annuity only to be told that she was entitled to much less than a man because women tended to live longer.[31]

While by all accounts successful in the Detroit office, Smart struggled to maintain his standing within the Equitable company after moving to Manhattan, occupying various positions, such as salesman, manager, and investigator. He was often too ill to go to work, and when he did go to the office, he always came home for lunch, all the way from 120 Broadway to 165 West 82nd Street. Gardener recalled that when it came to his job, Smart was so "leisurely (possibly lazy might be used by most) that I often wondered (and feared) that they did not dismiss him entirely for a well man who would reach the office promptly and remain all day." Even President Hyde did not come home for lunch,

Gardener exclaimed.[32] Gardener's reputation as a writer and speaker soared throughout the 1880s, but her public acclaim and book sales did not translate into a salary that could comfortably support the couple.

Gardener's greatest disappointment in New York, however, was not financial or romantic. It was intellectual. After years of critiquing the Bible for its treatment of women, she had come to believe that science offered a rational antidote to biblically sanctioned misogyny. According to Gardener, women who were "fortunate to live in the same age as Charles Darwin" had "better stick to nature . . . [because] nature may be exacting, but she is not partial."[33] In her 1886 keynote lecture at the American Secular Union Congress, Gardener even proposed that "the education of women in the sciences is vastly more important to-day than the education of men" because science had the power to elevate women.[34] But she would soon be dismayed to find that nineteenth-century science, like religion, was a system run by men for men. That, too, would have to change.

7

Sex in Brain

When religious influence and dogma began to lose their terrors, legal enactments were slowly modified in woman's favor and hell went out of fashion. Then, Conservatism, Ignorance, and Egotism, in dismay and terror, took counsel together and called in medical science, still in its infancy, to aid in staying the march of progress.

—HELEN HAMILTON GARDENER, 1888

NOT LONG AFTER her arrival in Manhattan, Helen Hamilton Gardener tried to register for science classes at Columbia University, not far from her apartment on 82nd Street. But in the 1880s, women could enroll only in the special Collegiate Course for Women, not in the University's science classes.[1] For the rest of her life, she proudly claimed to have done postgraduate work in biology at Columbia, but in reality she would have had to sit silently in the back of the class as an auditor.

In the long tradition of Thomas Paine, nineteenth-century freethinkers viewed science as the apotheosis of rational thought. Gardener, a voracious reader and autodidact, joined them in enthusiastically championing science. Atheists and agnostics had long dismissed biblical literalism, and the new science of evolution promised to substantiate their critiques with evidence. At the same time, the broad-based acceptance of evolutionary theory helped bring the freethought movement comfortably into the mainstream. Freethought conventions and publications regularly celebrated Charles Darwin—especially upon his death in 1882—and discussed the latest scientific and technological developments. Religion could not explain modern marvels like electricity, photography, or the telephone. Science could. Freethinkers believed that such advancements heralded the eventual triumph of a secular worldview.

For Gardener and other female freethinkers, evolutionary theory offered the additional benefit of debunking the Adam and Eve creation story. For generations, the lessons drawn from this myth circumscribed women's opportunities, justified their ill treatment, and diminished their self-confidence.[2] Eve was created from Adam's rib to be his help-mate; thus, it was preordained that women should be subservient to men. Eve introduced sin into the world by eating fruit from the Tree of Knowledge; thus, women were not to be trusted and sin was their fault. For her transgression, God cursed Eve and all women after her to suffer painful childbirth and be "ruled over" by their husbands. But as Elizabeth Cady Stanton observed in the freethought periodical *Lucifer the Light-Bearer*, "What would be the tragedy in the Garden of Eden to a generation of scientific women? . . . Scientific women [would] relegate the allegory to the same class of literature as Aesop's fables."[3]

Despite feminists' expectations that evolutionary theory would revolutionize thinking about the supposedly preordained differences between men and women, scientists did not welcome women into their ranks or have encouraging things to say about their capabilities. To the contrary, science was enlisted to explain why women were "naturally" unfit to enter college, the professions, and public life. The contrast between what science offered women in theory and how it was deployed by some male scientists inspired Gardener to probe the nature of science itself. Just a few years after she had challenged the (mostly) all-male preserve of the church for its foundational misogyny, she went

on to the second most powerful all-male preserve—science—and confronted the masculine bias at its core.

IN SEEKING ADMITTANCE to Columbia University, Gardener entered
the most heated women's rights debate of the late nineteenth century:
should women go to college? After the Civil War, more and more
women had begun enrolling in colleges because there were no longer
enough men to fill the seats or enough men to marry. But educators and
medical experts feared the consequences of this unprecedented social
experiment. In particular, they worried that higher education would
"unsex" women.

The debate over whether or not women should go to college was
shaped by the best-selling book *Sex in Education, or a Fair Chance
for the Girls* (1873), written by Harvard professor and physician Edward
Clarke. According to Clarke, the physical strain of menstruation was so
taxing that it should preclude higher education. Women who dared to
go to college while menstruating risked becoming infertile. Pioneering
doctor Mary Putnam Jacobi debunked Clarke's thesis with what was
then the largest and most comprehensive study of menstruation, but
Clarke simply shifted tactics and began arguing that women should not
go to college because of the structure of their brains.[4] Women's brains,
he asserted in his next book *The Building of a Brain* (1874), were fundamentally different from men's and thus not suited for higher education
or careers.

To substantiate his arguments about sex differences in brains, Clarke
turned to the work of William A. Hammond, the former surgeon general of the U.S. Army and past president of the American Neurological
Association.[5] Hammond claimed to have treated scores of young women
who had had their nervous systems "woefully disturbed" in the effort
to master subjects that "could not possibly be of use to them," such

as "algebra, geometry, and spherical trigonometry."[6] Hammond came to believe that teaching women the same subjects as men—especially science and math—overtaxed their delicate systems and led to mental breakdown.

After years of study, Hammond claimed that there were nearly twenty physiological differences distinguishing the brains of men from those of women. Male brains, he declared in *Popular Science Monthly*, weighed more, had higher specific gravity, and had better developed frontal regions. These distinctions supposedly revealed why men excelled in intellectual and professional pursuits and women did not.[7] As a result of their differential brain structure, women, according to Hammond, should stick with subjects relevant to their job as mothers—such as music, painting, and literature.[8]

Gardener was an avid reader of *Popular Science Monthly*, and she puzzled over Hammond's article, "Brain-Forcing in Childhood," published in the April 1887 edition. She had repeatedly asserted that science had propelled women's gains thus far, and here science (like the Bible) was being used to naturalize women's permanent inferiority. Something did not jibe. Hammond cataloged sex differences in brains as if these were well-known, established facts. But Gardener believed that Hammond worked from the unquestioned assumption that women were naturally inferior to men and based his research on substantiating this premise, rather than interrogating the premise itself. In other words, Hammond had his own Garden of Eden story. What was new in this retelling was the claim that female inferiority could be measured by scales and microscopes. Fine, Gardener demanded, let's measure.

Undaunted by Hammond's superior status in the scientific community, Gardener decided she would set the record straight. As a woman, she lacked a degree, a laboratory, and the ability to study brain specimens herself. So she wrote down a list of twenty questions—Do the brains of infants differ by sex? If so, were these differences observable by sight? If yes, did these differences increase with age? Was there "unanimity of opinion" among scientists about these questions?—and sent them to the leading neurologists and brain anatomists in New York City.[9]

She then queried the man she had heard was the nation's premier neurologist, Edward C. Spitzka, the former president of the New York Neurological Association and the man who would soon found the American Anthropometric Society, to collect and examine the brains of accomplished individuals. Having "previously discovered that even brain anatomists are subject to the spell of good clothes," Gardener put on her "best gown" and went to meet the esteemed doctor. Though Spitzka did not support women's rights, he was committed to modern scientific methods. His office was filled with all sorts of specimens, microscopes, and journals to which most people lacked access. According to Gardener, Spitzka, unlike Hammond, was "too thoroughly scientific to allow his hereditary bias to color his statements of facts on this or any subject." Spitzka confirmed that, contrary to Hammond's assertions, it was impossible to differentiate brains by sex. Gardener and Spitzka became lifelong friends.[10]

After having collected a wealth of data and immersed herself in the subject, Gardener rebutted Hammond's findings with a letter to the editor in the June issue of *Popular Science Monthly*. Hammond's theory about sex differences in brains, she charged, was based on "assumption and prejudice," not "scientific facts and discoveries."[11]

Gardener challenged Hammond to a public test. She would provide twenty brains from Spitzka's collection, and if Hammond could distinguish them by sex, she would concede. Hammond refused. He countered, smugly, that calculating averages, not examining individual brains, was the way "all such determinations are made by those who know what they are about." He dismissed Gardener's challenge as resulting from the "defective logical power" so "characteristic of most female minds." Not only would a sample of male brains always weigh, on average, more than female brains, Hammond dared Gardener to find just one female brain that exceeded 53 ounces, a mark of greatness met by several eminent men.[12] Gardener and Hammond sparred in the pages of *Popular Science Monthly* for the next several months. In October, the editors declared the debate over and granted Hammond the last word.[13]

Gardener's brain essays attracted international attention. Even scientists took note of her research and intellectual creativity. The *Physicians' and Surgeons' Investigator* republished her findings "with pleasure," boasting that this "talented young woman has bearded the lion in his den . . . the investigations set on foot by Miss Gardener open up an entirely new field, in which we hope she will continue her work."[14]

At the same time, *Men, Women, and Gods* continued to sell so well that it had recently appeared in a new edition. Yet the unrelenting stress of life as a reforming lecturer and writer with no steady paycheck drained Gardener. Since settling in New York, Smart's income and health proved even more unstable than Gardener's, exacerbating the couple's struggles. What's more, her brother Alfred Chenoweth died in November 1887, leaving Gardener with just one remaining sibling—Kate, with whom she was not in contact—to link her to the long chain of ancestral Chenoweths. In late 1887, Gardener, now thirty-four years old, suffered a health breakdown. This one lasted several months. The physical and emotional strain of becoming and performing Helen Hamilton Gardener had overwhelmed her.

In December, the conclusion of her first full year in New York, *The Truth Seeker* reported that Gardener was "too ill to respond to invitations to lecture, or to conduct correspondence." The paper proclaimed that "her heart is in the cause of liberty, but her body is too feeble to bear her to the front." When she recovered, the editors promised, "her voice will again be heard throughout the land."[15] And indeed it would. Not six months later, Gardener would deliver the speech that defined her career.

GARDENER SPENT the winter of 1887 as "an invalid confined to her room in New York," according to one colleague.[16] But in early 1888, an enticing invitation from her friend Elizabeth Cady Stanton, whom she had come to know on the freethought lecture circuit, hastened her return to the podium.

Born in 1815, Stanton was nearly the same age that Gardener's mother would have been. Gardener revered her as a role model and lovingly referred to her as "Mother Superior."[17] Stanton had been active in reform work since before Gardener was born—famously co-organizing the 1848 Women's Rights Convention at Seneca Falls, New York, and drafting the meeting's Declaration of Sentiments and Resolutions, which demanded, among other reforms, women's right to vote. Long considered the century's most prominent feminist thinker, Stanton's fearless writings about the misogyny undergirding marriage, religion, and social customs shared much in common with Gardener's. But by the late 1880s, Stanton's outspoken critiques of the Bible met with increasing resistance within the National Woman's Suffrage Association (NWSA), the group she cofounded and led with Susan B. Anthony.[18] Stanton was looking for new allies, and she found an enthusiastic one in Gardener.

Together with Anthony, Stanton was planning a historic international gathering of leading women from western Europe and North America—the biggest ever held in the United States—to take place

Elizabeth Cady Stanton, the freethinking friend who introduced Gardener to the women's rights movement.

during the spring of 1888 in Washington, D.C. For what they called the International Council of Women (ICW), Stanton and Anthony aimed to bring together "all women of light and learning . . . all associations of women in trades, professions and reforms, as well as . . . those advocating political rights."[19] Ultimately, women representing fifty organizations and eight countries converged in Washington on March 25 for the elaborate eight-day event. President Grover Cleveland welcomed the group, and a number of senators held receptions in their honor. Many attendees stayed on an extra day to address legislators in Congress, emphasizing that suffrage was the ultimate goal of the proceedings and of the women's rights movement.[20]

The ICW was organized under the auspices of the NWSA, one of two national suffrage groups competing for priority in the nineteenth century. In organizing the ICW, Stanton and Anthony hoped to shore up their preeminence by celebrating the fortieth anniversary of the Seneca Falls Women's Rights Convention, a decision that obscured the movement's earlier roots in abolition and the accomplishments of their rival group, the American Woman Suffrage Association (AWSA). As savvy organizers, Stanton and Anthony believed that for their cause to prevail, they also had to shape their own legacies, even to the point of compiling the movement's history themselves.

Stanton, Anthony, and Matilda Joslyn Gage had just completed step one of this mission by writing the first three volumes of the *History of Woman Suffrage*, which detailed the accomplishments of the NWSA and marginalized the AWSA (which worked for the vote on a state-by-state basis and was headquartered in Boston). Stanton and Anthony saw the ICW as the next phase of their legacy project. According to historian Lisa Tetrault, the ICW "worked to bring the women's movement in line behind the story Stanton and Anthony had given ten exhausting years to constructing" in the *History of Woman Suffrage*.[21] The two aging leaders hoped that a shared origins narrative would move female reformers, who by then disagreed on many issues and strategies, toward the singular goal of securing a federal suffrage amendment.

Stanton had an additional motive. She also wanted to use the ICW to entice women to join her *Woman's Bible* Revising Committee, a project to compile and provide commentary on all sections of the Bible that mention women.[22] Stanton had long voiced anticlerical and anti-orthodox sentiments, and after finishing the suffrage histories, she turned her full attention to *The Woman's Bible.* Believing this to be her most significant contribution to women's rights, Stanton had begun inviting women to her Bible project as early as 1882, but she was having a hard time securing Revising Committee members. Most of the women she approached over the years turned her down, their rejection letters producing, in her words, "a most varied and amusing bundle of manuscripts."[23]

The Woman's Bible was very similar in scope to Gardener's *Men, Women, and Gods,* and Gardener was one of a small handful of eager Revising Committee members. When Stanton first approached her in the summer of 1886, Gardener gladly accepted, declaring, "I consider this a most important proposal." If the two busy women could "ever stay on the same side of the Atlantic long enough," Gardener promised, "we will join hands and do the work."[24] Gardener agreed to chair the historical committee, and she provided regular updates about the project to interested readers of *The Truth Seeker.*[25] But she understood that her true job was to "bring the wit" to *The Woman's Bible.*[26]

Stanton's hopes of securing a large cadre of Revising Committee members at the ICW never came to fruition. What the gathering revealed instead was that the vast majority of female reformers remained deeply religious even though they held divergent beliefs about denominations and doctrines. Foreshadowing the book's later reception among suffragists, *The Woman's Bible* generated only controversy at the ICW.[27]

GARDENER, HOWEVER, TRIUMPHED. Her appearance at the ICW opened up a new chapter in her public life and introduced her to a wide network of international women. When brainstorming her ideal roster of speakers, Stanton had first proposed that Gardener speak during the session devoted to religion, but after reading Gardener's 1887 essays in *Popular Science Monthly*, Stanton suggested instead that Gardener deliver "one speech on our heads, as to their size and contents." Stanton told the other organizers that Gardener "was logical and at the same time amusing" and a "very pleasing little woman."[28]

Even though she had never attended a women's rights meeting before, Gardener was allotted a Saturday evening keynote spot at which to deliver her new lecture, "Sex in Brain." Stanton introduced Gardener, explaining that "the last stronghold of the enemy is scientific." And one would have been hard-pressed to overestimate the power of science in shaping public opinion about what women should and should not be able to do. "Men have decided that we must not enter the colleges and study very hard; must not have the responsibility of government laid on our heads," Stanton thundered, "because our brains weigh much less than the brains of men." But after fourteen months of investigation, Gardener, Stanton promised, would "show to us that it is impossible to prove any of the positions that Dr. Hammond has maintained."[29]

After a hearty round of applause, Gardener rose to the podium and looked out over hundreds of the world's foremost women. Emphasizing the serious purpose and historic nature of the ICW, the grand stage was festooned with flags from each U.S. state and several foreign countries, along with evergreens and flowers.[30] Every aspect of the ICW was designed to present women as capable citizens, up to the tasks of voting and crafting public policy. According to Stanton, "the order and dignity of the proceedings proved the women worthy [of] the occasion."[31]

Adorned in her favorite black velvet dress with a scarf of red Canton crepe across her chest, Gardener beseeched the women to add science to their agenda.[32] Women's opportunities, she explained, were "very greatly influenced" by those "two conservative molders of public opinion—clergymen and physicians." In those heady days of rapid scientific discovery and technological invention, few educated men still quoted the Genesis creation story to justify their treatment of women.

Now they turned to science. After biblical literalism had gone "out of fashion," Gardener contended, "Conservatism, Ignorance, and Egotism, in dismay and terror, took counsel together and called in medical science, still in its infancy, to aid in staying the march of progress."

Scientists like Hammond, she charged, let their religious and cultural biases taint their research and mar their conclusions, noting that "a man's religious leanings inevitably color and modify all of his opinions, and govern his entire mental outlook." Scientific experiments would not be free from sexism without checks in place to counter the ingrained prejudices of scientists themselves. As it stood, women "had hailed science as their friend and ally" only to be met with "pseudoscience" that "adopted theories, invented statistics, and published personal prejudices as demonstrated fact."

Beyond simply debunking Hammond's brain research, Gardener sought to impress upon her audience that science was both a vital fulcrum in debates about women's rights and a potential ally for feminists. "Educators, theorists, and politicians readily accept the data and statistics of prominent physicians, and, in good faith, make them a basis of action," declared Gardener, while women, the "victims of their misinformation," remained helpless. Few were confident enough to question scientific findings; fewer still had the anatomical and anthropological information required "to risk a fight on a field . . . held by those who based all of their arguments upon scientific facts, collected by microscopes and scales and reduced to unanswerable statistics."[33]

Women needed to participate in science, Gardener proclaimed. After so many scientists and news outlets uncritically accepted Hammond's findings, Gardener had been shocked to discover that there was in fact no scientific consensus on the existence or significance of sex differences in brains. "This being the case," Gardener implored, "it will be just as well for women themselves to take a hand in the future investigations and statements."[34] And Gardener had a very specific form of participation in mind. The brain of "no remarkable woman" had ever been studied. Scientists made sweeping claims about the differences between male and female brains, but their studies compared the brains of great male leaders and intellects against anonymous "female tramps, hospital subjects and unfortunates."[35]

Surrounded by the most prominent women in the United States, Canada, and western Europe, Gardener sought a few specimens. "I sincerely hope that the brains of some of our able women may be preserved and examined by honest brain students, so that we may hereafter have our Cuviers and Websters and Cromwells," she concluded. "And I think I know where some of them can be found without a search warrant—when Miss Anthony, Mrs. Stanton, and some others I have the honor to know, are done with theirs."[36]

Stanton was galvanized by Gardener's address. The next day she declared: "The paper read last night by Helen Gardener was an unanswerable argument to the twaddle of the scientists on woman's brain. The facts she gave us were so encouraging that I started life again this morning, with renewed confidence that my brain might hold out a few years longer."[37] In her autobiography, Stanton singled out just one speech from the eight-day ICW, describing "Sex in Brain" as "one of the best speeches" of the week.[38]

Gardener's brain research cemented her friendship with Stanton and prompted the two freethinkers to swear an oath to each other. The previous summer, Gardener wrote Stanton to urge her to donate her brain to science so that researchers could, for the first time, study the brain of a "great woman." She explained that she had instructed Smart to donate her brain too, but Gardener feared that because of her small stature and poor health her brain might not measure up as well as Stanton's presumably larger and heartier specimen. Gardener further enjoined Stanton to make sure that her children would honor her wishes and signed her letter "Heathen Helen." Stanton submitted her signed brain bequest form to Cornell University's Burt Wilder Brain Collection. And on the back of Gardener's letter, she instructed her children: "You must save my brain for Heathen Helen's statistics."[39]

Gardener even published a humorous poem imagining their brains living on together at Cornell, a creation she especially cherished because

FORM OF BEQUEST OF BRAIN.

I, *Elizabeth Cady Stanton*

now of *New York City*

student of _____ from _____

to _____, and graduated from _____

in _____, recognizing the need of studying the brains of educated and orderly persons rather than those of the ignorant, criminal or insane, in order to determine their weight, form and fissural pattern, the correlations with bodily and mental powers of various kinds and degrees, and the influences of sex, age and inheritance, hereby declare my wish that, at my death, my brain should be entrusted to the Cornell Brain Association (when that is organized) or (pending its organization) to the curator of the collection of human brains in the museum of Cornell University, for scientific uses, and for preservation, as a whole or in part as may be thought best. If my near relatives, by blood or by marriage, object seriously to the fulfilment of this bequest, it shall be void; but I earnestly hope that they may interpose neither objection nor obstacle. I ask them to notify the proper person promptly of my death; if possible, even, of its near approach.

Signature *Elizabeth Cady Stanton*

Date *Feb-4-2nd /900*

Witness *Edith Lyman White*

NOTES.—1. A duplicate copy of this form should be filled out and retained by the testator.

2. The bequest should be accompanied by a photograph and a sketch of life or character, or a reference to published biography. (*See -*)

3. The testator should notify the undersigned of any change of address, not merely on account of the bequest but also in order that copies of circulars or other publications may be sent.

4. A brain is most safely transmitted in a tin pail of *saturated* brine, the lid secured with surgeon's adhesive plaster; the pail should be addressed as follows: *Anatomical Department, Cornell University, Ithaca, N. Y. Specimen of Natural History. Perishable.*

5. Copies of provisional diagrams of the fissures will be mailed upon application to the undersigned. For a brief statement of reasons for the study of the brains of educated persons, see Buck's Reference Handbook of the Medical Sciences (Wm. Wood & Co., New York) VIII, 163, and IX, 110.

BURT G. WILDER, M.D., Professor of Neurology,

Physiology, and Vertebrate Zoölogy, Cornell University, Ithaca, N. Y.

At "Heathen Helen's" request, Stanton pledged her brain to Cornell University's Burt Wilder Brain Collection.

it "shocked the elect."[40] Gardener mused that "Corked in a decanter on a shelf so high, their brains at Cornell, their souls 'on the fly.' Elizabeth Cady and Helen so small, Hold converse with scientists, all 'round the wall." The pair shared the space with an assortment of interesting male brains—doctors, lawyers, an admiral, and a poet—but Gardener's brain told Stanton's, "None can more deeply delight me than you."[41]

After 1888, speaking invitations poured in from women's and reform groups eager to hear from Gardener. Degree or no degree, Gardener retained her enthusiasm for science and continued to encourage women to enlist science as an ally. A few years after the ICM, she spoke at an event called the Science Sermons Society and declared that "had it not been for the birth of the scientific method of thought I would not stand here—no woman would be represented here tonight." Without science, women would be "where superstition and authority placed [them]— under the feet of man!" And it was the "strictly scientific method of thought alone," Gardener promised, that would free woman from "the bondage which barbarity bound upon her."[42] Decades later when she entered suffrage work, Gardener told a younger colleague that "in and through and with all of my scientific work, at all times, I have applied it to the feminist movement and especially to suffrage in America."[43]

But the experience of debating Hammond had also revealed to Gardener the limits of statistics, science, and reason. As it turned out, she learned with dismay, many people did not really care about statistics, science, or reason. After the publication of "Sex in Brain," Gardener's essay writing slowed. As she continued to struggle with her own health, romantic drama, and finances, she increasingly turned to fiction. In fiction, Gardener could reveal truths about her own life, and the lives of women more broadly, that otherwise went unspoken.

8

The Fictions of Fiction

The fictions of fiction have contributed to disarm us . . .
We wait for the orthodox denouement. It does not come. We
pray . . . we sit down and wait but no rich relation dies and
leaves us a legacy, nor does the prince appear and wed us.
—HELEN HAMILTON GARDENER, 1890

B EFORE THE VOGUE of the memoir, writers often turned to fiction
to voice the shameful truths about their own lives and the things
that no decent person was supposed to openly acknowledge. Between
1888 and 1894, Helen Hamilton Gardener published three novels and
at least nineteen short stories. With a fake husband and a complicated,
scandalous past, Gardener had much with which she needed to come
to terms. Not all of her novels and short stories were autobiographical,
but she often spoke of her fiction in autobiographical terms, sometimes
even revealing to friends the names of the real-life people represented
by characters in her stories.[1]

Gardener described her turn to fiction in two distinct ways. She told
friends that for years her New York literary contacts had encouraged
her to try her hand at storytelling. Then one night she awoke with the
"theme and the diction" of a story coming to her, so she stayed up the

rest of the night and wrote it all down. In the morning, she mailed the story to Donn Piatt, the editor of *Belford's Monthly Magazine*, with a letter instructing him to return it if the story were not up to his standards. Piatt recalled that in a "musical rustle of feminine drapery," she brought the story to him in person and that he was struck by her "girlish face and figure" and her "dark, luminous eyes . . . shadowed with pain, as if touched with the reminiscence of suffering, common to lifelong invalids." Regardless of how he received the story, that evening Piatt sent Gardener a reply, saying simply "Tip Top" and enclosing a check for $100.[2]

Other times, Gardener recounted more intellectual reasons for writing fiction. It was only in fiction, she explained, that one could both tell the truth and compel readers to understand the truth. "It is an interesting mental condition," she began the preface to her first novel, "which enables people to know things and not know them at the same time; to be perfectly familiar with the facts, and yet fail to grasp their significance until it is put before them in dramatic form."[3]

The problem with most fiction, she thought, was that it had been written from a male point of view. "Much of life means one thing to men—quite another to women," she explained. "Literature has yet to picture life from her standpoint."[4] Popular works advertised as "safe stories for girls" generally depicted a husband as a woman's ultimate salvation and marriage as a guaranteed happily-ever-after. At the other end of the spectrum sat stories decrying "fallen women" and the varied ways these women came to their sad demise. Neither mainstream romances nor cautionary tales depicted love and sex from a woman's point of view. Gardener dismissed such stories as "rubbish."[5]

"Every hapless girl who reads such a story is led to believe that she is the household fairy who will meet the prince and somehow (not stated) redeem her father's family from want and despair," opined Gardener. "We pray . . . we sit down and wait but no rich relation dies and leaves us a legacy," as she knew all too well, "nor does the prince appear and wed us." According to Gardener, the most dangerous "fiction of fiction" was also the "one that dominates" the genre: "the idea that woman was created for the benefit and pleasure of man, while man exists for and because of himself."

Fiction did not prepare women, the majority of novel readers, for "real people . . . for the exigencies of life that come; for the decisions and judgements we are called upon to make." Instead, Gardener contended, "the fictions of fiction have contributed to disarm us." Women deserved novels that provided them with "the armor of truth and the ability to adjust it to life."[6]

In response to an editor who complained about women's tendency to write "immoral and erotic literature," Gardener suggested that authors like herself had simply "ventured to portray passion and pleasure, virtue and vice, or joy and sorrow from an outlook considered by men either nonexistent or unmentionable from the established male critics' position."[7] Just as she had done on the freethought podium and in the pages of *Popular Science Monthly*, Gardener sought to break down institutionalized sexism through her writing. But to write openly about sex, she had to turn to fiction.

THE FIRST SHORT STORY published under the name Helen Hamilton Gardener appeared in *Belford's Monthly Magazine* in October 1888. "The Time-Lock of Our Ancestors" introduced readers to a forward-thinking, witty, and attractive woman named Florence Campbell who would star in two subsequent short stories, "Florence Campbell's Fate" and "My Patient's Story." In all of Gardener's short stories and novels, Florence Campbell is the only repeat character. Campbell was Gardener's literary doppelgänger.

Neighbors and friends perceive Florence Campbell as a beautiful, charming woman who "spoke as if she were very old, although to look at her one would say that she were not twenty-eight." She was one of "those Dresden-China women" who "often carry their age with such an easy grace—it sits upon them so lightly—in spite of ill-health, mental storms, and moral defeats, that while their more robust sisters grow haggard and worn, and hard of feature and tone, under weights less terrible and with feelings less intense, they keep their grace and gentleness of tone in the teeth of every blast." Campbell was also a woman "who either did not know, or did not care to investigate too closely, the career of her husband," a charming but unreliable man named Tom.[8]

"Time-Lock" centers on a conversation between Florence and her young friend Nellie, who had been living with Florence and Tom since she was orphaned. Overcome by emotion, Nellie tries to summon the courage to confess a transgression. Florence comforts her by explaining that, in reality, right and wrong were often difficult to distinguish—"as if there were but one 'right'!" Nellie would learn in time, Florence intimates, that the line between right and wrong was arbitrarily drawn, especially for women.

After much prodding, Nellie admits that she slept with Florence's husband Tom, in the Campbell's own home. Nellie feels tremendous guilt for betraying Florence, but explains that she was charmed by Tom's attention and promises of love. Florence is not surprised by Nellie's confession. Emphasizing that Nellie is not to blame, Florence sends Tom to Europe the next morning and asks that Nellie remain with her because "no one— no one in all the world has ever loved me truly."[9]

In this story, Gardener can be read as both Florence, a world-weary woman slow to judge others, and Nellie, a young woman begging forgiveness from an older woman whose husband she has stolen. As she observed in an essay entitled "The Fictions of Fiction," one of the most "insidious" and harmful themes in literature was the idea that "the good are so because they resist temptation, while the bad are vicious because they yield easily."[10] In her experience, the demarcation had not been so clear. No one outside of Ohio knew about her extramarital affair with Charles Smart, and even those who had witnessed it may have been convinced that Smart did eventually divorce his wife so that he could marry her. Only Gardener and Smart knew the truth, and this shared secret bound them together in spite of illness, economic uncertainty, and the constant weight of having to lie to their increasingly wide circle of New York friends and acquaintances.

Unable to confide in anyone, Gardener created characters whose experiences mirrored her own and whose troubles she could resolve, for better or for worse, within a few short pages. Gardener drew on her own experiences with Smart and inserted as characters the people closest to her. Through her fiction, Gardener attempted to change the way men and women thought about heterosexual relations. She also endeavored to make peace with her own life choices, settle a few scores, and, ultimately, create a more fitting backstory for herself.

THE PUBLICATION of Gardener's first short story collection in June 1890 marked her turn away from the lyceum circuit and toward writing as a vehicle for social change. By the summer of 1890, "Ingersoll in Soprano" had become "a writer with purpose." A *Thoughtless Yes* contained nine short stories (most previously published in magazines) and went into at least ten editions, the first of which sold out in just eight days. Ingersoll declared that Gardener had found her field because in fiction "her dramatic genius can better reach the people than by direct preaching."[11]

Yet fiction, as some reviewers observed, did not come as naturally to Gardener as essay writing. In her earliest stories, the narration often confusingly switches from omniscient third person to first person, and characters come and go with little introduction. Other readers complained that Gardener's fiction was too heavy-handed. Donn Piatt, the editor who solicited her first short story, entreated Gardener to "write me a love story but don't put anything in it—any thought. Don't suggest any ideas." But Gardener insisted on writing fiction "for a purpose."

Piatt eventually stopped championing her work and told her, regretfully, "you are a rare genius ruined by sincerity."[12]

In her short stories, Gardener cast about for themes and tried to secure for herself a permanent place in the crowded landscape of late nineteenth-century reform literature. After the unprecedented success of Harriet Beecher Stowe's Uncle Tom's Cabin (1852), reform fiction reached a historic highpoint. The same year that Gardener started publishing short stories, Edward Bellamy's Looking Backward (1888) became one of the top-selling books of the century and inspired a mass movement of Bellamy Clubs throughout the nation. The temptation for ambitious reformers to turn to fiction was great, but the competition overwhelming. To gain a foothold in this publishing environment, an author needed a distinctive voice and an issue to call her own.

Gardener's short stories clustered around a few core themes: the failings of men in marriage; society's tendency to misjudge women; folksy, nostalgic, and, to modern eyes, racist Southern stories; heredity; and the injustices of capitalism. Her strongest pieces centered on the issue she knew best: the romantic plights of middle-class white women. Here her powers of subtle observation and empathy offered original takes on sexual assault, courtship, and matrimony. Women with stingy husbands turn to theft, only to watch their children become thieves; women with brutes for husbands die from the strain of not being able to obtain a divorce; a young stepmother, so eager to please her new family that she sacrifices visits to her own parents, has a son with an uncontrollable urge to run away. Even seemingly happy marriages are plagued by husbands who lord their power over their wives in every small household decision. No princes save the day in Gardener's stories. Male doctors often figure as benevolent narrators, but women either rescue themselves or die.

Gardener's reform fiction reached an apotheosis in her first novel Is This Your Son, My Lord? published in November 1890, just six months after her first story collection. This novel changed the trajectory of Gardener's career and introduced her unique blend of feminine frankness to readers across the country.

ONE THING that continued to irk Gardener about the challenges facing women who wanted to go to college was the unquestioned, and often unappreciated, access to higher education enjoyed by young men of privilege, including her own nephew, Ernest Bernard Chenoweth, son of her brother Bernard. After Bernard died in China in 1870, his widow, Caroline Van Deusen Chenoweth, settled in Boston and sent her two boys to the city's best schools. The Chenoweth sons were one generation removed from wealth—on their mother's side—but they enjoyed all its trappings nonetheless.

Ernest B. Chenoweth, who went by Bernard like his father, entered Harvard in the class of 1888. Even though he and his rich friends were the chosen acolytes of famed Boston minister Phillips Brooks, young Bernard was expelled from Harvard for bad behavior. For a young man of privilege, this was not a cause for alarm. Life offered a long series of safety nets and second chances. Bernard moved to New York, right around the same time that his radical aunt was auditing classes at Columbia, to pursue his own career as a writer.[13] Through her nephew and the men in her New York reform circles, Gardener became acquainted with the social customs of the Ivy League elite.

An aspect of this rarefied male culture Gardener could not abide was the encouragement young men received to "sow their wild oats" before marriage, often with prostitutes or by enticing lower-class women into sex with the promise of favors and gifts. For Gardener's premarital affair, she had been fired and run out of town. The contrast galled her. Even more appalling, such male behavior was endorsed by parents, ministers, teachers, and even police officers. Who had decided, Gardener demanded in an essay titled "Sex Maniacs," that providing a sexual outlet for men justified the "regulated slaughter (social, moral, and actually physical) of hundreds of thousands" of young women?[14] Gardener used fiction to draw attention to the physical and psychological ravages that resulted from rape, unwanted pregnancy, and sexually transmitted disease—all of which women were supposed to endure in silence.

Readers were familiar with stories of "ruined women" meeting their unfortunate, yet deserved, ends, stories that had for decades "served to sharpen and supply the novelist's pen." But hardly anyone had been moved to empathize with the fallen woman's perspective, much less defend it. Female purity reformers in the Woman's Christian Temperance Union had begun campaigning for a single sexual standard in the 1880s, but few Americans thought that anything would ever change the seemingly natural and inevitable custom whereby men could do as they pleased sexually with little or no consequences while for women the consequences of extramarital sex could not have been more severe. With *Is This Your Son, My Lord?* Gardener challenged the tradition of young men "sowing their wild oats" by telling the story of a man's "first false step."

"This novel was not written as history," she proclaimed in the preface to the second edition, "but there is not a material point in it which is not based on fact."[15] She later revealed to her friend Adelaide Johnson, the sculptor, that she knew elements of the story firsthand from Charles Smart, who had been asked by a friend in Michigan—the superintendent of schools in Muskegon—to accompany his young son to New York so that he could lose his virginity. Gardener also confessed to Johnson that the villain of the novel, Fred Harmon, was based on her nephew Bernard and that Fred's scheming, social-ladder-climbing mother was modeled on her sister-in-law, Caroline Chenoweth.[16]

Is This Your Son, My Lord? centers on the activities of three young Harvard graduates: Fred Harmon, Preston Mansfield, and Harvey Ball. Preston had fallen victim to an epidemic common among "young fellows who had been too intimately crowded together." He had "harmed himself" with "certain unwholesome practices." Preston had become a masturbator. Aghast, Preston's father, the head of the local school board, begs the family doctor to accompany the boy to New York City and help him "pick out a good dove."

After the doctor thwarts this plan, the father takes matters into his own hands by raping a lower-class, fifteen-year-old girl whom Preston had befriended in order to blackmail her into having sex with his son. Preston then fathers two children with her, and the girl becomes a prostitute. Wracked with guilt, Preston ultimately kills himself. Preston's friend Fred, the character based on Gardener's nephew Bernard, feels no such moral compunctions about his analogous lifestyle. At the urging of his mother, he marries for money, becomes an Episcopal priest for the social standing, and continues to cavort with prostitutes after hours.

Sales of *Is This Your Son, My Lord?* surpassed Gardener's and the publisher's wildest expectations. The novel quickly sold over 35,000 copies and went into multiple editions.[17] One journalist described the book as having taken "an almost unprecedented hold upon the thinking public."[18] Suffrage leader Carrie Chapman Catt recalled reading the novel, as a young woman, behind closed doors because few dared outwardly acknowledge the issues Gardener so fearlessly raised. According to Catt, Gardener's novels "stirred consciences underneath the surface from the Atlantic to the Pacific."[19] Advertisements for the novel proclaimed it to be "a fascinating story of radical truths on religion and social matters."[20] Another ad promised it was "without question the most radical and, in many respects, the boldest assault on the respectable conventionality and immorality in high places that has ever been written."[21]

In a roundtable review in *The Arena* magazine, Elizabeth Cady Stanton praised the book, written by a "representative thinker among women," for highlighting to women that "the stronghold of their slavery lies in social customs." As for its merits as a story, however, Stanton frankly surmised that "one can see the able essayist, and the clever pamphleteer, but not the born novelist."[22]

The harshest criticism came from Gardener's former publisher, Donn Piatt, who characterized the novel as "a fierce plunge into the horrible" that "turns on an impossible crime." Piatt charged that the problem with Gardener and other women reformers was that they had been "shielded in the home from the cradle to the coffin by fathers, brothers, sons, and husbands." Women, he proclaimed, "laugh at wounds but have never felt a scar." Piatt further insisted that the father's rape of the young woman was unthinkable.[23] This turned out to be a dividing line among readers: women thought the crimes depicted by Gardener were realistic, commonplace even, while some men denied such horrors existed.[24]

Gardener claimed that the reviews she prized the most were those she had received from young men themselves. Men thanked her for opening their eyes to an evil all around them, and men confessed they wished they had read her novel years before. She asked one young man if he thought the novel was "overdrawn." He reported that he was just twenty-three and yet he could think of at least fifty cases like the ones she dramatized. With pride, she recounted a review published in Princeton's literary magazine, which concluded that "it comes very close to any college boy who has kept his eyes open. When we finish we may say, not 'Is this Your Son, My Lord?' but, Is it I? Is it I?"[25]

In March 1891, Gardener traveled to Boston to promote her novel, which, a local paper reported, "in spite of its crudeness and its plain-speaking, it is said to be selling at the rate of 1000 copies a week."[26] While there, she embarked on a tour of nearby Salem, visiting the home of the writer Nathaniel Hawthorne, author of *The Scarlet Letter* (1850), and the famous Witch House. Gardener observed that had it not been for the scientific revolution, she likely would have suffered the same fate as the misunderstood witches of Salem, to say nothing of Hester Prynne, the adulterous protagonist of *The Scarlet Letter*.[27]

In what was becoming a common pattern, Gardener's professional triumph as a novelist was followed by another physical collapse. After the banner success of *Is This Your Son, My Lord?*, *The Truth Seeker* reported in June 1891 that she had decamped to Florida to restore her health.[28] Gardener fulfilled her promise to be the woman who dared voice things others could not express, but this audacity came at a price.

———

CHARLES SMART also continued to struggle with his health and in his post at the Equitable Life Assurance Society. On October 27, 1891, he received a friendly but admonishing letter from Henry Hyde—the fiercely admired company president and one of the richest men in America. Just what, precisely, had Smart been up to the past several months, Hyde inquired. In all the office memos that survive in the Equitable Life Assurance files, this is one of only two instances in which Hyde involved himself in such a relatively small personnel issue. Smart must have been doing a remarkably bad job to prompt such a letter.

Smart immediately replied in a plaintive, three-page-long missive written in drowsy, loopy cursive. No one, Smart asserted, worked harder to promote the success of the Equitable Life Assurance Society than he had. "I challenge any man under the officers of our great society to show more earnest loyal incessant personal effort to add to the Equitable success," he stressed, "than I have always given when not disabled by unavoidable sickness." Smart had "worked up" several promising contacts, men who could afford $10,000 policies or more, but "the unusual expenses . . . incurred by illness" left him without the money to close the deals. He told Hyde that he did not even have enough for postage or street car fare to make it to the office or to meet with his prospective clients. "I am working all the time at a disadvantage past telling," Smart rationalized. And if he could access the little money he needed—"not a gift, I work for all I get"—he was sure he could make his monthly allotment.[29]

A company memo prepared for Hyde the next day showed that Smart had already taken out several cash advances and owed the Equitable $4,562.40. Smart had written just $11,000 in policies for the year 1891, and of those, he had collected on only $1,000.[30] Smart continued to be listed in New York City directories with a business address at the Equitable's Broadway headquarters until 1894, but given his lackluster performance, it is unlikely that he worked there very often. The modern insurance industry, especially the world-leading Equitable did not tolerate weakness and failure.

To survive, then, Smart relied on Gardener's earnings as a lecturer and writer, which strained their relationship and her health. By the close of 1891, she was writing at a faster clip than ever before. Back in

New York, the couple took a night off to attend the first annual banquet of the new Vegetarian Society, where they enjoyed a "meatless feast" of boiled parsnips, potato pancakes, and cream of celery soup.[31] But otherwise Gardener was consumed by her writing and the pressure to support herself and the ailing Smart. Later in life, she described to her friend Adelaide Johnson the "dreadful conditions" in which she wrote her second novel, "under tight contract and with Smart constantly under foot."[32]

In April 1892, her second short story collection, *Pushed by Unseen Hands*, was released. It contained nine short stories and an endorsement from Robert Ingersoll. This book called into question the many social and moral problems that were governed by the "unseen hands" of the past, including the passing on of traits to offspring, outdated laws, and unexamined customs. Gardener characterized the overriding theme of the stories as "heredity," but modern readers might better understand the theme as "why people do what they do." Gardener did not believe in a strict definition of biological heredity, but rather one that included social and environmental forces, an idea she would continue to develop.

All the while, Gardener was scrambling to finish her second novel, *Pray You Sir, Whose Daughter?*, published just two months after *Pushed by Unseen Hands*. She desperately hoped that her second novel would sell even more than the first. But the literary quality of the novel reflects the stressful conditions in which Gardener finished it. Though she improved formally as a writer—for example, the narrator remains constant in the second novel—the plot lacks the verve of *Is This Your Son, My Lord?* Elizabeth Cady Stanton was right: Gardener was not a born novelist. Nevertheless, the book went into thirteen editions and sold more than 25,000 copies.[33]

With *Pray You Sir, Whose Daughter?*, Gardener also found her signature reform: raising the age of sexual consent for girls, which in 1890 was twelve or younger in thirty-eight states. In Delaware, it was seven.[34] Stanton wrote the preface and proclaimed that she had long waited for a novelist to do for women what *Uncle Tom's Cabin* had done for the enslaved—a book that would "paint the awful facts of woman's posi-

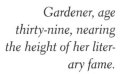

Gardener, age thirty-nine, nearing the height of her literary fame.

tion in living colors that all must see and feel." In so vividly describing the "dark shadows" lurking in "everyday life" and in "every household," Stanton declared, Gardener had come close to realizing her dream.[35]

The novel revolves around a wealthy New York family, the Fosters, and their twenty-year-old daughter Gertrude, a college student. Smart but sheltered, Gertrude longs to learn about life as it really is—not as men explain it to women, whom they deem too delicate or too stupid to understand. Volunteering at a neighborhood settlement house, Gertrude befriends two working-class fourteen-year-old girls, Francis King and Ettie Berton, both of whose fathers work for the local party boss and serve in the state legislature at his behest. Much to her traditional father's chagrin, Francis refuses to play the part of the wide-eyed naïf. Ettie, however, learned from a young age that the easiest way for women to get along in the world is to act how men want them to act—pleasing, self-effacing, and self-denying.

Always ready with a smile and an affirmation of male wisdom, Ettie is seduced and impregnated by an older man during a visit to Coney Island. Gertrude's father insists that she stop seeing Francis and Ettie lest she be found guilty by association of being a "fallen woman." "The test of respectability of a woman," he informs Gertrude matter-of-factly, "is whether a man of position will marry her or not. A man's respectable if he's out of jail."[36] Shunned by her father, the pregnant Ettie dies alone in the room she shares with Francis, paid for by Gertrude.

Indignant, Gertrude protests that society was wrong to condemn Ettie as a "fallen woman," when really she had only behaved precisely how she had been taught her whole short life. She soon learns from her suitor Selden Avery that the New York State Legislature had been meeting in secret session to lower the age of sexual consent from fourteen to twelve. Worse still, the bill had been introduced by Ettie's own father. The glaring hypocrisy of the situation inspires Gertrude and Selden to action, and they succeed in stopping the bill's passage. The novel concludes with Gertrude and Selden promising to marry in ten weeks so that they can move to Albany, the state capital, in advance of the next legislative session.

Reviewers praised *Pray You Sir, Whose Daughter?* as "a novel with a purpose." Some even heralded Gardener as the "Harriet Beecher Stowe of Fallen Women." B. O. Flower, editor of *The Arena*, declared it "the strongest work which has yet come from the pen of this gifted lady" and concluded that "if the white ribbon army should make it the 'Uncle Tom's Cabin' of their noble crusade, it would, I believe, accomplish more in one year than their present efforts will realize in a decade."[37] The freethought, birth control journal *Lucifer the Light-Bearer* praised the book for revealing "many unpalatable truths," declaring the work an "unexcelled . . . 'eye-opener' for women." The reviewer speculated that "if angels ever weep, it would be to see mothers who know that their seven- and ten-year-old daughters are being ravaged by men and yet claim that women have all the rights they need.[38]

More orthodox readers objected to Gardener's brazen choice of subject matter and suggested that she title her next book *Do You Know Where Your Husband Is, Madam?*[39] Unfortunately for Gardener, she knew precisely where Smart was nearly all the time: loafing about the apartment. But around the time of *Pray You Sir's* publication, Gardener discovered that Smart could serve narrative, if not functional, purposes.

PRIOR TO 1892, Gardener had never referred to Smart as her husband in print. Friends considered them to be husband and wife, but *The Truth Seeker* always referred to her as Miss Gardener, and none of her book prefaces mentioned a husband.[40] That is, not until the publication of *Pray You, Sir.*

Surprisingly, given what she later confessed to Adelaide Johnson about how Smart hindered her writing process, Gardener dedicated *Pray You, Sir* to her husband. She did not name him, but she gushed that he "was ever at once her first, most severe, and most sympathetic critic, whose encouragement and interest in her work never flags; whose abiding belief in human rights, without sex limitation, and in equality of opportunity leaves scant room in his great soul to harbor patience with sex domination in a land which boasts of freedom for all."

In a flurry of reviews and profiles of Gardener, Smart began to appear as an affectionate, egalitarian, and modern husband. A widely reprinted profile entitled "Helen Hamilton Gardener is Smart" announced that Smart was Gardener's real name and "she lives up to it." The article also stated, incorrectly, that Col. Smart was "a gentleman known in New York legal circles."[41] Other profiles emphasized the romance of their marriage. A friend from Michigan wrote to the *Saginaw Courier-Herald* to testify that he had visited Gardener in her New York home and hosted her on summer holiday. Unfortunately for her "masculine admirers," the man related, "she is married to a man she loves devotedly."[42]

Another profile raised a question no doubt on many readers' minds: how could a woman write about the sexual experiences Gardener detailed "unless she has a personal experience of the things of which she writes"? But according to the reviewer, this was an absurd assumption. No one would dare suggest such a thing of Shakespeare or Dickens or argue that the preacher "who depicts the torments of the damned must have had these torments." To further deflect attacks against Gardener's womanly character, the article reported that her "home life with her parents was markedly simple and happy and pure and as free as possible from the troubles and ills of the world"—an odd summation of a life that included the loss of three homes, two fortunes, two parents, three brothers, and one sister in the wake of the bloodbath of the Civil War. Moreover, the author declared, Gardener's "marriage or domestic life is simply ideal." Her husband, a "college-bred professional gentleman," was "in entire harmony with all her work and all she desires to do, as she is with all he thinks and does. She has no more earnest admirer and at the same time no more careful critic."[43]

For a freethinking woman with an interest in sex reform, having a devoted husband provided respectability and social validation. In writing about extramarital sex, statutory rape, and seduction, Gardener violated many taboos. Nearly all reviews and profiles described her feminine charms, idyllic home life, and polished manners in part to make her novels acceptable: If an upstanding woman wrote them, the novels could not be judged as impure. The fictive Charles Smart chronicled in the press allowed Gardener to present herself as an upstanding, happily married woman who abided by the normal rules of society even as she wrote about the many trespasses against them. In addition, this version of Smart-the-husband provided a rare model of an egalitarian marriage for other nineteenth-century women who were on the lookout for alternatives to the patriarchal marriages they had grown up with.

Having a husband who supported her career wholeheartedly also allowed Gardener to continue traveling the country—often alone—to do her work. She may have chafed against this reality, but at some level she knew that her career was bolstered by the public's perception of Smart. Single women traveling alone were highly suspect, but if everyone knew that Charles Smart waited at home, happily cheering on his intrepid wife, who could fault Gardener for venturing out? Regardless of what he actually contributed as a partner, the public Charles Smart allowed her to go about the world by herself, voicing her iconoclastic ideas.

By the end of 1892, travel was what Gardener needed the most. After the publication of four books in two years, she had become a literary sensation, a writer known far beyond the confines of the freethought movement, and a woman in need of a break. On December 24, *The Truth Seeker* reported that Gardener had left New York for the West, return date unknown.[44]

From December 1892 through July 1893, Gardener traveled the country researching her third novel, *An Unofficial Patriot*, which would be published in 1894. Outwardly, this was her most autobiographical novel, as she told everyone who read it, but it also involved a fair amount of fiction. In an inscribed gift copy, she wrote: "You may care to know before you read it that this 'story' is both historically and sociologically true and was fully verified in the records of the secret service department years ago. Only the names are changed."[45] The main character "'Griffith Davenport' was my beloved father," she divulged to another friend. "For the public it was a 'novel based on the secret history of the Civil War period,' for those who know it is also the soul of my home."[46]

To recount her father's heroism, Gardener headed west and south to see to what extent her memories could be verified. By February 1893, Gardener arrived in Locust Lodge, Kentucky, to visit General Thomas A. Harris, a Confederate veteran and politician. From there she traveled on to Louisville before going to Indianapolis to meet with May

Wright Sewall, the organizer of the World's Congress of Representative Women. The two conferred about the upcoming World's Columbian Exposition to be held in Chicago that May. Gardener explained to Sewall that she would have to play her arrival by ear because "I am West on a business trip—verifying material for my next literary work—I am compelled to govern my next movements by what I learn in each succeeding place."[47]

After meeting with Sewall and conducting some research in Indianapolis, Gardener took the train to Toledo, Ohio. In March, Clara Bewick Colby, her colleague on the *Woman's Bible* Revising Committee and the publisher of the Stanton loyalist paper the *Woman's Tribune*, hosted a reception in Gardener's honor at her home in Nebraska. The two may have had something else in common besides loyalty to Stanton and abhorrence of orthodoxy. Colby's husband was notoriously unfaithful (the couple divorced in 1906), and Gardener later told a mutual friend that "any doctor and every man know instantly upon looking at her that she has the worst form of the worst disease."[48]

An Unofficial Patriot is markedly different from Gardener's other fiction in that it has nothing to do with women's rights or sex reform. The novel profiles Rev. Griffith Davenport, his decision to manumit the enslaved people he inherited, his family's move west, and their experiences during the Civil War. Thirty years after the end of hostilities, the novel highlights the moral complexities of the war—the heroism and righteousness of her father, the racism of their Indiana neighbors, and the havoc that the war caused her family. While it condemns slavery, the novel also describes the structural barriers in place to freeing individual slaves, as well as nostalgic—and racist—depictions of the "peculiar institution." She gives no agency to the African American characters, none of whom are well developed. Instead, Gardener's work reflects a shared culture of whiteness among North and South to which white readers responded positively.

One critic hailed *An Unofficial Patriot* as "the most remarkable historical novel of the Civil War."[49] The *Los Angeles Herald* concurred with *The Arena's* assessment that the novel was "history instead of fiction" and a "story which will live in permanent literature."[50] The *Pittsburg Press* observed that *An Unofficial Patriot* "forms part of the summer reading of the best readers of the country."[51] Apropos of nothing, this blurb also included the information that Gardener weighed less than 100 pounds and wore a size 5¼ glove. "There is nothing in it to offend the traditions of an honest man, North or South," declared the *Chicago Times*.[52] Allegedly, both Fitzhugh Lee, son of Robert E., and Robert Lincoln, son of Abraham, enjoyed it, testifying to the book's appeal to white readers on both sides of the Mason-Dixon Line.[53]

"I am a Chenoweth of Virginia," Gardener had proudly declared upon settling in New York in 1886. There is no evidence that she visited Virginia since leaving as an infant in 1854 or that she kept in touch with any Virginia relations until much later. But she longed to reconnect with this storied heritage, and writing about it offered her one way to do so. More than anything else, *An Unofficial Patriot* established Gardener's reputation as a Southerner. In addition to her petite frame, youthful appearance, and loving husband, profiles now mentioned her Virginia birth and her long line of Chenoweth ancestors going back to Lord Baltimore.[54] A Louisville paper praised her for elevating "the literary profile of the South."[55] For the first time, some reviews even described Gardener as speaking with the twinge of a Southern accent.

Between 1888 and 1894, Gardener used fiction to make sense of her romantic past, enhance public sympathy for fallen and complicated women, and connect with a Southern way of life that she had not experienced firsthand. Throughout, she used the press generated by her novels to craft an appealing—if not altogether accurate—persona for herself.

Several months before the publication of *An Unofficial Patriot*, Gardener fulfilled her promise to May Wright Sewall to participate in the World's Congress of Representative Women in Chicago. This invitation provided Gardener with an opportunity to debut her revised self on the most prominent stage in the nation.

9

The Harriet Beecher Stowe
of Fallen Women

*If it were not often tragic and always humiliating, it would
be exceedingly amusing to observe the results of a method of
thought and a civilization which has proceeded always upon
the idea that man is the race and that woman is merely an
annex to him and because of his desires, needs, and dictum.*

—HELEN HAMILTON GARDENER, 1893

I N MAY OF 1893, Helen Hamilton Gardener joined hundreds of leading women in Chicago for the week-long World's Congress of Representative Women, held at the World's Columbian Exposition, the
second world's fair to be held in the United States. The Columbian
Exposition highlighted American innovation and industrial prowess
and commemorated the 400th anniversary of Christopher Columbus
landing in North America. In a grueling and deadly test of endurance,
over 40,000 skilled workers hastily constructed an all-white city of temporary buildings to welcome over 27 million visitors—more than one-
third of the entire U.S. population—who arrived by rail and by stage

every day for six months.[1] Not only were the buildings all white, so, too, were the fair's organizers, speakers, and exhibitors. To protest the exclusion of African Americans from this international celebration of American progress, black leaders Ida B. Wells and Frederick Douglass published and distributed thousands of copies of a pamphlet entitled "The Reason Why the Colored American is Not in the World's Columbian Exhibition."

Along with exhibits showcasing the advancements of more than eighty countries and thirty-eight states, the exposition hosted many smaller events, including a different thematic congress each week. The World's Congress of Representative Women was held just a few weeks after the fair opened, and many remarked that it was by far the most organized and informative of all the congresses, thanks to the leadership of May Wright Sewall, who had recruited Gardener to her Science and Philosophy Committee. The women's congress showcased white women's achievements in the arts, industry, the professions, and the home. The Woman's Building, which hosted exhibitions by and about women, was even designed by a female architect—twenty-four-year-old Sophia Hayden, the first woman to graduate from the architecture program at the Massachusetts Institute of Technology.

Helen Hamilton Gardener, now age forty and at the height of her literary fame, delivered at least four keynote addresses. Some women recalled her giving six or eight, more than any other American woman. The New York *Sun* reported that next to Susan B. Anthony, Gardener created "the profoundest sensation."[2]

"In one of the halls where Helen Gardener and Miss Anthony were to speak there was such a tremendous crowd," according to one eyewitness, "that they finally had to station two policemen to keep order."[3] Jennie June, the pen name of Jane Cunningham Croly—one of the most renowned female journalists of the nineteenth century, observed in her popular column that "there was one woman who, whenever she addressed an audience, was listened to with an intensity of interest accorded to no other speaker and attracted such crowds that the largest halls could not suffice for their accommodation." Everyone at the fair "wanted to hear this one woman; to secure her as a speaker, no matter how widely the central idea might differ from their own."[4] This woman, of course, was Helen Hamilton Gardener.

Not only did Gardener's speeches electrify, so, too, did her outfits. For generations, opponents of women's rights had characterized adherents as being short-haired women and long-haired men. The specter of the mannish spinster shaped audiences' expectations of what feminist reformers might look like, and Gardener delighted in few things as much as upending expectations. Reporting on the surprising presence of many attractive and fashionable women at the World's Congress, the Minneapolis *Star Tribune* featured Gardener as the first case in point. The paper even printed a "pen picture" of her to prove how stylish she was. "We've all more or less read her startling theories," the author declared, but what about her as a person? Was she serious? One look and the author could tell, yes indeed she was. "Imagine a slender, dainty figure, dressed in quiet yet elegant manner, refined features, large dark eyes and such a clear bird-like voice," described the correspondent. "Again picture this dainty, well-bred creature discussing the unmentionable social vices before a mixed audience as calmly as if delivering a literary critique. One might question her discretion but not her honesty or valor."[5]

Even though she had resented reviews of her freethought lectures that focused on her looks, Gardener also understood that female reformers could—whether they liked it or not—amplify their messages by looking attractive. She later criticized Elizabeth Cady Stanton's decision to include a frumpy picture as the frontispiece to her memoir. The photo, Gardener charged, "does not do her credit. It has a look that people, who do not know her, would say, 'Women who do things look like that. I should be afraid of her and I could not love her, however much I might admire her ability.'"[6] For her part, Gardener always strove to cushion the shock of her unconventional ideas by wrapping them in an attractive package.

AFTER SIX YEARS of writing fiction nearly exclusively, the magnificent occasion of the World's Columbian Exposition brought Gardener back to the podium and the polemical essay. To satisfy popular demand, she reprised her 1888 lecture "Sex in Brain" and delivered three new talks. The most significant was "Woman as an Annex," the speech she gave on Thursday, May 18, the day sponsored by the National American Woman Suffrage Association (NAWSA).

Since Gardener had last spoken to the suffragists back in 1888 at the International Council of Women, she had fallen even further out of step with the movement's leaders. Together with Stanton, Gardener objected to the 1890 merger of the National Woman Suffrage Association (NWSA), Stanton and Anthony's group, with the American Woman Suffrage Association (AWSA), led by Lucy Stone and her husband, Henry Blackwell. For Stanton and Gardener, the merger represented the ascendency of a more conservative faction of women's rights advocates—women who opposed Stanton's *Woman's Bible*; women who shied away from discussing divorce and sex; and, perhaps most irksome, women who promoted temperance via the Woman's Christian Temperance Union (WCTU), by far the largest women's organization of the nineteenth century.

As an outspoken agnostic, Gardener rejected the creep of Christianity into American public life (the era witnessed a surge in legislation proposing Sunday closing laws, Bibles in schools, and declarations that America was a Christian nation) and now into the women's rights movement.[7] And she opposed temperance as an infringement on individual liberty. Rather than outlaw vice, she suggested that "we . . . train young people to be strong and self-directing and self-respecting citizens," set the age of consent for drinking (and for the other "social evil," prostitution) at twenty-one, and let people make their own choices.[8] She also resented the stereotype often promulgated by temperance advocates that women were naturally more moral than men. She believed that female temperance advocates resorted to "a hatchet and a prayer" because they lacked a voice within the law.[9]

Back in October 1889, Gardener had spent the day with Stanton at her vacation home in Hempstead, Long Island, brainstorming what to do about the inevitable merger.[10] Matilda Joslyn Gage, another free-thinker and longtime suffrage leader, had suggested the formation of a new national liberal society that would combine the interests of the feminists with those of the freethinkers, in opposition to the proposed NAWSA merger, which she feared would bolster the church. Gardener and Stanton "talked the matter over, pros and cons" and agreed that a new organization would be best. Still in the midst of drafting *The Woman's Bible*, however, Stanton clarified that Gage would have to organize this group herself. Though she would reluctantly accept a more-or-less honorary position as the unified NAWSA's first president, Stanton declared herself beyond organizations. Henceforth, she would be a "free lance to do and say what I choose and shock people as much as I please."[11]

Gage's group failed to get off the ground, so Gardener, like Stanton, remained a "free lance" in relation to women's rights organizations, writing about feminist issues but not actively involved in women's rights groups. In March 1890, for example, Gardener published an essay in *The Arena* advocating divorce reform. Divorce, she argued, was not a religious matter but a matter of general welfare with particular urgency for women. While a man might suffer in a bad marriage, a man in a bad marriage "still owns his own body." "For these and other reasons," Gardener asserted, "an unhappy marriage can never mean to a man what it must always mean to a woman."[12]

With her emphasis on secularism, divorce, and sex, Gardener's writing represented precisely the sort of arguments not welcomed in the reunified NAWSA. In her 1890 NAWSA presidential address, Stanton proposed a set of resolutions, and the very first one advocated a wife's right to seek divorce. "Liberal divorce laws are for wives what Canada was for the slaves," Stanton proclaimed, "a door of escape from bondage." And it was absurd for the government to consider changing divorce laws "until woman has a voice" in government.[13] After Stanton stepped down as president of NAWSA in 1892, the group's annual meetings featured no more keynotes about divorce.

Despite never having attended a NAWSA meeting, Gardener was allotted a keynote spot—right after Susan B. Anthony, the group's patron saint—on NAWSA's day at the 1893 world's fair. At 10 a.m. on Thursday, May 18, "Aunt Susan" delivered the opening address to roaring applause. Next, Gardener took to the podium to deliver "Woman as an Annex."

"If it were not often tragic and always humiliating," Gardener began, "it would be exceedingly amusing to observe the results of a method of thought and a civilization which has proceeded always upon the idea that man is the race and that woman is merely an annex to him and because of his desires, needs and dictum." While Genesis encoded female subservience, nature itself imparted no such message. "Bigotry or sex bias and pride does not carry this theory below the human animal," Gardener asserted. "Among scientists and evolutionists, and, indeed, even among the various religious explanations of the source and cause of things, the male and female of all species of animals, birds and insects come into life and tread its paths together and as equals."[14] For decades, women had advanced many arguments against patriarchy, but Gardener was among the first to argue that it was not natural.

Gardener also delivered two speeches on heredity, which developed ideas from earlier essays. Evolutionary theory was revolutionizing scientific thinking about heredity, and reviewers praised Gardener simply for talking about a concept as yet so poorly understood. For the rest of her life, biographical sketches described her as "an expert in heredity." But Gardener was not really interested in the precise mechanisms of trait transmission. Rather, she invoked the intellectual prestige of hereditary science to warn women that the sexually transmitted diseases they contracted from their husbands could be passed on to their children.

Gardener was especially concerned about syphilis because it could result in children with seizure disorders, unsightly "syphilis teeth," and even blindness, to say nothing of the horrors the disease visited upon unsuspecting wives.[15] Ridding the world of the sexual double standard, of rape, and of prostitution, Gardener believed, would have far greater intergenerational consequences than just about any other reform. To those who protested that women must remain ignorant of vice, Gardener countered that before a woman became a mother, she should be brave enough "personally to demand and to obtain absolute personal liberty of action, equality of status and entire control of her great and race endowing function of maternity."[16]

Gardener's speeches at the world's fair proved so popular that she decided to quickly release them in book form. Just weeks after she left Chicago, newspapers reported that *Facts and Fictions of Life*, containing her world's fair addresses plus a few greatest hits, would be on sale in July. An advertisement for the book declared "a thinker has been let loose upon us."[17]

After her blockbuster performance at the World's Columbian Exposition, Gardener returned home to New York to prepare for the publication of what she considered her best book, *An Unofficial Patriot*. Over the next several months, she became more involved in the Woman's Press Club of New York, an organization led by her friend Jane Cunningham Croly; attended a women's rights meeting at the home of her friend Mary Phillips; and headlined a conference in Atlanta.[18] But back in New York, Gardener's public life as a celebrated author and reformer collided with her reality as a woman with limited income tethered to a feckless man.

CHARLES SMART'S PROSPECTS at the Equitable Life Assurance Society had continued to dim since his plaintive letter requesting a loan back in 1891. Even more stressful than their financial woes, Gardener caught Smart in a lie that changed the direction of their relationship and of her career.

At some point in 1894, Smart told Gardener that he had to go out of town for company business. Seeing as he generated so little business, she suspected that this was a lie. She confronted him, and they had the "first real and lasting quarrel we ever had." Smart cried, accused Gardener of being unfair, and suffered "heart failure." The couple summoned a doctor who warned that any further excitement would surely kill Smart. So Gardener "nursed him out of it—as usual." She never mentioned his mysterious trip again, but in her heart she knew he had betrayed her. From that point on, Gardener withdrew from him "*as a wife*, from any and all possible relations." She was "in a sense his mother from 1894 until his death," as she later confided to her friend Mary Phillips, "*but never his wife.*"

For the next several years, she told Phillips, her life became "simply a round of work and outside interest." But after Smart's deception, Gardener was no longer able to produce "really fine, *imaginative* work. . . . No one ever knew why—except him," she recalled. "I lost confidence and that crippled my faculties."[19] Even as Gardener attacked the laws and social customs that kept women dependent on men, she was not entirely immune to these customs herself. She had evaded traditional marriage, by choice or by circumstance, and she supported herself and Smart with her earnings, but at some level, she still depended on Smart's affection and fidelity for her self-confidence and for her public persona. Moreover, all evidence suggests that in spite of everything they went through together, she loved him deeply. She had not insisted that Smart marry her, but she had insisted that he love her the most. She was devastated by his betrayal. *An Unofficial Patriot* would be her last book.

IN JUNE 1894, Gardener took a chance on a new opportunity—to move to Boston so that she could coedit *The Arena*, a magazine in which she regularly published. While New York remained her favorite place to live, the financial precariousness of the writer's life weighed on her.

Plus, she had been writing constantly since 1888—six books in as many years—and welcomed a respite. Boston was a major metropolis but with a slower pace of life than New York and a guaranteed paycheck.

For years, Smart had claimed that he could not stay at the Equitable office all day because he missed Gardener and felt "so lonely I can't work."[20] To combat this problem in Boston, Gardener arranged a job for him as the business manager of The Arena at a salary of $75 per week.[21] Once settled, Gardener recalled that she "handled" the problem of Smart's lackadaisical work ethic by "going to the office myself and doing double work to keep him at it—and he did then work hard and faithfully."[22]

In Boston, the couple settled into a handsome apartment at 185 Huntington Avenue, near Copley Place.[23] The Arena offices were located in the Pierce Building downtown, and the couple mingled on the fringes of Boston Brahmin society, with Gardener occasionally giving talks to Boston women's clubs.[24] But mostly, they worked at The Arena. Founded by B. O. Flower in 1890, The Arena rapidly established itself as one of the nation's premier reform publications. As Flower recalled, his aim was "to give all-around discussions, by the ablest and most authoritative writers, on vital questions relating to the social, economic, political, ethical, psychological, philosophical, educational, literary, dramatic, and artistic life of our age, giving special emphasis to the liberal or progressive ideals or the newer or more unconventional thought of the day."[25] With fewer than 30,000 subscribers, though, The Arena's broad reformist goals were somewhat hampered.

But Arena readers sprang into action for what would become Gardener's signature reform. While the masthead still listed B. O. Flower as editor, Gardener took the reform publication in a new direction. Under her leadership, The Arena became devoted to the single issue of raising the age of sexual consent for girls, a problem she had frankly dramatized in her first two novels.

Gardener announced this new campaign in a special January 1895 edition titled "The Shame of America." Anti-vice crusader Aaron Powell, of New York, wrote the contextual essay, which explained that until very recently the age of consent in most states had been ten or twelve, following the precedent of English common law. But in 1885, British journalist William T. Stead went undercover in London's brothels and learned, among other things, that men regularly paid upward of 13 pounds to deflower child virgins. Outraged, Stead published an exposé entitled "The Maiden Tribute of Modern Babylon" in the *Pall Mall Gazette.* As public concern mounted, the British parliament raised the age of consent to sixteen. American reformers, led by Powell's group and the Woman's Christian Temperance Union (WCTU), took up the effort. By 1894, twenty states had raised the age of consent to fourteen, an improvement but far short of the reformers' goal of eighteen. Eight states refused to raise the age above twelve, and only in Kansas and Wyoming—where women had at least partial suffrage—was it raised all the way to eighteen.

Reformers were also motivated by the desire to curb prostitution, often cited as the inevitable next step for "fallen women," and to reduce the spread of sexually transmitted diseases. The so-called purity movement fought proposals to regulate prostitution, believing that government sanction of "the social evil" would only hurt women and children. They demanded instead that men abide by the same standard of sexual morals as women. Other contributors to the "Shame of America" issue of *The Arena* included the pioneering female physician Emily Blackwell and Frances Willard, president of the WCTU, who pronounced "strong drink and the degradation of woman" to be the "Siamese twins of vice."[26]

Gardener's mission was to highlight not only the grievous sexual crimes against girls but also the links between women voting and women being able to control what happened to their bodies, much as she had done in her essays about divorce reform and heredity. When asked to explain why she so adamantly advocated raising the age of consent to eighteen, Gardener replied that she might as well be asked why one should be opposed to the "practice of cutting the throats of his neighbor's children whenever that neighbor happened to not be at home to protect them." Simply put, "There is no argument. There is no basis for a difference of opinion." Maintaining that the problem stemmed, in part, from women's lack of voice in government, she declared that "no legislature on earth, if its discussions were open to women, if women were present at its sessions, would ever have passed such acts."[27] Further emphasizing the links between sexual and political autonomy, Gardener praised, in a later issue of *The Arena*, an Illinois proposal to disenfranchise and bar from public office men convicted of having sex with girls under fourteen.[28]

Developing skills she would later use to advocate for the vote, Gardener compiled a map of the United States indicating the age of consent in each state as well as a blacklist of states that had failed to raise the age of consent. She also pointed out that some states had technically increased the age only to add amendments stating that the crime exclusively pertained to cases where girls could prove they had previously been virgins. In a letter to Gardener, William Stead emphasized the absurdity of such clauses, noting that he had never met "a dissolute man who was not prepared to declare on oath . . . that he had not been first."[29]

Most of the blacklisted states were in the South. These states refused to raise the age of consent because, as the historian Estelle Freedman has established, Southerners viewed such reforms as challenges to white supremacy and to white men's prerogative to sexually assault black females without recourse. In 1904, for example, Mississippi state senators blocked efforts to raise the age of consent from ten to fourteen because they did not want black girls to be able to charge white men with a crime. Even when Southern states did raise the age of consent, several inserted clauses clarifying that statutory rape laws only applied to white girls or to girls who could prove, in the words of the Georgia law, that they "knew the difference between good and evil."[30] Gardener lobbied ardently to raise the age of consent in all states for all girls, and she even clarified that her ultimate goal would have been to pass legislation that applied equally to boys and to girls under the age of eighteen.[31] But the larger movement defined its goal as ending "white slavery," testifying to the extent to which reformers were mainly concerned about young white working-class and immigrant women.[32]

Next, Gardener rallied her troops to action. She and her team of volunteers sent personal letters to the 9,000 men (and a few women in Colorado) who served in the country's state legislatures, asking for their positions on the age of consent. She claimed to have received 6,000 letters of support, and only two men went on record in opposition. She printed these two letters in entirety. She also arranged to have autographed copies of her novel *Pray You Sir, Whose Daughter?* sent to each member of the legislature in states, including Kentucky and Illinois, where consent legislation was pending.[33]

Gardener's efforts to raise the age of consent for girls and to advocate for a uniform moral standard among men and women brought her into an unlikely alliance with purity reformers and anti-vice crusaders, including the WCTU and Anthony Comstock. NAWSA members occasionally praised efforts to raise the age of sexual consent at their annual conventions, and state chapters helped with petition drives, but in the 1890s, the organization was not actively engaged in sexual reform efforts.[34] Thus, Gardener allied with the people she believed to be most forcefully fighting for fallen women and against the sexual double standard, even if she disagreed with them on core issues, such as censorship, the role of religion in American life, and the roots of vice.

While Gardener shared the anti-vice crusaders' interests in protecting women from sexual assault and in holding men accountable for sexual crimes, at every opportunity she stressed that her motivation was not the same as theirs. She even chafed at the terms *moral reform* and *purity campaign*. Codifying a woman's right to consent to sex, Gardener proclaimed, was not a moral issue but a "vital, social, and economic measure" related to public health, justice, and the rule of law.[35] It was not illegal to burn down another man's house because arson was immoral. It was illegal because the state recognized the property rights of the homeowner. For the same reason, she declared, it should be illegal to have sex with a young girl; she should have the right to protect her own person, which the state should guard even more fiercely than a right to mere property. Moreover, Gardener clarified, this right should not be voided if the girl had already been unchaste. A woman's body was sacredly her own, no matter what.[36]

At the First Annual National Purity Congress, held in Baltimore in October 1895, Gardener explained that she came to sex reform via science and because she wanted women to be protected by law, not Christian ideals. "I shall ask this Congress to look at the question with which I shall deal," Gardener began, "upon strictly natural and scientific grounds." To her audience of devout Christians, this would have come as a startling request. To them, the whole point of reform was to make communities align more closely with what they perceived to be God's vision for America. Gardener invited them instead to think in terms of heredity, environment, and the intergenerational transmission of traits.

Nor, she stressed to her Christian audience, was marriage a sacred institution. To the contrary, marriage provided the vector through which the majority of women contracted syphilis and gonorrhea, which they then passed on to their children in visible and invisible ways. Purity and anti-vice reformers, Gardener charged, focused altogether too much on what happened outside of marriage—among young men in boarding houses and in popular places of entertainment—and not nearly enough on what happened inside the "marriage bond" where most "crime and disease" originated because of husbands who were "living lies."[37]

From Baltimore, Gardener and Smart traveled on to Atlanta, Georgia, where she headlined several meetings held in conjunction with the 1895 Cotton States and International Exposition. After listening to Booker T. Washington's "Atlanta Compromise" speech, Gardener delivered a keynote address on October 17, which was NAWSA's Suffrage Day.[38] Even though she had headlined several of the group's national events since 1888, Gardener was still not a member of NAWSA. In fact, at their next annual meeting, NAWSA members would vote to officially disavow the recently published Woman's Bible, prompting Gardener to editorialize against the decision.[39] The NAWSA censure, Gardener prophesied, would set the cause back years and prove to detractors that women should not be voting because they were incapable of logical thought. When nearly every biblical passage pertaining to women was so degrading, Gardener pondered, "how anyone can be an absolutely orthodox Christian and a woman suffragist at the same time is always one of those conundrums that I have to give up."[40]

Brewing controversy aside, Gardener delivered a "brilliant and inspiring" speech at NAWSA's Suffrage Day in Atlanta. Entitled "A Theory in Tatters," her lecture eviscerated the premise that women should not be educated alongside men because their delicate brains could not handle it and because their bodies were destined only for maternity. Gardener cited the successes of the first generation of women to graduate college and those who pursued so-called masculine careers in fields such as mathematics. Now, she urged, it was time to grant women the political rights that matched their educational and professional attainments. As a woman of the South, she suggested that Southern men "prove your chivalry by deeds that will shame your Northern brothers into justice."[41] This was not quite as radical as her suggestion that purity reformers focus on science, not religion, but it was a close second.

After her NAWSA speech, Gardener and Smart stayed on in Atlanta for a few additional weeks so that she could attend the meeting of the International League of Press Clubs, along with her friend Jane Cunningham Croly ("Jennie June"), president of the New York Woman's Press Club. Being in Atlanta afforded Gardener the opportunity to highlight her Southern heritage and femininity. She mentioned her Southern birth multiple times in her talks, and Atlanta newspapers welcomed her as one of their own.[42] One profile of this "truly noble" Virginian described Gardener as a "well-born and well-bred" woman who came "from a long line of fighters and writers." In conclusion, this profile proclaimed, "she is happily married and is an excellent housekeeper."[43] When she was not busy writing and lecturing, Gardener had a great knack for public relations and was not one to let the facts get in the way of her self-making.

LATER THAT FALL, Gardener and Smart returned to Boston, where she concluded her legislative advocacy to raise the age of sexual consent for girls. In November 1895, she published a revised national map and blacklist, showing the many states that had raised the age to at least sixteen. In her closing report for 1895, Gardener rejoiced that "we feel like congratulating the country upon the fact that so much more than we hoped for has been accomplished by concerted action." She also expressed her hope "that no state will rest content to have it said that her lawmakers wish, and her men are willing, to take legal advantage of the girl children whose guardians and protectors they claim they are and should be."[44]

Gardener's involvement in the age of consent campaign further convinced her not only that women needed the vote but also that the nation needed women officeholders, an idea at the vanguard of radical reform in the 1890s. She repeatedly observed that men "who are fathers, husbands, and brothers have met in secret session and passed" laws legalizing the rape of girls. If women could vote and hold office, Gardener believed such laws would never have been enacted. "I yield to no one in my belief that women should take active part in legislative as in all affairs of life," Gardener proclaimed in *The Arena*.[45] Proving her point, that same year, Colorado state representative Carrie Holly—one of three women elected to the state legislature after women attained the vote in Colorado in 1894—proposed a bill to raise the state's age of consent to eighteen. At the annual NAWSA convention, suffragists noted with pride that this was the very first bill introduced by a woman member of any state legislature.[46] Suffragists may have differed on tactics and policies, but they all agreed that women voting and holding office would surely lead to women attaining bodily autonomy.

Back in Boston, Gardener attached her name to a petition demanding municipal suffrage for women—though Massachusetts voters, male and female, resoundingly rejected this nonbinding referendum—and she published a sarcastic review of an anti-suffrage treatise. What that book had succeeded in demonstrating, Gardener declared, was that men alone cannot "legislate wisely and successfully and fairly for both sexes."[47]

Gardener's efforts to raise the age of consent provided the ideal preparation for her later suffrage activism. Indeed, the national age of consent campaigns, even more than individual state suffrage referenda (which overwhelmingly failed), foreshadowed the issues—namely racism and Southern intransigence—that would handicap congressional passage of the federal amendment. In the 1890s, Gardener followed the progress of consent bills in several states, monitored the shifting positions of legislators, figured out who knew whom and how to best target the men whose votes she desired, compiled extensive lists and maps, and organized a large team of volunteers to keep the pressure on individual elected officials, all the while mobilizing publicity. Gardener published thousands of words on the issue, dispatched untold numbers of letters, and succeeded in her first legislative crusade. But because NAWSA rejected *The Woman's Bible* as well as Gardener's unorthodox critiques of marriage, she did not yet see a place for herself among the suffragists. Instead she decided to continue raising public awareness of the unspoken (and unspeakable) problems women often encountered in marriage, perhaps inspired by yet another crisis brewing in her own home.

10

Wee Wifee

The woman of the street may *own herself, she* may *change her
life, she* may *refuse to continue in the course which has lost
her her self-respect. The unwilling wife is helpless. She has lost
all. She has no refuge.*

—HELEN HAMILTON GARDENER, 1890

WHILE SHE CONTINUED to publish essays and coedit *The Arena*
and *Free Thought* (previously *Freethinkers'*) magazines, by
the end of 1896 Gardener shifted her focus to marriage, divorce, and
maternity reforms.[1] She was appointed chair of the National Congress
of Women's Divorce Reform Committee, and in December, she "held
the audience in closest attention" when she spoke about divorce at the
Woman's Congress in Boston.[2] Would a legislature ever consider writing a law about the railroad without consulting railroad companies,
Gardener demanded? For a woman, whom to marry was often the only
major life decision she got to make, yet she had no say over the terms of
her marriage, and once enacted, the bond was nearly irrevocable. Worse
still, in marriage women lost control over their own bodies, including
even the decision of when to have children.[3] Since the 1870s, female

reformers had been advocating for "voluntary motherhood"—a wife's right to refuse to have sex with her husband—but marital rape would not be recognized as a crime for another hundred years.

Gardener's work on behalf of divorce reform, her writings on heredity and the sexual double standard, and her efforts to raise the age of consent were of a piece. All three issues pivoted on a woman's right to determine what happened to her body, when to have sex and with whom (though she did not go so far as to argue for women's right to have sex outside of marriage, as she herself had been doing for the past twenty years), and to reproduce only when a baby would be welcomed and well cared for. At the end of the nineteenth century, such arguments were still very much at the vanguard of American reform; unlike Gardener, the women who demanded voluntary motherhood generally did not also talk openly about divorce, venereal disease, and female sexuality.[4] While many nineteenth-century women no doubt entered reform movements with their own personal stories of cheating husbands, unhappy marriages, and unplanned pregnancies, Gardener explicitly inserted these private concerns into the larger program for women's political rights.

In February 1897, Gardener presented her case for female autonomy in an unlikely venue: the first annual National Congress of Mothers, a group that grew out of the kindergarten movement.[5] Eager to discuss how mothering practices might be improved to reduce social problems and produce healthier children, women from across the country traveled to Washington, D.C., for the event. Attendance exceeded all expectations, and at the last minute, a larger venue had to be rented to accommodate the unexpectedly large crowd. Facing an audience of women intent on discussing childhood feeding, educational best practices, music for children, and other pleasant aspects of motherhood, Gardener spoke instead about the inherent right of women not to be mothers—the path she herself had chosen. "I fear that I shall strike a less pleasant note than those who have preceded me," Gardener began, "who have so generally dealt with ideal motherhood, who have sung the praise side of the song. My theme is scientific." Marshaling evidence from the natural and social sciences, she demanded that women—including mothers—first and foremost be considered as individuals.

Gardener enumerated the countless ways mothers were praised on stage and in literature but noted that "in the building and maturing of this ideal, there runs ever and always the one thread of thought that self-sacrifice, self-abnegation, self-effacement are the grandest attributes of maternity; that in order to be a perfect, an ideal wife and mother, the woman must be sunk, the individual immolated, the ego subjugated." What if that were not true, Gardener posed? What if forcing women to lie to themselves and to their husbands, to deny their intellects and their desires was actually bad for women, bad for marriages, and bad for children? Women who could not take care of themselves nor determine the conditions into which they would bring children surely did not endow their offspring with the best possible traits. Throughout much of human history, women had lacked control over their own bodies. But now, Gardener charged, when women were more educated and engaged, "she who permits herself to become a mother without having first demanded and obtained her own freedom from sex domination and fair and free conditions of development for herself and child will commit a crime against herself, against her child, and against mankind."[6]

The *Chicago Tribune* characterized Gardener's address as the conference's "pièce de résistance," noting that "enthusiastic plaudits were frequent in some parts of the house and dubious looks among the orthodox."[7] Scientists quibbled with her discussion of "heredity," particularly the way she blended the passing on of traits with the passing on of diseases. To scientists the difference between a trait and a disease mattered a great deal.[8] To Gardener, it mattered not if "syphilis teeth" were considered a trait or a disease—it only mattered that they were passed on to unborn children whose mothers had no say in the matter.

Gardener's unusually explicit emphasis on the frequency of venereal disease transmission to unsuspecting wives might have indicated a personal familiarity with gonorrhea or syphilis. Smart's ongoing health struggles and her focus on the disease suggest he may have had syphilis, but it is impossible to document with certainty. Untreated syphilis can severely damage the heart and brain, both of which impacted Smart. The presence of venereal disease may also account for why the couple did not have children—either by choice or because of disease-related infertility. Even if Smart did not suffer from venereal disease, Gardener was closely attuned to the ravages such infections caused other women and was among the most vocal in linking women's sexual health to their political position.

Gardener's relationship with Smart and the couple's economic prospects continued to deteriorate after their move to Boston in 1894. By the summer of 1896, they were no longer even getting paid by their employer, *The Arena* magazine. Even worse, on the evening of February 17, 1897—just as Gardener would have been socializing at the Mother's Congress reception in Washington, accepting compliments for her talk that morning—Police Inspectors Bogan and Abbott arrived at her home in Boston to arrest Smart for committing fraud as *The Arena's* business manager.

To OUTSIDE OBSERVERS, *The Arena* contained a disproportionate number of advertisements for the books that its in-house publishing arm printed. Eventually, disgruntled authors came forward alleging that the Arena Publishing Company was essentially a Ponzi scheme whereby authors fronted the money for a first edition of 2,000 books— covering all expenses and, unbeknownst to them, a 20 percent profit for Arena. The Arena Publishing Company then advertised the books in *The Arena* magazine, but beyond a few big sellers like Gardener, most authors never sold the 2,000 books. In 1895, authors and employees sued the company for fraud and back pay. But by then, *The Arena* was far too indebted to pay either its authors or its own staff. In 1896, the magazine declared bankruptcy, and B. O. Flower was forced out as editor. Gardener and her friend John Clark Ridpath, the famous historian whom she had known from Greencastle, Indiana, continued as editors of the struggling magazine for a few more months.

On January 23, 1897, all Arena property was sold at public auction, and the book plates were sold for scrap. Gardener alone retained her book plates and unsold books.[9] As Arena employees, Smart and Gardener filed claims for unpaid compensation totaling $406.20 and $1,384.60, respectively. The court decreed that employees would receive an amount not exceeding $100 each, meaning the couple lost over $1,500 (the equivalent of $45,000 today).[10]

Then, on February 17, Smart and B. O. Flower were arrested for selling $2,700 of worthless stock to H. D. Campbell and Co. of Lynn, Massachusetts. The two men were held in jail until friends arrived to pay their $3,000 bail.[11] Imagine Gardener's shock at receiving word of Smart's arrest the very day she had given a stirring speech in Washington about women's right to live as independent humans. After all the years of watching him struggle at Equitable Life, she had tried so hard to arrange for Smart a job that he could do, no doubt using her own reputation as a chit, only for him to preside over *The Arena's* bankruptcy and then get arrested for fraud.

Over time, Gardener placed blame for the magazine's demise and financial improprieties on B. O. Flower, whom she later described as a man "who stands by nothing . . . who for personal gain will throw away person or idea, who borrows money knowing" that he could never return it. She considered Flower to be "corrupt at the foundation." Nevertheless, she was floored by *The Arena's* collapse. The Arena incident "hurt me," she reflected. "It hurt my capacity to do good work."[12]

By late March, Smart and Flower were "honorably discharged" of the accusations.[13] But the damage had been done. The fifty-eight-year-old Smart would never work again. Gardener received an invitation to headline the fourth annual Pacific Woman's Congress at the end of April. Papers reported that the California women had raised over $600, far above the norm and more than $18,000 today, to sponsor Gardener's first trip to the West Coast because they believed she would "undoubtedly create more of a sensation than any other woman lecturer who has recently visited San Francisco."[14] The couple hastily put their belong-ings in storage in New York. On April 12, Smart rented his own storage trunk, in secret, from the Garfield Safe Deposit Company.[15] Shortly thereafter, they took the new express train from New York to San Fran-cisco, which, in a miracle of industrialism and ingenuity, took only three and a half days. The couple arrived in San Francisco on April 25, where the mayor welcomed the "bright particular star" at her hotel.[16] Gardener told reporters that she and Smart had traveled to California for a much needed rest, planned to stay several months, and had "no definite plans for the immediate future."[17]

IF PINK CARNATIONS could pay for clothes, food, and hotel rooms, Gardener would have been rich. After she shared her favorite flower with a reporter, loyal readers and enthusiastic hosts regularly sent her flowers and gifts.[18] As it was, carnations could not be traded for food or lodging, calling into question how Gardener and Smart financed their extended stay in California. Gardener's friend Mary Phillips suspected that Smart had a secret stash of money, but Gardener doubted this—he could barely keep a job, how could he have harbored cash?[19] Gardener published essays at a brisk pace throughout 1895 and 1896, and she told her California hosts that she regularly received $100 per talk.[20] Whether or not this was her rate on the East Coast, her West Coast friends read-ily acceded. Needless to say, while in California, Gardener scheduled many talks.

Her speaking tour began on Thursday, April 29, when she delivered the Woman's Congress keynote address, reprising "The Moral Respon-sibility of Woman in Heredity," a talk she had first presented at the 1893 world's fair. Preconference publicity touted her "pronounced convic-tions and courage," promising that Gardener, now forty-four, was "not yet middle-aged" and "decidedly pleasant to look at." The *San Fran-cisco Call* reported that "long before the hour of opening the street was crowded with an impatient throng anxious to secure the best possible seats."[21] From there, she and Smart traveled to Palo Alto so that Gardener could deliver an address on heredity at Stanford University, where she was introduced by Stanford president David Starr Jordan.[22]

After two days at Stanford, they returned to San Francisco for Gardener to read from *An Unofficial Patriot* at a benefit for the Woman's Congress held at Golden Gate Hall. Newspapers reported scant attendance at this event, but one notable audience member listened eagerly: army colonel Selden A. Day.[23] Colonel Day's wife had attended the first Pacific Coast Woman's Congress in 1894 but died in 1895.[24] Perhaps Day had befriended the organizers and continued attending the annual event or perhaps he came just to see Helen Hamilton Gardener, whose father reporters claimed he had known during his Civil War service in Virginia. In a remarkable coincidence, Day may also have heard about Gardener from his old comrade in the Ohio 7th Infantry: Isaac Mack, the editor of the *Sandusky Daily Register* and the man who broke the story of her affair back in 1876.

Whatever the impetus, Day arrived at Gardener's reading on May 7, 1897, ready to participate. After Gardener, dressed in "cream colored something and lace," read from her book, Charles Smart piped up to tell the audience that the novel was a true story, based on Gardener's father. Then, according to news reports, Day, "who as a youngster served in West Virginia during the war, told in a few words the dangers and difficulties of the expeditions through the rugged mountain passes and of the value to the Army of intelligent, competent, and patriotic guides."[25] The historical record does not reveal whether Day and Gardener socialized after her talk, but something between them surely transpired. The two remained in touch after her California trip.

Gardener delivered a couple more lectures in San Francisco, traveled to Stockton to address another Woman's Congress, and returned to the city to visit with friends.[26] Meanwhile, in Boston, her nephew Bernard—the nefarious inspiration for the lead character in *Is This Your Son, My Lord?*—died, just shy of thirty-two.[27] Remarkably, her last surviving sibling, Kate Chenoweth Roehl, died on the very same day.[28] For as much as Gardener prized her status as a Chenoweth of Virginia, she was now the only remaining Chenoweth sibling.

By July, Smart and Gardener were in Southern California, staying at swank hotels—the Van Nuys, the Miramar, the Windermere, and the Governor's Cottage, finally settling in for a few weeks at the new Coronado resort in San Diego—likely paid for by her hosts and her speaking fees.[29] Along the way, she gave occasional talks, generally revivals of her greatest hits such as "Sex in Brain," and was feted at various parties. But mostly she and Smart relaxed. She visited beekeepers to learn about beehives and spent countless hours observing the peculiar habits of the California red woodpecker.[30] Why did Americans travel to Italy or France to restore their health, Gardener wondered, when one could partake in "rambles in olive groves" and the "grape-cure" right in California, all the while staying in "fine hotels, well and healthfully appointed, with every luxury in easy call." California, according to Gardener, was literally the "land of milk and honey."[31]

Gardener thrived in the West. Compared with the East Coast, she appreciated the West's more democratic way of life, especially the comparative freedom western states afforded women. In an article about the California woodpecker, she approvingly observed that in California it was impossible to tell a man's station in life by his job, his outfit, or his diction. In San Francisco, she had even witnessed Harvard men driving streetcars. For a woman constantly making and remaking herself, the openness of the West appealed. Reluctantly, in late October, the couple returned to New York and an uncertain future.[32]

WITH THEIR PINCHED FINANCES, Gardener and Smart could not return to their beloved Upper West Side. Instead, they rented a room on West 38th Street from their friend Mary Phillips, later moving several miles and many streetcar stops north to 519 West 123rd Street.[33]

Throughout 1898, Gardener prepared for the opening of the play

The Reverend Griffith Davenport, based on her 1894 novel *An Unofficial Patriot* and starring the celebrated actor and playwright James Herne and his wife Katherine. Gardener was thrilled to work with Herne, who also adapted the novel for the stage.[34] Herne had made his stage debut in 1859 in a theatrical adaptation of *Uncle Tom's Cabin* and earned his reputation as a dramatist with his 1890 play *Margaret Fleming,* which scandalized audiences when the titular character nursed the illegitimate baby born of her husband's young mistress. Just like Gardener's character Florence Campbell, Margaret Fleming scorned the errant husband and embraced the baby (the mistress died). According to his daughter Julie, Herne was fonder of *The Reverend Griffith Davenport* than anything else he wrote, save perhaps *Margaret Fleming.*[35] In Herne, Gardener had found an ideal partner.

But Herne made many changes to Gardener's novel—including adding in a brother who remained loyal to the Confederacy (played by a relative of John Wilkes Booth, the man who assassinated Abraham Lincoln)—and risked "lavish expenditure" in demanding costly sets, which prohibited short runs in smaller cities and scared away investors.[36] The New York engagement, reportedly costing $30,000, ran only four weeks in the fall of 1898. Nevertheless, Herne insisted on taking the play on the road.[37]

The Reverend Griffith Davenport opened at the Lafayette Theater in Washington, D.C., in January 1899. The *Washington Post* reviewed it favorably, marveling at the elaborate sets and army of actors, including more than forty speaking parts.[38] But a few days later, the *Washington Times* reported that the play had received a "condemnatory verdict" and would likely have to close early. Herne invested so much money in the production that he must have expected it would be "a masterpiece," but it was "too complicated, too modern, and too abundant" to succeed.[39] Because the play sent nuanced messages about war, heroism, and race relations, audiences were not sure what to make of it. "While it is exceedingly possible that an adaptation of *An Unofficial Patriot* could be made enjoyable," another reviewer wrote, "there seems to be little probability of such a change."[40]

The play had its final run in Stamford, Connecticut, in May 1899.[41] Herne wrote just one more play before dying of pneumonia in June 1901 at the age of sixty-two. Gardener recalled that she was bereft after his death because "had he lived we had planned much work for the future and to me he was a very great playwright as well as a good friend. His death was a real blow to me both financially and sentimentally."[42]

To Gardener, the stage debut of *The Reverend Griffith Davenport* had major personal and professional significance. She appreciated the opportunity to enact her Chenoweth-of-Virginia heritage, but the play's failure, coupled with the untimely death of Herne, dealt her another grim disappointment. In conjunction with the Washington performance, a local paper interviewed Gardener in her room at the Ebbitt Hotel. She reflected on the personal resonance of the play: "My story has been a part of my life and I have felt keenly every line I put into it." She shared that her brothers would be joining her in her box seats that evening. Bernard had been dead since 1870, William since 1882, and Alfred since 1887.[43] Did the reporter write this in error, or was this wishful thinking on Gardener's part? *An Unofficial Patriot* had remade Gardener as a Chenoweth of Virginia in the public mind, but there were no Chenoweths of Virginia left with whom to share this thrill. Nor could she expect another moment on the stage, as her writerly output had drastically diminished since 1894. The failure of *The Reverend Griffith Davenport* represented the end of two of Gardener's lifelong dreams: to reconnect with the Chenoweths and to be a career writer.

BACK IN NEW YORK, Charles Smart's mental faculties declined, and Gardener struggled to take care of him and keep the couple afloat financially. From 1898 through 1900, she occasionally lectured and published, but she mainly rehashed old speeches and essays. She also sought new organizational homes and attended a few public events—sitting at the head table at the Eclectic Club luncheon and organizing a

flag booth to benefit children orphaned by the cataclysmic 1900 Galveston, Texas, hurricane. [44] In April 1899, she joined her closest friends, the
historian John Clark Ridpath, Elizabeth Cady Stanton, and Dr. Edward
C. Spitzka, in forming a new Psychic Study Club to scientifically investigate spiritualist séances, which were then in vogue. But if this club
survived past its first meeting, no records remain.[45] Even her favorite
group, the Woman's Press Club of New York, was undergoing an internal struggle that put Gardener once again on the outside of women's
organizations. For years, Gardener had been a confidante of the group's
adored president Jane Cunningham Croly, but after Croly's death, the
Press Club fractured. Gardener ran for a club office in 1899 but was
defeated by the new guard.[46]

The second-to-last short story Gardener ever published captures her
lonely life during her final few months in New York City. "The Man at
the Window" recounts the sad story of a man's demise in the big city.
A female narrator, not unlike Gardener, rides the elevated express train
downtown and every day observes a fastidious man at work at his desk
near the Fiftieth Street stop. As the weather cools, she notices that he
does not move or put on his coat for several days. Fearing the worst, she
exits at his stop and tells a policeman her suspicion. Together, they enter
the man's room and find him dead. "He had evidently been dead some
days, in sight and hearing of hundreds," the narrator recounts, "with his
door unlocked in a house full of people, and no one had suspected that
anything was wrong!" A person could die of loneliness and starvation
with hardly anyone noticing because "the great metropolitan heart"
was "so absorbed . . . with the throb of its personal pulse beat."[47]

As Gardener wrote this story, she contemplated the death of Smart,
for whom she could no longer care at home. She had referenced his
declining health since 1893, but the historical record does not indicate
a clear diagnosis. His symptoms—heart trouble, fatigue, mood swings,
depression, and eventually dementia—match any number of ailments,
including the nineteenth-century epidemics of neurasthenia and late-
stage syphilis. Like the heroine of "The Lady of the Club," her best
short story, Gardener had learned that the "the keenest agony that mor-

tals ever bore" was the combination of love plus poverty. In the story, the wife refuses to hospitalize her ailing husband, even after his mental deterioration causes violent fits of rage. Instead, she poisons him and then herself.[48] Depressed and enervated as she was, Gardener chose a different course.

UPON THE RECOMMENDATION of their physician, Dr. John A. Wyeth, a Confederate veteran and surgical pioneer who was elected president of the American Medical Association in 1902, Gardener "took [Smart] by the hand" and reluctantly checked him into the Westport Sanitarium, in Westport, Connecticut, 45 miles away. Housed in a four-story gothic-style white building, the Westport Sanitarium specialized in the treatment of chronic diseases, which in Smart's case were dementia and heart trouble. Smart had obscured from others the "the truth about why he was there" and "who sent him," perhaps indicating a stigmatized condition. Smart selected the highest-priced room, and Gardener agreed, even though she had no money to pay for it. To fund Smart's stay, she moved farther north, all the way to West 142 Street, and went into debt.[49]

Gardener visited Smart three times a week. During what was to be her last visit, he received a letter. She asked if he wanted her to read it to him. He declined, saying he would read it himself eventually. Later, Smart returned from the water closet saying he had read the letter and that it was from an old friend in Detroit. The very next day, January 11, 1901, Smart died, just shy of his sixty-second birthday. Gardener found the letter in his death bed pocket. It was not from an old friend in Detroit. It was from his daughter Cora, and it referenced their life together. Smart had told Gardener that both of his daughters had died (only Iva had, in 1892), and she had no idea that he had stayed in contact with his wife and daughter all these years. She learned that Love and Cora had settled in West Virginia. Gardener realized that this must have been where Smart disappeared to in 1894, one other time when he told her that he had gone fishing for four days, and possibly other instances she had not discovered. This revelation was shocking. She had an especially hard time comprehending his liberty to travel since "he had only the money I gave him."[50]

Even on his death bed, after a bout of "aphasia" so severe that he could not connect words, Smart had mustered the wherewithal to lie to Gardener about this letter. "Great God!" she exclaimed to her friend Mary Phillips, "what a strange thing the human brain (and heart) is!" Gardener reflected that her predicament was utterly baffling, "for in many ways he was a wonderfully good man and his love for me was tremendous in every way except the one of absolute truthfulness."

"On what possible grounds could this have gone on for a quarter of a century with a family tie *that was in any conceivable operation* elsewhere?" Gardener pondered. "It seems to me quite impossible." And yet there it was. When she found the letter "in his poor dead pocket," she looked at his face for hours "but no light came to me." So, she packed up his belongings and sent them to his daughter because she knew that the daughter "most likely believed and trusted him as I had my own dear father."[51] Even in her shock and grief, Gardener behaved like the model women in her short stories—casting out the husbands and siding with the wives, mistresses, and daughters.

In the sanitarium's logbook, under the column for "married," Smart's entry simply reads "yes." All the other entries in this giant book list the spouse's name. Smart could not possibly have explained his complicated marital status in this small bureaucratic box. Friends claimed that Smart had told Gardener he had divorced Lovenia decades ago; and he and Gardener had lived together as husband and wife for nearly twenty-five years. To whom was he referring when he checked "yes" on his marital status? His legal wife or his day-to-day wife? Smart's precise cause of death was also murky. The *New York Herald* ran a short death notice for him noting only that he died of heart failure. His death certificate, signed by the director of the sanitarium, lists "chronic myocarditis," which often results from an infection, as the primary cause of death and "angina pectoris" as the secondary cause.[52]

After a small, private service consisting only of classical music— "including his favorite *Träumeri* by Schumann"—Smart was cremated. His ashes remain at the Fresh Pond Crematory in Long Island, where Robert Ingersoll had been cremated just six months before. At the time, cremation was an uncommon and controversial practice, but free-thinkers, none more so than Gardener, believed that they must carry their convictions with them to the end. Gardener had criticized other freethinkers who caved on their death beds and allowed a Christian burial.[53] With Smart's funeral and interment, she put their, or at least her, freethinking beliefs into action.

Gardener's situation grew more complex several weeks later when Smart's wife Lovenia resurfaced to claim that she was his rightful heir. Legally, of course, she was. Gardener recalled that she and Smart had written their wills together on the eve of their trip to California in 1897, leaving everything to each other and, in the case of mutual demise, to Mary Phillips (because Gardener liked her and because they owed her money).[54] When Gardener had announced plans to draft her will, Smart insisted on writing his, too, though he owned nothing, Gardener remarked, except some clothes and the watch she had given him. So, after his death, when his will could not be found, Gardener did not "disturb myself about it." After all, she believed his will to have been "a mere formality and done to satisfy his own sense of 'dignity' when I made my own will."[55] But Gardener soon learned that Smart had drafted another will, back in 1893. As Gardener was making her way home after dazzling audiences at the world's fair in Chicago, Smart had traveled to Charleston, West Virginia, to visit his family. While there, he filed a will naming his wife Love as his sole heir.[56] After Smart's death, Love appointed H. C. Bailey, her son-in-law, as executor and sent word to New York that she had Smart's will in hand.

Love also demanded possession of Smart's belongings. This is when Gardener learned that he had rented a secret storage trunk the week before they had departed for California. The claim receipt stated that the trunk contained clothes and papers.[57] What papers? With Gardener's reputation at its tenuous peak, Love's claim threatened to make public Gardener's twenty-five years of illicit cohabitation with Smart.

In an obituary for Smart published in *Free Thought* magazine, the editors acknowledged that even though they had never met Smart, everyone knew that "his religion was the Religion of Humanity, and the god he worshipped was Helen H. Gardener, his brilliant literary little wife" whom he lovingly called his "wee wifee." The obituary also quoted women's rights advocates who referred to Smart as a "Knight of the New Chivalry" because anyone who saw Gardener "with eyes and cheeks burning with that electric fire which makes her books so vital and so compelling standing . . . under the wing of her giant husband, whose joy and delight it was to protect her and further her work in every possible way, will realize what a loss his death will be to Helen Gardener."

Gardener wrote the magazine to thank freethinkers for the hundreds of condolences she had received, and her letter was included in the published tribute to Smart. She proclaimed that "my husband was a king among men, both in look and deed—over 6 feet 2 inches in height, firmly built and with a fine mind, cultivated, courteous, and always above all else my devoted lover."[58] In spite of everything, she never once let on that he was not her real husband or that he had deceived and disappointed her in every conceivable way.

Despite her strong public face, Gardener suffered another breakdown. Smart's death came just months after the deaths of Ingersoll, her longtime champion, and John Clark Ridpath, her oldest friend. Elizabeth Cady Stanton had recently celebrated her eighty-fourth birthday, and Gardener knew that Stanton, too, was not long for this earth. Financially insolvent and broken in mind and body, Gardener placed her belongings in a spare room at the Ridpaths' New York home and left instructions for her trusted confidante Mary Phillips to reclaim the secret trunk and sort out Smart's tangled probate, promising to repay her the money she owed.

Just as Gardener's adoring memorial to Smart was published in *Free Thought* magazine in March 1901, she was on her way to Puerto Rico to visit the army hero who had recently planted the first U.S. flag on the island: Col. Selden Allen Day, the very same man who had spoken about his Civil War experiences at her 1897 reading in San Francisco. Seventeen years had passed since Alice Chenoweth had emerged, like a butterfly from a cocoon, on the nation's stage as Helen Hamilton Gardener. More phoenix than butterfly this time, Gardener would remake herself once more.

PART THREE

Two Calling Cards

1901–1925

11

Around the World with the Sun

In case you use (in print) any of the points, kindly use my name as Helen H. Gardener, only. I never use Day in print—for literary work.

—HELEN HAMILTON GARDENER, 1903

A S HELEN HAMILTON GARDENER nursed Charles Smart through his final illness at the Westport Sanitarium in the winter of 1901, their family physician expected to hear one of two things: that "she had gone insane or had been killed by one insane." He admitted, she recalled, that "he was not prepared to see her come through a whole and balanced woman."[1] If she hoped to save herself, the doctor advised her to "neither read, think, nor try to write. If you do, your mind, if not your life, will pay the penalty."[2] He warned that her next break would be her last and advised her to seek a change of scenery.

So, just weeks after Smart's death, Gardener embarked for Puerto Rico to visit Col. Selden Allen Day, accompanied by a woman she referred to only as "Mrs. B."[3] It would have been unseemly to visit Day by herself. She explained to Elizabeth Cady Stanton that her New York friends, together with Colonel Day, had conspired together and "put me on an army transport and shipped me" to a more hospitable climate.[4] Gardener went to Puerto Rico to rest her mind and cure her tattered nerves because it was cheaper to live there than in New York and because she hoped that Day might offer her a lifeline.

After she had settled in Puerto Rico, Gardener wrote her New York friend Mary Phillips, on Day's "Chief Ordnance Officer" letterhead, to process her complicated emotions. "I still feel too stunned to think it out very clearly," Gardener confessed. "It is a queer old world, Little Phil!"[5] After a quarter century together, Smart had left Gardener with nothing but potentially humiliating probate issues. Having had her heart and her livelihood destroyed by a tempestuous relationship, Gardener was drawn to what she perceived to be the solid orderliness of Day.

Born in Chillicothe, Ohio in 1838, Day, like Smart, was the same age that her beloved eldest brother Bernard would have been. Also like Bernard, Day was a celebrated Civil War hero. At the outbreak of the war, Day, then a dentist, immediately organized a unit of volunteer troops before ultimately enlisting with Company C of the 7th Ohio Volunteer Infantry. At the first battle of Winchester (Gardener's birthplace), Day helped capture Confederate General Stonewall Jackson's brother-in-law and earned his first medals. He served until the end of the war and was then tasked with guarding the cell of Confederate President Jefferson Davis, who was held prisoner at Fort Monroe in Hampton, Virginia.[6] For the "generosity and consideration" Day extended to his famous captive (he even arranged to get Davis a rocking chair so that he could sit comfortably), he became lifelong friends with the Davis family and other prominent Confederates.[7]

After the Civil War, Day remained in the army but continued his education, graduating from medical school in South Carolina in 1880. He was also an amateur inventor who improved upon the "dum dum" bullet (an expanding bullet) and who had a penchant for moving vehicles, trying for years to "perfect flying machine parts." During the Spanish-American War, Day fought in Cuba and then Puerto Rico, where he hoisted the American flag over El Morro Castle and fired the national salute on the final day of occupation in October 1898.[8]

For a man in his early sixties, Day remained quite handsome and fit,

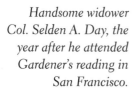

*Handsome widower
Col. Selden A. Day, the
year after he attended
Gardener's reading in
San Francisco.*

especially in his military uniform. He stood 5 feet 8 inches tall, a full 6 inches shorter than Smart, with light brown hair, sparse at the top, kind gray-blue eyes, and a cropped white beard with handlebar mustache.[9] According to her letters to Phillips, Gardener's relationship with Day was not immediately romantic, though the couple had several pictures taken of themselves during this initial trip.[10] Gardener described Day as a nice older man who had taken a special interest in her, not unlike the many other prominent men who had helped her over the years, including Ingersoll, Spitzka, and Ridpath. "He is lovely to me and has done everything possible for me," Gardener wrote Phillips. Gardener reciprocated by keeping Day company. "Between ourselves," Gardener revealed, "he is utterly alone here, two miles from town and other folks. It is *very bad* for him." Day needed "people with him and clings to those he likes as if his life depended on them."

When she mentioned leaving Puerto Rico, Day "simply went into hysterics." He begged Gardener and Mrs. B. to accompany him to his next post, wherever it might be, and "'run' his place." Gardener told him that "would not do" but he "can't seem to see it." After so many years of army life and living in "the frontier country," Day was "ill fitted for other life." Gardener was torn. She appreciated the warm weather and slower pace of life in Puerto Rico, but she worried that she would not be able to regain a foothold as a writer there. Gardener told Stanton that she wanted to return to New York but didn't know how she could make a living there.[11] She had been writing historical sketches to accompany a series of paintings by the artist Edward Moran and desperately hoped to be paid for the work. Ultimately, Moran compensated her with a painting that she proudly hung in her home, a prized possession that did not pay the bills.[12]

Just weeks before Day was to depart Puerto Rico, Gardener had not yet decided if she would stay in Puerto Rico without him, accompany him to his next post, or return to New York in the hopes of restarting her career. Further complicating her options, Gardener had not been forthcoming with Day. He knew nothing about her debts, Smart's probate issues, or that she had been, strictly speaking, Smart's mistress and not his wife. "He knows only the surface of my affairs so far as the within matters go," Gardener divulged to Phillips. "Of course I can trust you in all this," Gardener confided. But she did not trust completely. At the top of this seven-page-long confessional letter, she instructed Phillips: "*Best Destroy This Letter.*"[13]

In October 1901, Day departed for Fort Williams, in Maine—a cold and sleepy post compared with Puerto Rico. He was "very sore" about what was to be his last official duty before retiring. Gardener decided not to accompany him, at least not yet. Instead she set up "housekeeping" in Washington, D.C., with her friend LaSalle Corbell Pickett, the widow of the famous Confederate general George Pickett, the man who led "Pickett's Charge" at the Battle of Gettysburg.

As Day settled into his post in Maine just before the first snow, Gardener and Sister Pickett, as she called her, selected a suite of five rooms at the Cumberland Hotel on Thomas Circle. "Floored" by the trip back from Puerto Rico, Gardener was too weak to go to New York to oversee the transfer of her belongings, so she sent detailed instructions to Mary Phillips. "We need my two beds immediately—the mahogany one and the little green iron one," Gardener commanded. "Also all of my good chairs, rug, bookcase, pictures, table ware, etc etc. Mrs. P. has no table things hardly and we are going to keep house."[14] The two women had likely met years before in New York, where Pickett had moved after the death of her husband in 1875 to restore her reputation and that of the Confederacy. In addition to mythologizing her husband's questionable military prowess, Pickett wrote apologias for the "Lost Cause" that popularized racist depictions of happy slaves, benevolent slave owners, and idyllic life on the plantation.[15] Though her ultimate aim differed significantly from Gardener's, Pickett had also remade herself, in a calculated blend of fact and fiction, through her writing.

As they settled in to life in Washington, the two women joined the League of American Pen Women, a group of female writers, journalists, and artists founded in 1897 because women were denied membership to the all-male National Press Club.[16] Gardener also began to enter Washington society, serving as a hostess at various events and entertaining callers at the flat she shared with Pickett.

Gardener's favorite Washington activity, however, were her "daily drives" on one of the two white Andalusian horses, Kayo and Bayo, that Day had brought back from Puerto Rico. In this she made a "conspicuous figure," according to D.C. society pages.[17] Just as other women had recently discovered the freedom of movement afforded by the newly invented bicycle—including WCTU President Frances Willard, who published a book chronicling her enthusiasm for cycling—Gardener took to the streets with abandon on her white horse.[18]

But living with Pickett began to grate. For one thing, she spent lavishly on "absurd and cruel" offerings of hospitality without concern for where the money would come from.[19] Gardener sought a better domestic arrangement. In April 1902, she announced that she would marry Colonel Day. The couple recited their vows in a small private ceremony at the Cumberland, witnessed only by Sister Pickett, the matron

Gardener created a memorable impression riding her beloved Andalusian horses through the streets of the nation's capital.

of honor, and her son George, the best man. In deference to Gardener's freethinking beliefs, the wedding was officiated by Judge Seth Shepard of the D.C. Court of Appeals.

One society page described the event as "a curious mingling of sentiment with advancing years." The bride, nearly fifty, was a "wonderfully well preserved woman" who wore a cream-colored crepe dress, embroidered in white daisies, forget-me-nots, golden bees, butterflies, and wheat. Made in Paris, the extravagant dress was a gift from Pickett. At the conclusion of the brief ceremony, Gardener thanked Judge Shepard for his service, and Day proclaimed the wedding as "the happiest, proudest day of [his] life." Invitations to a late afternoon reception had been sent to friends as far away as Sandusky, Ohio, but the party was canceled due to the illness of Day's sister. Instead, the newlyweds boarded an afternoon train to Fort Williams, Maine, so that Day could return to his post.[20]

Life in Maine did not suit the couple, so Day arranged for a slightly early retirement, and they returned to Washington within weeks. Day began lobbying, unsuccessfully, for a promotion so that he could retire at a higher rank. In June, Gardener accompanied her friend Senator William Mason (R-IL) to the White House to meet, for the first time, President Theodore Roosevelt.[21] And in August, she began regular visits to the sculptor Adelaide Johnson's Washington studio so that she could be molded in clay for the "gallery of eminent women" Johnson hoped to create. Though she had only been in residence a few months, Gardener was already establishing herself as a Washington insider.

Born in Illinois in 1859, Adelaide Johnson was a highly skilled seamstress who longed to be an artist. As a young woman living in Chicago, she fell 20 feet to the ground from an open elevator shaft, broke several bones and gained a permanent limp, but received $15,000 in damages. With this windfall, Johnson traveled to Rome to study sculpture. She returned to the United States in 1886, joined the women's movement, and soon had the opportunity to sculpt Susan B. Anthony. Her bust of Anthony received wide acclaim, and Johnson was commissioned to sculpt busts of movement leaders to be displayed at the 1893 world's fair in Chicago. Johnson had found her lifelong calling as "the sculptor of suffrage."[22]

Johnson wrote Gardener in March of 1902, explaining that she wanted to "tell the tale of strength and delicacy knit into one" by sculpting Gardener's bust in clay. Gardener thanked Johnson for her kind words, noting dolefully, "It is such words and feeling from such fine and brave women as you that keep some of us from despair, sometimes."[23] When Gardener returned to D.C. in the summer of 1902, she immediately arranged to sit for Johnson. A devotee of the philosopher François Delsarte, Johnson believed that she had to understand her subjects' inner selves in order to capture their outer likenesses, so her method involved in-depth personal conversations with her subjects.[24] Following each of their twenty-six sittings, conducted between August and November 1902, Johnson carefully recorded what they talked about in a handwritten log, in teeny script, spanning thirty-four pages. While Johnson's Gallery of Eminent Women never materialized, her "sitting notes," preserved at the Library of Congress, offer a unique window into the personal lives of women reformers, including Gardener as she struggled to maintain her equilibrium in a new, somewhat hasty marriage.

When Johnson asked Gardener for her definition of love, Gardener replied that "as husbands go," "as homes go," marriage was "doing as someone else wishes," while, the women agreed, "having the heroic power to save your own very soul from disintegration at the same time." At their first session, Johnson noted that Gardener did not seem like herself and clung "to the reasonable hope that the state may be the result of . . . her long strain and pressure in the care of Col. Smart." As the weeks went on, Johnson increasingly fretted over her friend's well-being, observing that "she is letting go of something herself. It began when she married the second time and so soon. She cast away an ideal. It has hurt her with herself. How will she be able to stand that is the question and a tremendous test."[25]

Though his first wife also supported women's rights, Day assumed a more traditional role as husband than had Charles Smart—perhaps because, unlike Smart, he actually was Gardener's legal husband. During their first few months together, Gardener was working on a book called *Woman in the Saddle*, which detailed her love of horseback riding. But when she asked her husband to look at the book's illustrations, he nitpicked her choices.[26] Another day, she showed Johnson photographs of her ungloved hands that she had intended to use in the book and complained that Day had insisted on photos with gloved hands because that was more "horsemanlike."[27] *Woman in the Saddle* was never published.

While part of Day's appeal may have been his steady government paycheck, Gardener soon found that he was not very good with money. She related to Johnson his "most evident incapacity to cope with the combination of her and his own new position of having but a limited income and out of which all the necessities of life must come." For forty years, Day had lived in army housing, with many of his necessities paid for or subsidized. Now, living on his army pension, he had taken on a wife with her own needs, and he himself harbored "the desires of a gentleman of leisure and financial freedom." As a new wife, Gardener said nothing to Day but worried about her prospects tied to another man whose financial acumen she did not trust. Listening to these and other similar tales, Johnson observed that "it is clear that there is a culmination of events and Helen Gardener is trying to hold out." Johnson concluded, "My feeling is that her heart is crying out."[28]

DAY AND GARDENER spent several weeks touring Virginia on their horses in the fall of 1902, but hastily returned home on October 29 when they received the news that Gardener's close friend Elizabeth Cady Stanton had died.[29] Stanton's death was not entirely unexpected, but it came as a blow to Gardener nevertheless. Following the death of their mutual friend Robert Ingersoll in 1900, Stanton and Gardener pledged that they would speak for each other at their graves, in part to explain their unusual brain donations. Gardener had fully prepared to go to New York to speak at Stanton's memorial service. She even reached out to Dr. Edward Spitzka to confirm whether or not the brain of any educated woman had been studied since she wrote "Sex in Brain" back in 1888 (she hoped Stanton's would be the first).[30] But Stanton's children blocked Gardener from speaking at the memorial. Stanton's daughter, Harriot Stanton Blatch, herself a prominent suffragist, also denied her mother's brain bequest, announcing, "My mother never did anything to pain those nearest to her and whom she loved, and I am quite sure she would never have done this."[31] For years, Gardener remained hurt that she had been shunned from the service and that Stanton's "mediocre commonplace children," as Johnson described them, had thwarted Stanton's brain donation.[32]

"Mrs. Stanton asked me, in case she should go into the silence before me, if I would speak for her—at her grave," Gardener proclaimed at a separate, smaller event held in Washington. "I have come here tonight, in part to keep my promise to the dead." Gardener explained that Stanton wished it known that she "died as she had lived, a fearless, serene agnostic." Stanton knew that scientists examined the brains of great men, and yet "science had learned about woman through its hospital subjects, its paupers, its 'unknown' dead." Stanton felt that "a brain like hers would be useful for all time in the record it would give the world, for the first time—the scientific record of a thinker among women." Thus, she wanted to leave her "splendid brain" to the world as "her last and holiest gift." Revealing that just three days before her death Stanton had penned an essay in favor of easier access to divorce, Gardener hailed Stanton as the world's "greatest woman, noblest mother, and clearest thinker." Gardener prophesied that women around the world would light a candle to Stanton "in the years to come when the mothers of the race shall, for the first time on earth, be reckoned as self-respecting, self-directing human units, with brains and bodies that are sacredly their own."[33]

Within the span of two years, the most important friends in Gardener's life had died—Robert Ingersoll, Charles Smart, and Elizabeth Cady Stanton. With no new books since 1894, she felt it was increasingly unlikely that she could restart her career as a writer. Though she had steadied herself somewhat by marrying Selden Day, Gardener remained at a personal and professional crossroads. She still considered herself a writer and a reformer, but she had hardly published anything and rarely attended reform conferences since her 1897 trip to California. Nor did she feel comfortable embracing her new role as the wife of a celebrated army veteran. If she could not participate in radical social change, she needed one herself. In November 1902, she and Day announced that they were embarking on a multiyear "journey around the world with the sun."[34]

AFTER SPENDING the holidays in New York with Dr. Spitzka, his family, and the writers Herbert Casson and his wife Lydia Commander, Gardener and Day took the train to California to visit Day's family and his property in Point Loma. As Gardener spent her days "pleasuring and resting" along the coast in preparation for her world travels, Mary Phillips was stuck in New York trying to sort out Charles Smart's increasingly complex probate matters.[35]

Back in April 1901, H. C. Bailey, Smart's son-in-law and the executor of his West Virginia will, had traveled to New York to meet with Phillips and see about Smart's trunk, held in lien at the Garfield Safe Deposit Company because Smart had not bothered to pay the rent. Phillips initially dismissed Bailey as a hayseed who "had never been before" to New York and asserted that he agreed to let her have the trunk. But several months later, Bailey threatened to file papers in New York claiming the trunk and establishing the primacy of the West Virginia will.

On March 7, 1903, Phillips wrote to her lawyer, M. Cleiland Milnor, to discuss "a matter connected with Helen Gardener and of the greatest importance."[36] Phillips feared what would happen if the contents of the mysterious trunk became public and aimed to protect her friend from disgrace. Smart and Gardener also owed Phillips money. Phillips did not seem to care about the money, but she used this debt as leverage to assert her priority over the trunk. As she explained to her lawyer, "I do not think [the trunk] has anything of value in it to a stranger. My object is to keep the papers it may contain from falling into strange hands."[37]

In Phillips's retelling, years ago Smart had shown Gardener papers ostensibly proving that he had divorced Love in Ohio. In light of Smart's West Virginia will, Phillips now entertained the idea that the alleged divorce papers had been forged and thought they might be in this secret trunk. "The copy of the will is astonishing, yet if a bogus divorce was secured years ago by Judge Hardin of Ohio—or bogus papers shown to my friend," Phillips reasoned, "the old sinner may have been obliged to write this will to prevent suspicion by no. 1."[38]

Unbelievably, the extensive correspondence between Phillips, her lawyer Milnor, and Bailey also suggests that Smart's original family did not know he had been living with Gardener for the past twenty-five years. In confessing a small ruse to Milnor, Phillips revealed that she "did not want Mr. Bailey to know that no. 2 was Helen H. Gardener so do not bring her name up to him if possible to prevent it."[39]

Even though Gardener never produced a marriage certificate (which certainly would have been helpful as Phillips was attempting to establish her claim to Smart's estate), Phillips remained convinced that her friend believed she had been married to Smart. "I have great compassion for Helen Gardener," she told her lawyer, "and believe her to have been entirely innocent of the true condition of affairs." If any of the papers in the trunk could tarnish her reputation, Phillips pledged "I am willing to inconvenience myself" to keep them out of the wrong hands.[40]

Phillips thought that the most likely scenario was that Smart had married both Love and Gardener. She doubted that his family wanted "the scandal of Smart's having been a bigamist aired in [West] Virginia," so she suggested that her lawyer bully them into submission. Observing that several different hands had composed one of Bailey's letters, Phillips told Milnor, "They are poor people, and all seem to lack general intelligence." Phillips proposed to Milnor that he "put on a bold front" and threaten suit in West Virginia, believing that this would "frighten them all."[41]

Phillips, Milnor, Bailey, and Garfield Safe Deposit Company executives sent dozens of letters, increasingly threatening in tone, back and forth throughout the spring and summer of 1903. But the paper trail regarding the trunk and the West Virginia will goes cold after July 1903, perhaps because Lovenia died that summer (her obituary described her as Charles Smart's widow).[42] Nothing was ever revealed in the press about Smart's family in West Virginia. Gardener continued to claim—in private, in public, and even in Day's official army pension file—that she had been married to Smart since 1875. Mary Phillips and her "bold front" succeeded in keeping her friend's scandalous life secret. Meanwhile, Gardener spent a "charming" winter in California, blissfully unaware that her reputation teetered on the precipice of ruin back in New York.[43]

ON JUNE 12, 1903, Gardener and Day boarded the *Maru* for the six-day journey from California to Hawaii. In 1903, travel to Hawaii was still new and exotic. When Gardener and Day arrived, they were treated like the novelties they were. "Distinguished Authoress Here" proclaimed a local paper, and Gardener boasted to Mary Phillips that she did not have a chance to call on Mary's friends in Honolulu because she was so busy being feted elsewhere. Gardener shared with reporters that she had suffered a breakdown three years before and had not attempted to do much work since. Accordingly, this was a "pleasure trip," though she planned to research the people she met on her travels. "I expect to study the characteristics of the people of the countries we visit," Gardener said, "the family life; its sociological, political, and educational features. I am not writing a book, simply taking notes and absorbing knowledge."[44]

Gardener's goal for this trip, her first international travel, was to see the world, not like a tourist, but from "the inside." When they first imagined this trip "around the world with the sun," as Gardener referred to it, the couple predicted they would be gone for a year or two. In the end, they were abroad for four years, visiting twenty-two countries in total. In particular, Gardener could not wait to step foot in Japan. In both New York and Boston, she had employed Japanese servants and become fascinated with Japanese culture. According to Gardener, it was customary for highly educated Japanese men and women to spend a year or two "in service" in the United States to learn Western ways. Most people who encountered Japanese servants had no idea that they were rising stars in their home country. Gardener admitted that only after he left her home did she realize that one of her servants had recently received his PhD from a German university.[45] On June 26, 1903, after a runaway team of mules nearly catapulted their wagon over a Hawaiian cliff (breaking several of Gardener's ribs), they boarded the passenger ship *Korea* and sailed for Japan.[46]

Thanks to the men and women who had been Gardener's servants, she and Day lived among the locals in a lovely rented home in Tokyo. Her former cook Kussaka managed "one of the great banks," another servant had become a doctor, another was the son-in-law of the prime minister, and still another was the minister to Siam. These connections enabled the couple to, as she related to Mary Phillips, "get right at the heart of things through our various friends who are taking pains to have us see Japan of the Orient not Europeanized Japan."

To this same letter, Gardener attached a private postscript, intending for Phillips to share it with their mutual friend Gertrude Aguerre. Apparently, Gardener owed both Aguerre and Phillips money. She had written, under contract, a script for the actress Lillian Burkhart and hoped to use that money to repay Aguerre the $125 that Charles Smart had "wrongfully used of hers." But Burkhart returned the script without paying for it. This "discouraged me dreadfully," Gardener wrote, "but I am just trying my very best to get well, absorb new things, and come back with 'earning power' to pay that and you." (In her 1919 will, Gardener allotted $1,000 for Mary Phillips to "serve her in a time of need as she served me."[47])

Even though they had now been married more than a year, Gardener confessed to Phillips that she had "said no word to Col. D. of either debt." She then instructed Phillips to write "this sort of thing" on a separate sheet of paper because Day often asked her to read her mail aloud. Gardener concluded her chatty letter with the question, "Did ever anything come of the trunk?"[48] So far from her mind was the trunk that it merited only a one-sentence afterthought to a three-page letter.

Gardener and Day traveled extensively throughout Japan, often accompanied by the popular American singer Emma Thursby and her sister.[49] Gardener took copious notes and over 1,500 photographs, a new hobby for her and thousands of others at the turn of the century.[50] "Their food is good," she reported to Dr. Edward A. Spitzka (the son of her friend, Edward C., who had become a favorite correspondent), "whether it appeals to the European taste or not." Gardener was also impressed by Japanese children, who were so kind to each other, especially the older children who carried the younger ones on their backs. "Their quiet dignity and their almost omnivorous eagerness to learn—to develop mentally," she wrote, "makes of it a nation that has sprung forward 500 years in the last 40."[51] Gardener loved to boast about Japanese culture because, to her, such examples exposed the hubris underpinning American missionary ideology (though she praised the American imperialist efforts she witnessed in Puerto Rico and elsewhere). She had critiqued the missionary enterprise since the 1880s, noting that "in the abundance of our ignorance and self-righteousness we have presumed to send missionaries to the Japanese."[52]

The Days stayed in Japan six months longer than planned, spending nearly a year there in total. During this extended stay, Gardener penned anonymous pro-Japanese articles for the American press and made inroads among the Japanese scientific elite, passing along information about Japanese brains to Spitzka and helping the Imperial University of Tokyo establish its own brain collection.[53] Between her ethnographic note-taking, anonymous writing, amateur science studies, and enthusiastic picture taking, Gardener was beginning to return to her old self. She would also bring back to the United States several pieces of valuable Japanese lacquer, 400 or more years old, which became among her most prized possessions. But that was not all Gardener planned for her return. She told Phillips that "we shall bring home hundreds of lantern slides and I hope to be able to do some fairly good and intelligent and appreciative work in America that may be a help toward a better understanding of the nations of the east."[54]

FROM JAPAN, Col. and Mrs. Day sailed on to Manila, Malaysia, then China and Hong Kong. In China, Gardener visited the cities of Peking, Shanghai, Canton, Chefoo, and Tientsin. She also traveled along China's rivers to visit rural villages and farmlands, and she took pictures of herself on the Great Wall. Having long argued that Western gender roles were unnatural, Gardener delighted in seeing Chinese women captaining river boats as well as "nurses, chambermaids, 'hired-girls,' and washerwomen" who were all men.[55] More poignantly, she visited the grave of her beloved brother Bernard, who had died in China more than thirty years before.

At the end of October 1904, the Days traveled to Ceylon (now Sri

Among her many adventures, Gardener rode a camel
across Egypt, all the way to the Nile.

Lanka), via Singapore. Though they stayed only four weeks in Ceylon, Gardener took more notes and photos there than in any other country, documenting the trees, spices, tea, fruits, elephants, and people. Gardener marveled at Ceylon's railroad engineering and at the beauty of its ancient cities, which she speculated must have rivaled any in Europe. She did not approve, however, of the "ugly practice" whereby "girls marry at 12—grandmothers at 30."[56]

Next, the Days sailed past the Maldives and up the Red Sea to Cairo, Egypt, where they were detained unexpectedly for several weeks because Day got sick.[57] Gardener enjoyed some of her best adventures in Egypt, visiting mosques, watching whirling dervishes, admiring the engineering wonder of the Suez Canal, and observing the ritual of the Holy Carpet departing Cairo for Mecca. She especially enjoyed riding a camel through the desert to see the famed pyramids and the Nile River. While crossing the "desert of Sahara we came upon the home of a Bedouin—and the footprints of John D. Rockefeller," Gardener joked. "The main furniture of that happy home was two Standard Oil cans!"[58]

AFTER EGYPT, the Days traveled to Paris to begin the western European portion of their world tour. At the suggestion of Spitzka, Gardener contacted the renowned French anthropologist Léonce Pierre Manouvrier. In April, she and Day visited Manouvrier and his brain collection. This prompted Gardener to invite Manouvrier to accompany her on a visit to Day's old friend "Buffalo Bill" Cody and his Wild West Show, which was then in Paris for a two-month run. "Since 'Bill' and Col. Day are very old time comrades in arms and scouting," Gardener gloated, "we go and come as we see fit, show time or any other."[59] A few days later, Manouvrier and Gardener met with Buffalo Bill, watched the show, and measured the heads of thirteen Native American performers, including the famous Chief Iron Tail, of the Oglala Lakota Nation.[60]

*After measuring skulls, Gardener (center) posed with Chief Iron Tail,
Dr. Leonce Pierre Manouvrier, and others at "Buffalo Bill"
Cody's Wild West Show (Paris, 1905).*

Throughout the nineteenth century, skull and brain measurements
had been used as justification to limit the opportunities of women and
people of color. In the early to mid-nineteenth century, phrenology—
the study of bumps on the head—promised to reveal one's personal
strengths and weaknesses, as well as important differences according
to sex, race, and ethnicity. After phrenology fell out of favor, scientists
such as William Hammond contended that it was not bumps but brain
weight and visible brain structures that could reveal the differences
between the sexes and among races. In the early 1900s, the first generation of female social scientists—including Helen Thompson Woolley
and Leta Stetter Hollingworth, who had been trained by John Dewey
at the University of Chicago and Edward Thorndike and Franz Boas at

Columbia—established that differences between people were cultural, not natural.[61]

Gardener worked at the border between these two worlds. She knew that something was inherently wrong with Hammond's biological determinism, but the pioneering studies of cultural difference coming out of Columbia and the University of Chicago had not yet entered the mainstream, so she was unlikely to have encountered them. Most of her travel photos depict schools, families, and religious ceremonies. Her notes puzzled over how societal customs, not nature, inculcated cultural and gender norms. If women steered riverboats in China but not in America, certainly one could not say that it was "unnatural" for women to steer boats. Also, her travel writings, far from touting white American superiority, critiqued it by emphasizing the unique contributions of each culture she encountered. Thus, she studied the skulls of the Native American performers as part of her quest to better understand the various peoples of the world, perhaps not realizing that she was simultaneously naturalizing difference.

While in Paris, Day "got the auto fever." A lifelong tinkerer, he "bought a machine and is now practicing as his own driver," Gardener announced to Spitkza. "The Colonel always wanted to buy an elephant and ride across India. Not doing that he invested in a horse of a different breed here and proposes to ride (or drive) it instead," she reported. Gardener admitted that she was "rather afraid of the antics of the machine but I never back out of any place where others can go so I am whistling gaily and holding my breath." Gardener feared what the car might portend but faced this new challenge in good cheer. "You may get my brain," she joked to Spitzka, "by having to gather it from the branches of some wayside tree in France or Italy."[62]

After Day passed his French driving exam, a feat he considered more harrowing than any battle in which he had fought, the couple embarked on a twenty-month-long auto tour of Europe through Belgium, France, Switzerland, Spain, Italy, Corsica, Monaco, and Germany.[63] In this, the Days pioneered a brand new form of adventure travel. As the couple zoomed from France to Italy, American novelist Edith Wharton also bought a car and drove around France with her husband, her brother, and her friend Henry James. In 1908, Wharton published an account of her travels titled *A Motor-Flight through France*, in which she claimed that "the motor-car has restored the romance of travel." According to Wharton, the beauty of the car trip was the freedom of the open road, freedom from "all the compulsions and contacts of the railway" and the "delight of taking a town unawares, stealing on it by back ways and unchronicled paths."[64] Although Gardener lamented the expense and unreliability of Day's "elephant" and the difficulty of writing with "hotel pens . . . and an auto crank looking at his watch every two seconds," she, too, was drawn to the open road.[65]

By January 1907, the couple had returned to Paris. They had already stayed abroad three years longer than planned, but Day had just learned that the money he invested in California real estate had been lost.[66] Without the financial safety net they had counted on, they were not sure what to do. From their room at the Hotel Louis le Grande, at the Place Vendôme, they counted their pennies and plotted their next move.

Day had fallen head over heels for the "auto" and decided the couple would rent a cheap place in the French countryside so that he could build his own car. "I explained this would render me helpless to *do* anything," Gardener confided in her diary, "but am quite willing to do whatever is best for his work."[67] Her attempts to conform to the self-sacrificing wife ideal she had long critiqued were half-hearted at best. For weeks, Day and his friend scouted cars and homes while Gardener stayed at the hotel, taking French lessons, having regular "depil" (hair removal) appointments, and writing.

She lost patience, though, on January 21, 1907, her fifty-fourth birthday. "Nothing done or said to welcome it by *any* one," she vented in her diary. "Feel as much as sad and alone as if on a desert island. What a sad mistake it is not to be gentle and loving in all the little ways of life. The loss is terrible—the gain, what?" While her husband was out looking at cars, Gardener "spent the day alone in hotel. No recognition of any kind of birthday. I wrote article."[68] The next month she noted that February 24 would have been "C.S.S.'s" birthday, "a day I always made much of with little gifts and many attentions and efforts to create happiness. Xxx."[69] For all his many failings, Charles Smart still compared favorably as a husband next to Day. At least they had celebrated birthdays together.

When he wasn't out looking for and driving cars, Day spent much of February and March sick with the "grippe," or flu. But he refused to see a doctor and, Gardener complained, "flies at me if I urge it." His coughing spasms kept the couple up most nights and made it impossible for them to do much during the day. Occasionally, Gardener snuck away to the theater or to socialize without Day. In her few free afternoons, she managed to visit with a fascinating array of Americans—from the Baroness de Chabonlou to the Confederate veteran, congressman, and writer Henry Watterson to the wife of the American-British department store magnate Harry Gordon Selfridge. Her personal charms had been restored.

Unable to reach a deal on a rental house, Gardener concluded they "best go home."[70] On Easter Eve 1907, the couple set sail from le Havre to New York on the steamship *La Lorraine*, which Gardener depicted as an "old tub, acts like an empty barrel in the bottom of a runaway wagon."[71] Rough seas kept most of the passengers, including Day, inside for much of the nine-day voyage. But Gardener preferred to be outside in the fresh air. As they prepared for the next chapter—the first time they would really live together on U.S. soil as husband and wife—Day remarked to his wife, "When we get home we won't see so much of each other anymore. You'll have your friends and all, and I my work." Gardener confided in her diary that it "sounds as if he felt rather jealous of it. Keeps asking why I don't love him more." If he asked her again,

Gardener confessed "I will say something ugly!"[72] In this her first real marriage, Gardener had found a semblance of security but she longed for independence.

The couple docked in New York and took the first train to Washington, D.C. They arrived back at Sister Pickett's apartment on April 9, their fifth anniversary and "five years from the day we left home." Several days later, Day's auto arrived on a separate ship. Soon he added a second car to his collection; Gardener still preferred their Andalusian horses. The couple spent the summer in a rented house in Mountclair, New Jersey, visiting with friends, especially Mary Phillips, and relatives. Gardener enjoyed reconnecting but fretted over missing vital hours of work, lamenting to her diary, "I can do *no* work with people here."[73]

They also debated where to settle. Gardener hoped for a home "where I may have roots" and yet still "go and come as I like." The colonel maintained that New York was too cold for his bronchial problems, so Gardener fancied "either Washington, Va or California may be the final choice. I would greatly prefer the former, since it may not be New York City."[74] In October, the couple moved to Washington, D.C., settling in at the Ontario to "live on Day's pay as a retired officer."[75] Gardener may have lost the battle for her husband's attention to his new cars, but she had won the war in terms of selecting their home city.

Throughout their five-year journey, Gardener grappled with how to reconcile her desire for independence with her role as a wife, as evidenced by the variety of ways she signed her name in letters, oscillating between Mrs. Col. Selden Day, Helen H. Gardener, and Helen H. Gardener-Day. But she had saved her soul. This extended trip abroad fortified Gardener in mind and body (she gained more than 15 pounds), transformed her into a woman of the world, and enabled her to think about writing and working once again.[76] Upon returning to the United States, Gardener was eager to resume her public life, though she was not yet sure precisely how. Hints of what was to come can be seen in the hundreds of photographs she took on her travels. The vast majority

Gardener standing proudly beside Joan of Arc,
another fearless fighter, Paris, ca. 1906.

of her images depict the people and places she encountered; only a few
include Gardener. The most revealing one shows her posing proudly in
front of the statue of Joan of Arc in Paris. Descended from a "long line
of fighters and writers," Gardener had returned home to fight and write
once more. [77]

12

Mrs. Day Comes to Washington

*Woman has no voice in her own government, nor in fixing
the standards by which she is judged and controlled. She is
a dependent morally, mentally, financially and physically.
It is all very well—and very silly—to say that women control
society and make the moral standards that govern it.*

—HELEN HAMILTON GARDENER, 1891

AFTER FIVE YEARS of global travel, Helen Hamilton Gardener
struggled to settle into life in Washington, D.C., as the wife of a
retired army colonel. When she had last lived in the United States, she
was famous in her own right as a popular author, lecturer, and reformer
in New York City. But during her travels, she "died out as a 'seller'" of
books, and, as she recalled years later, her "literary life ceased." She had
to be "'born again' into quite another life."[1] But it was not immediately
clear just what this new life would be. Now fifty-four years old, Gardener looked for new social circles, new groups to join, and yet another
new sense of self. Illustrating her internal struggle, she even had two
calling cards printed: one for Helen Hamilton Gardener and one for
Mrs. Selden Allen Day.[2]

A worldly Gardener promoting her lecture series "Ourselves and Other People."

During her first several months in Washington, Gardener tried to reestablish herself as a writer and lecturer. She organized her travel notes and lantern slides into a lecture series called "Ourselves and Other People." Gardener advertised this series, consisting of fourteen distinct talks, to university extension programs and other educational institutions, including the Brooklyn Institute of Arts and Sciences. Gardener was embarrassed by the boorish, pompous attitude that Americans often took toward other countries and other people. She wanted to promote

international peace and understanding though her lectures on such topics as "Some Moral and Religious Ideas of the Japanese," "Egypt: Old
and New," and "China as I Saw It: Inside the Home."[3]

But the constant hustle of promoting herself and booking these
talks proved overwhelming. In January 1909, she asked Dr. Edward A.
Spitzka (her younger friend) to help her schedule lectures in Baltimore
and Philadelphia. The very next week, she told him not to bother.[4] "I
don't know whether I am a bit lazy or whether my physique is too much
depleted by the grave, *plus* the strains of earlier days, *plus* its original
lack of robustness," she had disclosed to him months before, "but some
or all of these reasons keep me always so far behind the goal I set for
achievement that I seem to accomplish almost nothing anymore."[5]

After a busy lecture season in New York in the fall of 1910, the answer
to Gardener's identity crisis came in the form of a new house. Colonel
and Mrs. Day bought a three-story home at 1838 Lamont Street, in the
Mount Pleasant neighborhood of Northwest Washington, an invest-
ment that stretched the limits of Day's army pension but enabled the
next phase of Gardener's life. From her back porch, she could hear the
animals at the nearby National Zoo, and Day could plant a tiny back-
yard garden. Her large home provided ample room for visitors and for
hosting events, and she could easily travel downtown, to Virginia, or to
New York City. Her wish for a home with "roots" from which she could
still "go and come" as she pleased had come true.

The place of pride in Gardener's new home was occupied by two
glass-door bookcases, filled with books written by her friends and
inscribed to her. She called this her "rogue's gallery," treasuring her intimate connections with so many writers. In addition, her walls proudly
displayed artwork given to her by her painterly friends, including "The
Viking's Daughter," by Frederick Church, and an early version of
Edward Moran's classic painting depicting the burning of the U.S.S.
Philadelphia. Her drawing room, which she referred to as the Louis
XVI salon, was furnished in Italian carved wood and matching drapery. And she could luxuriate in the claw-footed tub in her bathroom
adorned in hand-painted tile, featuring blue and pink floral bouquets.[6]

Gardener even modeled her new dining room on the wood-paneled one she had admired as a boarder in the Widow Melville's house in Sandusky, Ohio. Where the Widow Melville had decorated her dining room with paintings, however, Gardener displayed her treasures from Japan—antique black lacquer, hand-painted screens, and cushions. One reporter described Gardener's dining room "as much like a Japanese interior as modern building conditions on this side of the world will permit." Gardener "delighted" in entertaining friends in the traditional Japanese style, she enthused to a visiting reporter, and her home was always filled with the "literati" and other interesting people. While practicality did not permit her to require her guests to sit on the floor, per Japanese custom, Gardener did encourage everyone to eat with chopsticks, as she had become expert at doing during her travels.[7]

Gardener's most noteworthy new friend proved to be her next-door neighbor, Rep. James "Champ" Clark (D-MO), a presidential contender in 1912 and, from 1913 to 1918, Speaker of the House of Representatives. With her lovely new home, prominent neighbor, and an address book full of Colonel Day's old army buddies—men and their sons who had gone on to fill important posts in Washington—Gardener's next chapter began to come into focus.

For nearly twenty years, Gardener had skirted the edges of Manhattan society, but she found that world nearly impenetrable, based as it was on inherited wealth and old family names. A lapsed Chenoweth of Virginia carried little prestige among the Astors, Roosevelts, and Vanderbilts of New York. But in Washington, a person could distinguish oneself through a charming personality, social connections, and political savvy. This Gardener could do. She would be the suffragists' inside woman in the nation's capital. Mrs. Day had come to Washington to stay.

IN THE EARLY 1900s, the national suffrage movement, represented by the National American Woman Suffrage Association (NAWSA), was in the doldrums. Since 1896, no new states had enfranchised women, and the organization perpetually lacked funds. After the death of Susan B. Anthony in 1906, suffragists also lacked a charismatic guiding spirit. While women led reforms in several other sectors—from temperance to labor to food safety—it was not clear precisely what the relationship was between these progressive reforms and woman suffrage. In general, progressive reformers supported the vote for women—mainly because they hoped women voters would expedite the passage of reform legislation—but woman suffrage itself had not yet emerged as a pressing national policy goal. In her rousing remarks at the 1898 NAWSA convention, the group's future president, Carrie Chapman Catt, surmised that the "chief obstacle" to the ballot was "that large body of suffragists who believe that the franchise will come, but that it will come in some unaccountable way without effort or concern on their part."[8]

The suffrage movement was so marginal that from 1903 to 1910 NAWSA's national headquarters were located in a room in the courthouse in Warren, Ohio, the hometown of NAWSA treasurer Harriet Taylor Upton. NAWSA president Anna Howard Shaw, a gifted lecturer, preferred life on the hustings to office work and tasked Upton and her secretary with the day-to-day running of the organization.[9] The suffragists' position in Washington, D.C., looked especially bleak. Carrie Chapman Catt led the group's Congressional Committee, which had organized hearings before Congress every year since 1883. The Congressional Committee had no budget, no mandate beyond the perfunctory annual hearings, and no members who resided in Washington. At the 1908 NAWSA convention, Catt reported that the previous year's congressional hearings had absolutely no effect. When the NAWSA Congressional Committee asked President Theodore Roosevelt in 1908 if the signatures of 1 million women would convince him to support a federal suffrage amendment, he harshly told them to "go, get another state."[10]

For decades, suffragists had debated whether to pursue a state-by-state or federal path to enfranchisement. The state-by-state approach was considered less controversial by white NAWSA leaders because it sidestepped the question of black women voting in the South. In addition to being exclusionary, the one-state-at-a-time method was inordinately costly and exhausting. Prior to 1910, suffragists had succeeded in getting referenda on dozens of state ballots, but only four states had extended the franchise to women. Ultimately, there would be a whopping fifty-five state referenda to add woman suffrage amendments to state constitutions, the vast majority of which failed, and many of those that prevailed had to overcome subsequent legal challenges.[11] A federal approach would be strategically more focused, less time-consuming, and, at least ostensibly, more inclusive.

Officially, NAWSA pursued both strategies—state referenda and federal amendment—simultaneously, which appeased white Southern members but drained resources, leaving virtually nothing for the federal amendment. After 1908, however, the federal strategy gained momentum. For the first time, every presidential candidate in 1908 was asked his position on woman suffrage, and NAWSA leaders lobbied, unsuccessfully, the two major political parties to insert a suffrage plank in their respective platforms. To help the movement work more successfully with the press, Mrs. Alva Belmont, a multimillionaire socialite from New York, donated the funds for the NAWSA headquarters to relocate from Warren, Ohio, to New York City.[12]

Also between 1908 and 1912, the group's message shifted in ways that appealed to the freethinking, sex-reforming Gardener, who had opposed the merger that created NAWSA in 1890 and who resented the group's slights of her friend Elizabeth Cady Stanton. By the time Gardener moved to Washington, NAWSA's internal debates about religion had receded and speakers regularly critiqued the sexual double standard at the group's annual meetings. Gardener could now see a place for herself within the suffrage movement.

By 1910, Gardener had moved into closer contact with NAWSA. She attended the group's annual convention, held in Washington that

April, and established herself as a woman who could get things done in the nation's capital. Carrie Chapman Catt had completed a petition drive in support of a federal amendment, resulting in 404,825 signatures, which she planned to deliver to Congress via a large procession of cars. As the wife of an early automobile enthusiast, Gardener knew just about everyone in Washington with a car. So she arranged for fifty cars, "handsomely adorned" with American flags and suffrage banners, to transport these petitions to the Capitol.[13]

By 1912, Gardener had bolstered her position as NAWSA's go-to volunteer in Washington. In March, she helped organize a high-profile suffrage event at the Columbia Theater, the largest yet held, featuring members of Congress and their wives speaking on behalf of women voting.[14] Then, at the annual NAWSA hearings before Congress in April, Gardener recruited Rep. Edward Taylor of Colorado to talk about the effects of women voting in his state. His address characterized woman suffrage as an "unqualified success" and delineated 150 bills passed in Colorado at the behest of women since they first voted in 1894. Gardener made excellent use of Taylor's remarks, becoming expert at navigating congressional printing and mail rules. She prided herself on persuading members of Congress to "frank"—mail for free—the speech because "Uncle Sam does not take orders on credit." Ultimately, she sent out over 300,000 copies of Taylor's speech.[15] NAWSA officials took note of this "most efficient volunteer worker in Washington," and Gardener pronounced 1912 the year that "the states discovered I was back in Washington."[16]

As Gardener and Day settled into life in Washington, their Civil War ties became increasingly pronounced. During the two decades that Gardener lived in New York, there is no evidence that she visited her Virginia relatives, even as she dramatized her Southern heritage in fiction. Likewise, when Day was posted in the West and in Puerto Rico, he did not have occasion to attend Civil War reunions or see his army colleagues along the East Coast. But being in Washington allowed the Days to visit Virginia regularly and to renew ties with his army friends. The Civil War became the defining element of their social life, just as it continued to set the parameters of national politics, including debates about women voting.

The couple began spending several weeks each year with Gardener's Virginia cousins—the Peales and Keezells, who had taken up arms for the Confederacy—and touring, either by car or on their prized Andalusian horses, the battlefields on which Day had fought as a young soldier. Day also enthusiastically attended the annual reunions of the Blue and Gray who had survived the Battle of Cedar Mountain.[17] During this week-long festivity, old men who had once been young enemies became friends. The *Washington Herald* described the group's fiftieth anniversary gathering, held in August 1912, as a "love feast."[18] The aged soldiers toured the battlegrounds, shared stories of privation and danger, and bonded as white men who had fought in the nation's defining conflict and lived to tell the tale. The "blue and the gray are coming from Cal. and Texas, from Ohio and NY," Gardener announced to Day's cousin. "Some with one arm, others one leg etc. It is a sad, a tragic and an inspiring thing to see them together and to hear them talk it all over!"[19]

At the same time, the Days' Lamont Street home was a popular destination for their Virginia relatives—including Day's cousin, the writer Paul Kester, and Gardener's Peale nieces—along with Civil War veterans and their families, such as Caroline Greene Noble, daughter of Gen. Duff Greene, a Southern Democrat once kicked out of the White House for speaking rudely to Abraham Lincoln. While Day tinkered with his cars, Gardener hosted social events, often with her next-door neighbor Genevieve Clark, for Civil War memorials and veterans.[20]

In June of 1911, the Days welcomed the colonel's old friend, former Confederate general and Mississippi congressman Charles Hooker. Infamous as one of the most rabid secessionists, Hooker had been a close friend of Confederate president Jefferson Davis, whose jail cell Day guarded at Fort Monroe, and that is how he came to know Day.[21] On this, Hooker's last visit to Washington, Day and Senator John Sharp Williams (D-MS) escorted the eighty-six-year-old Confederate around the Capitol, where he walked with a "triumphal march." Washington newspapers covered the "one-armed General's" visit to the Days because it symbolized the healing of tensions between white men from the North and South. As the *Washington Herald* reported, "those first bitter days after the Civil War, now so happily forgotten as the one-armed old Confederate and the lame Federal veteran hobnob on the porch or drive to the Capitol."[22]

WHITE UNION AND CONFEDERATE veterans came together to social-ize and consolidate power in the decades following the Civil War, but this reconciliation came at the expense of African Americans, then suf-fering record levels of violence, segregation, and discrimination. The Compromise of 1877, in which Republicans agreed to stop enforcing the Fourteenth and Fifteenth Amendments in exchange for the pres-idency, was just one example of a larger pattern through which white Americans preserved their wealth and status rather than the ideals of the abolition movement and Reconstruction era.[23]

At the same time, white suffragists grappled with what the war had meant for women. On a practical, demographic level, the Civil War spurred white women's entry into college, the professions, and paid labor on a large scale. (Women of color also entered college and profes-sions during this time, and the vast majority worked outside the home, although most often they were limited to working in domestic service). But on the levels of politics and ideology, the Civil War and its after-math shaped the suffrage movement in vitally important yet often con-tradictory ways. Whereas white women had fought alongside African Americans for "universal suffrage" before and during the Civil War, after the war many white women sought the political support of white men at the expense of people of color.

Fifty years after the war, some white women still saw a federal suf-frage amendment as the Civil War promise they had been denied. Up until the ratification of the federal income tax amendment in 1913,

NAWSA members referred to the suffrage amendment as the Six-teenth Amendment, believing that it would logically and rightfully follow the Fifteenth Amendment (which guaranteed that race could not be used to deny voting rights but which had not been enforced since the end of Reconstruction). Nearly all NAWSA conventions and publications referenced the Civil War in some way, often bitterly prior-itizing the claims of white women over those of black men, obscuring black women and their rights altogether. The leaders of NAWSA—who desired but did not have a strong presence in the South—walked a fine line regarding race, generally claiming that they themselves were not racist but that they dared not publicly align with black women lest they offend potential white allies in the South, a necessary contingent if woman suffrage was ever going to pass Congress. While some NAWSA officers, notably Jane Addams and Mary Ware Dennett, forcefully defended the right of African American women to vote, NAWSA as a whole did not, prompting some historians to conclude that Northern leaders of NAWSA used deference to Southern racism as a convenient cover for their own.[24]

Officially, NAWSA let individual chapters determine membership requirements, which in practice meant that affiliates could deny African American women membership. Individual African American leaders, including Mary Church Terrell and W. E. B. DuBois, were occasion-ally invited to speak at NAWSA events, but NAWSA leaders generally ignored their insights and refused to work together in meaningful, coor-dinated ways. Beyond NAWSA, black women actively worked for the vote, along with a host of other civil rights causes, through black wom-en's clubs, churches, and reform organizations.[25]

Debates regarding racism within the movement, state versus federal strategy, and how the suffragists should engage with elected officials in Washington all came to a head in March 1913 when NAWSA produced the largest suffrage event ever organized—and one that might have transpired very differently without the contributions of Helen Hamil-ton Gardener.

AROUND THE SAME TIME that Gardener became active in NAWSA, another enthusiastic volunteer joined the organization: Alice Paul. A twenty-eight-year-old Swarthmore College graduate, Paul had recently returned to the United States after spending time in England with the more militant British suffragettes, led by Emmeline Pankhurst, whose motto was "deeds, not words." While in London, Paul was arrested for civil disobedience, went on a prison hunger strike, and was force-fed. Inspired by the bravery of the British women, she returned home determined to expedite ratification of a federal suffrage amendment and disrupt the "old fogies" of NAWSA who, to her mind, had been politely and ineffectually circulating petitions for more than fifty years.

At the 1910 NAWSA convention, Paul delivered a speech detailing her experiences with the English suffragettes, and, at the 1912 NAWSA convention, she proposed a radical idea to reinvigorate the American movement. Paul suggested that NAWSA leaders let her take over the more or less dormant Congressional Committee with the goal of organizing a massive procession of women suffragists to coincide with the first inauguration of President Woodrow Wilson in March 1913.

On December 5, 1912, NAWSA secretary Mary Ware Dennett wrote Paul to let her know that NAWSA leaders had tentatively approved her plan, as long as she raised all her own money and submitted a formal proposal. Paul wasted no time. Within a week, she had begun soliciting funds and convened a series of meetings in Washington with local officials and suffragists to ascertain the feasibility of her bold idea. The third Washington woman Paul sought out was Helen Hamilton Gardener. Paul recalled that Gardener was "very cooperative," though she seemed "very displeased that a young whippersnapper such as myself should be the chairman, because she talked about 'Well they don't have much sense about who they put in charge' and 'all these undertakings which need great experience' and so on. I think she probably thought she should have been made the chairman, but nobody had known I suppose that she would even think of it."[26]

Paul's intuitions were correct. Gardener had not made herself NAWSA's "most efficient" D.C. volunteer for nothing. At first, the two iconoclasts worked together warmly, but the parade set up a lasting rivalry between Paul and Gardener, which played out over the next six years, to determine who would be the suffragists' most effective emissary in Washington.[27]

From the outset, Gardener was Paul's most constant helper at the makeshift parade headquarters at 1420 F Street, NW. As Paul recalled,

Alice Paul and Gardener worked around the clock to organize the biggest women's march the nation had ever witnessed.

Gardener was the only person besides herself who "came in every day and stayed all day . . . and never budged."[28]

As Press Committee chair, Gardener was back in her old element, calling on her skills and contacts from her days as a writer and member of the New York Woman's Press Club and the League of American Pen Women. Morning, afternoon, and evening, she talked to reporters all over the country and distributed press releases and photos. She placed pithy quotes in newspapers and steered editorials in NAWSA's favor.[29] Paul excitedly told a friend in February that "the Washington papers are full of our procession. The Inaugural procession seems almost forgotten. . . . I do hope we can measure up to what seems to be expected of us."[30] Even in her oral history conducted more than sixty years later, Paul credited Gardener with securing tremendous press coverage and commended her as a "super-whiz at this. . . . certainly she was 100% wonderful, I thought. Didn't see how anybody could have been better."[31]

Gardener told a friend in late February that she had been "working every day at the desk here from nine o'clock often until eight in the evening and when I go home I am too tired to sit up a moment beyond what is necessary. The poor Colonel has to attend to the home and get along the best he can without me and he is doing the very best he can to make it easy for me to be away and keep things going."[32] Through her stellar press work, Gardener became, once more, a woman whose name was printed in periodicals across the country. Dozens of newspapers profiled the women who had charge of the parade, often focusing on their "beauty" and including photos as proof.[33]

In addition to running the press operation, Gardener used her network of well-placed D.C. contacts to secure the necessary permits for the procession and related open-air meetings. Initially, the D.C. chief of police, Richard Sylvester, refused to endorse a parade on March 3, the day before Inauguration. Next, he denied the suffragists permission to walk down Pennsylvania Avenue from the Capitol to the White House, suggesting instead that the women proceed along 16th Street, a popular shopping thoroughfare but one that would not guarantee a large, inaugural audience. To persuade Sylvester of the merits of their case, Gardener brought groups of prominent women—including congressional wives—to his office, met with his superiors (all the way up to President William Howard Taft), and wrote a slew of charming letters. She explained that the marchers would be the "leading women of every state" representing "women of splendid standing and dignity, college women, professional women, homemakers (mothers), and workers." All the women requested, Gardener emphasized, was that D.C. police keep Pennsylvania Avenue open for the procession. "Is that so much to ask?"[34]

Gardener also engineered a clever strategy to secure Pennsylvania Avenue by getting the Speaker of the House and the president of the Senate to grant the suffragists permission to assemble for the parade at the Peace Monument, on U.S. Capitol grounds. If the women received congressional approval to assemble at the base of Pennsylvania Avenue, surely the D.C. chief of police could not insist they march down 16th Street. By mid-January, the suffragists had received all the necessary approvals to hold the procession when and where they wanted.

Next, Gardener began assembling a high-profile "advisory committee" of elected and appointed officials and their wives, beginning with Genevieve Clark.[35] As NAWSA officials grew increasingly concerned that Alice Paul and her collaborator Lucy Burns wanted to bring English-style protests to America, Gardener tempered Paul's militant instincts with her exceedingly polite outreach to congressmen and their wives. She also helped enlist members in a D.C. Men's League for women's suffrage, a group that included her husband, Selden Day, as a charter member.[36]

Paul recruited dozens of women to help mount the procession, organize costumes and floats, solicit pledges, contract with platform builders, raise money, create a beautiful souvenir book, and stage tableaux. She ordered 1,500 costumes by famed designer Lanzilotti and thought carefully about the timing of the parade and the music, which included several bands and an orchestra.[37] She even convinced pageant creator Hazel MacKaye to write and direct the tableaux and then dispatched Gardener to New York City to persuade famous actresses to participate.[38] The legendary actress Lillian Russell agreed. Her manager/hus-

Gardener, Alice Paul, and NAWSA parade volunteers outside the makeshift parade headquarters at 1420 F Street NW.

band told Gardener that "she'd rather do it than eat." But the timing did not work with Russell's New York performance schedule.[39]

More than 5,000 women from across the nation arrived as planned and assembled themselves in an orderly fashion to participate in what was to be the largest and most dignified procession of women the world had ever seen. The massive parade consisted of seven large sections, each with hundreds of women organized by theme, to tell the international story of women's quest for full citizenship. The first section highlighted the countries where women could vote. The second section paid homage to the pioneers of the U.S. movement, featuring the few surviving women riding in cars. The other sections argued for suffrage by showcasing women's achievements throughout history as well as in the professions, in reform work, and in the home. Gardener chose to march in the professional women's section on a float labeled "Molding

Public Opinion," wearing a costume identifying her as a "writer." She rode on a chair on top of newspapers and magazines, holding a tablet and a pencil to make her point that "An Enlightened Press is Making an Enlightened People."[40]

Though the parade included women from across the country, the participants were nearly all white. The virtual exclusion of black women from this iconic event made visual their larger exclusion from the mainstream suffrage movement as a whole. Initially, Paul imagined that perhaps a few black women would march alongside white women as they had done in previous suffrage marches in the North.[41] But Washington women urged her to reconsider the ramifications of an integrated parade in what was essentially a Southern city on the eve of the inauguration of the first Southerner to be elected president since the Civil War.

In January, Paul got wind that the *Woman's Journal*, the official paper of NAWSA, was contemplating running a story about African American women in the procession. Paul asked Gardener, because she hailed from Virginia, to write Alice Stone Blackwell, the journal's editor, and explain their position. Gardener began by detailing how hard they had fought to get permission for the parade in the first place, emphasizing that they had only tenuously succeeded by using the "utmost diplomacy" and by promising that they would not raise any other issues beyond equal suffrage, as if equal suffrage did not also pertain to black women. Bringing in the right of black women to vote, Gardener feared, would cost the group "absolutely all we have gained and more. It will prevent the parade, ruin us, and do nobody the least little bit of good— and least of all the negroes." Gardener reminded Blackwell, a Bostonian, that "Washington is not Boston—nor even New York—and our wisdom and discretion now means much, much, much for our cause."

Though she published a few Southern nostalgia stories in the 1890s, Gardener had not previously written much about race in the United States beyond praising her family's abolitionism and critiquing the racism she witnessed when she lived in Boston.[42] Her main point in such writings seemed not so much to critique racism itself but to argue that racism was an American—not just a Southern—problem. In her efforts to raise the age of sexual consent for girls, she insisted that such laws must apply equally to all girls, regardless of race, which distinguished her among most of her reform colleagues. But after settling in Washington, she seems to have unquestionably adopted the dominant NAWSA positions that white women's rights took precedence over African American rights and that it was out of the question to simultaneously lobby for the enfranchisement of black women.

Gardener ended her letter to Blackwell by emphasizing her own unique heritage as the daughter of a Virginian who had emancipated his slaves "when it was against the law of his State to do so—who gave up his property, his friends and his home for the principle of human liberty." Attuned to charges of racism within NAWSA, Gardener attempted to deflect criticism of her racist position by pointing out her anti-racist heritage. "With his blood in my veins and the record of nearly forty years of work, myself, for human rights I need not remind you that it is not the appeal of a coward or reactionary." She hoped that Blackwell would support their efforts to prevent "the color question from appearing in *any form* in this demonstration."[43] Blackwell agreed not to raise the issue in the *Woman's Journal*.[44]

Paul remained concerned about black women marching. At the top of one letter from a hopeful participant, someone at headquarters wrote in pencil, "please see if these are negroes."[45] And Nellie Quander, president of the Alpha Kappa Alpha sorority at Howard University, had to write twice in order for her group to participate because no one replied to her first letter.[46] Paul's position was quietly to allow black suffragists to apply to march, hope that few would actually do so, and stall when they did.[47]

But Paul was not following an official directive from NAWSA. To the contrary, NAWSA leaders urged Paul to welcome African American women into the march. At the outset, Mary Ware Dennett, Paul's chief liaison to the NAWSA board, sent a pointed letter saying she had heard that a group of African American women had been asked to withdraw their application to participate. According to Dennett, it would be "absolutely impossible to rightly endorse any such plan" to discriminate. "The Suffrage movement stands for enfranchising every single women [sic] in the United States," Dennett proclaimed, and "there was no occasion when we would be justified in not living up to our principles."[48]

Then, just a few days before the March procession, Dennett sent a frantic night telegram to Paul. "Am informed that Parade committee has so strongly urged Colored women not to march that it amounts to official discrimination which is distinctly contrary to instructions from National headquarters. Please instruct all marshals to see that all colored women who wish to march shall be accorded every service given to other marchers."[49] But on the day of the parade, state delegations received conflicting messages regarding NAWSA's policy on black women marching. Illinois leaders reluctantly informed the journalist and anti-lynching crusader Ida B. Wells that she would have to march at the back of the parade, thinking that was NAWSA's directive. Declaring she would "not march at all unless I can march under the Illinois banner," Wells waited among the crowd on Pennsylvania Avenue until the Illinois delegation passed and then took her rightful place under the banner.[50]

Some forty black women did ultimately march alongside white women in the procession, but there is no telling how many more women of color were discouraged from marching by headquarters' volunteers or by NAWSA's conflicting messages.[51] In response to a critical article in *The Crisis*, the magazine of the National Association for the Advancement of Colored People (NAACP), Paul insisted that she had received no letters of protest and issued no segregation order but conceded "the point concerning a cool reception, is, I suppose, true."[52]

As the controversy regarding black women's right to participate in the parade indicates, the legacy of the Civil War and Reconstruction was highly pronounced in the March 3 procession. Wilson's election had been hailed as a victory for the latter-day Confederacy. His move to Washington highlighted the Southern character of the nation's capital and the ascendency of Southern Democrats—many of whom had once been leading Confederates or were sons of Confederates. In the 1912 election, Democrats also won control of both chambers of Congress, prompting one NAWSA leader to lament that it seemed as if congressional leaders spoke a different language because their Southern accents were so pronounced.[53]

Paul chose to end the procession by placing a quote from Abraham Lincoln on the final float. Women dressed in white, representing light, walked around a black float, depicting the states where women had no vote. The float was adorned with a banner that read: " 'No country can exist half slave and half free.' Abraham Lincoln."[54] White NAWSA leaders drew connections between themselves and enslaved people, all the while discounting or ignoring the rights of black women and the continued disenfranchisement of black men in the South.

DESPITE THE MISGIVINGS of NAWSA headquarters that the scope of the parade might be too militant or too ambitious, Paul, Gardener, and their small team had organized the biggest and highest-profile suffrage event in history. But just as the procession began, hostile men crowded onto Pennsylvania Avenue, obstructing the path of the marchers for several blocks, often reducing the parade to a single file. The men pressed up against the marchers, called them unprintable names, spat on them, tripped them, and assaulted them. Few policemen could be seen, and many simply joined the crowd. For almost two hours, thousands of women stood virtually unprotected against an angry, intoxicated mob. The procession stood at a standstill, from 6th to 14th Streets, until the U.S. Calvary was called in to clear Pennsylvania Avenue and restore order.[55]

In the short term, the police snafu succeeded in getting the suffragists an immediate audience before Congress. Just days after the procession, the Senate Subcommittee on the District of Columbia convened hearings to determine what had gone wrong and whose fault it was. The

*Thousands of angry men blocked the suffragists'
parade for nearly two hours.*

hearings lasted several days—nearly as long as the suffragists had ever testified before Congress over the past fifty years combined—and generated a tremendous amount of written material and photos. The women blamed Washington officials, Police Chief Sylvester, and his bosses, while Sylvester blamed individual officers themselves. Sen. Clyde Tavender reported that he and his wife saw just six policemen along the entire procession and long periods when absolutely no police could be seen to guard the "dignified women" against the "jeering hoodlums."[56] Another witness, William E. Ambrose, described police efforts to clear a path for the procession as "the efforts of a boy to stop a waterfall by using first one hand and then the other."[57]

Gardener testified extensively about her involvement in the planning of the parade and what she experienced along the route. She explained to the senators that she had repeatedly asked Sylvester for additional protection and that Sylvester had refused, insisting that his staff could handle the parade, even though he had initially denied women the right to march on the grounds that his staff could not adequately protect them from the Southern "riff raff." Gardener told the senators that men came right up to her float, took away the newspapers she had used for decoration, and pushed the groomsmen who were driving the float. The police "did nothing" except say "go back" to the sidewalks in a nonauthoritative manner. "I am used to Army life," Gardener declared. "I am used to tones of authority and conduct that means authority. I did not see any of that." Instead, the police "seemed to be quite entertained."[58] As a result of the Senate hearings, thirteen men were arrested and a subsequent investigation of Chief Sylvester resulted in his termination in 1915.[59]

Although the women's plans for a flawless procession had been ruined, the violent protesters and police failures vividly made NAWSA's point for them: women needed the vote to protect their interests from unscrupulous and incompetent men. Senator Tavender declared that "more votes were made for women suffrage in the city of Washington on the afternoon of March 3 than will perhaps ever be made again in the same length of time so long as the government stands."[60] Even Anna Howard Shaw, whose letters were not generally marked by optimism, told Paul that the violent disruption of the procession "has done more for suffrage and will do more for suffrage in the end than the parade itself would have done."[61]

As the suffragists rejoiced in capturing positive national media attention for the first time, tensions simmered between Alice Paul's faction—now called the Congressional Union—and NAWSA. NAWSA leaders sensed, correctly, that Paul's plans were much larger than one parade. What Paul wanted was to organize women across the nation to advocate for the federal amendment and against Democrats, the party in power. At the time, NAWSA was engaged in several state campaigns, had virtually no money, and was strictly nonpartisan, so everything about Paul's plans threatened the organization's existence.

All sides agreed that meaningful suffrage action had finally focused on Washington and the federal amendment, but the essential struggle came down to this: which suffrage group would represent the national movement in D.C., and who would be that group's spokesperson? From behind the scenes, Helen Hamilton Gardener moved confidently to counter Alice Paul and represent the suffrage movement in Washington.

13

Old Fogies

You do not allow us women to give our consent, yet we are governed . . . no one who lives, who ever lived, who ever will live understands or really accepts and believes in a republic which denies to women the right of consent by their ballots to that government.

—HELEN HAMILTON GARDENER, 1914

I N THE WEEKS immediately following the March 3, 1913, suffrage procession, Helen Gardener and Alice Paul worked on a variety of meetings, petitions, and visits to Congress to keep up the pressure for the federal amendment that the parade had invigorated. But in a split that would shape the final years of the suffrage movement, they followed increasingly divergent paths. Gardener endeared herself to NAWSA leadership and embraced its policy of nonpartisanship, while Paul doubled down on protest tactics targeting Democrats. Ironically, that summer a syndicated newspaper article profiled Gardener and Paul, with photos, describing them as the "two busiest women in the capital," not realizing they were often working at cross-purposes.[1]

Unofficially, Paul began to build a national organization that would work solely for the federal amendment. Within days of the parade, she wrote to suffrage leaders in various states requesting their mailing lists and asked NAWSA secretary Mary Ware Dennett to share the addresses of the group's life members. Several respondents, including Dennett and Harriet Taylor Upton, of Ohio, warily replied, "You don't wish to ask for money, do you?" Indeed she did. Paul even approached the *Woman's Journal* to see if the NAWSA paper of record would consider relocating from Boston to Washington, D.C., so that it could better report on the federal amendment.[2] NAWSA leaders refused most of Paul's requests because resources—both financial and temporal—were scarce and because they correctly sensed that Paul was staging a revolt.

Paul intended nothing less than a wholesale redirection of the national suffrage movement and a takeover from the "old fogies." As the year progressed, she and Lucy Burns set up their own newspaper, *The Suffragist,* and national organization, first called the Congressional Union (CU) and later the National Woman's Party (NWP). Paul proposed that she would both run the CU and remain a member of the NAWSA Congressional Committee. But NAWSA leaders deplored Paul's strident tactics and especially her partisan attacks against Democrats. While they recognized Paul's brilliance and tried to find a way to work together, NAWSA officials repeatedly warned Paul that her militancy would not be tolerated and would only hurt the cause.[3] No one felt this more urgently than Gardener.

For the first few months of 1913, Gardener had been energized by working alongside Paul—a young firebrand not unlike herself thirty years earlier. But long before NAWSA leaders figured out that Paul posed a threat to the organization and its reputation, Gardener cooled relations and began to separate herself from Paul. Over time, Gardener positioned herself as the seasoned D.C. antidote to Paul's militant, partisan upstart. Paul may well have been the "smartest woman in America," as Gardener once characterized her, but she lacked Gardener's lobbying skills, varied life experiences, contacts, and personal charms—all of which would prove crucial in securing the federal amendment.[4]

As Paul began lining up her forces to challenge Democrats in upcoming elections, Gardener approached her friends in Congress, often through their wives, beginning with Rep. Edward Taylor (D-CO)—the suffragists' staunchest ally—and Rep. John Raker (D-CA), to see about establishing a House Committee on Woman Suffrage. Such a committee had long been a goal of NAWSA, and it became an even more pressing need as the federal amendment gained ground because it was the necessary procedural mechanism to advance the amendment to the House floor for a vote. The Senate had had a Committee on Woman Suffrage in place since 1883, and each year this committee held hearings and provided women the chance to testify. But the House had no such committee, so suffragists were forced to plead their case before the House Judiciary Committee, where they were stymied, rebuffed, or ignored.

On March 28, 1913, Lucy Burns, Paul's second in command, reported to Paul that Gardener was "working nobly" for the House committee and that her personal lobbying "may be very well to secure a Suffrage committee in the House."[5] The following month, NAWSA tapped Gardener to testify before the Senate Woman Suffrage Committee. At the hearings, Gardener deployed her signature humor to win new converts. She quoted members of Congress who had recently praised America's founding documents before pointing out that in denying women political rights, the congressmen acted much like the king whom the colonists had deplored. Were women people, she demanded to know, and if so, how could congressmen justify women's exclusion from democracy?[6] The *Washington Times* reported that Gardener's "witty speech attacked various arguments against suffrage" and was delivered amid "laughter and applause."[7] On May 14, 1913, the Senate Woman Suffrage Committee reported favorably on women voting for the first time in twenty-one years.[8]

Nevertheless, on May 22, Paul wrote Mary Beard complaining that it was "almost hopeless" to get action from the House Judiciary Committee. She predicted that "it is going to be a very hard fight" to get a suffrage committee in the House.[9] Gardener had a different read of the situation.

By June, Gardener was giddy with excitement over the prospects of the House committee. She informed NAWSA board member Harriet Laidlaw "sub rosa" that "Mr. Underwood (leader of the House of Representatives) has just assured me he will try to get us a hearing (right away) making the Rules Committee to agree to the appointment of a House Committee on Woman Suffrage. It now *looks* as if we'd get it! If we do, it will be the first hearing before it (and a tremendous advance step, nationally, when the [NAWSA] Convention comes)." She was "almost bursting with delight" over her congressional inroads but cautioned that her behind-the-scenes work "must not be spoken of or get into print."[10]

In July, Gardener, accompanied by the wives of four pro-suffrage congressmen, met with the chairman of the House Rules Committee to plead the case for a woman suffrage committee. Rep. Robert Lee Henry (D-TX) told the women that a hearing on such a topic could only be held during the regular session of Congress, which would be in December, so Gardener turned her attention to that.[11]

Throughout the summer and fall of 1913, Gardener and Paul worked independently for the House committee. Their parallel efforts caused much confusion among members of Congress, the press, and even other suffragists, because, as Gardener lamented to Paul, it was "very difficult" to get people to understand that not all suffrage groups were one and the same.[12] As it stood, several factions of suffragists—the Federal Equality Association (led by Elizabeth Cady Stanton's longtime ally Clara Bewick Colby), the National Council of Women Voters, the College Equal Suffrage League, NAWSA, and now Paul's Congressional Union—all requested meetings with the White House and Congress. The men simply could not keep track of who was who. NAWSA tried to establish itself as *the* voice of the suffrage movement but was repeatedly thwarted by congressmen's lack of attention to detail and especially by Paul's highly publicized statements that presented her as the voice of the national movement.[13]

For her part, Gardener endeavored to sustain NAWSA's Congressional Committee as an entity distinct from Paul's Congressional Union, which, confusingly, still worked out of the NAWSA office at 1420 F Street. Gardener distanced herself from Paul after the Senate hearings and regularly decamped to visit friends and family in Virginia, leaving her desk at the headquarters untouched for weeks at a time.[14] Gardener lamented to Illinois suffrage leaders that for years she had functioned as the de facto NAWSA Congressional Committee and now the officially appointed committee, still led by Paul, seemed poised to take the lead just "when things are ready to boil over."[15]

OWING TO HER KEY ROLE in the March parade and her effectiveness as a D.C. liaison, Gardener was appointed, in June, to the NAWSA Convention Program Committee and tasked with coordinating events with the White House and Congress to take place that December, a plum assignment. However, this job, too, was beset by confusion. Alice Paul had asked another Mrs. Gardner—Mrs. Gilson Gardner—to set up D.C. meetings for the Congressional Union. The resulting mix-ups prompted NAWSA president Anna Howard Shaw to exclaim in frustration, "I wish women had the good sense to stick to the names by which they were labeled when they were born. Then we might be able to tell them apart."[16]

Within a few weeks, Gardener had secured sixteen senators, eight from each party, representing the "cream of the Senate," to speak on behalf of "our bill" at the Senate hearings in December. She also invited President Wilson to welcome the convention on its opening night, even though "Sunday is a very bad time to ask Presbyterians to do such a thing."[17] He declined.

With much of the NAWSA convention planning completed, Gardener left town in November on a clandestine trip to New Orleans. Her husband, Selden Day, told Paul that Gardener had gone south for her health, but really she went to New Orleans to represent NAWSA at the meeting that formed the Southern States Woman Suffrage Conference, on whose letterhead she was subsequently listed (though her name was misspelled "Gardiner," perhaps indicating that she was never asked her permission).[18]

Southern suffragists, led by Kate Gordon, had become increasingly frustrated by NAWSA's redoubled focus on the federal amendment and formed this group to continue working for the vote one state at a time.[19] Southern women threatened to leave NAWSA (and several eventually did) if forced to advocate for a federal amendment because the strategy was too reminiscent of the Fifteenth Amendment and because they did not want black women to vote. Gardener was dispatched to represent the national organization in New Orleans, she recalled, because "I am a Southern woman and was, therefore, supposed to be able to speak 'without offense' to those who insisted upon waiting for the action of their states."[20]

At the meeting, Gardener gave a speech—later revised and published as the NAWSA pamphlet "Woman Suffrage: Which Way"— arguing that it was in the South's best interest to match their Western counterparts in chivalry and grant women the vote before the federal government forced them to via a constitutional amendment.[21] She did not focus on the merits of the federal amendment, as she did elsewhere, but rather on its inevitability. NAWSA's efforts to enlist Southern support for the federal amendment became the group's central challenge moving forward, and Gardener, soon the group's highest-ranking Southerner, would play a crucial role.

Back in Washington, generational tensions flared between the CU and NAWSA. Just days before the annual convention began, Lucy Burns was arrested by D.C. police for chalking sidewalks with suffrage messages. Anna Howard Shaw begged Burns to pay the fine, walk away, and "from this on to the Convention, see that nothing of this kind comes up." Anticipating Burns's objections, Shaw conceded, "You may think we are all a set of old fogies and perhaps we are; but I, for one, thank heaven that I am as much of an old fogy as I am, for I think there are certain laws of order which should be followed by everybody and that one never loses by doing so." Shaw rejected the idea that following the rules signified cowardice. "It requires a good deal more courage to work steadily and steadfastly for forty or fifty years to gain an end," she contended, "than it does to do an impulsive rash thing and lose it."[22]

While much of the NAWSA convention proceeded along typical lines—speeches, workshops, hurried meals—the highlight was the December 3 hearing before the House Rules Committee about the creation of a House Committee on Woman Suffrage. Over two efficient hours, the women presented their case for the committee, and Gardener ensured that many congressional wives and daughters also attended. Highlighting her insider credentials, Gardener proclaimed that "those of us who live here and have known Congress from our childhood know that an outside matter" such as suffrage has less of a chance to get before the House Judiciary Committee than "the proverbial rich man has of entering the kingdom of heaven." Next she compared the plight of women to that of American Indians. Before the existence of the Committee on Indian Affairs, Gardener caustically declared, American Indians were under the province of the War Department, whose general position was that "the only good Indian was a dead Indian." With their own committee, American Indians began to get "schools, lands in severalty and the general status of human beings." Women demanded the same consideration before Congress—their own committee and the consideration afforded to independent human beings. "This is not much to ask," Gardener concluded, "and it is not much to give."[23]

The discussion eventually centered on the relationship between the proposed woman suffrage amendment and the Fifteenth Amendment. Then, over the next three days, the anti-suffragists, mostly men, addressed the Rules Committee. Some of them spoke for nearly an hour each about the risks to family and nation if women were to leave the domestic sphere. Nevertheless, NAWSA members remained hopeful that the Rules Committee would report favorably on the creation of a woman suffrage committee. Gardener considered this hearing—the very first of its kind—a signature triumph.[24]

Gardener's second coup was organizing a high-profile reception featuring an array of pro-suffrage Washington insiders at the home of Sen. Robert and Belle La Follette, cohosted by "four Cabinet ladies, about 20 Senate ladies, and 50 House ladies."[25] Gardener stressed to the editor of the *Woman's Journal* that she had organized this event "through my personal friends in the Congressional Circles" and that "nothing of the kind was ever done before."[26] While social events did not carry the same weight as votes, Gardener believed that the more she could bring congressmen in contact with NAWSA members and the more she could entice congressmen to appear publicly in support of federal suffrage, the faster the amendment would pass.

The next Monday, ninety-four suffragists went to the White House for what was only their second official meeting with the president (Alice Paul had arranged the first one following the March procession). This second meeting lasted just ten minutes but produced an important result. Wilson declined to endorse the federal amendment, but, to the suffragists' delight, he affirmed that creating a woman suffrage committee in the House was "a proper thing to do."[27]

The support of the president was not enough to sway the House Rules Committee, however. The committee tied, four to four, regarding whether or not to report favorably on the creation of the woman suffrage committee. In advance of the vote, Paul had encouraged her followers to bombard the committee chair with letters, and the Congressional Union announced that members would work to defeat Democrats in the 1914 elections. Following Paul's campaign announcement, the suffrage committee question unexpectedly went before the House Democratic caucus, which voted 123 to 55 that suffrage was a state, not a federal, question, derailing the chances that the House committee would be created.[28]

NAWSA viewed this as a devastating and unnecessary defeat triggered by Paul's showy, partisan tactics. NAWSA Congressional Committee vice chair Antoinette Funk confided that Rep. Robert Henry had promised a favorable report but had been "a good deal harassed, I understand, by Miss Paul. On one or two occasions he has had to leave his office when she came in because of her insistence with reference to his conduct."[29] Gardener's year of careful relationship building with members of Congress and their wives had been for naught.

AT THE DECEMBER NAWSA convention, Paul presented a report covering the Congressional Committee's activities, highlighting the historic March 1913 parade. She received overwhelming applause from the members. But NAWSA leaders remained piqued that Paul had not submitted a detailed budget—which Paul found curious, since, to her mind, NAWSA financial records were in perpetual disarray—and they did not like her plan for the upcoming year, which proposed that she and Lucy Burns continue to lead the Congressional Union and simultaneously serve on the NAWSA Congressional Committee.[30] NAWSA leaders feared this scenario would lead to more confusion in Washington and that it would be too hard for them to keep Paul and Burns in check.

Because the "National ha[s] not yet accepted me on 'my terms,'" Burns wrote a friend, she declined to remain on the Congressional Committee.[31] Instead, Burns, Mary Beard, and Paul aggressively courted "the more intelligent younger women" who recognized "the danger of siding with the old fogeys."[32] They succeeded in recruiting Doris Stevens, a terrific young organizer who had been working on the Ohio ballot initiative with Harriet Taylor Upton. Stevens was excited to leave behind the "old fogeys," enthusing to Burns, "I dare say you and Miss Paul even now have a most level-headed and far-reaching scheme to outwit the Dear Ladies."[33]

For several weeks following the 1913 convention, NAWSA's Congressional Committee and Paul's Congressional Union (CU) attempted to find a way to work together—with the Congressional Committee organizing women in the states to lobby their congressmen at home and the CU lobbying in Washington. But this tenuous compromise proved to be a "terrible ordeal."[34] The CU would not agree to follow NAWSA's policy of nonpartisanship and chafed at the prospect of having the old fogies approve their every move. Congressional Committee chair Ruth Hanna McCormick, appointed in early 1914, described her tenure as "one of the most disagreeable tasks I have ever performed."[35]

In a letter on the topic of who was best positioned to argue the case for the federal amendment in Washington, Gardener warned the NAWSA secretary about the dangers of ceding such vital work to Alice Paul. The existence of two suffrage groups with offices in the nation's capital would, Gardener warned, "go far to tie the hands of the [NAWSA] Committee and to continue the 'befuddling of the brains and understanding' up at the Capitol." Far more dangerous, the men on the Hill "do not like the kind of 'lobbying and lobbyists' the Union will provide and has provided so far." And "they 'dodge' [Paul] whenever they can." Women with personal charm and connections, Gardener urged, "will do more with the men on the Hill to help us in a week than Miss Paul could do in a year."[36]

At the same time, Paul flatly refused to accept NAWSA's invitation to return to the Congressional Committee if Helen Gardener remained on it. She and Burns maintained that Gardener opposed the federal amendment and supported the states' rights position popular among Southern suffragists. In a letter to CU member Mary Beard, Burns described Gardener as "very shaky" on the federal amendment and "flirting a little with both sides of the question."[37] Gardener never wrote anything publicly or privately in support of the states' rights argument (and she wrote much in favor of the federal amendment), so it is more likely that Burns misinterpreted Gardener's adroit lobbying or her attendance at the New Orleans meeting. But Paul's ultimatum stood.

Thinking she had the final compromise agreement in hand, Ruth McCormick met with Paul in January 1914 to get her signature. In the hours since they had last spoken, however, Paul had seen a NAWSA press release listing the names of the women nominated for the Congressional Committee. This list included Gardener. Paul withdrew her support for the compromise plan. Desperate to save the deal, McCormick phoned NAWSA headquarters, and leaders agreed to rescind Gardener's nomination. But the damage had been done. Paul refused to sign an agreement with NAWSA, and Gardener was later reappointed to the committee.[38]

The Congressional Union and the NAWSA Congressional Committee formally parted ways in February 1914, but for years to come, they continued to be conflated by members of Congress, the president, the press, and the general public.[39] To her growing frustration, much of Gardener's lobbying and publicity work would focus on distinguishing the NAWSA Congressional Committee from the CU.

AS THE ONLY MEMBER of the Congressional Committee who lived in Washington, Gardener hosted a few events in early 1914 and testified before the House Judiciary Committee that March.[40] Gardener, a woman who had helped make sexual consent a national issue in the 1890s, used her congressional testimony to demand women's right to consent to their government through voting. She critiqued the "aristocracy of sex" that denied women this constitutional right by invoking a speech given the previous day by Secretary of State and three-time Democratic nominee for president William Jennings Bryan. Bryan had argued that the cornerstone of democracy was the consent of the governed. The irony enraged Gardener. "You do not allow us women to give our consent," Gardener informed the members of the House Judiciary Committee, "yet we are governed." She concluded: "No one who lives, who ever lived, who ever will live understands or really accepts and believes in a republic which denies to women the right of consent by their ballots to that government."[41]

Amplifying the connections between political and sexual autonomy, earlier that week Gardener had answered the question "Why I'm a Suffragist" in the *Washington Herald*. "Because I am an adult human unit who has not forfeited the fundamental right to life, liberty and the pur-

suit of happiness," she declared. Besides all the usual reasons for want-
ing the vote, Gardener claimed for women one particular reason: to
protect themselves from the unwanted advances of men. "As a last resort
men can and do resort to brute force," Gardener professed; thus women
needed the vote to protect themselves and to have a say in the laws that
governed relations between men and women.[42]

After the March 1914 congressional hearings, Gardener was largely
sidelined from suffrage activities as a result of illness, travel, and inter-
necine drama (though she continued to send out franked congressional
speeches).[43] All things considered, 1914–1915 was a good time to sit out
of suffrage activities. NAWSA records suggest this was a year of particularly extreme infighting at the national headquarters, still in New
York City.[44] And according to the *History of Woman Suffrage*, 1914 will
"always be noted for the long controversy over what was known as the
Shafroth national suffrage amendment," which was a proposal to make
it easier to get state suffrage referenda on the ballot and to distinguish
NAWSA from Paul's Congressional Union.[45]

Gardener spent much of 1914 and 1915 in Virginia and traveling. On
New Year's Eve, she and Day sailed from New York for Panama. They
spent several weeks in the Canal Zone before traveling to California to
visit Day's siblings and attend the 1915 world's fair in San Francisco. By
April 1915, the Days were back in Washington. Gardener testified before
the Senate Woman Suffrage Committee on April 16 but did not actively
participate in other Congressional Committee activities that season.[46]
With the NAWSA Congressional Committee not actively lobbying in
Washington, Gardener bided her time.

That November, the NAWSA annual convention was held in Washington, and Gardener was again tapped to help organize the event.[47]
Two major events transpired at the convention that propelled Gardener
toward the pulse center of suffrage activities. First, the members deci-
sively rejected any further attempts to push the Shafroth-Palmer amendment.[48] In the 1915 elections, all four state suffrage ballot initiatives
failed, underscoring the challenges of the state-by-state method. Second, NAWSA president Anna Howard Shaw, who had never been keen

on Gardener, stepped down after eleven years at the helm. NAWSA members recruited former president (1900–1904) and international suffrage leader Carrie Chapman Catt to lead the organization in what everyone believed would be the final push for the federal amendment. Catt reluctantly accepted and laid down her terms, which included stepping up efforts in Washington and enlisting the states in an all-out effort for federal enfranchisement.[49]

Catt immediately recognized that the main impediment to NAWSA's efforts in Washington was the ineffectual Congressional Committee. As Catt surveyed the national scene, she "found many big tasks awaiting it and nothing was in order anywhere. The most obvious thing to do at once was the Congressional Committee work in Washington." Catt was surprised to learn that Chair Ruth McCormick had resigned several weeks earlier and that Vice Chair Antoinette Funk had essentially stopped working the previous June. Nothing at all had been done to prepare for the incoming Congress. The NAWSA board appointed Mrs. Jennie Roessing as chair, but Catt had another leader in mind. She reached out to Boston organizer Maud Wood Park, the woman who had founded and led the very successful College Equal Suffrage League, and instructed her to "pack your grip" and "obediently leave for Washington."[50]

As Catt continued to analyze the situation in D.C., she was further dismayed to find that "the National Association is losing its federal amendment zealots to the Congressional Union merely because we do not work on that job hard enough." According to Catt, NAWSA "never has really worked for the Federal Amendment. If it should once do it there is no knowing what might happen."[51] To turn her prophecy into a reality, Catt built an all-star team in Washington. Initially, Maud Wood Park served as vice chair of the Congressional Committee, but she traveled frequently and still considered New England her home. Chairwoman Roessing, too, commuted from Pennsylvania. Catt needed a Washington insider to be her conduit, and she found that person in Helen Hamilton Gardener.

14

NAWSA's "Diplomatic Corps"

No one more sincerely regrets, deprecates and opposes the heckling of the President by the militant, English branch of the suffragists, than do the real suffragists of America who have carried the woman suffrage banner, with dignity and good sense, from the early days to the splendid showing of complete triumph in twelve states and its promise of very early success in several others.

—HELEN HAMILTON GARDENER, 1916

BACK IN THE 1890s, Helen Hamilton Gardener and Carrie Chapman Catt had been on opposite sides of the women's rights movement. After all, it was Catt who spearheaded the official censure of Elizabeth Cady Stanton's *Woman's Bible* at the 1896 NAWSA convention.[1] Yet, Catt had long respected Gardener's intellectual bravery and winning personality, recalling decades later that she had been awed by Gardener and her bold novels. And it turned out that these were the qualities she was looking for in a Washington ambassador. Gardener's seemingly disparate life experiences—freethinking lyceum speaker, sex reformer, secret fallen woman, daughter of the Civil War, wife of a Civil War veteran—all came together in this her penultimate role as

NAWSA's inside woman in Washington. Technically, she remained a member of the Congressional Committee, but her colleagues began referring to her as NAWSA's "Diplomatic Corps," a title that more aptly captured her true role.

After Catt took over as NAWSA president in late 1915, Gardener and Selden Day left D.C. to winter in California. Gardener's first assignment was to interview Californians about the Congressional Union's (CU) campaign against Democratic incumbents in the upcoming 1916 election. A main source of contention between NAWSA and Alice Paul's CU remained the CU's policy of holding the party in power—since 1913, the Democrats—accountable as long as the federal amendment had not passed. Shockingly to NAWSA, the CU even campaigned against Democrats who actively supported suffrage. In a lengthy memo, Gardener reported to Catt that every Democrat opposed by the CU in California had also been a suffrage ally. She struggled to see the wisdom in such a plan. If the CU policy had succeeded in converting other Democrats to suffrage, Gardener reported, this "has yet to be disclosed."[2]

Gardener was also aghast to learn more about Paul's lobbying tactics, especially her dealings with President Woodrow Wilson. To Gardener, Paul's efforts to reach the president bordered on harassment. CU members had even followed Wilson to a lunch on the nineteenth floor of the Biltmore Hotel in New York and promised to trail him everywhere he went, all over the country. To Gardener, an intellectual radical who had long relied on her good manners to push her unorthodox agenda, such methods tarnished all suffragists by association and simply would not do. What Gardener did not mention and perhaps failed to even realize was that Paul's aggressive tactics had made woman suffrage front-page news, attracted the attention of political leaders, and provided an opening for her.

When Gardener returned to Washington, she immediately set out to counteract the damage she felt had been done to the cause by Paul and her followers.[3] On July 5, 1916, she wrote to Joseph P. Tumulty, Wilson's secretary, who functioned more like a chief of staff, to introduce herself and to clarify that "the real suffragists of America" had nothing whatsoever to do with the young militants who had recently started heckling the president at his public appearances. She enclosed an "outpouring of my wrath" decrying the Congressional Union and explaining the differences between NAWSA and Alice Paul's group, suggesting that he and the president use her memo in any way they saw fit. "Our old, original Constitution forbids any 'partisan' action by our Suffrage Organization," she explained, "and our leaders deplore it now as always."

Along with her missive, Gardener included her calling card, a photo, a list of references, and a 1915 NAWSA letterhead listing her position "since you may never have heard of me." She emphasized her political contacts, noting, "if you wish to ask Senators Williams, Sutherland, Thomas, Smoot or Representatives Taylor (Col.), Champ Clark (or his secretary Mr. Bassford) you will find who and what I am." Of the scores of letters that Tumulty and Wilson regularly received from various factions of local, state, and national suffragists, something about Gardener's letter stood out. Perhaps it was because her letter was typewritten and easily legible. Perhaps it was her telltale charm, honed over decades of writing such letters to powerful men. Or perhaps her letter stood out because, rather than ask Tumulty for a favor, her memo provided something useful to him. Whatever the reason, Gardener's letter made an impression on the White House and distinguished her from the many other women who wrote the president about the vote.

To that same letter, Gardener penned a postscript for the president's new wife, Edith Bolling Galt, whom he had married—just a few months after the death of his first wife—in December 1915. "As the wife of an Army Officer," Gardener declared, it would "give me pleasure to call."[4] Mrs. Wilson invited Gardener for tea at 10:15 a.m. the very next day. Political observers and Washington residents had scoffed at the president's hasty marriage to Galt, sixteen years his junior, and the First Lady must have welcomed some friendly company. Though she remained opposed to the federal amendment, Edith Wilson, the daughter of another impoverished "first family" of Virginia and the first woman in Washington to drive a car, immediately warmed to Gardener.[5]

Several days after Gardener introduced herself to Tumulty and befriended Mrs. Wilson, Carrie Chapman Catt requested a meeting with the president to ascertain his thoughts on the newly approved Democratic Party platform, which included a statement in support of suffrage, but only if granted state by state. The Republican Party adopted a similar plank (after hundreds of suffragists, including Gardener, gathered at their convention in Chicago to demand action). Catt had lobbied for party platforms that endorsed the federal amendment, and she wanted to discuss the prospects of such an amendment with the president.[6]

Before accepting Catt's request for a meeting, Wilson pressed Tumulty for more information about the women of NAWSA. "Are these ladies of the 'Congressional Union' variety?" the president inquired.[7] Even after more than three years in office and multiple meetings with suffrage groups, Wilson still could not distinguish the various suffrage factions, nor did he realize that NAWSA was the nonpartisan, national voice of women suffragists. Drawing on Gardener's instructive July 5 letter, Tumulty assured the president that these women were not of the "'heckling' variety" (Gardener's letter was later inserted into the Congressional Record to help congressmen differentiate between suffragist groups).[8]

Wilson gladly accepted the meeting: "OK Tuesday at 2 p.m.—office." In agreeing to meet with NAWSA leaders, President Wilson hoped to avert a crisis among women and to tamp down the protests against him. By the summer of 1916, it was clear that the upcoming presidential election would be very close. Wilson did not want to further enrage the women who could now vote in twelve states and who helped determine 91 electoral votes. Wilson's Republican opponent, Supreme Court Justice Charles Evans Hughes, enthusiastically supported a federal amendment to enfranchise women and eagerly courted Paul's Congressional Union.

For Gardener, forging a relationship with the White House was both strategic and personal. Twenty years ago, she had been one of the most prominent and respected women in America. By 1916, though, most of the younger suffragists with whom she worked had never even heard of her and knew nothing of the personal hardships she had endured for her bold feminist ideas. Since moving to Washington, Gardener, now sixty-three, had watched as younger and, to her mind, less qualified women received choice suffrage posts and public acclaim for advancing ideas she had articulated decades earlier. She knew that Carrie Chapman Catt was hoping to identify a strong NAWSA leader in Washington. Gardener wanted to be that leader.

FOLLOWING THEIR cordial August meeting, Catt invited President Wilson to address the members of NAWSA at their upcoming annual convention in Atlantic City, New Jersey, to be held in early September. After both political parties declined to endorse the federal amendment in their platforms, Catt moved up the convention from December to September as an emergency measure to regroup and strategize. Wilson readily agreed, the first president to do more than offer tepid welcoming remarks at a NAWSA convention.

Thrilled to be at the center of suffrage activity but worried that her health might prevent her from attending the convention in person, Gardener sent Catt a nine-page memo detailing the situation in Washington and including a ten-point plan. Finally, someone valued Gardener's opinion about how to lobby for the amendment in Washington. For starters, Gardener implored Catt to move the NAWSA headquarters from New York to D.C. and to move herself so that she could personally oversee things. Without Catt at the helm, Gardener feared "the National will fall into a decidedly second place in suffrage and trudge along at a consistent disadvantage that will be of its own making as it has been in the past. It was this blind refusal to see the perfectly obvious that resulted in the C.U." Catt, Gardener urged, needed to be on hand to meet with the "political leaders of the nation. She could and should dominate the situation."

Also, publicity would be much improved if NAWSA were headquartered in Washington, as Gardener well understood from having handled the press for the 1913 parade so masterfully. National papers and syndicates sent their "picked men" to Washington, Gardener explained. These men looked for suffrage news and found only the Congressional Union. To make NAWSA truly the voice of the national movement, the organization's headquarters needed to be fully staffed in Washington by the best paid workers available ("otherwise employed, or overworked women, cannot in these strenuous days carry the burden alone") and stocked with pamphlets and educational material.

Next, Gardener suggested that Catt appoint a "Diplomatic Agent" who understood that "both the political and social etiquette of Washington is often precisely the opposite of that employed in any other American city, for the simple reason that a part of it was adopted from France and much has been adopted and adjusted to meet foreign diplomatic needs and requirements." Therefore, NAWSA needed someone "to prevent 'collisions' or mistakes in procedure that might seem trivial to an outsider (or be entirely unknown) but which might spell failure as against success if gone at the wrong way or at the wrong time." Gardener reminded Catt that NAWSA had frequently "lost out" because, historically, the group had not looked to women who understood the ways of Washington.[9]

The 1916 NAWSA convention marked a turning point in suffrage history. The women focused with renewed zeal on the federal amendment because they understood that the European war would place new responsibilities on women and because they knew that to abolish the sexual double standard, women needed the vote. A portion of the program was dedicated to "public morals" and prostitution. Katherine Bement Davis, the reformer and social scientist who would later compile groundbreaking statistics on women's sexual activity, delivered an address (which President Wilson listened to before giving his own talk), arguing that women voters would help eliminate prostitution—not because women were inherently more moral (as some purity reformers had argued), but because "all down the ages women have paid the price of vice and crime." For generations, Davis explained, men had been taught that they could do "some things which a woman may not." Men then wrote these sexual double standards into law and decided how to enforce them. Drawing on her years of working in the penal system, Davis observed that the woman's "point of view has no representation," and thus, women alone were punished for sexual vice, even their own sexual assault.[10] Ideas that Gardener helped normalize in the 1890s had become a standard feature of women's demands for the vote.

In his address, Wilson reiterated his preference for the state-by-state method, which did not endear him to his audience. But the women were glad to have this show of presidential goodwill nevertheless. After remarking on the comparatively swift progress of suffrage, Wilson explained that he had not come to tell the women to "be patient" because they had been patient already but to "congratulate them" that they would soon be victorious. They just needed to wait a little longer.[11]

But in her presidential keynote, Catt declared that women would wait no more. Catt's speech, "The Crisis," argued that the time had come for women to vote. Catt called for a "mobilization of spirit," telling NAWSA members that they had become too accustomed to being patient. Now was the moment to act.[12] To crystalize her thoughts, Catt drafted a comprehensive "Winning Plan," which would guide the movement over the next four years. Her multipronged strategy involved working for the federal amendment along with targeted state referenda—because she rightly predicted that a few more state victories would force federal action—while at the same time preparing for ratification in the required thirty-six states.[13] Catt shared her plan with the NAWSA board and state chairs, vowing that she would resign unless thirty-six state chairs committed themselves to her plan by signing a compact.[14] Everyone signed on.

The Washington-based elements of Catt's "Winning Plan" included many ideas detailed in Gardener's August memo. The NAWSA board approved plans to open a large office in Washington (while retaining the official headquarters in New York). But Catt herself refused to move, preferring to delegate the day-to-day dealings in Washington to

Maud Wood Park and Gardener. Finally given official license to do what she had wanted to do all along, Gardener took to the task with her father's evangelical zeal.

IN OCTOBER 1916, Gardener approached Wilson, via Tumulty, with her first major request. In the upcoming November election, two states— South Dakota and West Virginia—had woman suffrage on the ballot. Catt had tasked Gardener with asking the president to write notes in support of these two measures. But Gardener stressed that the president could do much more than just write two letters because "when you want things to happen you don't confine yourself to official communications." As a young man, Wilson had once written that hearing women speak in public left him with a "chilled, scandalized feeling."[15] As a presidential candidate he had remained silent on women's rights, and as president he avoided the suffragists as best he could for as long as he could. But Gardener saw room for hope in this distinguished educator, who had (reluctantly) begun his teaching career at the all-women's college Bryn Mawr and who was a devoted father to three daughters.

Gardener strove to convince Wilson of the folly of the state-by-state method. She described to him in painstaking detail the labor that women had to undertake to get referenda on ballots in states where they could not vote. "To win the attention of the voters in a matter so far removed from their own interests and experiences," Gardener related, women had to collect signatures through "a house to house canvas which involves calling upon men in their homes,—yes and in their lodging houses, at night." For dramatic effect, Gardener recalled how the previous summer she had "groped my way up a dark stairway" only to have her knock answered "by a colored man in his underclothes. . . . And with that man in a dark hall-way, half undressed, I had to discuss my right to vote." Worse, "even young girls must do it."

These were highly charged words in the era of unprecedented lynching of black men on the false pretense that they had sexually assaulted
white women. Gardener made no other references to direct canvasing herself—that was not her specialty—and it is more likely that she
invented this story to stir up Wilson's racial animus. She resorted to
dangerous racist stereotypes to ask Wilson who was more deserving of
the vote, the black man in his underclothes or the white woman who
sat before him at the White House? Since the collapse of the universal
suffrage coalition in the late 1860s, white suffragists had often invoked
such stereotypes to argue that educated white women were more deserving of the vote than men of color.[16] Gardener never espoused the states'
rights position or the whites-only voting provisions advocated by some
other Southerners. But she did use her whiteness to endear herself to
male leaders and to prioritize the rights of white women over those of
African Americans.

Gardener further emphasized to Wilson that "we do not have to go
through these state referenda just once." To the contrary, "since 1867
there have been no less than 43 suffrage referenda taken, of which only
seven carried." Wilson must have understood the stakes, at some level,
because he had heard from dozens of New Jersey women regarding the
1915 ballot initiative in his home state. Wilson voted for the measure,
but it failed to carry. Gardener lamented, "It is the life of leading spirits
of two generations of women which is being spent upon the unreason-
able task of asking to be allowed to take their part in the world as full-
fledged human beings." She did not name names, but she may have
been thinking of her own compromised health or that of labor lawyer Inez Milholland, the so-called "most beautiful suffragist." Astride a
stunning white horse, Milholland had dramatically led the 1913 suffrage
procession, but just a few weeks after Gardener sent Wilson this letter,
she died from anemia and exhaustion brought on by constant travel for
the Congressional Union. She was just thirty years old.

Worse, Gardener told Wilson, the disenfranchisement of women
squandered a vast amount of human power "while every social abomi-

nation that can be conceived by wicked women and men stalks through the land." Finally, Gardener hinted that there would be "political advantages" to Wilson taking a more public stance in favor of suffrage. Doing so would keep his Republican rival, Justice Hughes, from claiming that he was the candidate of women voters. And it would give lie to the impression that the Democratic Party stood in the way of women voting. "Mr. President," Gardener implored, "your performances have been so much greater than your promises that I hope the same may prove true in the present case. . . . I hate to have you only come in when our fight is won."[17]

Per Gardener's request, Wilson signaled his support for the pending suffrage ballot measures in West Virginia and South Dakota; nevertheless, both failed. Wilson himself was just narrowly reelected over Justice Hughes. Alice Paul took credit for keeping the presidential election so close, though Wilson won in eleven of the twelve states where the CU campaigned against him.[18] The 1916 election also marked the victory of Jeannette Rankin of Montana, the first woman elected to the House of Representatives.

In December 1916, Gardener helped plan a party to celebrate the grand opening of the new NAWSA Washington office at 1626 Rhode Island Avenue. The sixteen-bedroom "Suffrage House" featured a grand second-floor space for entertaining and plenty of offices, along with extra rooms to rent out to visiting suffragists. It was to be "as much of a club and a gathering space" for suffragists as it was a workspace.[19] Several members of the NAWSA Congressional Committee boarded there, including Maud Wood Park, who moved to D.C. after the 1916 convention and soon became chair.

Each day over breakfast, Congressional Committee members shared their plans for the day, then departed for Capitol Hill, returning at dinnertime to compare notes. A few secretaries kept charge of the office, and volunteers took turns as greeters so that visiting suffragists, reporters, and politicians would always be welcomed by someone friendly and knowledgeable. Suffrage House became everything Gar-

Gardener and Maud Wood Park (center) hosting one of many events
at NAWSA's Suffrage House in Washington, D.C.

dener imagined when she outlined for Catt her ideal Washington headquarters back in August.

Similar to the event she organized in 1913 at the La Follettes' home,
Gardener invited a "who's who" of Washington's political, military,
and legal officials to the grand opening. The suffragists expected
hundreds of guests, but only a handful attended, and many of those
were on their way back from another party. Gardener, "as slender and
appealing as the crescent moon" in her white and silver dress, remained
undaunted.[20] She set about getting the prominent invitees to serve on a
new NAWSA Advisory Council—not that she necessarily wanted their
advice. What she wanted was a letterhead listing all the elected and
appointed officials who favored the federal amendment to make its passage appear inevitable.[21]

Park recalled attending her first Congressional Committee meeting at Suffrage House. After appraising the 531 congressional files, one

for each member of Congress, meticulously compiled by NAWSA volunteers, Park left feeling intimidated by the task ahead. As she stood waiting for a streetcar, she "was joined by a small woman with gray hair, who had sat throughout the evening without a question or remark. She told me that she was Helen Hamilton Gardener and that she had been a member of the Congressional Committee for some time." That was Park's first memory of "a woman of genius who was to teach me almost everything of value that I came to know during those years in Washington."[22]

Thus, 1916 drew to a close. The Democratic and Republican Parties offered lukewarm endorsements of suffrage on a state-by-state basis, and all states that voted on suffrage referenda denied women the vote. But with Catt's "Winning Plan" and the opening of Suffrage House, NAWSA members felt hopeful about the federal amendment. Gardener's stature in Washington continued to rise.

WITH NAWSA MATTERS in hand, Gardener turned to another legislative challenge during the winter of 1916–1917: securing a long-sought promotion for her husband, Col. Selden Day, before it was too late. Day had served in the army for forty-two years, from the outbreak of the Civil War straight through his retirement in 1902. He had been wounded several times, fought in two wars, and requested active duty in the Philippines, too. But he had spent twenty years at the level of lieutenant colonel because of the "regimental promotion" system whereby officers used favors or even cash bribes to attain promotions. As a result, Day retired at the rank of colonel when he believed he should have been brigadier general, a title accompanied by a larger pension.[23]

Day's health was failing, so Gardener attempted to fix things without her husband knowing while he wintered in California. (No longer sidelined from suffrage, Gardener declined to go west with him this year.) She began with her friend, Sen. John Sharp Williams of Mississippi, who had once referred to her on the Senate floor as a woman "whom we all know as a very intellectual, bright woman."[24] Williams had been orphaned during the Civil War, which connected him to Gardener, who, while not technically orphaned, had also lost her family and home as a result of the war. Gardener socialized with Mrs. Williams, hosted their daughter Sallie, and exchanged books with the senator, whom Maud Wood Park characterized as "the most erudite member of the Senate."[25] So, it was to him she turned for help in her secret mission to get Day promoted before he died.

Williams enthusiastically came to Gardener and Day's aid, repeatedly lobbying his colleagues on behalf of Day's private bill. He praised Day as a "sweet and lovable" man who had given his entire career to serving his country, never asking for anything in return. During the Civil War, Williams declared, Day "was not only a brave, but chivalrous enemy of my people."[26] Gardener underscored the importance of the Civil War in securing her relationship to Williams, noting that "we appreciate your really fundamentally helpful and kind way of making us feel that the men of the South and the men who fought on the other side were and are 'brothers under the skin' and nearer to each other than are the generation which has no memories of the great struggle to make them understand."[27]

Sen. Atlee Pomerene (D-OH) introduced Day's promotion bill, S. 8088, but the War Department disapproved, dooming its chances. The experience did, however, further bond Gardener to Williams and their shared experiences of the Civil War. Throughout 1917, she curried favor with members of Congress by pressing them on Day's bill—legislation that had nothing to do with women's suffrage but instead reminded congressmen that Gardener was the devoted wife of a Civil War hero. Gardener understood the give-and-take of negotiations. She knew that men in Congress rarely thought about one issue in isolation, but rather viewed each issue in light of the others they were simultaneously considering and in the context of their personal relationships. While unrelated to women voting, Day's bill advanced Gardener's NAWSA lobbying efforts nonetheless.

NAWSA's MAIN GOAL during the winter of 1917 was to court increasingly public shows of support from President Wilson. Now that Wilson finally understood the difference between the rival groups of suffragists, he welcomed opportunities to cooperate with NAWSA and cold-shoulder the CU, now known as the National Woman's Party (NWP).

Alice Paul rang in the New Year by requesting an immediate meeting with Wilson to present him with resolutions passed at the recent memorial services for Inez Milholland. From his typed memo to staff, one can almost hear Wilson groan, "Please say that the days and the hours named are impossible. I would like to avoid seeing them altogether, but if I do see them, it will be at a time of my own selection." Paul wrote back to demand a meeting "for the earliest date" possible. Wilson reluctantly agreed to meet on January 9 but then learned that Paul planned to bring along 300 NWP members. Wilson instructed his staff to tell Paul that he could meet with only a single representative.[28] She sent three.

The next month, NWP representatives requested a meeting with the president in advance of his March inauguration. This time he was even less welcoming. He instructed Tumulty to "please say to these ladies that it would be literally impossible for me at such a crowded time to do what they ask."[29]

As Paul's efforts to reach Wilson were increasingly rebuffed, Gardener's relationship with the White House grew closer. In the early months of 1917, she asked for and received several favors from Wilson. In January, she phoned the White House to ask the president to please pen a birthday greeting to Dr. Anna Howard Shaw. She even took the liberty of suggesting he write that Shaw "has lived to see the Cause in which she has spent her life so near to its fulfillment and expressing the hope that she may live to be its full beneficiary."[30] Implicit was a subtle plea that the president ought to do everything in his power to enable

Anna Howard Shaw to vote before she died. Wilson promptly sent the greeting as instructed.

Later that month, Catt and Gardener reached out to Wilson, along with several congressmen, to request letters in support of Oklahoma and North Dakota's pending measures to extend women limited franchise, which he gladly wrote.[31] Gardener even convinced the president's staff to rewrite the North Dakota letter to her specifications and send it "out from the White House with a flourish of trumpets."[32] Catt's "Winning Plan" was beginning to bear fruit; in just seven months, suffragists had increased the number of electoral votes cast in states where women had at least partial suffrage from fewer than 100 to 172.[33]

Next, Gardener took the opportunity to offer Catt, who admitted she was no publicity expert, a tip on how to promote her new book, *Woman Suffrage by Federal Constitutional Amendment.* Why not send autographed copies to every member of Congress, Gardener suggested? As an "old-time editor," Gardener explained that a man was twice as likely to read a book if his own name was written in it. "I worked that on the legislators in putting out *Pray You, Sir, Whose Daughter?* in raising the 'age of consent' in 34 states," Gardener revealed. Catt followed her advice.[34]

Gardener enjoyed doing "inside" work for suffrage, but she chafed against her lack of official position. Catt relied on Gardener as her emissary in D.C., regularly asking her to write and sign letters under Catt's signature, but Gardener regretted that she had no proper title in the movement. After reporting to Catt that she convinced several members of Congress to issue statements praising the victory in North Dakota, she suggested that Catt write her own thank-you notes. "You see I have no 'standing in court' officially and no title and all the rest of it," wrote Gardener, "so it is only my personality, and social side, that can speak to them and for you and suffrage." Catt replied by instructing Gardener to go ahead and write and sign all the notes for her.[35]

After the flurry of activity in getting Day's promotion bill introduced and in coordinating various suffrage messages in Washington,

Gardener was "laid up in bed for repairs" for much of February and early March.[36] As she told Senator Williams, "the Grim Reaper has been swinging his Scythe back and forth in front of me for the past ten days . . . but missed me at every stroke!"[37] She invited her friend Caroline Noble to come help with her correspondence, prompting Noble to observe to Catt that Gardener was a "powerful human Dynamo to hold in check, as you may imagine."[38]

From her sick bed, Gardener "adopted" five members of Congress by signing them up for subscriptions to the *Woman's Journal*. Senator Williams initially thought Gardener had meant to send the paper to his wife, but then laughed when Gardener confirmed it was for him. He promised to "read that blessed paper" as best he could.[39] Gardener's "adoption" plan was so popular that suffragists in two other states followed suit.[40] Gardener returned to full health just as the nation prepared to enter World War I.

ON APRIL 2, 1917, Congress convened for a special war session, and President Wilson addressed both Houses concurrently, signaling the U.S. entry into the war in Europe. Earlier that same day, suffragists gathered at the Capitol to greet Jeannette Rankin. The NAWSA Congressional Committee requested fifty seats in the gallery, via Gardener's next-door neighbor Speaker Champ Clark, and the women all wore the suffrage colors, yellow and purple, to welcome Representative Rankin. Gardener sat on the Speaker's bench, as she often did, to take in the momentous occasion. Prior to the swearing in ceremony, NAWSA hosted a breakfast in Rankin's honor at Suffrage House, and a "personal escort" composed of Gardener, Catt, Park, and Harriet Laidlaw, of New York, accompanied Rankin to the Capitol in a "decorated auto parade."[41] The sense of new possibilities for women was palpable.

At home, the outbreak of war also impacted Gardener. Day was disappointed that his promotion bill had not passed, and he struggled to find purpose, which no doubt distressed Gardener, too. After serving in the army for nearly his whole adult life, Day longed to rejoin the action. Perhaps watching his younger wife so actively engaged in her own battles exacerbated the sting of his futility. Just days after Wilson's declaration of war, Day, age eighty, hurried home from California so that he could volunteer for military service. He wrote two letters to the Secretary of War asking to be placed on the "active" list "for any duty as may be desired."[42] Gardener confided to Senator Williams that Day's "past treatment cut him to the quick, but the present call of his country—like the one in 1860, finds him first of all a soldier of freedom."[43] Day's offer was kindly rebuffed.

Day's health seems to have rapidly deteriorated following his return from California. He drops out as a presence in Gardener's letters and in the society pages. Though she did not write about it, nursing Day— as with Smart before—must have taken a toll. To help care for Day and herself, Gardener welcomed her favorite great-niece and namesake, Helen Gardener Crane, of St. Louis, into their home.

War preparations prompted major shifts in NAWSA strategy, which pushed Gardener into closer contact with the White House and Wilson into a more outspoken suffragist. First, NAWSA leaders began encouraging Wilson to demand the enfranchisement of women as a war measure. Anna Howard Shaw implored the president to call on Congress, in his special April 2 address, to pass the federal suffrage amendment because, otherwise, how could the government "without shame, call upon its women citizens to perform patriotic duties while depriving them of the fundamental right of all free people in a Republic—the right of self government?"[44] The president declined to do so that day, but the suffragists would continue to press this strategy for the next two years.

Harkening back to Elizabeth Cady Stanton and Susan B. Anthony's decision to suspend women's rights activism during the Civil War, Gardener suggested to the NAWSA board in April that "no drive should be undertaken during the Extra [war] Session of Congress." The board unanimously approved. To demonstrate their patriotism, NAWSA members worked on behalf of the Women's Overseas Hospital Committee, which sent all-female hospital staff to care for patients in France, and Wilson appointed both Shaw and Catt to influential wartime volunteer posts.[45] NAWSA also organized its own three-person committee, including Gardener, who ostensibly understood military preparedness because of her husband's career, to coordinate women's war work with the government.[46] As Catt would point out time and again, American women could be so helpful in the war effort because they had already been so well organized for suffrage.[47]

Yet, suspension of efforts was not exactly what Gardener and the NAWSA Congressional Committee had in mind. Rather, they valued the appearance of suspension while continuing to work behind the scenes for the suffrage amendment. Gardener aimed to use the special wartime session of Congress to establish, finally, the House Committee on Woman Suffrage, the vital infrastructure suffragists would need to get their amendment to the floor for a vote. She spent March 13, 1917, in Speaker Champ Clark's office, meeting with congressional leaders and discussing plans. "I believe that we now have the chance of a lifetime to secure a position that will enable us to push our work successfully and rapidly," Gardener reported to Catt. The congressmen assured her that the election of Jeanette Rankin would bolster the suffragists' case for the House committee and that NAWSA could "pretty nearly name its membership."[48]

Gardener's legislative work often began on her front porch, which adjoined that of Speaker Clark, who lived at 1836 Lamont Street.[49] Over 6 feet tall and a natural raconteur, Clark was "the dominant personality in the House." Though the Speaker was a proud Southerner whose thick accent made Maud Wood Park pine for an interpreter, he had long been on record as a supporter of the vote for women.[50] As Park recalled, "having the Clarks next door furnished opportunities that Mrs. Gardener used to our advantage. Occasionally she had her cook make Southern delicacies to be handed to their cook over the back fence. . . . If she wanted to get a bit of information from him or to convey some without the formality of a call at his office she would sometimes wait, with coat and hat on, until she heard the door of the next house slam after him. Then she would appear, as if by accident, on her own steps; and during the moment of friendly chat that was sure to follow she would adroitly drop in her question . . . but she was far too wise to do that too often."[51]

Even though Clark had signaled his approval of the House committee, he told Gardener that the final authority rested with Rep. Edward W. Pou of North Carolina, the powerful chairman of the House Rules Committee. Clark further intimated that even though Pou opposed the federal amendment, he might be swayed by the president.

Gardener went immediately to Wilson, who had offered tentative, verbal support of a House committee back in 1913. This time, she justified her appeal in terms of the war, NAWSA's cooperative spirit, and President Wilson's chivalrous, principled nature. Emphasizing that this was the *"only* request that the National American Woman Suffrage Association has made of this session of the Congress," Gardener implored the president to help the women "secure to us the machinery of future work for which we have pled in vain for years." Gardener concluded by reminding Wilson that Shaw and Catt were, at that very moment, busy with national defense work and that "with this added bit of legislative machinery . . . we can all the more freely and happily give of our services in other directions to our country."[52] Again, Gardener's combination of timing, flattery, and logic worked. Wilson responded, "It will give me great pleasure to write to Mr. Pou as you suggest."[53] This was, by far, the biggest request NAWSA had yet made of Wilson, and the outcome hinged on the close relationships Gardener had built with Wilson and his staff.

That same day, Wilson wrote to Chairman Pou. He noted that while "strictly speaking, it is none of my business, and I have not the least desire to intervene in the matter" he had heard from Gardener that his opinion could be of significance in determining whether or not the House should establish a Committee on Woman Suffrage. Wilson informed Pou that such a committee "would be a very wise act of public policy, and also an act of fairness to the best women who are engaged in the cause of women suffrage."[54] In his estimation of the "best women," Wilson surely drew on his impressions of Gardener, the suffragist he liked most and the one most frequently in his office.

AS WAR PREPARATIONS pushed NAWSA into closer contact with the White House, Alice Paul and the NWP employed new methods to capture the president's attention. Frustrated by Wilson's brush-off in January, NWP activists began staging daily protests at the White House. On January 10, twelve "silent sentinels" adorned with colorful sashes and banners stood at the Pennsylvania Avenue gates demanding: "Mr. President, What Will You Do for Woman Suffrage?" and "How Long Must Women Wait for Victory?" The vigil continued, six days a week, rain, snow, or shine. Then, on March 4, the eve of Wilson's second inaugural and harkening back to the 1913 parade, Paul planned a massive demonstration at the White House.

Paul, a Quaker, objected to the U.S. entry into World War I. Once the United States officially declared war, she highlighted the hypocrisy of Wilson's statement that the nation was fighting to "make the world safe for democracy" while simultaneously denying democracy to more than half the population at home.[55] Initially, the president greeted the "pickets" with good cheer. He invited them inside for warm drinks and instructed grounds staff to provide the women with warm bricks for their feet. But over time he became increasingly irritated with the NWP. He wrote his daughter Jessie that "they certainly seem bent upon making their cause as obnoxious as possible."[56]

Meanwhile, Gardener and Catt worried that the "misguided women who have been picketing the White House" would undermine their efforts to establish the House committee, just as they believed Paul's strident tactics had cost them the committee back in 1913.[57] After Gardener and Maud Wood Park testified before the House Rules Committee on May 18 about the merits of their proposal, they expected a solid "yes" vote. But one representative unexpectedly issued a statement declaring that he would approve no such committee while women picketed the White House in a time of war.[58] In response, Catt published an open letter to Alice Paul, deploring the protests and distancing NAWSA from them, warning that "there is now clear proof that the presence of the pickets is hurting our cause in Congress."[59]

On May 25, Gardener forwarded Catt's letter to President Wilson. In her cover letter, Gardener explained that NAWSA feared that "in spite of your cordial endorsement of our request for a suffrage committee in the House, the Rules Committee may deny us this help because of their resentment toward a wholly different group of women."[60] Wilson again signaled his support, and the Rules Committee reported favorably. Worried that additional members of Congress would speak against the proposed committee when the measure came to the House floor, Gardener again approached Wilson on June 10. This time she asked him to send a "word or note" to Rep. James Heflin of Alabama, whom she described as "one of the two most dangerous and persistent opponents on the floor." As requested, Wilson wrote Heflin and advised that it would be a very wise thing "both politically and from other points of view" for the House to approve a Committee on Woman Suffrage. Heflin replied that he had read Wilson's letter several times and that even though he opposed women voting, he would "not oppose the creation of a Committee in the House on Woman Suffrage."[61]

The next day, Alice Paul sent out a fundraising letter incorrectly claiming that the National Woman's Party was the only suffrage group "working on Congress that has not been turned aside by the war, but is still, as an organization, putting all its effort into the suffrage movement."[62] She likely had no idea what Gardener had been doing behind the scenes and how close she was to finally securing the House committee. But Paul did know that the NWP needed cash. The NWP had many wealthy benefactors, such as Alva Belmont, but after 1917, the NWP did not have the resources to function on the same scale as NAWSA.

What enabled NAWSA to redouble their efforts for the amendment in 1917 was a huge bequest from Miriam Leslie, a magazine publisher who donated her multimillion-dollar fortune to NAWSA to do with as Catt saw fit. With this windfall, Catt increased the number of NAWSA paid staff (though Gardener remained a volunteer), purchased the *Woman's Journal*, and set up the Leslie Bureau of Suffrage Education in New York, which grew to comprise six departments and a staff of twenty-four.[63]

Throughout the summer of 1917, the NWP picketers intensified their efforts. In July, several women were arrested and sentenced to jail. President Wilson issued a pardon, but the women refused to accept it. Meanwhile, Gardener and Maud Wood Park continued to meet with White House and congressional representatives to press for the creation of the House Committee on Woman Suffrage. On any given day, Gardener shuttled between congressional offices, committee rooms, the House floor, and the White House, gaining what information she could along the way.[64] Speaker Clark informed her that the time to vote on the suffrage committee was inopportune because of the White House picketers, while Pou claimed that the new committee could not be taken up until all war measures had been dealt with.[65] Desperate, Gardener and Park implored Speaker Clark for more help, only to be told that they should "Sit tight and trust in the Lord!"[66]

A major concern was the fact that members of Congress still could not differentiate between NAWSA and the NWP pickets. To most congressmen, all uppity women were one and the same. In an effort to stem the conflation of suffragists in the public mind, Gardener met with White House press staff and various national press representatives to entreat newspapers to leave out the word "suffrage" or "suffragist" when reporting on the NWP protesters so as to not inadvertently impugn the reputation of NAWSA. The NWP, which had become so adept at promoting suffrage through the nation's newspapers, resented this press blackout.[67]

At the end of July, Gardener scheduled a meeting between the president, herself, and Carrie Chapman Catt. A giddy Gardener wrote Catt, instructing, "Now, lady, think up all the pretty, strong, and fine arguments in the world to put up to him. Ask him to put it in a 'message' the moment he feels he can wedge it in to advantage as a war measure and that this will let us free to work for 'our country' instead of for our own freedom, etc etc. If you can, I think it will be pretty wise to put a lot of your points in type and leave them with him. He is a very absorbent party." Gardener also indicated that the press situation had much improved since President Wilson had pardoned the picketers and since reporters had been more careful to distinguish the NWP from NAWSA.[68]

Through their regular canvasing, Gardener and her colleagues learned that the House would vote on their suffrage committee in September and that the strongest case for the committee could be made by representatives from suffrage states. So the women got to work shoring up their male allies from the West. The work proved exhilarating. After so many years of politely circulating petitions from the margins, NAWSA members reveled in their newfound insider status. One Congressional Committee member wrote to a colleague that "We are having a most delightful time and I find it almost as good as a vacation."[69] After two weeks of nonstop persuading, however, she grew weary. Her next chatty report bemoaned that "life has been dragging lazily on . . . even the best men, we find, will bear constant watching."[70]

With the impending suffrage committee vote, Gardener dispatched a few more frantic pleas to Tumulty, asking him to use the power of the White House to get a few more House Democrats to fall in line.[71] Finally, after years of meetings, arm-twisting, and memo writing, the House scheduled a vote on the Woman Suffrage Committee for September 24, 1917. Various representatives impugned the suffragists—especially the pickets—as "nagging . . . iron-jawed angels" and "deluded creatures with short hair and short skirts." Then Judiciary Committee chairman Edwin Webb (D-NC) insisted that voting rights were a state issue and denied that President Wilson had endorsed the committee. To prove that the committee had the president's backing, Chairman Pou brandished the letter that Wilson sent him at Gardener's request. The House voted, 181 to 107, to establish a Committee on Woman Suffrage. The creation of this committee was a landmark victory in the quest to secure the federal amendment. NAWSA credited Gardener with it.[72]

Gardener and Park rushed from the House gallery to thank their friends, beginning with Speaker Clark. "We trusted in the Lord and He stood by us," Gardener exclaimed, quoting the Speaker's own words. Clark grunted, "The Lord didn't have anything to do with it. Tended to it myself."[73] Gardener spent the next several days back at the Capitol, orchestrating the composition of this new committee.[74] She also wrote to Chairman Pou to thank him for his support and welcome him and his wife to the NAWSA Advisory Council. She knew he did not support votes for women, but she really wanted his name on her letterhead.[75]

As Gardener detailed in a subsequent NAWSA report, hers was "the silent work of dealing with certain officials of both parties, securing their cooperation in expediting our various plans." What made this work so challenging was that alliances constantly shifted and every few years the party in power changed. "To secure and hold the confidence and respect, the goodwill and cooperation of opposing administrations, and of men who are fighting night and day 'to get the best of' the other faction or party," Gardener asserted, "is a work that few, indeed, can do successfully."[76] Gardener's efforts to expedite the creation of the House Committee on Woman Suffrage testify to her deft lobbying of allies and adversaries alike.

Getting a suffrage amendment out of this new committee—the goal of setting up the committee in the first place—proved tricky. Judiciary Committee chairman Webb informed Gardener and Park that only the Judiciary Committee could forward constitutional amendments. Indignant, Park and Gardener went to see Clark, who confirmed that this was true. Park blurted out, "Why didn't you tell us this before?" to which the Speaker replied, "You didn't ask me." Once outside the Speaker's office, Park "broke into denunciations of the Speaker's treachery." Gardener, however, took a different view. She surmised that the Speaker had not previously known that constitutional amendments had to originate in the Judiciary Committee. "That old man is so conceited that he would rather have us think he double crossed us," Gardener said, "than admit that he didn't know an important fact about the procedure of the House."

Next Gardener orchestrated the solution. Park researched the issue in *Hinds' Precedents* and found that it was possible for constitutional amendments to come through committees other than Judiciary. Rather than correct the Speaker themselves, Gardener called Clark's secretary, Mr. Bassford, "whom she had previously made a devoted friend," and explained the situation. Bassford agreed to place *Hinds' Precedents*, open to the precise page, on the Speaker's desk so that he would see the correct rule and act accordingly.[77]

After many such encounters, Park recalled that "no other lesson that I learned in Washington stood me in as good stead as my growing realization of the value of Helen Gardener's help."[78] Drawing on Gardener's tactics, Park codified, somewhat humorously, a list of "dos and don'ts" for the NAWSA Congressional Committee to follow as they lobbied Congress, including "don't nag; don't boast; don't threaten; don't stay too long; don't lose your temper; don't talk about your work in corridors or elevators; don't tell everything you know."[79]

The NWP continued protesting at the White House throughout the summer and fall, even after several women were arrested and imprisoned at Occoquan Workhouse. In a mass mailing to members, Paul pronounced picketing the White House as "our most effective method of voicing to the Administration the protest of women against their disfranchisement." She asked for volunteers who were "prepared for imprisonment."[80]

By the end of October, Paul herself was sentenced to six months in jail, an unheard of punishment for a white, middle-class reformer. After her demands to be treated as a political prisoner were refused, Paul led a hunger strike, which resulted in forced feedings and numerous other abuses, creating a national outcry. Earlier that summer, when Wilson had pardoned other NWP protesters, he hinted that the D.C. police had gone too far. But he never put the full weight of his authority behind the release of the prisoners and many took his relative silence as an endorsement of the women's cruel treatment.[81]

Nor did NAWSA come to the defense of the imprisoned NWP protesters. Publicly, NAWSA leaders continued to distance themselves from
the NWP and, privately, to press Wilson for help, often by reminding him
that they were not like the NWP. Catt was especially concerned that the
pickets would harm the chances that the woman suffrage referendum
would pass in New York State that November. Her canvassers informed
her that men were saying they would never vote for suffrage because of
"the pickets." Catt dismissed this as a "plain case of male hysteria," but
to hedge her bets she tasked Gardener with "another 'diplomatic service,'
and this is perhaps the most important yet." Would Gardener ask the
president to issue a public statement saying that he hoped the New York
measure would pass and that "no man will be influenced in his decision
by 'the pickets'"? Since Wilson was the only man to have been directly
picketed, Catt reasoned that his words would "carry weight."[82]

Gardener again worked her magic, via Tumulty.[83] Within a few hours
of receiving her request, Wilson sent the following message to the voters
of New York: "May I not express to you my very deep interest in the campaign in New York for the adoption of woman suffrage, and may I not say
that I hope that no voter will be influenced in his decision with regard to
this great matter by anything the so-called pickets may have done here
in Washington?" These women "represent so small a fraction" of suffragists, Wilson proclaimed, "that it would be most unfair and argue a very
narrow view to allow their actions to prejudice the cause itself."[84]

On November 6, New York enfranchised millions of women,
doubling the number of women voters nationally and substantially
increasing the number of congressmen who represented voting female
constituents (New York State had the largest House delegation, at 43
representatives).[85] Catt referred to the New York victory as the "Gettysburg of the woman suffrage movement."[86] And Gardener proclaimed
this win an augury that "national suffrage, through the federal amendment, is practically won."[87] She also sensed that President Wilson might
soon come out publicly for the federal amendment.

Ever since first meeting Wilson in the summer of 1916, Gardener
had intuited that the president wanted to do right by the suffragists.

She made it her mission to identify favors that he would be comfortable doing, increasing the significance of her asks one by one. To thank the president for his statement about the New York vote, Gardener requested a meeting at the White House on Friday, November 9.[88] Once at the White House, Gardener, Catt, and a couple of other NAWSA representatives informed the president that it was time for him to demand that Congress pass the federal amendment "in order that women may be saved the expense and long struggle which is involved in the States by the State referendum plan." They shared their strategy for the upcoming congressional session and asked for Wilson's help in seeing it through. Catt issued a statement—after Gardener first cleared it with Tumulty—announcing, "We believe [President Wilson] is going to do everything that he can to help us."[89] News reports described Gardener leaving the meeting exuding "triumph and gratification."[90]

In follow-up correspondence with Tumulty, Gardener detailed her

As NAWSA's "Diplomatic Corp," Gardener relied on her charm, her insider knowledge of Congress, and her discretion.

ideas for congressional passage of the amendment, emphasizing the decisive role that she hoped Wilson would play. She presented Tumulty with a copy of her book *An Unofficial Patriot* (1894) and boasted that Senator Williams had declared it the very best portrait of Abraham Lincoln in American literature. She then explained that her careful study of Wilson, another wartime president, had convinced her that he, too, would be remembered for expanding rights and that suffrage would ultimately be extended to women as a war measure, in spite of lingering Southern opposition. "Congress cannot, for long, ask of women to work alongside of men, to suffer together with men, to sacrifice more than any man is asked to sacrifice—the sons they bore—to finance the battle for justice and 'world democracy,'" Gardener stressed, "and at the same time refuse the benefits of all this work and suffering and sacrifice to one half of those who are called upon. It is too utterly illogical. It is too tragically and hideously unfair."[91]

CONFIDENT THAT their decades of toil were about to pay off, NAWSA members went into their December 1917 annual convention "full speed ahead" for the federal amendment.[92] Catt laid out detailed plans for congressional passage of what was now known as the Susan B. Anthony Amendment, a 1918 election contingency plan should it fail to pass during the Sixty-Fifth Congress, and a national ratification strategy to go into immediate effect following congressional victory. Maud Wood Park reported on the Congressional Committee's activities, giving special praise to Gardener: "The association is profoundly indebted [to Gardener] for constant advice and help, as well as for the most skillful handling of delicate and difficult situations. She has been called the 'Diplomatic Corps' of the committee and the name in every good sense has been well won by the important services which she has rendered."[93] As a testament to her contributions, Gardener was appointed a NAWSA vice president, a position that came with a coveted spot on the letterhead.[94]

While the suffragists convened at Poli's Theater, Gardener took a break from conferencing to meet twice with Tumulty at the White House. She shared with him NAWSA's tally regarding the odds of passage during the Sixty-Fifth Congress and asked if Wilson would personally persuade eight to ten more members to vote "yes." Drawing on a conversation she had with Tumulty the previous month, she observed that the women's main adversaries continued to be Southern Democrats.[95]

NAWSA officers had ideas about how to work with Southerners in Congress, but they still refused to partner with African American leaders or to publicly endorse the idea of black women voting. Thousands and thousands of black women continued to work independently for the vote and to sustain the core conviction that citizenship must include voting rights through their own organizations, as the historian Rosalyn Terborg-Penn and others have documented, but they were more or less shunned by NAWSA.[96] At an executive committee meeting following the December convention, NAWSA officers—a category that now included Gardener—considered an application for affiliate membership from the Northeastern Federation of Women's Clubs, an African American women's group. With three members dissenting, NAWSA leaders denied this application on a technicality.[97] Meeting minutes do not detail the discussion, but NAWSA leaders had long feared that openly joining forces with black women would doom the federal amendment's chances for congressional passage and ratification, both of which would require at least some support from white Southern officeholders. In the coming years, the question of black women voting would determine the trajectory of the Nineteenth Amendment, its reach, and its historical legacy.

15

Twenty-Two Favors

*There are some men of real vision and of lofty aim in
Washington political circles today, and there are others whose
personality and value to the nation could be poised upon the
point of a cambric needle and leave room for a jazz band.*

—HELEN HAMILTON GARDENER, 1919

WITH MOMENTUM from the creation of the House Committee
on Woman Suffrage, Wilson's increasingly public support, and
the passage of suffrage in New York, Helen Gardener and her NAWSA
colleagues entered 1918 expecting that the Susan B. Anthony Amendment would pass both chambers by the conclusion of the Sixty-Fifth
Congress, leaving plenty of time for ratification in advance of the 1920
election. But the women underestimated just how impenetrable the
"Southern Wall of Opposition," as Carrie Chapman Catt called it,
would be.

Southern politicians said they opposed the amendment on the
grounds that it infringed on "states' rights" to determine voter qual-
ifications. In actuality, they dreaded the enfranchisement of African
American women and the overall growth of the black electorate. White
Southerners deeply resented the Fifteenth Amendment, which made it

illegal to bar citizens from voting on the basis of race, and they under-stood the Nineteenth Amendment as inherently linked to it, as indeed it was. After federal troops withdrew from the region in the late 1870s, Southern states began to enact various state-specific laws—including poll taxes, property restrictions, and literacy tests—to bar black men from voting and void the Fifteenth Amendment. In the decades since, federal authorities had not challenged these discriminatory laws, which violated the spirit but not necessarily the letter of the Fifteenth Amendment.

As part of a larger movement to formally restrict voting rights in the early 1900s, some Southern congressmen even proposed repeal-ing the Fifteenth Amendment.[1] Repeal efforts did not succeed, but white Southerners worried that the Nineteenth Amendment would bring scrutiny to the ways states had gutted the Fifteenth Amendment and maybe even compel the federal government to enforce it. In this, Southerners were joined by several Northern and Western members of Congress who also declared that their fidelity to states' rights—code for racial exclusion—trumped any interest they might have otherwise had in women voting. As Maud Wood Park recalled, "If I had needed a lesson about the tendency of acquiescence in one injustice to breed tolerance of another, I should have learned it from the way so many of the men from the South saw other questions only in the light of their determination to keep the Negro from the ballot box."[2]

African American women also recognized that the Fifteenth and Nineteenth Amendments were "two fronts in the same fight," as histo-rian Liette Gidlow has established.[3] In a 1915 essay in *The Crisis*, Afri-can American leader Mary Church Terrell asserted that "the reasons for repealing the Fifteenth Amendment differ but little from the argu-ments advanced by those who oppose the enfranchisement of women."[4] But white suffragists no longer understood their struggle to vote as fun-damentally linked with that of African Americans. They fought for the Nineteenth Amendment knowing full well that black women would be barred from voting in Southern states just as black men had been, despite the guarantee of the Fifteenth Amendment.

NAWSA even published state-by-state population counts, show-ing that enfranchising Southern women would actually increase the white majority because white women outnumbered black women in most Southern states.[5] Throughout the early 1900s and especially after the ascendency of Catt, NAWSA leaders cooled relationships with the Southern women (such as Gardener's one-time friend Kate Gordon) who advocated explicitly racist proposals for whites-only suffrage and stood firm against such measures, but they stopped far short of embrac-ing African American women as their partners in the struggle for equal citizenship.[6]

Throughout her life, Gardener expressed tremendous pride in her father's and three brothers' Union service—a rare sacrifice among Vir-ginians and one that led to the premature deaths of all four men—and she idolized Abraham Lincoln, saluting his statue in the Capitol rotunda every time she passed it.[7] But she seems to have felt as though her family's valiant efforts to abolish slavery excused her from having to actively engage in the ongoing struggle for African American civil rights. Like many white progressives of her era, Gardener considered herself an ally of African Americans even as she held tight to white privilege and remained silent in the face of increasing violence and dis-crimination against African Americans.

As a proud Chenoweth of Virginia, Gardener also prioritized white reconciliation over the full incorporation of African Americans into American life. Gardener's social life in Washington, D.C., revolved around her Virginia relatives and Col. Selden Day's friends from the Civil War, both Union and especially Confederate veterans. As she watched white men from the North and South consolidate power through their shared wartime experiences, Gardener, who had also suf-fered greatly as a result of the Civil War, wanted in. Beginning with the publication of An Unofficial Patriot (which she regularly sent new friends through the late 1910s), she worked toward sectional reconcilia-tion in her own way.[8]

From behind the scenes, Gardener reached out to President Wilson and her Southern friends in Congress to dismantle the "Southern Wall of Opposition" to the Susan B. Anthony Amendment. In large part she did this by emphasizing that World War I, like the Civil War before it, was a fight to extend democracy and by applying the promises of America's founding documents to white women. She presented herself to NAWSA as a woman who could advocate for the federal amendment in the South, and she presented herself to Southern politicians as a Southern woman who understood—but did not agree with—their states' rights objections. Such a dual perspective proved instrumental in the final months of suffrage lobby work in Washington, but it also underscored the fact that NAWSA's priority remained the enfranchisement of white women.

WHEN CONGRESS CONVENED in January 1918, the House—thanks to the newly constituted Committee on Woman Suffrage—immediately took up the Susan B. Anthony Amendment. From January 3 to January 7, the committee held hearings and listened to testimony from supporters and opponents. A long-standing objection to women voting had been the fear that women would vote for Prohibition. But just weeks before, Congress had passed the Prohibition Amendment, neutralizing this argument. Antis had also claimed that women voting would destroy the family, voiced concerns about prostitutes voting, and insisted that most women really did not want the vote.[9] But after more and more states had granted women at least partial suffrage and none of these objections had been borne out, the singular sticking point remained states' rights. Having rebutted so many arguments over the years, Carrie Chapman Catt seemed almost relieved to now focus on just one.[10]

NAWSA members and their allies prevailed at the hearings. On January 8, 1918, the House Committee on Woman Suffrage reported favorably on the Susan B. Anthony Amendment, clearing the way for a floor vote. Anticipating the vote and knowing they would need every possible "yes," Park, Gardener, and their colleagues had spent the previous month "like a three-ringed circus in which our Congressional Committee had to perform hair-raising stunts in all the rings at practically the same time." Gardener organized another high-profile reception, while Park put together a suffrage steering committee in the House, chaired by Rep. Carl Hayden of Arizona, whom she claimed was "easily the most popular member of the House." Thanks to Catt's "Winning Plan," NAWSA internal polls showed tremendous gains in 1917. In one year, the number of confirmed "yes" votes had grown from 182 to 245. They needed at least 273.[11]

With the House vote looming, Gardener stepped up the pressure on President Wilson through his secretary, Joseph Tumulty. Even though he had assured her of his support, Wilson had yet to make a public statement in favor of the federal amendment. Now was the time, Gardener and other suffragists urged. Catt asked Wilson's son-in-law, the cabinet secretary William McAdoo, for assistance. And Elizabeth Bass, the head of the Woman's Bureau of the Democratic National Committee, appealed to Wilson for a public statement, promising that doing so "would enthrone you forever in the hearts of the women of America as the second Great Emancipator."[12]

Finally, on the eve of the House vote, Wilson summoned to the White House the Democratic members of the House Committee on Woman Suffrage and encouraged them to vote "yes" on the amendment (the committee vote had been procedural). This meeting had been arranged by Tumulty in consultation with Gardener, who was, by then, his daily correspondent. The president wrote his statement to the committee in his own hand and allowed it to be released to the press. It read, "The committee found that the President had not felt at liberty to volunteer to Members of Congress his advice in this important matter, but when we sought his advice, he very frankly and earnestly advised us to vote for the Amendment as an act of right and justice to the women of the country and of the world."[13]

Tumulty saved the handwritten scrap of paper for Gardener, a thoughtful testament to their close working relationship and to her role in cultivating Wilson's support of the federal amendment. She "thanked him from the bottom of [her] heart for thinking of it" and asked him to please "not fold it" and "ask [the president] to sign it and let me have it just as it is." Gardener predicted that the president's statement would be a "historic document," but it remains in an obscure folder in Tumulty's papers at the Library of Congress.[14]

On the morning of January 10, Gardener headed to the Hill and took her reserved seat in the House gallery, courtesy of Speaker Clark. Around noon, the Reverend Billy Sunday, who happened to be in town, opened the session with a prayer. After forty minutes of debate over committee jurisdiction, Rep. Jeanette Rankin offered the first floor speech in favor of the amendment. For the next five hours, Gardener listened anxiously while congressional opponents voiced objections and proposed various impediments. Rep. John Moon (D-TN) argued that in Southern states where black people outnumbered whites, giving women the vote would "produce a condition that would be absolutely intolerable. We owe something to the wishes and the sentiments of the people of our sister States struggling to maintain law and order and white supremacy." Rep. William Greene (R-MA) claimed he could not vote for the amendment because he objected to the NWP pickets. Rep. John Raker (D-CA), chair of the House Committee on Woman Suffrage, brought in hundreds of letters from Southern women demanding the vote and claimed that white women in the South far outnumbered black women, intimating that women suffrage would bolster white supremacy.[15]

Finally, the vote was called just before 5 p.m. Knowing the outcome would be close, Rep. James Mann (R-IL) traveled to the Capitol from his hospital bed, against doctor's orders, to vote "yes"; Rep. Henry Barnhart (R-IN) was wheeled in on a stretcher just in time to answer the second roll call and cast his vote in the affirmative; and Rep. Thetus Sims (D-TN), who had slipped on the ice and broken his shoulder that morning, refused treatment so that he could attempt to rally his fellow Southerners to approve the measure. Most poignantly of all, New York representative Frederick Hicks, Jr., took the train to D.C. immediately after the death of his wife, who had been an "ardent suffragist," and stayed just long enough to vote "yes." After recounts and last-minute challenges, the measure passed 274 to 136, meeting the two-thirds requirement with one vote to spare. Gardener and her colleagues in the House chamber were "jubilant" and broke out singing "Praise God from Whom All Blessings Flow."[16]

CATT FELT CONFIDENT about the amendment's chances in the Senate, but NAWSA's polling showed that they fell a few votes shy of the required two-thirds majority. Gardener went straight to work. She began with her old friend Sen. John Sharp Williams of Mississippi, whom her colleagues described as "hopeless." Gardener first inquired about Mrs. Williams, reminding the senator how they had celebrated her birthday dinner together the year before. Then she laid into him: "Did you analyze the vote on Suffrage in the House?" Did you, she pressed, notice that twenty-five state delegations were united in support of the amendment and only six states, including Mississippi, were solidly opposed? "*I want you to redeem that state*," she implored. "You are by far its leading citizen." Do not, she beseeched him, "insist upon remaining with a sinking ship" when everyone could see that "Democracy's hour has struck" for women.

In her four-page entreaty, Gardener also invoked white superiority as a reason to oppose Williams's preferred state-by-state method. To organize for a federal amendment, she emphasized, women had to lobby only the "picked men of the Legislature." Wasn't that enough? "Do you want to force the refined white women of your state to appeal to *all* of the individual voters there?" Surely, Gardener presumed, Williams must be "willing to save them from that humiliation." In this race-baiting argument, Gardener demanded that Williams rectify what to her mind was the fundamental unfairness of allowing all men to vote (at least in theory) when women—even educated white ones—could not.

Next, Gardener invited the senator, in so many ways her peer, to put himself in her position and imagine that "when the day comes (very soon now) when the Senate votes upon this question, I shall sit (as I did all day long in the House, as the guest of the Speaker) tense and anxious in the gallery, while men decided our fate." Gardener implored, "Remember that you are holding in your power *my* right to attain self-government by the shortest, best, and constitutionally prescribed method. Remember that I want it with all my heart with all my soul and with all my strength—whether or not any other women whose good will you value cares for it or not."[17]

The following day, Senator Williams sent his "Dear Friend" a candid reply: "If anything in the world *could* make me do the thing you want done it would be your letter." But even though he realized that women's suffrage was on the horizon, he could not do as Gardener wished. Mainly, Williams divulged, he could not vote for the Susan B. Anthony Amendment because it would, at least on paper, enfranchise the black women of Mississippi. This he could not abide, even if it meant disenfranchising his daughters and offending Gardener. If he lived in "any white state," he acknowledged, he would vote for suffrage, but not in Mississippi. Black women, he charged, "cannot be controlled, as the men can be, and they would almost all, without exception, go to the polls while a great many white women would not."

Referring to the "injurious" Fifteenth Amendment, Williams clarified that he considered the vote a privilege, not a right, and that it should be up to each individual state to determine who could cast a ballot. He then returned explicitly to race. "Of course, you know as well as I do, and if you do not I will tell you confidentially, that the real reason why negro men do not vote in the State of Mississippi, is not because of their legal disqualifications, but because *they are afraid* that if they do vote some of them might get hurt." But such violent tactics would not work with black women because "a woman is a woman after all, whether she be black or white." And even if "a few men of the very lowest sort" did use violence to scare black women from the polls, the "whole moral sense of the world would be set against the Mississippi white man."

Williams concluded that he would make no public statements on woman suffrage and that he had answered no other letters on the topic, only Gardener's because she was his friend. He preferred that his "no" vote on the Susan B. Anthony Amendment "be the sole answer I make."[18] Decades after Reconstruction, the Fifteenth Amendment still set the terms of debate regarding women voting and highlighted the lengths to which some white leaders would go to keep African Americans from the polls.

GARDENER MAY HAVE been disappointed by Williams's reply, but as a savvy lobbyist, she intended her letter to Williams for wider audience. She immediately sent a copy of it to Tumulty and asked him to share it with the president.[19] During these tense months of lobbying, Gardener repeatedly sent the White House copies of her letters to Southern Democrats, using this back channel method as a way to critique the states' rights position, which had until that month been Wilson's stance, without overreaching.[20]

A few days before the January 1918 House vote, Gardener had also given Tumulty a copy of a letter she had just sent to her friend Chief Justice Walter M. Clarke of North Carolina, a progressive Democrat who advocated woman suffrage and condemned lynching. She used this letter to make an argument to Wilson about the underlying party politics of suffrage. "The defeat by the Democratic Party of the suffrage amendment of this session of the Congress," Gardener warned Clarke, "will also be the *sure* defeat of the Democratic Party at the next Presidential election and the loss of the Congress of the House before that time." She asked him if the Democratic Party could "afford to allow a group of its backward-looking men [to] lose for it the opportunity of a generation." Gardener boasted that NAWSA members could easily unseat enough congressmen to ensure that the amendment would pass in the next Congress: "Two million well organized women with a goodly supply of financial and voting backing can accomplish quite a change in the face of things when they try, and the men in the Congress who have not yet 'got the hang of the Declaration of Independence' enough to apply its principles to one half of the population will doubtless 'return to the practice of the law' in large numbers."[21]

As Gardener's correspondence illustrates, the party politics of suffrage were often unpredictable and did not fall along straight partisan or regional lines.[22] Both the Republican and Democratic Parties had adopted planks in support of suffrage—if granted state by state—at their respective 1916 conventions. Although the most vehement and coordinated opposition to the federal amendment came from the South, several Western and Northern Republicans—including both senators from Massachusetts, one from Delaware, plus one from New York—were also virulent anti-suffragists, generally because they feared that women would vote for reforms that curbed the power of big business or because they, too, feared the growth of the black electorate.

Despite having antagonists on both sides of the aisle, Alice Paul and the National Woman's Party continued to oppose only Democrats, even pro-suffrage allies, as long as the party controlled both the Congress and the White House. To Paul, doing so showcased the ability of women to steer the congressional agenda.[23] NAWSA remained nonpartisan but worked closely with the Democrats in power. And Gardener, as Carrie Chapman Catt observed, "may be a non-partisan, but she is so well known to be a very enthusiastic Wilsonite that she passes for a Democrat."[24] The one and only time Gardener had voted, in California, she cast her ballot for the straight Republican ticket.[25] But her letters to Democratic leaders reveal that she was deeply invested in diminishing the power of the old guard of "states' rights" within the party. In this she found common cause with Wilson's influential secretary Tumulty, who joined Gardener in encouraging the president to champion the federal amendment.

PATIENTLY, over the eighteen months since she had first met Wilson in the summer of 1916, Gardener had alternated between publicly praising him and privately urging him to do more for women. In the spring of 1918, she told Tumulty that the time had arrived for Wilson's big push in the Senate. Gardener regularly provided the president with NAWSA's lists of senators who were for suffrage, against, and "doubtful" so that he could channel his influence accordingly.[26] Every time Gardener got a lead on a Democratic senator who might be swayed, she nudged Tumulty to get the president to reach out to the man in question.

Wilson initially resisted, noting that it had long been his policy to offer his recommendations to members of Congress only when they asked for his opinion. At one point he even resorted to a ruse. In March, he invited two senators from Gardener's list to the Oval Office on the pretense of discussing the Commerce Committee's investigation of the Shipping Board. A third senator was then invited and instructed in advance to ask the president his thoughts regarding women voting so that Wilson could subtly inform the first two senators that he wanted them to vote for the federal amendment without seeming to have invited them for the express purpose of arm-twisting.[27] But as the Sixty-Fifth Congress dragged on without the prospect of Senate passage, the president dropped such pretexts and began openly calling, writing, and telegramming individual senators.

Gardener also kept a lookout for other opportunities for the president to speak publicly in favor of suffrage. She used a statement he made in praise of the Women's Overseas Hospital Committee—a group supported by NAWSA—to promote the federal amendment.[28] And then she persuaded him to revise a letter he had written to French suffragists to include a statement urging immediate congressional passage of the amendment. His secretary Rudolph Forster marveled that this was the

Gardener (bottom right) and NAWSA officers leaving the White House armed with a letter from President Wilson urging congressional passage of the Nineteenth Amendment.

only time the president had changed a statement after it had left the White House. Together with other NAWSA officers, Gardener went to the White House to receive this letter so that they could publicize its message.[29]

Besides her skillful maneuvering to secure the House Committee on Woman Suffrage, Gardener's signature diplomatic achievement was the way she interacted with the president and his top aides. Nearly every time she wrote Wilson a letter, Gardener also included a cover letter to Tumulty or Forster or both, explaining her purpose, what she wanted the president to do, and how they could help. After a June 1918 White House visit, she thanked Tumulty for all his invaluable help and confessed that it had been hard on her to "seem so insistent and persistent" and that "if I had your job, I'd be crazy." Above all, she appreciated that he treated her with "sympathy and good will whatever I have to bring to you."[30]

Gardener frequently visited the White House in person and called on the telephone several times each week, becoming a regular and welcome presence during Wilson's second term. She positioned herself as providing insider information on suffrage and Democratic politics in the South. Ultimately, Wilson's staff came to view her as a partner and collaborator, not as a pesky supplicant. She sent apricots from her garden, effusive thank-you notes, and a heartfelt letter when Tumulty's father died.[31] Even NAWSA president Carrie Chapman Catt generally did not approach Wilson without first going through Gardener, and she often stayed at Gardener's house when in D.C. Catt once instructed Park, "Tell Helen to go in person about the President's message but I will write also and send the letter to her. No! She writes so much better than I do that she must write it and she may sign my name if she thinks it necessary. She will know what to say!"[32] By 1918, the White House had come to consider Gardener as the voice of NAWSA in Washington and as a friend.

NAWSA Congressional Committee chair Maud Wood Park recalled that Gardener's work with the White House proved invaluable during this final push in Congress. As NAWSA's White House emissary, "she was vastly better than anyone else," Park explained. "She was the one woman to whom the President was always willing to grant an appointment and whom Mr. Joseph Tumulty and Mr. Rudolph Forster, the secretaries in the executive office, were always glad to assist."[33] Gardener later boasted that she had asked the president for twenty-two favors and been granted twenty-one.[34]

In contrast, when the National Woman's Party requested a meeting to discuss the Senate situation in May 1918, Wilson's aide wrote a memo observing that "the case of these women presents a bit of a problem. They refuse to take 'no' for an answer. They come to the Executive Office with letters which they insist shall be brought to the President's attention at once . . . and remain in the Executive Office for hours." Wilson personally crafted the reply to this latest NWP appeal indicating that there was no reason for him to meet with them because "no

*Gardener and Carrie Chapman Catt leaving the White House after
one of their many meetings with President Wilson.*

further representations could make his interest in the suffrage matter
any deeper than it is now."[35]

Over the course of 1918, Gardener grew bolder. In addition to giving
the White House names of senators for the president to contact, she
began also providing talking points about suffrage as a war measure.
And the White House started sharing copies of the president's letters to
senators with Gardener.[36] At one point, she even sent Forster a bulleted
to-do list for the president.[37] Summoning her literary humor, Gardener
penned a July 4 poem to the President, which she claimed, tongue in
cheek, had been written by a soldier on the front:

We'll fight with all that's in us for justice to all mankind, but it takes our nerve and riles us, to know that such men behind can bully and flout our women who ask but their honest due—so we're asking, Woodrow Wilson, for another blast from you![38]

Gardener was literally trying everything she could think of to get the amendment through the Senate before the Sixty-Fifth Congress adjourned.

But by the summer of 1918, the suffragists still did not have enough "yes" votes in the Senate. Gardener, now sixty-five, was hospitalized for appendix surgery for much of July and August while Congress recessed. From her sick bed, Gardener pressured Wilson to move beyond writing letters to individual senators and to use his presidential authority to demand that Congress pass suffrage as a war measure. This was the strategy NAWSA had long worked toward, and Gardener attempted to get Wilson to put the full weight of the presidency behind it. One day she told him that her "good friend and yours" Sen. John Sharp Williams would "back the President in all war measures." So Gardener reasoned that "a 'war measure blast' from you is, I believe, our last best hope."[39] Another day, she gave Wilson a copy of Catt's open speech to Congress, which she delivered several times in 1917–1918, explicating the suffrage-as-a-war-measure argument.

Gardener spoke regularly with White House staff from the hospital phone, and she boasted to NAWSA colleagues that the White House sent her copies of the president's letters to senators while the ink was still wet.[40] In August, Wilson had staff send Gardener several dozen roses from the White House Conservatory. But nothing cheered her as much as Wilson's promise to grant her wish that he "say to the Senate and the country some of the splendid things you have said to individuals" about his support for the federal amendment.[41] This vow so exhilarated Gardener that even though "the doctor says I may go downstairs once a day, I have been down twice today."[42]

By September, NAWSA leaders believed they were just one vote shy in the Senate.[43] Gardener immediately arranged a meeting at the White

Gardener often presented President Wilson with instructive reading
material, sometimes even including "to do" lists.

House to discuss what Park described as their best prospects yet in the Senate.[44] The women implored the president to issue a public statement demanding that the Senate pass the Nineteenth Amendment as a war measure. "The hope and the fate of the women of the nation rest in your hands," Catt declared.[45]

With the proud, indulgent tone of someone bearing a great and unexpected gift, the president replied to Catt, "I did not do what [your letter] suggested, but I hope that you think what I did do was better."[46] What Wilson did was grant Gardener's sick bed wish that he publicly say some "splendid things" about suffrage. On September 30, he went to the Capitol to address the entire U.S. Senate, for only the second time in his presidency, accompanied by all but one member of his cabinet. Wilson told the senators that passage of the Susan B. Anthony Amendment was "vitally essential to the successful prosecution of the great war of humanity in which we are engaged." The nation had "made partners of the women in this war," Wilson implored, "shall we admit them only to a partnership of suffering and sacrifice and toil and not to a partnership of privilege and right?"[47]

Heeding the president's call to action, the Senate scheduled a vote on the amendment for the very next day. Once again, the question of black women voting anchored the debate. Senator Williams even tried unsuccessfully to add a clause limiting the vote to white women. Ultimately, the Senate fell short of passing the Susan B. Anthony Amendment by two votes. With "heads held as high as we could get them," Gardener, Park, and Mary Hay (of New York) went to thank their friends in the Senate for their help. More disappointed than at any previous defeat, Carrie Chapman Catt vowed never again to watch another vote.[48]

THE "SOLID SOUTH" accounted for most of the "no" votes, but the Southerners were joined by Massachusetts senators John W. Weeks and Henry Cabot Lodge, among others. "Nothing in the history of the Amendment," observed Maud Wood Park, "has been more amazing than the constant working together of Republican opponents from the north-eastern states and Democrats from the so-called solid south."[49] Wilson's advocacy may have failed to turn enough votes in the Senate, but it nevertheless bolstered the public perception that the Anthony Amendment was a vital war measure and emboldened the women of NAWSA to do everything they could to ensure its immediate passage.

NAWSA members focused their efforts on ousting two Senate opponents in the upcoming 1918 election, one from each party: Republican John Weeks of Massachusetts and Democrat Willard Saulsbury of Delaware. The fact that women could not vote raised obvious challenges to NAWSA's plan to defeat incumbent senators at the polls. NAWSA set up a special task force in Massachusetts to send speakers around the state and to distribute thousands of flyers to targeted groups, urging every woman to "get at least one" man to vote against Senator Weeks.[50] The suffragists and their husbands, fathers, and brothers succeeded. Weeks was defeated by a pro-suffrage Democrat and Saulsbury lost to a pro-suffrage Republican. As Catt gloated, "When Senators cannot change their minds, the Senators, themselves, must be changed."[51]

In an attempt to appear nonpartisan, the NWP threw its support behind two pro-suffrage Democrats who were vying to fill unexpired terms, but neither succeeded.[52] Meanwhile, all three suffrage referenda on state ballots passed, providing additional momentum. And as Gardener had predicted to Justice Clarke, Republicans won majorities in both houses of Congress, resulting in a divided government for the first time in years. With at least two new "yes" votes in the Senate, suffragists believed that—as long as they did not lose any votes and as long as they maintained strong relationships with the incoming Republican congressional leadership—the federal amendment would pass in the Sixty-Sixth Congress.

WITH CONGRESSIONAL PASSAGE in sight, Gardener set about establishing a place for women in world affairs. The week after the 1918
election, she wrote to Wilson suggesting that he appoint Carrie Chapman Catt, an international leader who had earned the goodwill of the
women of twenty-six countries during her tenure as president of the
International Suffrage Commission, as a member of the World War I
Peace Commission.[53]

Wilson replied that it was "not practicable" to appoint a woman to
the Peace Commission, "much as [he] would personally like to do so."[54]
Gardener informed Wilson that his reply "took courage out of" her
heart. This was the only favor he had refused her. She held out hope
that he would convince America's allies to appoint women to the Peace
Commission. And she did not share his refusal with NAWSA officers,
lest the women feel that when "they were sorely needed to help men
save man's own idea of civilization, all was asked of them and they gave
all; only to be denied even a small voice when they asked, in return, to
be represented and consulted as to the use to be made of the victory
they did so much to secure."[55]

In all the correspondence between Gardener and the president, this
was the only time she wrote sharply to him. But she had a lot on her
mind that November day. On top of her letter to Wilson, she placed a
handwritten note for Tumulty, informing him that she had written the
president from her husband's deathbed and thus was not in the proper
state of mind to judge the letter's appropriateness. She asked Tumulty to
destroy her letter to Wilson if he thought she had gone too far; he did
not.[56] The president asked Tumulty to assure Gardener that he would
mention the amendment in his upcoming speech to Congress, which
he delivered on December 2, the night before he left for Europe to
negotiate the end of World War I with the world's leading men.[57]

Col. Selden Day had lived to see the end of another U.S. war. On
December 22, 1918, he died at home, with Gardener at his side. The

cause of death was "cardiac decompensation" following years of heart problems. Day requested a private funeral conducted by his longtime friend Henry Couden, the "Blind Chaplain" of the House of Representatives. On Christmas Eve, the colonel was laid to rest with full military honors at Arlington National Cemetery.[58]

Gardener faced her loss virtually alone, except for a visit from Day's cousin, Paul Kester, a younger writer who lived nearby in Virginia. She revealed to Kester that she had kept Day's true condition secret over the past several months—he was mostly sedated on opiates—because she did not want their friends to know him as anything other than his best self. Other than Kester, Day's family did not visit or write. She never hinted at these personal struggles in her letters to her suffrage colleagues, much less her correspondence with the White House, always keeping cheery and funny, even when she herself was in the hospital or her husband was dying at home. In saying goodbye to Day, Gardener realized she was also closing another distinct chapter of her life. She reflected to Kester, "I seemed to have lived several totally separate ones."[59] She could never have anticipated that her favorite chapter was yet to come.

AFTER TAKING a month to mourn Day's death, Gardener launched straight into another legislative campaign. On January 25, 1919, she filed for her army widow's pension, which was granted at the rate of $25 per month. As the various documents certifying their marriage, Day's death, and the death of Charles Smart circulated through the government bureaucracy, the pension commissioner intimated that she might be entitled to more money.[60] Gardener got right to work. She contacted her friends in Congress, starting with Sen. Thomas Walsh, who chaired the Pension Committee. In her sworn testimony, she stated that since Day's death, she had absolutely no income and a $3,000 mortgage to pay on their Lamont Street home. Senator Walsh hastily calculated the numbers and introduced a legislative fix. On February, 22, 1919, both houses of Congress passed S. 5649, doubling Gardener's widow's pension, a nice bump but still not enough to pay her bills. On March 4, President Wilson signed the bill into law. At the time, so-called private bills were quite common, though Gardener's may have set a record for speed of passage. This was not the legislation that Gardener had planned to pass in 1919, but it was a promising start to the year.

The Sixty-Fifth Congress did not adjourn until March, and NAWSA leadership stubbornly refused to give up hope that the Senate might pass the Susan B. Anthony Amendment by then. If not, the measure would have to pass the House again in the Sixty-Sixth Congress, and ratification in time for the 1920 election would be much more complicated. Many state legislatures did not meet every year, so the more time between congressional passage and the 1920 election, the better the odds that thirty-six states could ratify in time. Catt, unflappable on the outside and in all public pronouncements, sent frantic letters to Park. "What more can we do?" she implored in November 1918. "I am on the verge of suicide."[61] Regarding the ongoing impasse in the Senate, she wrote Park again to say, "Of course everything is a whirl around the White House, but Helen *must* get something done there." She signed off, "If I don't hear from you about every ten minutes I'm crazy."[62]

By February 1919, Catt felt more sanguine. The chances for Senate passage had not changed, she told Park, "except by the additional earnestness of our friends and bitterness of our foes. . . . If fate perchances victory on our bedraggled and outworn banner, we shall all be glad and perhaps we shall even feel jubilant. We shall shed no tears at any rate." Catt prepared two editorials for *The Woman Citizen*—one for Senate victory and one for Senate defeat.[63]

The intense scrutiny on the Senate—and in particular on Southern Democrats—continued to keep Gardener busy and in regular contact with the White House. As a measure of Gardener's effectiveness, Park appointed her vice chairman of the Congressional Committee.[64]

Once again, hopes hinged on the unlikely possibility that Sen. John Sharp Williams might change his vote. On January 10, 1919, Tumulty

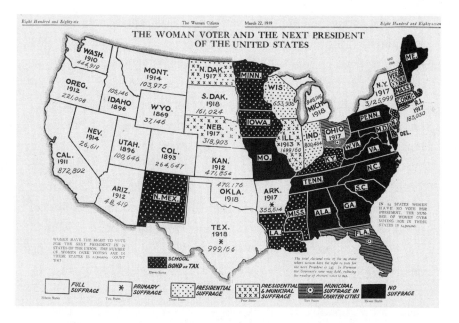

NAWSA *map showing the increasing power of women voters even before passage of the Nineteenth Amendment.*

suggested that Wilson contact him.[65] Wilson telegrammed Williams from France to express his hope that "a new survey of affairs may convince you the wisdom of [the Nineteenth Amendment's] passage." At the bottom of Wilson's telegram, Williams scribbled in pencil, "Not as long as they keep up their infantile and asinine bonfire performances in LaFayette Park."[66] As warmly as he felt toward Gardener, Williams despised the NWP protesters, though they certainly had succeeded in capturing his attention.

Paul and her intrepid followers had kept up their protests in increasingly creative ways, despite ongoing arrest and imprisonment. In August 1918, for example, they had demonstrated at LaFayette Square, only to be imprisoned at an uninhabitable abandoned workhouse near the district jail, where the women were sickened by tainted water and open toilets. Paul was sentenced to ten days simply for attending the protest; she led another hunger strike.[67]

Gardener tried to convince Williams that the "childish and offensive conduct of the women who perform on Lafayette Square" was not a legitimate justification for a "no" vote.[68] But deep down she knew that his real objection remained his desire to keep African Americans from the polls. To another friend, Gardener described Williams as a man with a "splendid" feeling for democracy as a "fundamental principle," but whose aristocratic blood and "slave-holding states' rights traditions tone down and modify certain of the fundamentals just as they did with Washington and Jefferson."[69]

Sen. William Borah (R-ID), the "Lion of Idaho," presented the most vexing obstacle of all. For years, he had spoken in Congress and in whatever state NASWA dispatched him to about the benefits of women voting in his home state. And yet he would not budge on the federal amendment. Catt and other NAWSA leaders targeted Borah in early 1918, after he voted for Prohibition, which, in the words of Catt, made his states' rights objection to suffrage "really quite unaccountable."[70] Borah finally told Catt that there was no point in further communication because there was no way he would change his mind.[71] By November 1918, Catt concluded, "Do not count on Borah for anything which calls for common sense or honesty. He possesses neither."[72]

Each time the Senate seemed ready to vote, Borah was deluged with letters and telegrams urging him to vote "yes" and a few thanking him in advance for voting "no." His home-state constituents were especially perplexed by his position. Idaho provided a prominent example of the benefits of women voting, so how could an Idaho senator be a stronghold of opposition? Borah even resisted an appeal from former president Theodore Roosevelt, with whose daughter, Alice, he carried on a lengthy affair and fathered a child in 1924.[73]

When constituents asked Borah why he would not support the federal amendment, he told them it was because he received "thousands and thousands of letters" from white women of the South, begging him to not let black women vote.[74] But this was not true, at least not according to what is saved in Borah's papers at the Library of Congress. To the contrary, in December 1917, Borah wrote to his friend James Callaway, a Confederate apologist who wrote a popular column for the *Macon*

(GA) *Daily Telegraph,* and asked to hear firsthand "the best thought of the women of the South" on the federal amendment "especially as it touches the race question."[75] Not only was Borah not bombarded with letters from white Southern women, he had to recruit the one such correspondent he had: a Mrs. J. B. Evans, of Selma, Alabama.

Mrs. Evans informed Borah that she was very fond of all her black servants. But she had no kind words for suffragists. She objected to suffrage, first of all, because it had grown out of the abolition movement, and to her mind, all suffragists had a "venomous hatred of the south, and the southern white people." Worst of all, the Susan B. Anthony Amendment would "bring . . . to life" the Fifteenth Amendment, which had "never been enforced."[76]

Borah elaborated on his position in a long letter to the chair of the Idaho Republican Party, which was later reprinted as anti-suffrage propaganda by the Georgia Association Opposed to Woman Suffrage. Enfranchising women would, according to Borah, "impose upon the South three million colored voters." This scenario would result either in violent civil chaos or in the federal government endorsing discrimination against black women voters, just as it had done in the case of black male voters since the end of Reconstruction. Neither scenario was acceptable to Borah. "I am asked to help write into the fundamental law that which would be to a large portion of the people of the country a cowardly lie," Borah asserted. "The north has sat still for forty years and witnessed the disfranchisement of the Negroes of the south and now they want their representatives to write another solemn clause into the charter and sit still for forty years or interminably while the negro women are disfranchised." Borah vowed he would oppose the federal amendment, even if doing so caused him to be voted out of office.[77]

On February 10, 1919, the Senate again voted on the Susan B. Anthony Amendment. This time, the measure failed to meet the two-thirds majority by one vote. Gardener, her NAWSA colleagues, and their allies in the White House had exhausted all possible leads, but their efforts were not enough to surmount the "Southern Wall of Opposition" in the Sixty-Fifth Congress.

ALL WINTER, NAWSA members had been frantically canvasing the incoming Sixty-Sixth Congress, and the numbers were still too close for comfort in the Senate. While the women counted just enough "yes" votes, their slim margin meant that one illness or one changed mind could signal another defeat. On April 30, 1919, as the president prepared to return from Europe for the opening of Congress, Tumulty cabled to let him know that his suffrage contacts, no doubt Gardener, informed him that they needed one more vote in the Senate. Tumulty suggested that Wilson track down Sen. William Harris of Georgia, who was also in Paris, and convince him to issue a public statement saying that he would deliver the vote. Three days later, he reminded the president, "It is urgent that you see Senator Harris about suffrage matter." Senator Harris issued the public statement as requested.[78]

Wilson then dispatched a message to Congress urging members to pass the suffrage amendment immediately upon convening, as part of his larger post-War agenda.[79] The Sixty-Sixth Congress assembled on May 19. Rep. James Mann (R-IL), who had come from his hospital bed to vote "yes" the previous January, assumed the chairmanship of the House Committee on Woman Suffrage. He assured a nervous Maud Wood Park that he had all the necessary votes lined up and that he intended to make the Susan B. Anthony Amendment the very first item on the House agenda.[80] Two days later, he did.

Gardener hurried excitedly to the Capitol on the morning of May 21, though she missed sitting in her reserved seats on the Speaker's bench. Under the new leadership, she and Park sat in regular seats on the Republican side. Wearing a black silk dress with a drop waist and a jaunty black straw hat, Gardener listened stoically as men debated whether or not women would be full citizens.[81] After several hours, the House overwhelmingly approved the amendment: 304 in favor to 89 against.[82] The vote had been called so hastily that not very many suffragists had time to get to Washington, so the celebration was more subdued than the previous year's. Maud Wood Park filmed a moving picture newsreel with Representative Mann, and pictures of Gardener, together with the rest of the NAWSA Congressional Committee, were cabled across the country to spread the historic news.[83]

Two weeks later, on June 4, the Senate scheduled a vote on the amendment. The heat was oppressive—this time, Gardener wore all white—and the discussion dragged on and on. Sen. James Reed (D-MO) delivered a three-hour filibuster about states' rights. And Sen. Pat Harrison (D-MS) introduced a measure to exclude black women from voting. Sen. Ellison Smith (D-SC) summarized the opposition when he protested that "the southern man who votes for the Susan B. Anthony Amendment votes to ratify the Fifteenth Amendment."[84] Finally, the vote was called. At 5:15 p.m., Senate president pro tempore Albert Cummins announced that the amendment had carried 56 to 25, narrowly meeting the two-thirds majority. In addition to the two "yes" votes the suffragists picked up in the 1918 election, Senator Harris kept his promise to Wilson, and Sen. Frederick Hale of Maine changed his vote to "yes" after Mainers agreed, in 1918, to let women vote in presidential elections. Speaking for the Southern Wall of Opposition, Sen. Edward Gay of Louisiana bitterly declared that "thirteen states will never vote for this measure unless you amend it to spare the South the problem of the negro woman vote."[85]

After the vote was announced, all rules of Senate decorum were ignored. The Senate floor and galleries erupted in cheers and "deafening applause" lasting two straight minutes.[86] The *New York Tribune* reported that the suffragists "indulged in a good old fashioned feminine kissing and hugging bee."[87] But Gardener could not spend much time celebrating; she had to rush to the official signing ceremony that she herself had planned.

IN ADVANCE OF the long-awaited Senate vote, Gardener had contacted the press, purchased a decorative gold pen, and organized a stately signing ceremony to take place in the Speaker of the House's office. Gardener stood next to Speaker Frederick Gillett (R-MA) as he signed the landmark amendment. The following day, she and Maud Wood Park flanked Vice President Thomas Marshall as he signed it as president of the Senate. Reporters, photographers, and even motion picture cameras caught these historic scenes. Countless women and several suffrage groups had fought long and hard for the amendment, and it was certainly not a given that any of them would be invited to the signing ceremony or that there would even be such a ceremony. But Gardener made sure that there was a momentous event to mark this achievement and that the members of the NAWSA Congressional Committee were there.[88]

Gardener saw her work as NAWSA's "Diplomatic Corps" as the culmination of her life's efforts to secure full autonomy for women. And she had personified the NAWSA Congressional Committee for nearly ten years. To members of Congress, to the White House, and to most

Gardener standing next to the Speaker of the House as he signed the Nineteenth Amendment with the gold pen she purchased just for the ceremony.

Gardener (right) and Maud Wood Park (left) as Vice President
Thomas Marshall signed the Nineteenth Amendment.

suffragists, Gardener had been, since 1910, NAWSA's most constant presence in Washington. As she reflected in her 1919 vice chairman's report, "I have served upon the Congressional Committee longer than has any other person, having been a member from the first, and having served under every chairman."[89] In the years before there was an active Congressional Committee, Gardener attended congressional hearings related to suffrage and circulated reports across the country. Gardener was there when the first NAWSA Congressional Committee office opened in 1913, and she would be the one to turn off the lights when Suffrage House closed its doors.

What made Gardener's tenure on the Congressional Committee so critical was her ability to infiltrate various settings that had long been closed to women and befriend male allies and adversaries alike, realizing that the boundary between the two was often arbitrary and tenuous. Gardener also possessed remarkable personal magnetism and social intuition—gifts forged over a long, varied life surmounting many obstacles in many places. In dealing with powerful men, Gardener relied on some old-fashioned womanly charm and a certain degree of dissemblance—skills practiced for decades on Charles Smart and Selden Day. She prided herself for understanding "human nature," and she harbored no illusions about the men with whom she worked. "The study of human nature in high places is more illuminating than an encyclopedia,—not always disappointing; sometimes inspiring," she proclaimed in her final report to NAWSA. "There are," Gardener granted, "some men of real vision and of lofty aim in Washington political circles today, and there are others whose personality and value to the nation could be poised upon the point of a cambric needle and leave room for a jazz band."[90]

Both Catt and Park credited Gardener's contributions as key to congressional passage. To the extent that NAWSA's Congressional Committee had succeeded, Park claimed, it was due to "Helen Gardener's gift for making and holding friends for the cause and to the influence of her advice and example upon the rest of us."[91] As Park elaborated, "her incomparable service, a service which no one else could possibly have rendered, came in the months when the efforts of the suffragists were centered upon the Congress of the United States. Then her knowledge of men in public life, her familiarity with official custom and legislative procedure, combined with her rare gifts of person and mind and character, made her the most potent factor in securing the passage of the Amendment by the Congress."[92]

Alice Paul, the woman whose agitation had propelled NAWSA to focus on the federal amendment and caused the nation to take notice, was livid that she and the other NWP leaders had been excluded from the signing ceremony. Even fifty-five years later, she wondered how Helen Hamilton Gardener had made her way to the "pen ceremony." In her oral history, Paul reflected on how suffrage history might have turned out differently had Gardener aligned with her, rather than NAWSA. "This one lady's resignation really hurt us," Paul recalled, "because if she had kept on with the publicity, we would have been much better off."

Paul then lamented that Gardener had been invited to the pen ceremony. According to Paul's recollection, the president "invited a group of women to be there for this ceremony of the proclamation, and among others was this Mrs. Helen Gardener, whom we hadn't seen all these intervening years . . . not one of us was invited or recognized in any possible [way], but all these opponents, every person who was there [had been] an opponent!"[93]

Gardener certainly opposed picketing, but she was no opponent of the federal amendment. Paul surmised, incorrectly, that Gardener and Wilson had bonded over a shared commitment to the state-by-state strategy, when, in fact, Gardener had been nudging the president to champion the federal amendment all along. Such efforts necessarily occurred behind closed doors and were never covered by the press, so only White House staff, individual congressmen, and Gardener's NAWSA colleagues understood the scope of her diplomatic work. For years Paul had led valiant protests outside the White House, not realizing that Gardener had used her opposition to Paul's tactics to charm her way inside.

The rivalry between Paul and Gardener, a microcosm of the larger organizational rift between the NWP and NAWSA, permeated the suffrage movement in its final years and continued to shape suffrage history as both sides—following directives from their leaders—took credit for the victory, distorting a more impartial understanding of the movement and obscuring the myriad contributions of women of color. Though their tactics contrasted, both the NWP and NAWSA contributed vitally to the passage of the Nineteenth Amendment, just as both organizations bear responsibility for the movement's failure to work with and for black women.

As it turned out, the pen ceremony was just the beginning of a much longer struggle over the meaning of women's suffrage. For the next five years, Gardener's efforts to secure the movement's history and her own personal legacy would prove nearly as challenging as getting the Nineteenth Amendment through Congress.

16

Our Heroic Dead

*Our Arlington is scattered over America in graves little
recognized, where lie the great commanders of our bloodless
revolution that freed womankind—Lucretia Mott, Ernestine
Rose, Julia Ward Howe, Lucy Stone, Elizabeth Cady
Stanton . . . and hundreds of others many of whose very names
would be new to many of you but whose deeds were mighty.*

—HELEN HAMILTON GARDENER, 1925

O
N JUNE 10, 1919, less than a week after congressional passage of
the Susan B. Anthony Amendment, Helen Gardener presided
over a victory celebration at Suffrage House. Carrie Chapman Catt
looked "queenly" in a "most Frenchy creation" of white lace with pink
rosebuds while a string trio serenaded members of Congress, congressional wives, and White House representative Joseph Tumulty.[1] The
party also marked the closure of Suffrage House. After the festivities,
Catt instructed Maud Wood Park to let Gardener have the best type-
writer so that she could continue on as NAWSA's one-woman office in
the nation's capital, working out of her home, while the rest of NAWSA
leadership turned to ratification.[2]

As the sole remaining NAWSA officer in Washington, Gardener's

Gardener, Carrie Chapman Catt, and Maud Wood Park at Suffrage House, where they helped make Catt's "Winning Plan" a reality.

first challenge was to figure out where to place the many relics displayed at Suffrage House, including a portrait of Susan B. Anthony. Gardener, a student of history and a writer, understood the importance of narrative and of memory. And she knew firsthand that the stories we tell about our past shape our present and our future. Gardener feared, rightly as it turned out, that the memories of women's rights activists were already being lost and that if the nation failed to commemorate them, future generations of women would be hampered in their efforts to participate in democracy and attain true equality.

Two days after the victory celebration, Gardener secured an introduction from the White House and reached out to William Ravenel at the Smithsonian to inquire about donating the portrait of Susan B. Anthony, along with other suffrage memorabilia. The previous year, the Smithsonian had turned down the very same portrait, noting "this is of no *special* interest to the Division of History. It might be regarded as a *desirable* addition to our series of portraits of noted Americans but exhibition space is in demand."[3] But when Gardener's letter arrived just days after congressional passage of the Susan B. Anthony Amendment, a portrait of its namesake now seemed more appealing. Curator William Holmes claimed that the painting was not of sufficiently good quality to adorn the National Portrait Gallery but suggested that it would fit in the Smithsonian's History Museum, since "Miss Anthony's life forms a most interesting episode in the history of woman's place in the nation."[4]

In addition to the portrait, many of the movement's most prized artifacts had come into the hands of Lucy Anthony, Susan's niece, and Lucy's partner, Anna Howard Shaw, the former NAWSA president, whose health was failing (she would die later that summer, several months before she would have been eligible to cast her vote).[5] The two women asked Gardener to find a suitable home for their collections. By the end of June, Gardener had compiled the items for the Smithsonian donation, including: the red shawl that Susan B. Anthony wore at suffrage conventions, a copy of the 1848 Declaration of Sentiments and Resolutions, the table on which Stanton drafted the declaration, photos of the congressional signing ceremonies, and the gold pen Gardener had purchased for the momentous occasion.[6] Lucy Anthony expressed great hope for the exhibit Gardener was working toward, describing it as "a crowning glory to everything."[7]

From the outset, Gardener insisted that the materials be donated to the Smithsonian, the nation's museum. Catt had initially asked her to place the Anthony portrait at the Corcoran Gallery, but in a rare instance, Gardener ignored Catt's directive, convinced that her plan was far better.[8] Gardener explained to her colleagues the unique mission of the Smithsonian, as a branch of American government, to house historical collections and the nation's most important artifacts. Seeing a portrait of the signing of the Declaration of Independence had convinced her that the Smithsonian "was the place for our Thomas Jefferson's portrait." Gardener's aim was to make suffrage history tangible to the thousands of "men, women and children, from all over the world, now and in the future" who would come to the Smithsonian to "gather inspiration and to come close to the great leaders of America, through seeing what they looked like, and what they were, and what they had, and what they did."[9]

Gardener detailed very specific conditions to Ravenel about the placement and significance of the relics she donated. She insisted that "above all else this exhibit be kept all together in the most suitable place you can prepare for it, because these few things that we now have sent will not be the end of the historic collection to show the origin and development of the greatest bloodless revolution ever known,—the achieving of political and financial independence by one-half of the people without a drop of blood being shed."[10]

And she emphasized, more than once, that the exhibit represented the work of the National American Woman Suffrage Association. The exhibit must never mention or be associated with, she instructed, the National Woman's Party.[11] Like the partisan version of events outlined in the *History of Woman Suffrage* a generation earlier, Gardener's exhibit presented the history of one faction as the history of the movement.[12] Thus, it came to pass that months before the Nineteenth Amendment was ratified, the Smithsonian debuted a new exhibit titled "An Important Epoch in American History." Gardener told Anthony that she did not think they could have had better placement within the museum. But more privately she confessed to Park that "I do think that the Smithsonian matter will never be finished and done right until they understand it and its meaning better than they do now."[13] Men seemed to understand history in terms of war; they underestimated and mis-understood the stakes and sacrifices of women's "bloodless revolution."

Organizing this exhibit was of great interest to NAWSA leaders, who all along had been concerned not just about attaining the vote but also about securing women's place in American history. To help increase awareness of the movement's significance, NAWSA distrib-uted copies of the *History of Woman Suffrage* to libraries across Amer-ica and to civic leaders. In 1909, the NAWSA education committee had surveyed history and civics textbooks to see how women were rep-resented. The committee chair had ruefully reported that textbooks conveyed the point that "this world has been made by men and for men."[14] Leaders hoped that familiarity with movement history would curb this tendency.

Gardener was especially keen for male leaders to have a copy of the *History of Woman Suffrage*. She asked Lucy Anthony to send her an autographed set of all volumes so that she could present it to Wilson to help him understand the "meaning and the magnitude of the suffrage work." Gardener regretted that men did not grasp the significance of the women's bravery and accomplishment. "We must see that [the men] do," she implored Anthony. "That work is ahead of the younger ones. Make 'history' tell the truth and make people visualize that history! Yes, it is a big job—but not as big" as the job of the women who had won the vote.[15]

WHILE STRATEGIZING ways to memorialize suffrage history, financial worries and ill health continued to plague Gardener. In August 1919, she retreated to Harrisonburg, Virginia, where "there is not a thing to do but eat and sleep." She hoped to return rested and "fit to do some useful work later on."[16] In addition to coordinating the exhibit at the Smithsonian and representing Carrie Chapman Catt at various events in D.C., Gardener continued to conduct diplomacy for NAWSA, which most often meant enlisting President Wilson's help in the ratification effort.[17] She delighted in such work, but it did not pay the bills. She confessed to Maud Wood Park that she had been ignoring various invitations and fundraising appeals from suffrage colleagues because she did not dare "exploit my flattened pocketbook." Rather than say no outright, she preferred to "draw into my shell a bit farther, even if they all think me rude and indifferent to the good things I'd love to do if I could."[18] She worried that she would have to sell her home and reluctantly accepted two cash gifts from Park.

Increasingly, Gardener's White House lobbying focused on securing prominent appointments for women. Having women employed by government at the highest levels would, she hoped, signal the larger changes in American life that suffragists imagined the vote portended. Throughout the fall and winter of 1919–1920, Gardener repeatedly contacted the White House to suggest women for various commissions and to gently scold when they were not appointed. As she explained to Tumulty in one characteristic letter, "I was afraid that the appointing power would not think of [a woman] at all—nor what such 'recognition' would mean to the women of the country at such a time. Think it over, oh, you clever political actor."[19]

Then, on October 2, 1919, President Wilson suffered a debilitating stroke that incapacitated him for the rest of his term. At the time, the White House obscured the gravity of his impairment, but historians now concur that his wife, Edith, and top staff, including Gardener's close friends Tumulty and Rudolph Forster, essentially ran his presidency for its final months.[20] Gardener focused her redoubled lobbying efforts on them. By the end of 1919, twenty-two states had ratified the Susan B. Anthony Amendment, but no women had been appointed to high-level government positions.

Gardener hosted Selden Day's nephew Sam Day and his cousin Paul Kester, the playwright, along with Maud Wood Park for Christmas. In a letter to Kester, she hailed Park as "my closest woman friend" because "she understands and has no place in her large and fine soul for the purely conventional."[21] Now in her late sixties, Gardener, ever young at heart, felt most at home around people decades her junior. Friends described her as the "personification of eternal youth."[22]

Gardener spent most of January and February 1920 working on the Smithsonian exhibit and then traveled to Chicago for the final NAWSA annual convention, which celebrated the legacies of pioneers Susan B. Anthony and Anna Howard Shaw. She gave a moving tribute to Anthony, and she updated members about the NAWSA exhibit at the Smithsonian, which she characterized as a "shrine" to the "great women leaders of liberty and civilization on the same broad basis accorded to men." She expressed her fond hope that this exhibit would be "an object of reverence and education to all American womanhood."[23]

The Chicago convention formally transitioned NAWSA chapters into chapters of the League of Women Voters (LWV), to be led by Maud Wood Park. Though voter education remained the top priority, the LWV also pledged to prioritize the eradication of prostitution, through the equal punishment of johns, and "venereal disease control."[24] Newly minted women citizens sought, among other things, to obliterate the sexual double standard and craft laws governing sexual relations from the perspective of women.

But Gardener did not spend much time discussing the institutionalization of her once radical ideals. She was too busy trying to obtain appointments for women in government. She took multiple breaks from the meetings to communicate with Tumulty. During the convention, rumors circulated that the president was thinking of appointing Mrs. Edith Owen Stoner, a D.C. suffragist aligned with the Southern states' rights faction, to the three-person U.S. Civil Service Commission. This would be by far the highest-ranking position ever held by a woman, rating just under a cabinet secretary.[25] NAWSA members considered the potential selection of Stoner to be a "calamity," according to Gardener, because she was "totally unfit" and "has no woman following nor influence." Before Gardener left for Chicago, she had met with Tumulty and Forster to discuss this post and felt confident that they agreed with her suggestions (Park and Mary Foy, of California) and that "there was not the slightest danger" of Stoner getting the prized nomination.[26] She urged Tumulty to please send her an assurance that these rumors were mistaken.[27]

Earlier in his presidency, Wilson had bowed to pressure from racist Southern senators and segregated the civil service, which had been the backbone of the black middle class in Washington for decades. Besides enlisting the federal government in support of segregation, this move also relegated African American employees to substandard working conditions and severely limited opportunities for advancement.[28] In appointing a woman civil service commissioner, the Wilson White House again sought to manifest an ideological position through government jobs. Such a high-profile post would acknowledge the contributions of female government workers (a category that had ballooned during the war) and publicly recognize white women's new civic status.

Gardener may not have realized that in addition to Stoner, several other women, themselves highly aware of the symbolism of the civil service appointment, had been actively lobbying the White House for the position. But Gardener's favor within the Oval Office stood out among the rest. In March of 1920, the president (or, more accurately, Tumulty and Forster acting on his behalf) nominated not Park or Foy but Gardener herself to Theodore Roosevelt's former seat on the Civil Service Commission, making her the highest-ranking and highest-paid woman in federal government. Overnight, Gardener became a national symbol of what it meant, finally, for (white) women to be full citizens.[29]

NEWSPAPERS AROUND THE COUNTRY devoted front-page coverage to this historic appointment, and suffragists cheered Gardener as the "right woman honored."[30] Many articles focused on the larger meaning of Gardener's new job. The *Atlanta Journal Constitution* observed that Gardener's nomination "marks the beginning of a new era of feminine activities in the government of our country." The civil service functioned, as Gardener explained, like a civilian branch of the military, fulfilling all the tasks that the government needed to function. Employing over 660,000 people, more than the army and navy combined, the civil service was the biggest employer in the world. Because about two-fifths of these employees were now women, the consensus was that it was only fitting for a woman to sit on the commission. Emphasizing the discrepancy between Gardener's diminutive stature and the enormity of the task at hand, several news accounts reported that, seated behind her stately desk, Gardener's feet did not touch the ground. She had to bring in a footstool.[31]

Gardener felt thrilled and daunted by the opportunity. She wrote to Wilson to thank him for placing his trust in her, noting that "all our lives we have heard of the 'office seeking the man' but it is something quite new in our experience for the office to seek the woman." Her first impulse, she confessed, was to ask him to withdraw her name, but "upon thinking it over I realize that since women are now, for the first time, to enter fully into the benefits of American citizenship, they must not refuse to take up such duties as are laid upon them." She understood that she alone would not be held accountable for her work. Rather, the "women of the country . . . will be on trial until I shall have proved myself efficient in this important and vital work."[32]

In more private letters to Paul Kester, she admitted that she felt "rather scared" by the "*big* job." She knew she "must not fail."[33] She told Wilson and Kester that her nomination had come "out of the clear sky," but she must have realized that throughout the many months she had been lobbying the White House to appoint women to prominent posts, she had also been lobbying for herself. She revealed to Tumulty that she suspected the idea to nominate her had originated in his "fertile brain" and that, after having dedicated her life to women's rights, she felt very fortunate to have the opportunity to "complete some of the work I dreamed of and began very many years ago." She promised to "do her level best."[34]

After being unanimously approved by the Senate, Gardener was sworn in as commissioner on April 13, 1920. That very day she began her first full-time paying job since she had worked as a teacher in San-

*At age sixty-seven, Gardener was sworn in as the
highest-ranking woman in U.S. history.*

dusky nearly fifty years before. But before Gardener could fully settle
into her new position, she had some vital NAWSA diplomacy to complete. During the spring of 1920, NAWSA leaders believed that either
Delaware or North Carolina would become the thirty-sixth and final
state to ratify the Nineteenth Amendment, so Gardener remained in
regular contact with Tumulty and Forster about ways the White House
could expedite the ratifications and thwart pending legal challenges,
just as she had done regarding congressional passage.[35] Neither North
Carolina nor Delaware ratified, though, and the governors of Vermont
and Connecticut refused to call special sessions of their legislatures.
The only chance to ratify in time for women to vote in the 1920 election, then, was Tennessee.

The Tennessee state legislature was not in regular session, so ratification would require the governor to call a special session, which he
initially refused to do because he claimed that constitutional amendments had to be approved during regular sessions. Gardener implored

Tumulty to get President Wilson to intervene. Wilson asked the Department of Justice to issue a report on the question. Once the department determined there was no constitutional basis for the Tennessee governor's refusal, Wilson urged him to call a special session, which he did in August.[36] As Carrie Chapman Catt, Alice Paul, and suffrage allies and opponents from across the country assembled in Nashville for the ratification session, Gardener was tasked with keeping a handle on things in Washington.

Anti-suffragists vowed to pursue various legal challenges that would prohibit the Nineteenth Amendment, once ratified by thirty-six states, from being signed into effect by the secretary of state. As the Tennessee vote drew near, Gardener waited by the phone for word of passage so that she could ferry the news to the secretary of state before any countersuits could be filed.[37] The Tennessee legislature ratified the amendment on August 18, and after various protests and recounts, the governor sent the official certificate to Washington on August 24. Gardener, the solicitor general, and Secretary of State Bainbridge Colby stayed up all night waiting for the paper to arrive, which it did at 4 o'clock on the morning of August 26. Not wishing to participate in the feuding signing ceremonies planned by Catt, on behalf of NAWSA, and Paul, on behalf of the NWP, Colby signed the proclamation by himself at home.[38] Catt arrived in D.C. by 8 a.m. and met up with Gardener and Park. The trio went first to see the signed document at the Department of State and next to the White House to thank President Wilson.

Though there had been many setbacks and surprises along the way, Catt's "Winning Plan" had succeeded more or less as she had planned. Women in the North and West and white women in the South would be able to vote in the 1920 election. A resident of the District of Columbia, Gardener had no representation in Congress, but she voted for James Cox, the Democratic nominee, for president.[39] He lost in a landslide to Warren G. Harding. As Sen. William Borah of Idaho had predicted, however, black women living in states with racist voter discrimination laws, along with other women of color, would have to wait another forty-five years for the federal government to enforce the Fifteenth and Nineteenth Amendments.

The members of NAWSA celebrated what they considered to be an unquestioned triumph with a "jubilee" at Poli's Theater in Washington on the night of August 26. Gardener and Catt attended, and the next morning Catt took the train to New York City, where women gathered to cheer her at every stop along the way. In Manhattan, Catt was treated to a hero's welcome and another huge victory party.[40] Gardener did not attend the New York events because she had a new job to do.

⎯⎯⎯

THE WORK OF a civil service commissioner was demanding and required Gardener to show up at the office, located on the sixth floor of 1724 F Street and overlooking the White House and Lincoln Memorial, six days a week.[41] Each day, the three commissioners gathered to discuss various appointments, firings, and disputes and come to consensus about how to proceed. They also communicated regularly with the White House—Gardener was appointed the special White House liaison—regarding high-level posts, rule changes, and statute interpretations. Gardener also met regularly with job seekers in her office and represented the Civil Service Commission at various events in D.C. and along the eastern seaboard.

She loved her job and the perks that accompanied it. Describing the work as "fascinating," she found it a "natural follow-up of my past work." She invited Kester to come see her in action at her stately new office, advising, "If they tell you 'she is in a board meeting' you just say loftily 'she asked me to send in my card' . . . strike an imposing tone and wait! I'll come."[42] Bursting with pride, Gardener relayed that she had her own secretary along with a Cadillac and driver at her disposal during the workday. Indeed, one of the reasons that Gardener, now sixty-seven, took the job was because she desperately needed the money. With her

Gardener loved her work as U.S. Civil Service commissioner,
barely missing a day during her five-year tenure.

comfortable salary of $6,500 per year (nearly $85,000 today), she paid
off her and Day's debts, purchased her own car, put her favorite niece
Helen Gardener Crane through college, and bought expensive gifts—
silk scarves, evening gowns, gloves—for her female friends.[43] For the
first time in her life, she "felt safe financially."[44]

To keep her household running smoothly, she and Helen Gardener
Crane welcomed in cousin Mrs. Kate Wyatt, who presided over the
cooking; a male friend of Mrs. Wyatt's; Day's nephew Sam Day, who
drove Gardener around town in her new Dodge; and her secretary,
Rena B. Smith (who went on to become prominent in the civil service
herself). Most nights Gardener came home late from work and went to
bed, but she did make time for her favorite pastimes—women's clubs and
theater. A lifelong theater buff, Gardener invested in the nation's first
all-women theater production company and regularly attended plays in
Washington (her favorite was *Lincoln,* by John Drinkwater, which she
saw at the National Theater at least three times).[45] She actively partici-

pated in events hosted by the Women's City Club of D.C., the League of American Pen Women, and the LWV (she was the first charter member of the D.C. chapter).[46] She also spent a few weeks each year in the Shenandoah Mountains of Virginia and in New York visiting with old friends, including the Ingersoll family.

These were the happiest years of Gardener's life. Thanks to her historic appointment, she returned to the podium as a sought-after lecturer and traveled up and down the East Coast speaking about the importance of women in government.[47] Her earlier letters frequently reference toil, heartache, and how she used humor to stave off the "mad house."[48] After starting her new job, the tone of her letters becomes giddy with excitement and pride. Her position also had a salutary effect on her health; after years of intermittent illness and frequent breakdowns, Gardener barely missed a day of work as commissioner.[49] When she went to the White House one day during President Harding's administration, his secretary said: "I went to the mat for you yesterday, Mrs. Gardener.

With her comfortable paycheck and own home, Gardener finally felt free. This was the last photo taken of her, 1924.

A man undertook to tell me that you are nearly seventy; but I said that if you are a day older than I am—I'm 54—I'd eat my hat." To which Gardener replied, "Then prepare for a diet of felt!"[50]

While she claimed that her top priority was finding the best person for each job, the issues Gardener championed as commissioner were equal pay for equal work and the right of women to work after marriage. She gave many speeches on pay equity and considered it a victory that the Classification Act of 1923 contained the following provision: "In determining the rate of compensation which an employee shall receive, the principle of equal compensation for equal work irrespective of sex shall be followed."[51] She also supported the creation of a Civil Service Advisory Council composed of half men and half women.[52] Over the course of her lifetime, women had increasingly entered business, teaching, and government work, but nineteenth-century prohibitions against married women working remained in effect. Such regulations were often justified by the need to give jobs to returning soldiers or by the argument that it was unfair for one family to draw two paychecks. Gardener did not buy these flimsy excuses and began her campaign with the Postal Service, the nation's largest employer.

"Will you tell me how it came to be the business of Post Master General Payne to regulate the home life and conduct of the wives of his clerks," Gardener demanded regarding a policy put in place back in 1902. What if a wife were a lousy cook, could hire a good cook for $15 per month, and could earn $100 per month herself as a "first class stenographer or book keeper." Who was the Post Master to arbitrarily limit her monthly family income by $85 while at the same time bestowing "indigestion and a constant fear of poverty" among two people who would otherwise be content? To the claim that the government could not employ two members of the same household, Gardener countered that enforcing such a provision would cause "a good deal of hardship to a number of officials whose fathers and sons chance to have an aptitude (or a pull) in the same kind of work." Gardener rejected the "colossal assumption of the masculine mind" that enabled men to "dictate to women how they shall occupy their time and ability the moment they marry; or how much a family may or may not earn." This, she concluded, represented the "bigotry and ignorance of a past age." Gardener's appeals on behalf of married women working garnered tremendous press coverage—one paper celebrated her efforts as a "square deal for the fair sex"—but she would not live to see the full adoption of this far-reaching reform.[53]

In her daily work as commissioner, Gardener excelled. On her six-month anniversary, her two fellow commissioners wrote to President Wilson to applaud him for the wisdom of her appointment, which they described as a "ten strike."[54] And on her third anniversary, the 400 employees at civil service headquarters surprised her with flowers and thoughtful tributes.[55] Throughout her tenure, newspapers across the country profiled her as one of the top women in government and claimed that her appointment heralded women's full participation in the nation's affairs.[56] Gardener gloried in the attention and in the satisfaction of finally becoming the prominent person she had always longed to be—a woman able to shape policy, be quoted in newspapers, and earn a paycheck.

———

BUT, AS ALWAYS, she kept one eye on the next chapter—which she suspected would be the grave. She revised her will, updated the exhibit at the Smithsonian to include a portrait of Elizabeth Cady Stanton, and worked with those who would memorialize Wilson in an ill-fated attempt to ensure that suffrage was included as one of the president's top achievements. She urged Tumulty to highlight in his memoir President Wilson's many efforts to help women to attain the vote, even in the face of the "picketing lunatics."[57] Tumulty did not mention suffrage.[58] Next, she encouraged Ray Stannard Baker, Wilson's official biographer, to "make plain" that Wilson was "the only President who ever turned his hand over to help women in their long struggle for emancipation— the only bloodless revolution ever fought."[59] With a few notable exceptions, history has not made plain the full spectrum of Wilson's efforts regarding suffrage.[60]

If presidential historians would not remember suffrage, Gardener hoped at least that younger women would. In what would be her last public speech, at the NAWSA "Looking Backward" luncheon in April 1925, Gardener delivered a poignant plea to remember the brave women who had led the bloodless revolution. With an uncharacteristically raspy voice, the only indication of her declining physical condition, Gardener began her speech, movingly titled "Our Heroic Dead." First she announced that merely calling the roll of the movement's deceased leaders would take more than her allotted time. But she was tempted to do so because so many of the pioneers' names were unfamiliar to "the workers of today." Most of their struggles already seemed distant. Gardener reminded her audience that the earliest women's rights leaders faced the "hardest of all tests to bear"—opposition from fathers, husbands, and sons. After having braved public scorn and overwhelming obstacles, these intrepid women faced "constant opposition at their own firesides," a challenge that would have defeated most women, including those gathered at the luncheon. Even though the pioneers "knew that the Promised Land was not for them," they nevertheless "bore the cross for you and for me."

Gardener pondered how suffrage would be remembered and what it would take for women's rights leaders to assume their rightful place among America's exalted statesmen in the nation's collective memory. In the early twentieth century, civic leaders had rushed to honor Civil War veterans, Union and Confederate, in a host of statues, parks, and monuments, including the Lincoln Memorial, which had been dedicated in 1922. And much of Washington's existing landscape paid tribute to the Revolutionary heroes. Gardener contended that Lucretia Mott, Susan B. Anthony, Elizabeth Cady Stanton, and Lucy Stone were "the George Washington, the Thomas Jefferson, the Alexander Hamiltons of the woman's revolution." It did not occur to her to include the names of the pioneering African American women she had encountered, such as Mary Church Terrell and Ida B. Wells. Where were the public shrines to these women? Who would pay homage to them?

Adelaide Johnson's gallery of eminent women never materialized, and she destroyed many of her sculptures before dying in poverty. During the ratification drive, the National Woman's Party commissioned Johnson to create a new bust depicting Anthony, Stanton, and Mott for inclusion in the Capitol building. After tireless lobbying, this statue, known as the Portrait Monument, was displayed in the Capitol rotunda for just one day before being dispatched one floor below to the area known as "the crypt" of the Capitol. In 1996, women raised the money to finally move it upstairs.[61] For decades, the limited Smithsonian exhibit that Gardener had orchestrated remained the principal public tribute to the suffrage movement.

From the "Looking Backward" luncheon ballroom, it was just a short trip to Arlington National Cemetery—"the great city of the dead heroes of many wars," in Gardener's description, where soldiers received "the Nation's homage year after year for what they did to free their fellowmen." Where were the brave soldiers of the women's rights movement commemorated? Gardener observed that "Our Arlington is scattered over America in graves little recognized." Even though the names of suffrage leaders had already become unfamiliar, they were women whose "deeds were mighty, whose courage, patience, and loyal achievement deserve the cross of honor, the distinguished service medal of achievement, and the hero's wreath from us all who should worship at their shrine and keep their memory green." Gardener concluded this, her final speech, by imploring her audience to "not forget and let us not allow our children and our children's children to forget, while we continue to give our cheers for our living heroes, to also mingle our tears for our heroic dead."[62]

Having lived through the Civil War, its reconciliation, and its commemoration, Gardener understood that how the nation remembered something was generally even more important than the thing itself.

She had attended parades for aging soldiers, participated in reunions of the Blue and Gray, and watched as Congress debated how to properly memorialize Lincoln. She wanted a spot for women in these national civic memories and maybe even a place for herself.

———

LESS THAN ONE MONTH LATER, on May 11, Gardener went to the Civil Service Commission for what would be her last day on the job. She was hospitalized for much of the summer. Friends believed she would make a comeback, as she had done so many times before. Gardener, too, thought she might go back to work. But by July, she was busily trying to confirm her replacement on the commission.[63] On July 25, she bid a few friends and her niece Helen Gardener Crane goodnight, closed her eyes, and died in her sleep.

Fulfilling Gardener's wishes, a simple, nonreligious service was held at her home on July 28. Rudolph Forster, President Wilson's former secretary, served as one of the honorary pallbearers, and the offices of the U.S. Civil Service Commission closed in her honor. Carrie Chapman Catt, Maud Wood Park, and her colleagues on the Civil Service Commission gave moving tributes to Gardener's strength of character and lifetime of achievement on behalf of women's rights. A few weeks before, Catt related, Gardener had told her that she was not afraid to die. "I have lived my life as well as I could day by day," Gardener said. "Whenever I am called, I am ready, and I have always been ready." Catt singled out "courage" as her friend's defining characteristic and claimed that Gardener was "one of the most all-round courageous human beings I have ever known." Had she lived in an earlier era, Catt imagined Gardener as a queen fearlessly leading her troops into battle. As it was, she lived at the turn of the twentieth century, "so she gave herself to what was . . . the most controversial of subjects . . . the emancipation of women." To the younger suffragists and career women in attendance, Catt emphasized that their opportunities resulted in part from Gardener's work, especially her brain research: "You who are younger never encountered [arguments like Hammond's]; you found the doors open and now it is a forgotten episode, yet it was Helen Gardener who blazed that trail."[64]

The night after Gardener's funeral, Catt wrote her close friend Mary Gray Peck expressing her loneliness and grief. "Maud and I loved Helen very much, and were proud that neither of us broke down in tears," Catt related. Gardener's grave may have been nearby, but "Washington will never be the same again. She was one of the world's wonders."[65]

Gardener updated her last will and testament on May 26, when she must have sensed that the end was near, leaving detailed instructions regarding the dispersal of her estate, which by then totaled over $17,000.[66] She wanted most of her savings, stocks, and prized possessions to be divided among the two nurses who had cared for her and Day, Rena Smith, Maud Wood Park, and her favorite nieces and great-nieces. When she made a cash gift to a male friend, she specified that the money was to be used for the education of his daughter. She also bequeathed her prized Japanese lacquer, the American flag Day hoisted over Puerto Rico, and other notable items collected during her world travels to the Smithsonian. Years later, more than 2,000 of her lantern slides and photographs wound their way there, too.[67] She also gave an unintentional gift to Helen Gardener Crane, her favorite niece and her will's executor. Crane ended up marrying Barnum L. Colton, the assistant trust officer at the District National Bank, where most of Gardener's assets were held. Throughout her final years, Gardener kept two separate bank accounts: one for Helen H. Gardener and one for Alice C. Day. She even signed her will in both names, lest there be any lingering confusion.

To Carrie Chapman Catt, who Gardener noted was well-off financially, she left her fifty-volume *Chronicles of America*, the series published in 1918 by Yale University Press. With volume titles such as "The Fathers of New England," "The Fathers of the Constitution," and "The

Masters of Capital," these were the grand masculine narratives of American history that Gardener tried to disrupt through her life's work, the Smithsonian exhibit, and her final speech.

Unfortunately for historians, Gardener's will also contained one very lamentable instruction. After clarifying that her nieces and Rena Smith should oversee the closing up of her Lamont Street home, she commanded them "to burn, *unopened*, my letters, personal papers, etc. . . . These are in drawers and boxes in the storeroom and in trunks and in the locked closet." As Gardener explained, "No one would understand many of the letters and papers. . . . Do not leave them to the eyes of strangers."[68] After having spent decades creating "Helen Hamilton Gardener," she wanted to control her narrative into posterity.

THE MOST UNUSUAL ELEMENT of Gardener's will was her stipulation that her brain be removed and transported to Cornell University, in fulfilment of her decades-old promise to provide a specimen of "a woman who thinks." Gardener explained in her will that Burt Wilder, then the director of Cornell's brain collection, had invited her back in 1897 to donate her brain as a representative of women "who have used their brains for the public welfare." After having spent her life "using such brains as I possess in trying to better the conditions of humanity and especially of women," she was happy to grant his request.[69] Because Elizabeth Cady Stanton's children had refused to fulfill their mother's brain bequest, Gardener went to extraordinary lengths to ensure that hers would not be thwarted. She reached out to Cornell's president in 1923 to confirm plans, designated in her will the doctor who would remove her brain (and provided a handsome $1,000 payment for the service), and consulted two different attorneys to make sure that her will was inviolate.[70] Her unusual bequest received intense national press coverage, including multiple front-page stories in the *New York Times*.[71]

By happenstance, Burt Wilder, the brain collection's founder and namesake, had died just a few months before Gardener. Newspapers reported that the two brains would be studied in tandem so that scientists might, for the first time, compare the brains of men and women who had grown up under similar circumstances. Unbelievably, the two brains weighed exactly the same, 1,150 grams, just shy of the mark of greatness set by William Hammond back in the 1880s. Though brain weight had long since been discredited as a marker of intelligence, the finding seemed significant. Dr. James Papez, the director of Cornell's Wilder Brain Collection, examined Gardener's brain in exhaustive detail and published his findings in a fifty-page report. After comparing every fissure, lobe, and curve of Gardener's brain against forty other specimens, male and female, Papez concluded that her brain exhibited sex differences "to a lesser degree" than did other female brains.[72]

Jettisoning the nuance of Papez's study, the *New York Times* headline proclaimed "Woman's Brain Not Inferior to Men's." The ensuing article reported that Gardener's brain "posthumously substantiated her lifelong contention that, given the same environment, woman's brains are the equal of man's."[73] Gardener would have been pleased. In changing her name, obscuring much of her early life, and destroying her papers, she sent the message that she wanted her brain to stand as her final legacy. And, for a little while, it did.

During its heyday, the Burt Wilder Brain Collection contained hundreds of specimens. Today it contains just eight that are identifiable and suitable for display. One of these eight brains is Helen Hamilton Gardener's. Jarred in formaldehyde, her brain floats in a glass case outside the Psychology Department, much like she imagined it might in her poem "Brains at Cornell." But Stanton is not there beside her. The other specimens are all male. Gardener's name is misspelled on the explanatory poster (though it is correct on her jar), and hardly any of the students or faculty who pass by each day know who she was or what prompted her unusual donation. Gardener was confident that once the brain of an educated woman had been studied, no one would dare claim that women's brains differed in any essential way from men's. She would be frustrated, but probably not surprised, to learn that one of

Gardener's brain remains on display at Cornell University, a final testament to her lifelong efforts to establish the equality of women.

the most persistent promises of modern brain research and of each new brain imaging technology has been that it will illuminate, once and for all, the differences between male and female brains.[74]

BEFORE TURNING HER attention to the vote in the 1910s, Helen Hamilton Gardener devoted her life to creating the preconditions that made the vote possible. She encouraged women to question the stories that taught that they were designed by God and nature to be subservient to men; she demanded that scientific studies of sex differences be accountable to evidence and reason, not predetermined by male bias; she insisted that women had more to offer than their virginity and that men be held to the same standard of sexual morality as women. Above all, Gardener hoped to establish that women, too, inherently possessed the unalienable rights to think for themselves, earn their own money, have a say in the laws by which they were governed, and pursue their own happiness. Throughout her seventy-two years, she challenged all the prevailing ideologies of her time, save one: white privilege. Gardener proved a valiant, yet imperfect, soldier in what she called the "greatest bloodless revolution."

In the years following Gardener's death, Rena Smith, her former secretary, hastened to write a biography of Gardener, whom she believed to have been one of the most remarkable women of her era. Likewise, Maud Wood Park strove to make sure Gardener's contributions would not be lost to history, suggesting her for inclusion in a series of historic commemorations and repeatedly writing down her own recollections of Gardener's achievements.[75] Sadly, much like Adelaide Johnson's sculpted bust of Gardener, these efforts were never completed.

No streets, monuments, or historical markers bear her name. But Gardener's ashes are buried next to Selden Day, in lot number 4072, at Arlington National Cemetery, "the great city of the dead heroes of many wars," as she described it. Characteristically, she insisted that both of her names be inscribed on her tombstone. Underneath Day's entry, it reads: "Helen H. Gardener, Born Alice Chenoweth-Day." She had returned to Virginia, as a Chenoweth, after all.

Acknowledgments

IF I LIVE TO WRITE TEN MORE BOOKS, I may not enjoy the process of writing another as much as I have enjoyed this one. Tracing the life of Helen Hamilton Gardener has proved to be a great adventure. In large part, this is due to the many wonderful people I have encountered along the way—from expert archivists, to local history enthusiasts, to Chenoweth descendants, to people who live in the houses where Gardener once lived, to fellow scholars. It is my pleasure to acknowledge and thank the many people who have helped make this book possible. I am only sorry that there is not room enough to name everyone who has helped bring this project to completion.

I first encountered Gardener in 2004 when I was flipping through the pages of old *Popular Science Monthly* magazines in the Perry-Casteñada Library at the University of Texas in Austin. I have been researching, thinking, and writing about her ever since. For encouraging my interest in Gardener at its very earliest phases, I thank Robert Abzug and Janet Davis, who have remained role models, readers, and friends all these years.

For their insightful comments on various conference papers related to Gardener, I want to thank Sarah Richardson, Kathi Kern, Lori Ginzberg, Carolyn Eastman, Catherine Cox, Debbie Weinstein, Elaine Leong, Rosalind Rosenberg, Lilian Calles Barger, Andrea Turpin, and Michelle Nickerson. Several other scholars and friends, including Carla Bittel, Sally Gregory Kohlstedt, Jenna Tonn, Daisy Hernandez, Alicia

Gibson, Matt Hedstrom, and Cindy Klestinec, have read sections of the manuscript at various stages and provided vital feedback. Thanks to Dan Bouk for helping me decipher Charles Smart's insurance company memos and to Barron Lerner for helping me puzzle through Smart's health ailments. I am especially grateful to Stacy Cordery, Mary Frederickson, Monica Schneider, Jim Tobin, Nancy Unger, and Susan Ware for their careful readings of the penultimate draft of this manuscript. It is much improved thanks to their expertise and feedback.

Special thanks are due to the growing band of suffrage historians whom I have come to know over the years and whose work continues to inspire me. Corinne Field, Lisa Tetrault, and Cathleen Cahill have read various drafts, asked probing questions, steered me to new sources, and sharpened my thinking.

My research has been enriched by feedback from colleagues, visiting scholars, and students at Miami University (MU), especially through MU Humanities Center programs. Special thanks to Tim Melley and John Altman. My departmental colleagues in American Studies and History have been very supportive, particularly Jana Braziel, Walt Vanderbush, Wietse de Boer, Cathie Isaacs, and Shawn Vanness. Sheila Sparks in interlibrary loan and Jenny Presnell, humanities librarian, have also provided invaluable assistance.

Together with a faculty improvement leave from Miami University, a Public Scholar Award from the National Endowment for the Humanities (NEH) supported the extended research leave that enabled me to finish this book in time for the 2020 suffrage centennial. (Any views, findings, conclusions, or recommendations expressed in this publication do not necessarily reflect those of the National Endowment for the Humanities.) I also received vital research funding from the 2017 Carrie Chapman Catt Prize for Research on Women and Politics, the MU History Department, and an MU Committee on Faculty Research Summer Research Grant.

I am grateful for many opportunities to share Gardener's life with audiences outside of academia through invited talks and as part of the Ohio Humanities Council Speakers Bureau. My thinking has been shaped by these discussions and by the chasm between what historians know about women's lives and the ways women are presented (or not) in our shared national narratives.

This project required visits both to archives and to places. Over the past several years, I have traveled to all the towns Gardener lived (with the exception of Dardenne, Missouri) to get a feel for her movements and surroundings. These have been my favorite research trips because I have met so many kind people and seen so many beautiful places.

Special thanks to Tom and Ronda Heckel and Sue Chenoweth for so warmly welcoming me to the Chenoweth Family Reunion in Elkins, West Virginia. Jon Egge, who helps coordinate the Chenoweth family website, answered many questions, shared genealogical research, and put me in touch with other Chenoweths. I was thrilled and honored to meet Gardener's closest living descendant, Helen Pate—the grand-daughter of Helen Gardener Crane and Barnum Colton—who gener-ously shared an afternoon and several Gardener artifacts with me.

At the Berkeley County (WV) Historical Society, Todd Funkhous-er's and Howard Butts's encyclopedic knowledge of the area and its people helped me put the Chenoweths in perspective. In Winchester, Virginia, I took advantage of the wonderful resource that is the Stew-art Bell, Jr. Archives Room at the Handley Regional Library. Of the many librarians and local history experts who have helped me trace Gardener, Margaret Hotchner at the Harrisonburg-Rockingham His-torical Society deserves special praise for helping me better understand the Peales and Keezells.

Thanks also to the staff at the Putnam County (IN) Probate Court records office. Diana Brumfield went above and beyond the call of duty to help me in the Genealogy Room of the Putnam County Library, and Larry Tippin, Putnam County historian, steered me to sources that illuminated the history of Greencastle. Wesley W. Wilson, Coordinator of Archives & Special Collections at the DePauw University Archives, shared numerous sources related to Reverend Chenoweth, his sons who attended Asbury, and family friend John Clark Ridpath.

While I have lived in Cincinnati since 2007, I did not previously know much about the history of the city. For teaching me about the Queen City in the 1870s, I am grateful to Anne Delano Steinert and the staff and resources at the Joseph S. Stern, Jr. Cincinnati Room, Cincinnati Public Library. Two librarians at the Cincinnati Public Library offered vital assistance at the early stages of this project. Jeanne Strauss–De Groote acquainted me with the library's local history holdings and put me in touch with genealogical whiz Amy Gresham, who helped me find news reports of Gardener's affair with Smart.

Of the many excellent public libraries this project has given me occasion to visit, the Sandusky (Ohio) Library ranks near the top. Dorene Paul helped me understand Sandusky in the 1870s and alerted me to the photo of Selden Day that appears in this book. Ron Davidson, Special Collections Librarian, enthusiastically answered many questions and provided feedback on the Sandusky section.

An added bonus of Gardener's many letters in the Paul Kester Collection was the opportunity to spend time in the Brooke Astor Reading Room of the New York Public Library. Thanks to Cara Dellatte for sharing her expertise and good cheer. Diane Dias De Fazio in the NYPL's Irma and Paul Milstein Division of Local History steered me to sources about Manhattan at the end of the nineteenth century.

Over many years, everyone in the Library of Congress Manuscript Reading Room has shared valuable knowledge and time, but Bruce Kirby deserves special praise for going out of his way to help me locate sources and for his enthusiasm for this project. Thanks also to Michelle Krowl, Janice Ruth, and Elizabeth Novara, who provided critical advice. Likewise, nearly every staff member at the Schlesinger Library, Radcliffe Institute, has aided this project in some way. It would have been impossible to write this book without the holdings and the expertise of staff at the SLRI. Ellen Shea and Diana Carey merit special mention and thanks.

Thanks to Katherine Crowe, Gina Rappaport, and Carrie Beauchamp at the Smithsonian's National Anthropological Archives for granting access to Gardener's many photos and for allowing me to view the objects—including her prized Japanese lacquer—that she donated. Lisa Kathleen Graddy, curator of political history at the National Museum of American History, kindly shared the files regarding the NAWSA exhibit. Tim Devoogd and Pamela Cunningham, in Cornell's Psychology Department, allowed access to Gardener's brain. Joel Klein, at the Huntington Library, scanned Edward Spitzka's newly received papers for mentions of Gardener, and Jocelyn Wilk, Columbia University Associate Archivist, helped me figure out what Gardener may have studied at Columbia. A very memorable archival trip involved going to the tippy top of the Suffolk County (MA) Courthouse to view the records of the Jones vs. Arena case. Many thanks to Elizabeth Bouvier, head of Archives, Massachusetts Supreme Judicial Court, for facilitating that request. Thanks also to Roderick Bradford, current editor of *The Truth Seeker*, for alerting me to the digitized editions of this valuable resource.

The people who live in the houses where Gardener once resided— in Sandusky, on 82nd Street in Manhattan, and at 1838 Lamont Street in Washington—have been unbelievably generous in opening up their homes to me: Ezell and Sharon Smith, George Beane, Louis Eby, Matthew Hall, Francesca, and Arthur. Thank you all.

Valuable research for various aspects of this project was completed by Brooks Tucker Swett, Sheila Dean, Chris Calcia, and two undergraduate associates at Miami University—Kate Ely and Heather Burich. Eric Adler provided professional genealogical assistance.

Of the many people who helped this book go from proposal to a bound copy, Natalie Dykstra and Stacy Cordery merit special mention for their guidance and for providing encouragement when I needed it most. Once I had the proposal (almost) in order, Geri Thoma at Writers House agreed to take me on. Her sage advice and enthusiasm has made all the difference. For steering this project from proposal to book, I thank Geri, Andrea Morrison, and the team at Writers House. Working with Alane Salierno Mason at W. W. Norton is a dream come true. Eternal thanks to Alane for seeing the potential in this project, for her insightful editorial advice, and for so willingly answering my myriad questions—big and small, day and night—along the way. It has also been a joy to work with William Willis, Mo Crist, and everyone at Norton.

Heartfelt thanks to the many friends who have hosted me, indulged me, and supported me, especially Maggie Dickenson, Kinda Serafi, Aine Zimmerman, Vera Soper, Kimberly Jones, Kerith Spicknall (and the Dr. Moms), Kristen Folzenlogen, Mary Frederickson, Elisabeth Horany Carrell, Amanda Diekman, Michael Link, Monica Schneider, and my tennis friends, including Jen Vatter and Laura Micciche.

Words cannot adequately express my gratitude to my parents, Ray and Kay Hamlin, who enthusiastically receive my daily calls and text updates, who have provided childcare for many trips, who have read and offered feedback on the entire manuscript, and whose unconditional love has enabled me to pursue my dreams.

My two children, Ruby and Elias, have grown up with this project and do not remember a time before it. They have sustained me at all times with their presence, love, and humor. My husband, Michael Christner, has supported me in this and all my endeavors, even when it means many trips and late nights. I thank my family from the bottom of my heart for their patience, love, and encouragement over the course of this project and always.

Finally, I want to thank Helen Hamilton Gardener for living such a bold and interesting life and for sharing it with me these past several years.

A Note on Sources

<hr />

THE ARTHUR AND ELIZABETH SCHLESINGER LIBRARY on the History of Women in America, Radcliffe Institute, Harvard University (SLRI) holds three separate collections of Helen Hamilton Gardener's papers. Her letters to Edward Spitzka are in Helen H. Gardener Papers, 1902–1909, A/G218b; some of her suffrage correspondence can be found in the Helen Hamilton Gardener Papers within the Woman's Rights Collection (WRC); and her 1907 diary, will, and other personal papers are cataloged as Helen Hamilton Gardener Papers. The correspondence between the SLRI and Gardener's heirs regarding her personal papers can be found in her accession file, RG XVIII, Series 2.1, box 23, SLRI. Another terrific source at the Schlesinger has been Rena B. Smith's unpublished biography of Gardener, which is in the Edna Lamprey Stantial Collection.

The National Anthropological Archives (NAA) at the Smithsonian Institution holds the nearly 2,600 photographs and lantern slides Gardener took on her world travels. Lot 98 contains the 1,500 lantern slides (along with notecards from her "Ourselves and Other People" lecture series); lot 97 contains more than 1,000 additional images. Many of these are viewable online through the NAA website.

Besides Gardener's own papers and photographs, the most important sources for this book came from Woodrow Wilson's papers and Adelaide Johnson's papers, both held at the Manuscript Division, Library of Congress (LOC). Wilson's correspondence regarding suffrage and with suffragists was mostly—but not entirely—archived as Case File 89, which corresponds to series 4, boxes 112–116 and microfilm reels 209–210. There are related Gardener materials in the papers of Edith Wilson, Joseph Tumulty, Rudolph Forster, and Wilson's biographer Ray Stannard Baker, all housed at the Library of Congress. I also searched the collections of all the members of Congress with whom Gardener corresponded. The most revealing of these letters are in the John Sharp Williams papers, chronological correspondence folders, at the Library of Congress.

There is extensive material regarding Gardener in the National American Woman Suffrage Association (NAWSA) Collection, including a few folders specifically on Gardener, chronological folders, and the records of the NAWSA Congressional Committee. These materials are housed at the Manuscript Division, Library of Congress, and also available via microfilm, as are the papers of the National Woman's Party, which detail Gardener's involvement in the 1913 suffrage procession. The papers of individual suffrage leaders contain some Gardener correspondence and references, especially the papers of Maud Wood Park (Library of Congress and SLRI) and Carrie Chapman Catt (Manuscripts and Archives Division, New York Public Library, NYPL). There are also several personal letters from Gardener to Paul Kester, Selden Day's cousin, in Kester's papers at the NYPL. When I found more than one copy of a letter, citations are to the original.

In addition to manuscript collections, I learned a great deal about Gardener from her voluminous writing—seven books and countless essays. Her books are readily accessible in many university libraries, and her articles can be found in digitized databases or through interlibrary loan. She contributed dozens of essays to (and was regularly profiled in) freethought and reform publications, especially *The Arena*, *Free Thought*, and *The Truth Seeker*, which have all been digitized and made available online courtesy of the International Association for the Preservation of Spiritualist and Occult Periodicals. *Free Thought* is also available via microfilm at the Library of Congress and in hard copy at the New York Public Library.

Before the advent of digitized historical newspapers, it would have been quite impossible to trace Gardener's comings and goings and tell her story. Newspaper databases, including the Library of Congress's Chronicling America (which is free), newspapers.com, and newspaperarchive.com identified hundreds of stories pertaining to Gardener. Genealogical databases, probate records, and local history centers provided important information about Gardener and her relatives.

U.S. government records, including Civil War pension records, military service records, records of the Senate and House Committees on Woman Suffrage, and Civil Service Commission records, were also very helpful in understanding Gardener and the men in her life. These are all housed at the National Archives and Records Administration (the civil service records at the Maryland branch, the rest at the D.C. branch).

This book is inspired by and indebted to the pioneering work of generations of historians of women's rights and woman suffrage, including: Aileen Kraditor, *The Ideas of the Woman Suffrage Movement 1890–1920* (New York: Columbia University Press, 1965); Eleanor Flexner and Ellen Fitzpatrick, *Century of Struggle: The Woman's Rights Movement in the United States* (Cambridge: Harvard University Press, 1959, 1975, rev. 1996); Ellen Carol DuBois, *Feminism and Suffrage: The Emergence of an Independent Women's Movement in America, 1848–1869*, with new preface (Ithaca, NY: Cornell University Press, 1978, 1999), and *Woman Suffrage and Women's Rights* (New York: New York University Press, 1998); Nancy Cott, *The Grounding of Modern Feminism* (New Haven: Yale University Press, 1987); Rosalyn Terborg-Penn, *African American Women in the Struggle for the Vote* (Bloomington: Indiana University Press, 1998); Marjorie J. Spruill Wheeler, *New Women of the New South: The Leaders of the Woman Suffrage Movement in the Southern States* (New York: Oxford University Press, 1993); Jean H. Baker, *Sisters: The Lives of America's Suffragists* (New York: Hill and Wang, 2005); and Ann D. Gordon, who led the team at Rutgers University that collected and published the six-volume *Elizabeth Cady Stanton and Susan B. Anthony Papers* (and the microfilm edition) and who has published numerous other related volumes.

Notes

Abbreviations

AHS	Anna Howard Shaw
AP	Alice Paul
CCC	Carrie Chapman Catt
HBS	Harvard Business School
HHG	Helen Hamilton Gardener
HOWS	*History of Woman Suffrage*
JSW	John Sharp Williams
LOC	Library of Congress
MP	Mary Phillips
MWD	Mary Ware Dennett
MWP	Maud Wood Park
NAA	National Anthropological Archives, Smithsonian Institution
NARA	National Archives and Records Administration
NAWSA	National American Woman Suffrage Association
NWP	National Woman's Party
NYPL	New York Public Library
PK	Paul Kester
SLRI	Schlesinger Library, Radcliffe Institute, Harvard University
WRC	Woman's Rights Collection
WW	Woodrow Wilson

Preface

1. HHG, "Elizabeth Cady Stanton," *Woman's Tribune*, November 21, 1902, 1; reprinted in *Free Thought*, January 1903, 3–10.

2. Maud Wood Park (MWP), "Remember the Ladies," 78, MWP Papers, box 15, Manuscript Division, Library of Congress, Washington, DC (LOC); MWP, notes for more "Rampant Women," 13, National American Woman Suffrage Association (NAWSA) Collection, reel 37, LOC; "Four Factors" in Maud Wood Park, "Hasty Summary of Congressional Work written in reply to Mrs. Inez Hayes Irwin's inquiry," copy, NAWSA reel 37, LOC.

3. Catt remarks, HHG funeral booklet, HHG Papers, Arthur and Elizabeth Schlesinger Library on the History of Women in America, Radcliffe Institute, Harvard University (SLRI).

4. HHG, "Our Heroic Dead," copy in Edna Lamprey Stantial Collection, box 5, SLRI.

1. A Chenoweth of Virginia

1. Details about the Chenoweth family ancestry from Richard C. Harris and Shirley D. Harris, *The Chenoweth Family in America: Some Descendants of John Chenoweth b. 1682*, 1994, 9–10, 347. Supporting records regarding John Chenoweth's home and slave ownership at Berkeley County Historical Society, Martinsburg, WV.

2. Harris, *The Chenoweth Family in America*, 360. John Chenoweth will recorded in Putnam County, Indiana, September 7, 1864, Will Record Book, 380, Putnam County Probate Office, Greencastle, IN.

3. Throughout her life, Gardener claimed that her novel *An Unofficial Patriot* was the true story of her family's life ("only the names are changed"). Since no letters survive from this period of her life, my impressions of her childhood are largely drawn from this novel and supporting public records. Quote from *An Unofficial Patriot* (Boston: Arena Publishing, 1894), 7–8.

4. Robert Abzug, *Cosmos Crumbling: American Reform and the Religious Imagination* (New York: Oxford University Press, 1994).

5. HHG, *Unofficial Patriot*, 36–37.

6. *Minutes of the Methodist Episcopal Church*, vol. III, covering the years 1829–1845 (New York: T. Mason and G. Lane).

7. Nancy B. Hess, "The Heartland 'Rockingham County,'" compiled for Rockingham County Extension Homemakers, October, 1976, 329–330. Copy residing at Harrisonburg-Rockingham Historical Society.

8. Works Progress Administration, Articles from Rockingham County, The Peale Homestead, 1936, 302–303. Copy residing at Harrisonburg-Rockingham Historical Society.

9. *Harrisonburg Rockingham Register*, June 18, 1885, 1. The article references the earlier trial.

10. In the Harris *Chenoweth* genealogy book and elsewhere, the Chenoweth

marriage is dated 1836, as is the birth of their first child Bernard. But official records at the Rockingham County Historical Society date their marriage to 1838. It is possible that Bernard was also born in 1838 (birth records were not officially kept in Virginia until the 1850s) or, less likely, that Bernard's birth predated their marriage.

11. Rev. W. M. Ferguson, *Methodism in Washington, District of Columbia* (Baltimore: The Methodist Episcopal Book Depository, 1892), 147.

12. Kate Masur, *An Example for All the Land: Emancipation and the Struggle over Equality in Washington, D.C.* (Chapel Hill: University of North Carolina Press, 2010).

13. HHG, *Unofficial Patriot*, 84, 70.

14. HHG, *Unofficial Patriot*, 90–91.

15. Putnam County Deed Books, Boatright Files, and Plat Books, Putnam County Public Library, Genealogy and Local History Room. 1860 Census enumerates the Chenoweths in house number 264.

16. Historical description from Putnam County Interim Report, 1982, Putnam County Public Library, Genealogy and Local History Room. In the 1860 census, John Chenoweth listed his occupation as "gentleman"—a rarity in Putnam County.

17. Jesse W. Weik, *Weik's History of Putnam County, Indiana* (Indianapolis: B. F. Bowen, 1910), 70.

18. Professor Joseph Tingley writing about his arrival in Greencastle in 1843, quoted in John J. Baughman, *Our Past, Their Present: Historical Essays on Putnam County, Indiana* (Greencastle, IN: Putnam County Museum, 2008), 30.

19. Report from *Western Christian Advocate*, November 9, 1854, quoted in Baughman, 31.

20. HHG wrote about her educational experiences in "Mental Panics," *Free Thought*, May 1889, 210–214; also described in biographical sketch of HHG, dated June 18, 1923, in National American Woman Suffrage Association (NAWSA) collection, reel 36, LOC.

21. *The McGuffey Readers: Selections from the 1879 Edition*, edited and with an introduction by Elliott J. Gorn (New York: Bedford/St. Martin's, 1998).

22. HHG, "English as She Is Writ," *The Truth Seeker*, March 26, 1887, 197.

23. "Report on Memoirs, Rev. Alfred Griffith Chenoweth [obituary]," *Minutes of the Thirteenth Annual Session of the North-Western Indiana Conference of the Methodist Episcopal Church* held at Delphi, Indiana, September 7, 1864 (Cincinnati: R. P. Thompson Printers, 1864), 18–19.

24. HHG, "How Mary Alice Was Converted," in *Pushed by Unseen Hands* (New York: Commonwealth Company, 1892). HHG told Adelaide Johnson that this was an autobiographical story. Adelaide Johnson Sitting Notes, eighteenth sitting, Friday, September 3, 1902, Adelaide Johnson Collection, box 71, Manuscript Division, Library of Congress, Washington, DC (LOC).

25. Profile of HHG, May 20, 1891, *Louisiana Review*, 2.
26. "A Kansas Soldier," *Leavenworth Times*, April 29, 1869, 2.
27. "Sex in Brains," *Los Angeles Herald*, July 16, 1897, 6.
28. Susan Jacoby, *Freethinkers: A History of American Secularism* (New York: Metropolitan Books, 2004), 41–42. Paine published the work in three stages, the last in 1807.
29. HHG, *Unofficial Patriot*, 148.
30. 1860 census; Indiana Ministers List, North, Northwest, South, and Indiana Conferences, 1800–1900, 135. Copy residing at DePauw University Archives.
31. Eleventh sitting of Helen Gardener, August 19, 1902, Adelaide Johnson Collection, LOC.
32. Baughman, *Our Past, Their Present*, 88–89.
33. "Bravest of the Brave," *St. Joseph Gazette-Herald* (St. Joseph, MO), August 10, 1900; "The Story of a Consul," *Hartford Courant*, May 3, 1869, 1; Harris, *Chenoweth Family in America*, 365–366; *Unofficial Patriot*, 159–179; *History of Buchanan County*, 1881, reprinted by Seward W. Lilly, 1973, courtesy of the Northwest Missouri Genealogical Society, 464–465. For a history of "bloody Kansas," see Nicole Etcheson, *Bleeding Kansas: Contested Liberty in the Civil War Era* (Lawrence: University of Kansas Press, 2004).
34. "The Story of a Consul," *Hartford Courant*, May 3, 1869, 1.
35. HHG, *Unofficial Patriot*, 178. Bernard, William, and Alfred's military service is substantiated in their Combined Military Service Records (CMSR), National Archives and Records Administration, Washington, DC (NARA).
36. Betty Skeens, "'Crossroad Farm' Was Civil War Hospital," *Daily News Record* (Rockingham County, VA), Dec. 19, 1992, 1. The home is now on the National Register of Historic Places. For a history of the war in the Shenandoah Valley, see Edward Ayers, *In the Presence of Mine Enemies: The Civil War in the Heart of America, 1859–1864* (New York: W. W. Norton, 2004).
37. Lyon Gardiner Tyler, ed., *Encyclopedia of Virginia Biography*, vol. III (New York: Lewis Historical Publishing Company, 1915), 356.
38. Dialogue from *An Unofficial Patriot*, 190–191. Gardener claimed to have verified her account with documents in the War Department. President Lincoln's extant correspondence does not contain letters to or from Chenoweth, but there are several letters from Gov. Morton recommending various Indiana citizens for war posts in line with Gardener's description of events.
39. HHG, *An Unofficial Patriot*, 225.
40. "Report on Memoirs, Rev. Alfred Griffith Chenoweth [obituary]," *Minutes of the Thirteenth Annual Session of the North-Western Indiana Conference of the Methodist Episcopal Church*, 18–19.
41. Bernard Chenoweth to General Grant, September 11, 1862, Bernard Chenoweth, CMSR, NARA.
42. "The Story of a Consul," *Hartford Courant*, May 3, 1869, 1; *Brown County World* (Hiawatha, KS), August 17, 1882, 3.

43. Harris, *Chenoweth Family in America*, 370; Alfred Hamlin Chenoweth, Pension file and CMSR, NARA.

44. HHG, *An Unofficial Patriot*, 312.

45. "Letter by Helen H. Gardener," *The Truth Seeker*, August 13, 1887, 515.

46. HHG to Paul Kester, July 31, 1912, Paul Kester Papers, Box 6, Manuscripts and Archives Division, New York Public Library. Astor, Lenox, and Tilden Foundations (NYPL).

47. Alfred Chenoweth obituary, *Minutes of the Northwestern Indiana Conference*, 18–19, Special Collections, DePauw University, Greencastle, IN.

48. HHG to Paul Kester, July 31, 1912, Paul Kester Papers, NYPL.

49. Harris, *Chenoweth Family in America*, 367. William Chenoweth Pension File and CMSR, NARA.

50. Nancy Woloch, *Women and the American Experience*, 5th ed. (New York: McGraw Hill, 2011), 189–195; Joan Hoff, *Law, Gender, and Injustice: A Legal History of U.S. Women* (New York: New York University Press, 1991).

51. Putnam County Probate Records, book 6, pp. 139–142; book 7, 302. Putnam County Office, Greencastle, IN.

52. S. M. Watson, "Growing Up on Dardenne Prairie," *History of St. Charles County, Montgomery and Warren Counties, Missouri*, 459; Bill Schiermerier, "Dardenne Prairie's First Settlers," *Cracker Barrel*, vol. 3, no. 507, December 5, 1984. All courtesy of the St. Charles (MO) County Historical Society.

53. St. Charles County Marriage Records, Courtesy of the St. Charles County Historical Society.

54. Putnam County Probate Records.

55. Watson, "Growing Up on Dardenne Prairie."

56. "A Kansas Soldier," *Leavenworth Times*, April 29, 1869, 2.

57. "The Late U.S. Consul in Canton," reprinted from *Harper's Weekly*, *Leavenworth Times*, September 12, 1870, 3.

58. Harris, *Chenoweth Family in America*, 366; "Caroline V. Chenoweth," *Brooklyn Daily Eagle*, November 30, 1890, 19.

59. HHG recounts "a case she knew herself," but does not name names, in HHG, *Men, Women, and Gods and Other Lectures* (New York: Truth Seeker, 1885), 4.

60. The 1870 census lists Alice as the third resident of Julia and Frederick Hatcher's household in Dardenne.

2. The Best and Cheapest Teachers

1. Some later biographical entries of HHG claim that she also graduated from high school in Cincinnati. She does not appear in the city directory until

1872, but it is possible she attended high school before enrolling in the normal school.

2. D. J. Kenny, *Illustrated Guide to Cincinnati and the World's Columbian Expositions, Ohio at the Great Columbian Exposition* (Cincinnati: Robert Clarke and Co., 1893), Cincinnati Public Library.

3. Robinson Atlas of Cincinnati, 1883–1884, plats 5–7; Sanborn Fire Insurance Map, 1904; the artificial limb companies have multiple ads in the 1872 *Stranger's Guide to Cincinnati*, hotel handbook. All courtesy of Cincinnati Public Library.

4. HHG, "Vicarious Atonement," *Men, Women, and Gods and Other Lectures* (New York: Truth Seeker, 1885), 52.

5. Nancy Woloch, *Women and the American Experience*, 5th ed. (New York: McGraw Hill, 2011), 270.

6. J. David Hacker, "A Census-Based Count of the Civil War Dead," *Civil War History* 57, no. 4 (December 2011): 307–348.

7. Beecher quoted in Woloch, *Women and the American Experience*, 127.

8. Carl F. Kaestle, *Pillars of the Republic: The Common School Movement and American Society, 1780–1860* (New York: Hill and Wang, 1983).

9. According to Cincinnati city directories at the Cincinnati Public Library, she later moved around the corner to 420 Baymiller Street.

10. Kenny, *Illustrated Guide to Cincinnati and the World's Columbian Expositions*.

11. "History of the Normal School" by Delia Lathrop (written for 1876 Centennial Exhibition), included in Henry A. Ford and Kate B. Ford, *History of Cincinnati, Ohio* (Cleveland, OH: Williams and Co, 1881), 194–195; John B. Shotwell, *A History of the Schools of Cincinnati* (Cincinnati: The School Life Company, 1902). Copies residing at the Cincinnati Public Library.

12. Lathrop in Ford, *History of Cincinnati, Ohio*, 194–195.

13. "Normal School Commencement," *Cincinnati Enquirer*, June 21, 1873, 8; Ford, *History of Cincinnati, Ohio*.

14. 1873–1874 Report of the Normal School by Delia Lathrop, for the *Common School Annual Report*, 89–90.

15. Ellen Carol DuBois, *Feminism and Suffrage: The Emergence of an Independent Women's Movement in America, 1848–1869*, with new preface (Ithaca, NY: Cornell University Press, 1978, 1999); Faye Dudden, *Fighting Chance: The Struggle over Woman Suffrage and Black Suffrage in Reconstruction America* (New York: Oxford University Press, 2011); Laura E. Free, *Suffrage Reconstructed: Gender, Race, and Voting Rights in the Civil War Era* (Ithaca, NY: Cornell University Press, 2015).

16. Ellen Carol DuBois, "Overcoming the Compact of Our Fathers: Equal Rights, Woman Suffrage, and the United States Constitution, 1820–1878," and "Taking the Law into Our Own Hands: Bradwell, Minor, and Suffrage

Militance in the 1870s," both reprinted in DuBois, *Woman Suffrage and Women's Rights* (New York: New York University Press, 1998).

17. "Our Lady Teachers," *Cincinnati Enquirer*, December 17, 1876, 9.
18. Lathrop, in Ford, *History of Cincinnati, Ohio*, 194–195.
19. Harris, *Chenoweth Family in America*, 366–368; William Chenoweth Pension File and CMSR, NARA.
20. "Woman's Weakness: An Intimacy That Ended in Shame and Death," *Cincinnati Enquirer*, March 30, 1878, 1; "Naughty Conduct of a Truly Good Man, Punishment Promptly Meted Out," *Cincinnati Enquirer*, August 28, 1873, 2.
21. See, for example, Nina Auerbach, "The Rise of the Fallen Woman," *Nineteenth-Century Fiction* 35 (June 1980), 29–52.

3. A Very Bad Beecher Case

1. Many later biographical entries on HHG state that she taught at the Ohio State Normal School in Columbus, but that school did not exist until 1899. The Sandusky school may have been a branch of the statewide system.
2. Introductory Remarks, *Sandusky Directory* (Sandusky, OH: Printed and published by I. F. Mack and Brother, 1884). Copy residing at the Archives Research Center, Sandusky Library.
3. "First Woman U.S. Civil Service Commissioner Recalls Early Days as Teacher in Sandusky," *Sandusky Star-Journal*, May 22, 1920, 6.
4. Catherine Melville-Milne obituary, *Sandusky Daily Register*, March 12, 1895. Helen M. Hansen, "At Home in Early Sandusky: Foundations for the Future," 1975, 36–37; copy given to the author by Ezell and Sharon Smith, of Sandusky.
5. "Teachers Meeting at the High School," *Sandusky Daily Register*, May 9, 1874.
6. "School Exhibition," *Sandusky Daily Register*, June 26, 1874.
7. Editorial, *The National Teacher, a Monthly Journal of Education*, vol 5, W. D. Henkle, editor and publisher, Salem, OH, 1875, 75.
8. Charles Smart, Twenty-Third Annual Report of the State Commissioner of Common Schools to the General Assembly of the State of Ohio, for the school year ending August 31, 1876 (Columbus: Nevins and Meyers State Printers, 1877), 40. United States Office of Education, 1876.
9. "Appointment of Teachers," *Sandusky Daily Register*, June 29, 1875.
10. "New Year's Day Open Houses," *Sandusky Daily Register*, January 1, 1875.
11. "Sex in Brains," *Los Angeles Herald*, July 16, 1897, 6; she also relates this story in the preface to *Facts and Fictions of Life* (Chicago: Charles H. Kerr, 1893); Ely Van De Warker, "The Relations of Women to Crime," *Popular Science Monthly*, November 1875.

12. Charles E. Frohman, *Sandusky's Editor* (Columbus: Ohio Historical Society, 1972).

13. "Notes and Comments," *Sandusky Daily Register*, April 28, 1876; "Board of Education," *Sandusky Daily Register*, April 29, 1876.

14. "Classical and English School," *Gallipolis Journal*, August 14, 1862; Ohio Biographical Sketches, 1876, ancestry.com.

15. Marriage license, ancestry.com; "School Opening Delayed," *Gallipolis Journal*, September 18, 1862.

16. Advertisement in *Jackson Standard*, February 21, 1867. Substantiated in Ohio Biographical Sketches, 1876, ancestry.com.

17. *Gallipolis Journal*, June 18, 1874.

18. *The Stark County Democrat* (Canton), September 3, 1874, 4; *Hamilton Examiner*, September 3, 1874, 2.

19. "Commissioner Smart," *Sandusky Daily Register*, July 21, 1876; the article in the original newspaper on file in Sandusky has been torn out, but it was reprinted in full in the *Highland Weekly News*, August 10, 1876, 1.

20. "Notes and Comments," *Sandusky Daily Register*, July 17, 1876.

21. *Springfield Republic* quote reprinted in "Commissioner Smart," *Sandusky Daily Register*, July 21, 1876; reprinted in full in the *Highland Weekly News*, August 10, 1876, 1.

22. Ohio News Items, *Cambridge* (OH) *News*, June 8, 1876, 1.

23. *The Eaton Democrat*, February 17, 1876.

24. HHG, "Men, Women, and Gods," in *Men, Women, and Gods and Other Lectures*, 11.

25. HOWS, vol. 3, 22; quoted in Lisa Tetrault, *The Myth of Seneca Falls: Memory and the Women's Suffrage Movement, 1848–1898* (Chapel Hill: University of North Carolina Press, 2014), 99.

26. In the Adelaide Johnson Sitting Notes, the preface to *Is This Your Son, My Lord* and the essay "The Fictions of Fiction," HHG describes her fiction as "true" and/or as autobiographical, sometimes even explaining who was who.

27. "Sex in Brains," *Los Angeles Herald*, July 16, 1897, 6; she also relates this story in the preface to *Facts and Fictions of Life* (Chicago: Charles H. Kerr, 1893); she tells a slightly different version in "Welcome Lady Commissioner," *The Federal Employee* 5, no. 24 (June 1920): 8.

28. Carol Groneman, *Nymphomania: A History* (New York: W. W. Norton, 2001).

29. Rachel P. Maines, *The Technology of Orgasm: Hysteria, the Vibrator, and Women's Sexual Satisfaction* (Baltimore: Johns Hopkins University Press, 1999).

30. Linda Gordon, *The Moral Property of Women: A History of Birth Control Politics in America*, rev. ed. of *Woman's Body, Woman's Right: Birth Control in America* (Urbana: University of Illinois Press, 2007), 74.

31. Thomas Laqueur, "Orgasm, Generation, and the Politics of Reproductive

Biology," *Representations: The Making of the Modern Body, Sexuality and Society in the Nineteenth Century* (Spring 1986): 1–41.

32. Helen Lefkowitz Horowitz, *Rereading Sex: Battles over Sexual Knowledge and Suppression in Nineteenth-Century America* (New York: Knopf, 2002), 360 –385.

33. Andrea Tone, *Devices and Desires: A History of Contraceptives in America* (New York: Hill and Wang, 2001), 3–5; Gordon, *Moral Property of Women*, 66.

34. Tone, *Devices and Desires*, 14–17.

35. "Commissioner Smart's Denial," *Jackson Standard*, August 10, 1876.

36. Reprinted in the *Sandusky Daily Register*, July 31, 1876.

37. *Sandusky Daily Register*, July 31 and August 7, 1876.

38. *Sandusky Daily Register*, August 7, 1876.

39. "School Commissioner Smart," *Jackson Standard*, August 17, 1876, 2.

40. *Jackson Standard*, August, 24, 1876.

41. *Jackson Standard*, September 7, 1876.

42. *Jackson Standard*, August 3, 1876.

43. Debby Applegate, *The Most Famous Man in America: The Biography of Henry Ward Beecher* (New York: Penguin Random House, 2007); Richard Wightman Fox, *Trials of Intimacy: Love and Loss in the Beecher-Tilton Scandal* (Chicago: University of Chicago Press, 1999); Barbara Goldsmith, *Other Powers: The Age of Suffrage, Spiritualism, and the Scandalous Victoria Woodhull* (New York: Harper Perennial edition, 1999).

44. *Sandusky Daily Register*, August 30, 1876.

45. From the *Chillicothe Herald*, reprinted in the *Jackson Standard*, October 16, 1876.

46. HHG, preface, *Is this Your Son, My Lord?* (Boston: Arena Publishing, 1890), xvi.

47. HHG, *Is this Your Son, My Lord?*, 38.

48. I have not found a marriage certificate after extensive research. Even if they did marry, it would not have been legal because Smart had not divorced Lovenia.

4. Purgatory and Rebirth

1. Orvin Larson, *American Infidel: Robert G. Ingersoll* (New York: Citadel Press, 1962), 117–120.

2. Quoted in Larson, 120; Susan Jacoby, *The Great Agnostic: Robert Ingersoll and American Freethought* (New Haven, CT: Yale University Press, 2013), 59–61.

3. Larson, *American Infidel*, 129–132.

4. Lecture as reprinted, Robert Ingersoll, *The Liberty of Man, Woman and Child* (New York: C. P. Ferrell, 1915), 396.
5. *Sandusky Daily Register,* July 7, 1877, 1.
6. *Cincinnati Enquirer,* July 26, 1877, 5; *Jackson Standard,* August 9, 1877.
7. *Sandusky Daily Register,* February 13, 1877.
8. "Ohio Legislature," *Cincinnati Enquirer,* January 16, 1878, 2; "Notes and Comments," *Sandusky Daily Register,* January 22, 1878.
9. "From Schools to Insurance," *Cleveland* (OH) *Leader,* December 20, 1883, 11.
10. *Jackson Standard,* January 24, 1878.
11. HHG, *Men, Women, and Gods,* 107.
12. As reported in *Jackson Standard,* January 24, 1878; 1878 Detroit City Directory, 80. Copy residing at Burton Historical Collection, Detroit Public Library.
13. Ann C. Chenoweth probate records, case 1447, Lincoln County (MO), Recorder of Deeds Office.
14. *Gallipolis Journal,* August 19, 1880; *Highland Weekly News* (Hillsboro), December 16, 1880, 3.
15. Detroit city directories listed the names of teachers in each school, but there are no teachers named Smart or Chenoweth between 1878 and 1883.
16. HHG, "The Fictions of Fiction," in *Facts and Fictions of Life* (Chicago: Charles H. Kerr, 1893), 34.
17. HHG, "Historical Facts and Theological Fictions," *Men, Women, and Gods,* 108.
18. Various ads in *Detroit Free Press,* March–April 1878, and in 1878 Detroit City Directory, 80; "Results of Tontine Policies," *Detroit Free Press,* December 19, 1879, 1.
19. "Sayings and Doings," *Detroit Free Press,* November 4, 1881, 1; "Triumph of the Equitable," *Detroit Free Press,* January 20, 1883, 1.
20. George W. Stark, *City of Destiny: The Story of Detroit, Illustrated* (Detroit: Arnold-Powers, 1943), 393–411. Copy residing at the Burton Historical Collection, Detroit Public Library.
21. "Griswold Hotel," www.historicdetroit.org accessed April 1, 2019; Griswold Hotel postcards, Detroit Historical Society online collections.
22. Ann C. Chenoweth Probate Records, case 1447, Lincoln County (MO), Recorder of Deeds Office.
23. HHG, "Vicarious Atonement," *Men, Women, and Gods,* 70. She also describes a son who broke his mother's will and charged her for room and board in HHG, "Men, Women, and Gods," *Men, Women, and Gods,* 4.
24. "Ingersoll," *Detroit Free Press,* November 9, 1882. She may have secured an introduction to Ingersoll via a man named James Redpath. Redpath served as Ingersoll's manager for a time, and in the 1850s, he published a Free Soil newspaper at the Kansas-Missouri border, through which he may have known Bernard Chenoweth. John R. McKivigan, *Forgotten Firebrand: James Redpath and the Making of Nineteenth-Century America* (Ithaca, NY: Cornell University Press, 2008).

25. HHG Speech at dedication of Ingersoll Portrait, Washington Law Library, May 8, 1921, reprinted in Rena B. Smith unpublished biography, Edna Stantial Collection, SLRI; M. T., "Helen H. Gardener: How her Successful Advent into Literature Began," *Sunday News* (Wilkes-Barre, PA), March 24, 1895, 14, widely syndicated; "Col. Ingersoll Done in Soprano," New York *Sun*, January 7, 1884, 1, states she showed him her writing "three years ago."

26. Several volumes of *Ladies Repository* are listed in Ann Chenoweth's estate inventory.

5. Ingersoll in Soprano

1. "Chickering Hall," New York City Chapter of the American Guild of Organists, www.nycago.org accessed April 1, 2019.

2. "From Schools to Insurance," *Cleveland* (OH) *Leader*, December 20, 1883, 11.

3. Alexander Hamilton lineage mentioned in Charles Smart entry, Ohio Biographical Sketches, 1876, ancestry.com.

4. HHG Speech at dedication of Ingersoll portrait, Washington Law Library, May 8, 1921, reprinted in Rena B. Smith unpublished biography, Edna Stantial Collection, SLRI; M. T., "Helen H. Gardener: How Her Successful Advent into Literature Began," *Sunday News* (Wilkes-Barre, PA), March 24, 1895, 14, widely reprinted.

5. T. H. MacQueary to Rena B. Smith, November, 16, 1926, reprinted in Rena B. Smith unpublished biography, Edna Stantial Collection, SLRI.

6. Ad, *New York Times*, January 6, 1884, 11. Foreshadowing later problems in documenting her life, the *New York Times* ad misspelled her name as "Gardner," which is how the press reported on her for much of the year.

7. "Chickering Hall," New York City Chapter of the American Guild of Organists, www.nycago.org accessed April 1, 2019.

8. Adelaide Johnson Sitting Notes, tenth sitting, August 18, 1902, Adelaide Johnson Collection, box 71, Manuscript Division, Library of Congress, Washington, DC (LOC). Manager named in ad, *Buffalo Commercial*, February 9, 1884, 2.

9. Ingersoll introduction reprinted in HHG, *Men, Women, and Gods*, x.

10. "Ingersoll in Soprano," *Chicago Tribune*, April 28, 1884, 8. This is a description of her Chicago lecture, but she gave the same speech and wore the same black velvet dress throughout this tour.

11. *New York World* review, reprinted "Christianity Crushed," *Detroit Free Press*, January 12, 1884, 3; *Buffalo Sunday Morning News*, February 10, 1884, 4.

12. "Ingersoll in Soprano," *Chicago Tribune*, April 28, 1884, 8.

13. HHG, "Men, Women, and Gods," *Men, Women, and Gods*, 14, 24.

14. *Wheeling Daily Intelligencer* (WV), April 30, 1884, 2. For more on women and American atheism, see Annie Laurie Gaylor, ed., *Women Without*

Superstition—"No Gods-No Masters": The Collected Writings of Women Freethinkers of the Nineteenth and Twentieth Centuries (Madison, WI: Freedom from Religion Foundation, 1997); Evelyn A. Kirkley, Rational Mothers and Infidel Gentlemen: Gender and American Atheism, 1865–1915 (Syracuse, NY: Syracuse University Press, 2000).

15. "Christianity Crushed," Detroit Free Press, January 12, 1884, 3.

16. "Col. Ingersoll Done in Soprano," New York Sun, January 7, 1884, 1; subsequent headlines shortened this to "Ingersoll in Soprano."

17. Leigh Eric Schmidt, Village Atheists: How America's Unbelievers Made their Way in a Godly Nation (Princeton, NJ: Princeton University Press, 2016); Susan Jacoby, Freethinkers: A History of American Secularism (New York: Metropolitan Books, 2004).

18. Ad, Buffalo Commercial, February 9, 1884, 2; Syracuse Sunday Courier, reprinted in The Truth Seeker, March 1, 1884, 137; "Wahle's Opera House," Buffalo Commercial, February 9, 1884, 3; "Miss Gardner's Lecture," Buffalo Commercial, February 11, 1884.

19. "Ingersoll in Soprano," Chicago Tribune, April 28, 1884, 8.

20. George E. Macdonald, Fifty Years of Freethought: Story of the Truth Seeker from 1875 (New York: Truth Seeker, 1929); Schmidt, Village Atheists; Roderick Bradford, D. M. Bennett: The Truth Seeker (Prometheus Books, 2006); Bradford, "D. M. Bennett: The Nineteenth Century's Most Controversial Publisher and American Free-Speech Martyr," Freethought Today 24 (May 2007).

21. HHG, "Lecture by the New Male Star," The Truth Seeker, April 2, 1887, 213.

22. Ads in The Truth Seeker began running August 2, 1884, 496.

23. The Truth Seeker, September 13, 1884, 584–585.

24. The Truth Seeker, September 20, 1884, 596.

25. The Truth Seeker, October 11, 1884, 654.

26. "Miss Gardener on the Characteristics of Her Sex," The Truth Seeker, January 24, 1885, 50–51.

27. Quoted in Lucy N. Colman, "Mrs. Slenker's Ghost-hunting," The Truth Seeker, May 9, 1885, 292.

28. E. A. Stevens, "Miss Gardener Scolded," The Truth Seeker, March 20, 1886, 183.

29. U.C. to Editor, The Truth Seeker, October 22, 1887, 683.

30. "Miss Gardener in Her Own Behalf," The Truth Seeker, May 30, 1885.

31. Lucy N. Colman, "Mrs. Slenker's Ghost-hunting," The Truth Seeker, May 9, 1885, 292. Theresa Sobieski also defended HHG, The Truth Seeker, May 16, 1885, 315.

32. Joanne E. Passet, Sex Radicals and the Quest for Women's Equality (Urbana: University of Illinois Press, 2003).

33. For example, Ingersoll refused to defend his friend D. M. Bennett, publisher of The Truth Seeker, when he was arrested for distributing a free love pamphlet, as described in D. M. Bennett to Ingersoll, May 31, 1879,

Ingersoll-Farrell family papers, Manuscripts and Archives Division, New York Public Library. Astor, Lenox, and Tilden Foundations (NYPL).

34. HHG, "Our Great Dead—Ingersoll," *Free Thought*, September 1899, 507–509.

35. Dedication page, Helen Hamilton Gardener, *Men, Women, and Gods and Other Lectures* (New York: Truth Seeker, 1885).

36. HHG to Paul Kester, October 26, 1921, Paul Kester Collection, NYPL.

37. "Helen Gardener on Social Heresies," *The Truth Seeker*, November 27, 1886, 755–756.

38. "Miss Gardener on the Characteristics of Her Sex," *The Truth Seeker*, January 24, 1885, 50–51. She signed off from St. Louis in this letter, *The Truth Seeker*, October 11, 1884, 654.

39. Alfred Hamlin Chenoweth, Pension File, National Archives and Records Administration (NARA); Harris, *Chenoweth Family in America*, 370.

40. C. S. Smart to H. B. Hyde, January 3, 1885, Equitable Life Assurance Society of the United States records, carton 12, Baker Library, Harvard Business School (HBS).

41. Samuel Putnam letter, *The Truth Seeker*, April 11, 1885, 229.

42. HHG, "Nobody Wants to Play," *The Truth Seeker*, April 25, 1885, 261; HHG, "St. Louis Clergymen Aroused," *The Truth Seeker*, August 1, 1885, 487.

43. HHG, "Library Vandals," *The Truth Seeker*, November 28, 1885, 758.

44. Samuel Putnam, "Advance Notice," *The Truth Seeker*, September 5, 1885, 573.

45. HHG, "Historical Facts and Theological Fictions," in *Men, Women, and Gods*, 93.

46. "The Albany Convention," *The Truth Seeker*, August 22, 1885, 536.

47. E. A. Stevens, Editorial Notes, *The Truth Seeker*, May 19, 1888, 313.

48. *Chicago Times* review, reprinted in *The Truth Seeker*, February 13, 1886, 110.

49. W. M. Chandler, Book Review, reprinted in the *The Truth Seeker*, November 21, 1885, 750.

50. A.B.B. (Antoinette Brown Blackwell), Book notices, *The Truth Seeker*, December 26, 1885, 830–831.

51. Zoa Topsis, "'Men, Women, and Gods' in Court," *The Truth Seeker*, May 26, 1888, 326.

52. Amarala Martin, Book Notices, *The Truth Seeker*, February 6, 1886, 94.

53. Review from *The Sociologist*, reprinted in *The Truth Seeker*, January 9, 1886, 30.

54. "Miss Gardener's Address to the Clergy and Others," *The Truth Seeker*, January 2, 1886, 6. She described her daily mail in a profile written by Emily Bouton for the *Toledo Blade*, reprinted in *The Truth Seeker*, May 23, 1891, 323.

55. HHG to Dr. E.F. Strickland, Feb. 6, 1894, Strickland Autograph Collection, SLRI.

56. Editorial notes, *The Truth Seeker*, March 20, 1886, 185.

6. The Cultured Poor

1. HHG, "Rome or Reason," *North American Review* 143 (November 1886), 519–521.
2. HHG to Edward Eggleston, April 26, 1886, Century Company Records, Manuscripts and Archives Division, New York Public Library. Astor, Lenox, and Tilden Foundations (NYPL).
3. Larson, *American Infidel*, 189, 210, 226–227, 264.
4. Society Page, *New York Daily Graphic*, February 12, 1887, quoted in Larson, 229; "at homes" described in Larson, 229–235.
5. "A Party at Colonel Ingersoll's," *The Truth Seeker*, February 26, 1887, 133.
6. Cora Rigby, "The Diplomatic Corps," *Woman Citizen*, May 2, 1925, 12–13.
7. HHG Speech at dedication of Ingersoll Portrait, Washington Law Library, May 8, 1921, reprinted in Rena B. Smith unpublished biography, Edna Lamprey Stantial Collection, SLRI.
8. "Clubs with Queer Names," *The Sun* (NYC), December 9, 1888, 3.
9. Christine Stansell, "When the Village Broke Free," *New York Times*, June 2, 2000, E29.
10. "The Liberal Club," *The Truth Seeker*, February 19, 1887, 117.
11. Correspondence, *The Truth Seeker*, September 24, 1887, 620.
12. Editorial Notes, *The Truth Seeker*, April 9, 1887, 233.
13. Blurb, *The Truth Seeker*, December 10, 1887, 791.
14. New York City directories (at NYPL and on microfilm at LOC) list the couple as follows: 1887 A. C. Smart home, W 82nd Street; 1889, A. C. Smart home, 185 W 82nd Street; 1890, A. C. Smart "clerk," at 185 W 82nd Street; 1891, A. C. Smart home, 185 W 82nd Street; 1892 A. C. Smart home, 185 W 82nd Street; 1893–1894, Alice C. Smart, 165 W 82nd Street. C. S. Smart business ("ins.") listed at 120 Broadway in the 1887, 1889, 1890, 1891, 1892, 1893–1894 directories. According to maps and images, 185 and 165 W 82nd Street refer to the same building. Later HHG addresses in NYC are taken from the addresses she wrote on her correspondence.
15. She describes one such stroll, HHG, "Men, Women, and Books," *The Truth Seeker*, January 15, 1887, 36.
16. Description of HHG's life in NYC in T. H. MacQueary to Rena B. Smith, November 16, 1926, reprinted in Rena B. Smith unpublished biography, Edna Stantial Collection, SLRI.
17. HHG described her Japanese servants and her disdain for American Christian missionary culture several times, including in her 1886 lecture "Pulpit, Pew, and Cradle," reprinted as a pamphlet (New York: Truth Seeker Publishing Company, 1892), 15–16. Microfilm copy available at Harvard University Libraries.
18. Letter, HHG, *The Truth Seeker*, August 13, 1887, 515.
19. Robert A. M. Stern, Thomas Mellins, and David Fishman, *New York 1880:*

Architecture and Urbanism in the Gilded Age (New York: The Monacelli Press, 1999), 745, 739.

20. HHG, "The Cultured Poor," *Free Thought*, May 1892, 271–276.
21. HHG, "The Boler House Mystery," first published in *The Truth Seeker Almanac 1890*, reprinted in *A Thoughtless Yes* (New York: R. F. Fenno, 1890), 127.
22. HHG, "The Lady of the Club," *A Thoughtless Yes*, 34.
23. HHG, "The Lady of the Club," 35–37.
24. HHG, "The Lady of the Club," 56.
25. "Miss Gardener in the Field," *The Truth Seeker*, July 10, 1886, 436.
26. Stern, 395.
27. Internal memo to Hyde, October 2, 1883, Equitable Life Assurance Society of the United States records (ELAS), carton 12, Baker Library, Harvard Business School (HBS).
28. Internal memo to Hyde, May 31, 1883, ELAS Collection, carton 12, Baker Library, HBS.
29. HHG, "Lawsuit or Legacy," *Popular Science Monthly* 31, July 1887, 339–345.
30. Dan Bouk, *How Our Days Become Numbered: Risk and the Rise of the Statistical Individual* (Chicago: University of Chicago Press, 2015).
31. HHG, "Woman as an Annex," *Facts and Fictions of Life*, 145–147.
32. HHG to Mary Phillips, August 11, 1901, Adelaide Johnson Collection, LOC.
33. HHG, *Men, Women, and Gods and Other Lectures* (New York: Truth Seeker, 1885), 24, 12.
34. HHG, "Pulpit, Pew, and Cradle," 19.

7. Sex in Brain

1. Author email correspondence with Jocelyn Wilk, Columbia University Associate Archivist; Rosalind Rosenberg, *Changing the Subject: How the Women of Columbia Shaped the Way We Think about Sex and Politics* (New York: Columbia University Press, 2004). Barnard College opened in 1889 and offered women the standard curriculum, not a special feminized version.
2. Kimberly A. Hamlin, *From Eve to Evolution: Darwin, Science, and Women's Rights in Gilded Age America* (Chicago: University of Chicago Press, 2014).
3. Elizabeth Cady Stanton, "Woman and the Church," *Lucifer the Light-Bearer*, July 17, 1891.
4. Carla Bittel, *Mary Putnam Jacobi and the Politics of Medicine in Nineteenth-Century America* (Chapel Hill: University of North Carolina Press, 2009).
5. Bonnie Ellen Blustein, *Preserve Your Love for Science: Life of William Hammond, American Neurologist* (New York: Cambridge University Press, 1991).
6. William A. Hammond, "Brain-Forcing in Childhood," *Popular Science Monthly* 30 (April 1887): 731.

7. Hammond, "Brain-Forcing," 731.
8. Hammond, "Men's and Women's Brains," *Popular Science Monthly* 31 (August 1887): 554.
9. For secondary sources on nineteenth-century brain size controversies, see Hamlin, *From Eve to Evolution*; Anne Fausto-Sterling, "A Question of Genius: Are Men Really Smarter Than Women?" in *Myths of Gender: Biological Theories about Women and Men* (New York: Basic Books, 1985): 13–60; and Cynthia Eagle Russett, *Sexual Science: The Victorian Construction of Womanhood* (Cambridge, MA: Harvard University Press, 1989).
10. HHG, "Sex in Brain," *Facts and Fictions of Life*, 104; Duane E. Haines, "Edward Charles Spitzka," American National Biography Online, 2000.
11. HHG, "Sex and Brain Weight," *Popular Science Monthly* 31 (June 1887): 266.
12. Hammond, "Men's and Women's Brains," *Popular Science Monthly* 31 (August 1887): 554–558.
13. HHG, "Sex and Brain Weight," 266–268; Hammond, "Men's and Women's Brains," 554–558; HHG, "More about Men's and Women's Brains," *Popular Science Monthly* 31 (September 1887): 698–700; Hammond, "An Explanation," *Popular Science Monthly* 31 (October 1887): 846.
14. "Sex in Brain," *The Physicians' and Surgeons' Investigator*, June 15, 1888, 6.
15. "Books and Periodicals," *The Truth Seeker*, December 24, 1887, 821.
16. Moncure Conway, "The International Council of Women," *Open Court*, May 3, 1888, 930–931; HHG described herself as "too ill to write" in a February 17 letter published in *The Truth Seeker*, March 3, 1888, 137.
17. HHG, "Mother Superior," poem written in honor of Stanton's eightieth birthday, October 5, 1895, *The Papers of Elizabeth Cady Stanton and Susan B. Anthony*, ed. Patricia Holland and Ann D. Gordon (Wilmington, DE: Scholarly Resources, 1991), reel 34.
18. Lori D. Ginzberg, *Elizabeth Cady Stanton: An American Life* (New York: Hill and Wang, 2009); Ellen Carol DuBois and Richard Cándida Smith, eds., *Elizabeth Cady Stanton: Feminist as Thinker, A Reader in Documents and Essays* (New York: New York University Press, 2007); Kathi Kern, *Mrs. Stanton's Bible* (Ithaca, NY: Cornell University Press, 2001).
19. "The Birth of the ICW," 1957, ICW papers, box 1, Sophia Smith Collection, Smith College, Northampton, MA; quoted in Leila Rupp, *Worlds of Women: The Making of an International Women's Movement* (Princeton, NJ: Princeton University Press, 1997), 15, note 11.
20. Lisa Tetrault, *The Myth of Seneca Falls: Memory and the Women's Suffrage Movement, 1848–1898* (Chapel Hill: University of North Carolina Press, 2014), 148–149.
21. Tetrault, *Myth of Seneca Falls*, 144.
22. Kern, *Mrs. Stanton's Bible*, 103–106.
23. Stanton, *Eighty Years and More: Reminiscences 1815–1897* (New York: T. Fisher Unwin, 1898), 467, 391.

24. HHG letter as quoted in Stanton, *Eighty Years and More*, 392.
25. HHG, *The Truth Seeker*, October 26, 1886. Stanton to Sara Underwood, April 13, 1887, reprinted in Ann D. Gordon, *The Selected Papers of Elizabeth Cady Stanton and Susan B. Anthony: Their Place Inside the Body-Politic, 1887 to 1895*, vol. 5 (New Brunswick, NJ: Rutgers University Press, 2009), 22–23.
26. "Among the Heretics," *The Truth Seeker*, August 27, 1887.
27. Kern, *Mrs. Stanton's Bible*, 106.
28. Stanton to Anthony, March 10, 1887, *Selected Papers*, vol. 5, 9–13; Stanton to Rachel G. Foster, January 12, 1888, *Selected Papers*, vol. 5, 77.
29. Stanton introduction reprinted in the *Woman's Tribune*, April 3, 1887, 4.
30. Tetrault, *Myth of Seneca Falls*, 148–149.
31. Stanton, *Eighty Years and More*, 412–413.
32. "The Women in Politics," *Chicago Tribune*, April 1, 1888, 13.
33. HHG, "Sex in Brain," *Facts and Fictions of Life*, 99.
34. HHG, "Sex in Brain," 123.
35. HHG, "More about Men's and Women's Brains," 699.
36. HHG, "Sex in Brain," 124.
37. Elizabeth Cady Stanton, remarks, *Report of The International Council of Women* (Boston: Rufus Darby Printers, 1888), 431.
38. Stanton, *Eighty Years and More*, 413.
39. Stanton's brain bequest form, Burt Green Wilder Collection, box 2, folder 4, Cornell University Archives. HHG to ECS, July 25, 1887, *The Papers of Elizabeth Cady Stanton and Susan B. Anthony*, ed. Patricia Holland and Ann D. Gordon (Wilmington, DE: Scholarly Resources, 1991), reel 25.
40. HHG to Spitzka, January 29, 1909, Helen H. Gardener Papers, 1902–1909. A/G218b, SLRI.
41. HHG, "Brains at Cornell," *Free Thought*, February 1900, 94–95.
42. HHG, "As a Man Thinketh So Is He," *The Truth Seeker*, November 18, 1893, 726–727. Reprint of her speech delivered at the Science Sermons Society on November 5, 1893.
43. HHG to Miss E. L. Waldo, October 23, 1913, National Woman's Party papers, microfilm, reel 5; Donald L. Haggerty, *National Woman's Party Papers: The Suffrage Years, 1913–1920* (Sanford, NC.: Microfilming Corporation of America, 1981).

8. The Fictions of Fiction

1. In the Adelaide Johnson Sitting Notes, the preface to *Is This Your Son, My Lord*, and the essay "The Fictions of Fiction," HHG described her fiction as "true" and/or as autobiographical, sometimes even explaining who was who.
2. Adelaide Johnson Sitting Notes, thirteenth sitting, Tuesday, August 26,

1902, LOC; Donn Piatt, "A Roman Catholic's View," *The Arena*, January 1891, 244.

3. HHG, Preface to the Second Edition, *Is This Your Son, My Lord?* (New York: R. F. Fenno, 1890), 1.

4. HHG, "The Immoral Influence of Women in Literature," *The Arena*, February 1890, 323.

5. HHG, "Fictions of Fiction," 20.

6. HHG, "Fictions of Fiction," 27, 22–23, 33.

7. HHG, "The Immoral Influence of Women in Literature," 322.

8. HHG, "Time-Lock of Our Ancestors," *Belford's Monthly Magazine*, October 1888, 646–649.

9. HHG, "Time-Lock," 655.

10. HHG, "Fictions of Fiction," 29.

11. "A Thoughtless Yes," *The Truth Seeker*, July 19, 1890, 457.

12. HHG to Moncure Conway, December 9, 1890, Helen Hamilton Gardener Papers, SLRI.

13. "Well Known in Journalism," obituary of Ernest Bernard Chenoweth, *Boston Globe*, May 23, 1897, 2.

14. HHG, "Sex Maniacs," part 1, *Woman's Tribune*, April 9, 1892.

15. HHG, Preface to Second Edition, *Is This Your Son, My Lord?*, iv–v.

16. Adelaide Johnson Sitting notes, twenty-first sitting, Wednesday, September 10, 1902, box 71, Adelaide Johnson Collection, LOC.

17. Sales figures confirmed in Roger E. Stoddard, "Vanity and Reform: B. O. Flower's Arena Publishing Company, Boston 1890–1896, With a Bibliographical List of Arena Imprints," *Papers of the Bibliographical Society of America*, vol. 76, 1982.

18. Emily S. Bouton, Profile of HHG, *Toledo Blade*, widely reprinted, including in *The Truth Seeker*, May 23, 1891, 323.

19. Carrie Chapman Catt eulogy, Gardener funeral booklet, 21–22, Gardener Papers, SLRI.

20. First ad for *Is This Your Son*, in *The Truth Seeker*, November 15, 1890, 736.

21. Ad for *Is This Your Son*, in the *Arizona Republic* (Phoenix), December 17, 1890, 4.

22. Stanton, "A Representative Thinker among Women," *The Arena*, January 1891, 240.

23. Piatt, "A Roman Catholic's View," *The Arena*, January 1891, 244.

24. The *Woman's Tribune*, for example, described the plot as a "sad story of human experience duplicated daily in large cities and aped in the smaller." Reprinted in "New Publications," *The Truth Seeker*, December 13, 1890, 791.

25. HHG, Preface to Second Edition, *Is This Your Son, My Lord?*, xii.

26. "Boston Letter," *The Critic*, March 28, 1891.

27. Trip described in HHG, "As a Man Thinketh So Is He," *The Truth Seeker*, November 18, 1893, 726–727.

28. *The Truth Seeker,* June 27, 1891, 409.

29. Smart to Henry Hyde, October 29, 1891, ELAS collection, carton 12, Baker Library, HBS. Smart paraphrases Hyde's initial letter, but it is not in the archive.

30. "Memo to Mr. Hyde," November 2, 1891, ELAS Collection, carton 5, Baker Library, HBS.

31. "A Meatless Feast," *New York Times,* March 16, 1892, 2.

32. Adelaide Johnson Sitting Notes, tenth sitting, August 18, 1902, Adelaide Johnson Collection, LOC.

33. Stoddard, "Vanity and Reform."

34. Ages cited by HHG numerous times, supported by Mary E. Odem, *Delinquent Daughters: Protecting and Policing Adolescent Female Sexuality in the United States, 1885–1920* (Chapel Hill: University of North Carolina Press, 1995), 13–15.

35. Stanton, preface, *Pray You Sir, Whose Daughter?* (Boston: Arena Publishing Company, 1892), vi–vii.

36. HHG, *Pray You Sir, Whose Daughter?,* 138.

37. B. O. Flower review, *The Arena,* June 1892, xxxiii–xxxv.

38. Review, *Lucifer the Light-Bearer,* August 12, 1892, 1.

39. *Atchison Daily Globe,* April 10, 1893, 4.

40. T. H. MacQueary describes his memories of them as a married couple in New York in the 1890s in a letter to Rena B. Smith, reprinted in Rena B. Smith unpublished biography, Edna Stantial Collection, SLRI.

41. "Helen Hamilton Gardener Is Smart," widely reprinted, for example, in *Oshkosh Northwestern,* April 21, 1894.

42. Reprinted in *The Truth Seeker,* December 31, 1892, 336–337.

43. "Helen Hamilton Gardener's New Book," *The Truth Seeker,* July 8, 1893, 430.

44. *The Truth Seeker,* December 24, 1892, 820.

45. HHG calling card, HHG Papers, SLRI.

46. HHG to Paul Kester, July 31, 1912, Kester Collection, NYPL.

47. HHG to May Wright Sewall, February 12, 1893, May Wright Sewall Papers, Indianapolis Special Collections Room, Indianapolis Public Library.

48. Society, March 8, 1893, *Omaha Daily Bee,* 4; Adelaide Johnson Sitting Notes, Tenth Sitting, Monday, August 18, 1902, Adelaide Johnson Collection, LOC.

49. Ad for *An Unofficial Patriot, Boston Home Journal,* reprinted in *The Arena,* November 1894, 12.

50. B. O. Flower, "Unofficial Patriot," *The Arena,* June 1894, i–v; review, *Los Angeles Herald,* June 10, 1894.

51. *Pittsburg Press,* July 15, 1894, 6.

52. *Chicago Times* and *Boston Home Journal* reviews, reprinted in ad for *An Unofficial Patriot* in *The Arena,* November 1894, 12.

53. Josephine K. Henry, Profile of HHG, *Courier-Journal* (Louisville), June 17, 1894, 10.

54. For example, *Pittsburg Press*, July 15, 1894, 6.; "Helen Hamilton Gardener," *Blue Grass Blade*, 1894.

55. Josephine K. Henry, *Courier-Journal* (Louisville), June 17, 1894, 10.

9. The Harriet Beecher Stowe of Fallen Women

1. Eric Larson, *The Devil in the White City: Murder, Magic, and Madness at the Fair That Changed America* (New York: Vintage, 2003), 4–5.

2. "Women in Convocation," New York *Sun*, May 28, 1893, 2. May Wright Sewall, ed., *The World's Congress of Representative Women*, vol. 1 (Chicago: Rand McNally, 1894). Contains the entire week's schedule and many excerpts from speeches.

3. Emily Ketcham, "Proceedings of the Twenty-Sixth Annual Convention of the National American Woman Suffrage Association," Washington, DC, 1894, ed. Harriet Taylor Upton, 138.

4. Jennie June, New Cycle column, reprinted in ad for *Facts and Fictions*, in *Lucifer the Light-Bearer*, February 23, 1894.

5. "Fair Sex," *Star Tribune* (Minneapolis), May 28, 1893, 15.

6. HHG, "Eighty Years or More," *Free Thought*, March 1900, 172–174.

7. Helen Lefkowitz Horowitz, *Rereading Sex: Battles over Sexual Knowledge and Suppression in Nineteenth-Century America* (New York: Alfred A. Knopf, 2002), 359.

8. HHG to Dr. E. F. Strickland, February 6, 1894, Strickland Autograph Collection, SLRI.

9. HHG, "The Danger of an Irresponsible Educated Class in a Republic," *The Arena*, August 1892, 311; HHG, "Liberalism: A Symposium," *Truth Seeker Annual* (New York: Truth Seeker, 1889), 33–36.

10. Stanton, *Eighty Years and More*, 417–418.

11. ECS to Matilda Joslyn Gage, October 19, 1889; Ann D. Gordon, ed., *The Selected Papers of Elizabeth Cady Stanton and Susan B. Anthony: Their Place Inside the Body-Politic, 1887 to 1895*, vol. 5 (New Brunswick, NJ: Rutgers University Press, 2009), 214–215.

12. HHG, "Divorce and the Proposed National Law," *The Arena*, March 1890, 413–417.

13. Susan B. Anthony and Ida Husted Harper, HOWS, vol. 4 (NAWSA, 1902), 165.

14. HHG, "Woman as an Annex," *Facts and Fictions*, 129.

15. HHG, "Heredity: Is Acquired Character or Condition Transmittable?," *Facts and Fictions*, 147, 150, 154.

16. HHG, "Moral Responsibility of Woman in Heredity," *Facts and Fictions*, 154.

17. "Helen Hamilton Gardener's New Book," *The Truth Seeker*, July 8, 1893, 430.

18. "Their Enthusiasm Growing," *New York Times*, April 19, 1894; HHG at Woman's Press Club, *The Truth Seeker*, March 31, 1894, 200; "Society," *Atlanta Constitution*, May 6, 1894, 6.

19. "Little One" [HHG] to "Little Phil" [Mary A. Phillips], August 11, 1901, Adelaide Johnson Collection, box 66, LOC.

20. "Little One" to "Little Phil," August 11, 1901.

21. Frederick J. Jones vs. Arena Publishing Company, Supreme Judicial Court for the Commonwealth of Massachusetts, April 16, 1898, 4. Massachusetts Supreme Judicial Court Archives, Boston.

22. "Little One" to "Little Phil," August 11, 1901.

23. Boston city directories, 1895–1897, LOC.

24. *HOWS*, vol. 4, 714; *The Truth Seeker*, January 26, 1895, 56.

25. B. O. Flower, *Reminisces*, 1914, quoted in Roger E. Stoddard, "Vanity and Reform: B. O. Flower's Arena Publishing Company, Boston 1890–1896, With a Bibliographical List of Arena Imprints," *Papers of the Bibliographical Society of America*, vol. 76, 1982, 274.

26. Frances Willard, "Arousing the Public Conscience," Shame of America Roundtable, *The Arena*, January 1895, 199.

27. HHG, "What Shall the Age of Consent Be," The Shame of America Roundtable, *The Arena*, January 1895, 196.

28. HHG, "A Battle for Sound Morality: Final Paper," *The Arena*, November 1895, 402.

29. Quoted in HHG, "Have Children a Right to Legal Protection," pamphlet (Boston: Arena Publishing, 1896), iv.

30. Estelle B. Freedman, *Redefining Rape: Sexual Violence in the Era of Suffrage and Segregation* (Cambridge, MA: Harvard University Press, 2013), 135, 142; see also Hannah Rosen, *Terror in the Heart of Freedom: Citizenship, Sexual Violence, and the Meaning of Race in the Postemancipation South* (Chapel Hill: University of North Carolina Press, 2009).

31. HHG, "A Battle for Sound Morality, II," *The Arena*, September 1895, 1.

32. Mary E. Odem, *Delinquent Daughters: Protecting and Policing Adolescent Female Sexuality in the United States, 1885–1920* (Chapel Hill: University of North Carolina Press, 1995).

33. "To Protect the Girl," *Chicago Tribune*, March 3, 1895, 4, notes that *Pray You Sir* was given out to members of Illinois State Legislature by the WCTU.

34. Based on descriptions of NAWSA convention speeches and resolutions, 1890–1900, in *HOWS*, vol. 4.

35. HHG, "Have Children a Right to Legal Protection," pamphlet (Boston: Arena Publishing, 1896), v.

36. HHG, "The Battle for Sound Morality, I," *The Arena*, August 1895, 353–354

37. HHG, "Heredity and Ethics," in *The First Annual National Purity Con-*

gress, Its Papers, Addresses, and Portraits, ed. Aaron Powell (New York: The American Purity Alliance, 1896), 99, 104.

38. Agnes Scott, "How I Saw Helen Gardener," *Free Thought,* January 1897, 3; revised as Scott, "Helen Hamilton Gardener," *The Woman's Voice and Public School Champion,* July 17, 1897, 3. "Woman's World," *Atlanta Journal,* October 17, 1895.

39. Described in Kern, *Mrs. Stanton's Bible,* 181–185.

40. HHG, "The Woman's Bible," *Free Thought,* June 1896, 400.

41. "Woman's World," *Atlanta Journal,* October 17, 1895.

42. Blurb, *Atlanta Constitution,* October 22, 1895, 6.

43. "A Truly Noble Woman," *Morning Telegram* (Eau Claire, WI), November 2, 1895, 3, widely reprinted.

44. HHG, "Battle For Sound Morality, III" *Arena,* November 1895, 415.

45. HHG, *The Arena,* September 1895, 29.

46. *HOWS,* vol. 4, 240. For an analysis of suffrage in the West, see Rebecca J. Mead, *How the Vote Was Won: Woman Suffrage in the Western United States, 1868–1914* (New York: New York University Press, 2004).

47. "Eminent Suffragists," *The Woman's Journal,* November 9, 1895, 1; HHG, "Shall Women Vote," *The Arena,* December 1895, 73.

10. Wee Wifee

1. HHG, "To the Evergreen Club," *Free Thought,* March 1896, 167; unsigned editorial (likely HHG), "Elizabeth Cady Stanton, the Woman's Bible, and the Resolution Passed at the Woman's National Convention," *Free Thought,* May 1896, 329; HHG, "The Woman's Bible, *Free Thought,* June 1896, 400; HHG "The Negro in the North," *Atlanta Constitution,* June 16, 1896, 4; HHG, "Where Had John Been," *Harper's New Monthly Magazine,* September 1896, 575–576; HHG, "Philosophers Afloat," *The Arena,* August 1896, 480; HHG, "A Bugle Note," *Free Thought,* November 1896, 717.

2. Listed as chairwoman in Mary Lowe Dickinson, "The National Council of Women of the United States," *The Arena,* February 1897, 496; "Woman's Congress Closes at Boston," *Chicago Tribune,* December 5, 1896, 6.

3. Excerpted in "Woman's World," *Weekly Wisconsin* (Milwaukee), January 26, 1897; revised version of "Divorce and the Proposed National Law," *The Arena,* March 1890.

4. Linda Gordon, *The Moral Property of Women: A History of Birth Control Politics in America,* rev. ed. of *Woman's Body, Woman's Right: Birth Control in America* (Urbana: University of Illinois Press, 2007), 55–72, 80–85.

5. LCW, "The Congress of Mothers," *Congregationalist,* February 25, 1897, 8.

6. HHG, "The Moral Responsibility of Woman in Heredity," *National Con-*

gress of Mothers: First Annual Session (New York: Appleton, 1897), 130–147. This is a revised version of the talk she gave under the same title at the 1893 world's fair, published in *Facts and Fictions*. In the 1893 version, she drew on then-popular racialized evolutionary arguments about "civilization" [such as those described by Gail Bederman in *Manliness and Civilization: A Cultural History of Gender and Race in the United States, 1880–1917* (Chicago: University of Chicago Press, 1996)], claiming that "civilized" white people had become less physically hardy than nonwhite races. The 1897 version focuses on education and autonomy.

7. "Mothers are the Rage," *Chicago Tribune*, February 19, 1897, 9.
8. Edward Drinker Cope, "Mrs. Helen Gardener on the Inheritance of Subserviency," *American Naturalist* 31, March 1897, 253–254.
9. Roger E. Stoddard, "Vanity and Reform: B. O. Flower's Arena Publishing Company, Boston 1890–1896, With a Bibliographical List of Arena Imprints," *Papers of the Bibliographical Society of America*, vol. 76, 1982, 279.
10. Frederick J. Jones vs. Arena Publishing Company, Commonwealth of Massachusetts, April 16, 1898, Massachusetts Supreme Judicial Court Archives.
11. "Flower Arrested, C. S. Smart Arrested too," *Boston Post*, February 17, 1897, 1; "Held in $3000 Bail Each," *Boston Daily Globe*, February 18, 1897, 10; *Lowell Sun*, March 17, 1897, 3.
12. Adelaide Johnson Sitting Notes, Day Three, August 9, 1902, LOC.
13. *Lowell Sun*, March 17, 1897, 3.
14. "Helen Gardener Coming to San Francisco," *San Francisco Chronicle*, March 30, 1897, 9; "The Women's Congress," *San Francisco Call*, March 31, 1897, 14.
15. Garfield Safe Deposit Company claim receipt, April 12, 1897, Adelaide Johnson Collection, box 66, LOC.
16. "Mayor Phelan Called on Her," *San Francisco Call*, April 26, 1897, 10.
17. "Sex in Brains," *Los Angeles Herald*, July 16, 1897, 6.
18. Agnes L. Scott, "How I Saw Helen Gardener," *Free Thought*, January 1897, 30–32.
19. "Little One" [HHG] to "Little Phil," [Mary Phillips] August 11, 1901, Adelaide Johnson Collection, LOC.
20. "Helen Gardener Coming to San Francisco," 9.
21. "Read Papers on Mental Training," *San Francisco Call*, April 30, 1897, 5.
22. "Lectures at Stanford," *San Francisco Call*, May 5, 1897, 4; *Stanford Daily*, May 6, 1897, 4.
23. "Helped to Save His Country," *San Francisco Call*, May 8, 1897, 5; "Extracts from the Latest Novel Will Entertain an Audience," *San Francisco Chronicle*, May 6, 1897, 8.
24. Mrs. [Marie] Selden Day reported attending the 1894 Women's Congress, *San Francisco Call*, May 14, 1894, 7. Various documents in Day's Pension File at NARA record her death in March 1895.

25. "The Story of a Patriot," *San Francisco Chronicle*, May 8, 1897, 5.

26. *Oakland Tribune*, May 15, 1897, 19.

27. "Well Known in Journalism," *Boston Globe*, May 23, 1897, 2; "Deaths of the Day," *New York Times*, May 23, 1897.

28. "Descendants of Catherine Chenoweth," genealogical research prepared by Chenoweth family, shared with the author by Jon Egge.

29. "At the Summer Resorts," *Los Angeles Herald*, July 25, 1897, 9, and August 4, 1897, 10.

30. HHG, "How the California Woodpecker Fattens his Pork," *Illustrated American*, March 19, 1898, 355–357; HHG, "A Queen Bee and Her Subjects," *The Arena*, June 1899, 683–699.

31. HHG, "Queen Bee," 683.

32. *Los Angeles Herald*, October 24, 1897, 10.

33. HHG wrote her address as 19 West 38th Street in a letter dated October 29, 1898, published in *Free Thought*, January 1899, 22–26. The 1900 census records their address on W 123rd Street.

34. HHG to Dr. E. B. Strickland, February 6, 1894, SLRI.

35. Herbert Edwards and Julie Herne, notes for biography of Herne, chapter 10, "Griffith Davenport," James A. Herne Collection, Raymond H. Fogler Library Special Collections Department, University of Maine, Orono, Maine.

36. "At the Theaters," *Evening Times*, January 17, 1899, 8.

37. Edwards and Herne, notes for chapter 10, "Griffith Davenport."

38. "Cut for a Fresh Deal," *Washington Post*, January 15, 1899, 25.

39. "At the Theaters,"*Washington Times*, January 17, 1899, 3.

40. "The Passing Show," *Washington Times*, January 22, 1899, 18.

41. Edwards and Herne, notes for chapter 10, "Griffith Davenport."

42. HHG to Paul Kester, June 10, 1912, Kester Collection, NYPL.

43. "The Theatrical Forum," *Washington Times*, January 22, 1899, 19.

44. "An Eclectic Afternoon," *New York Tribune*, May 10, 1900, 7; "For Galveston Homeless Orphans," *Montgomery Advertiser* (AL), October 21, 1900, 11.

45. "To Study Occult Sciences," *Evening Times*, Washington, DC, April 19, 1899, 4.

46. "Women's Press Club Torn by Factions," *New York World*, February 27, 1899, 2; HHG's involvement substantiated by minutes of the Woman's Press Club of New York City, Woman's Press Club Collection, Columbia University Rare Book and Manuscript Library, New York.

47. HHG, "The Man at the Window," *Free Thought*, September 1900, 520–523. Her final short story: "One Little Yankee Soldier—a Spirit Likeness," *Free Thought*, March 1901, 148–151.

48. HHG, "The Lady of the Club."

49. "Little One" to "Little Phil," August 11, 1901; eleventh sitting of Helen Gardener, Tuesday, August 19, 1902, Adelaide Johnson Sitting Notes, LOC. Address listed in her March 1901 letter published in *Free Thought* and in

itemized list of her property, by landlord Miss Van Buren, attachment to "Little One" to "Little Phil," October 8, 1901.

50. "Little One" to "Little Phil," August 11, 1901.

51. "Little One" to "Little Phil," August 11, 1901.

52. "Deaths in the Town of Westport" Record Book, Courtesy of Westport Sanitarium; Death notice, *New York Herald*, January 12, 1901; Smart's State of Connecticut Death Certificate, Selden Day Pension File, NARA.

53. Smart obituary, *Free Thought*, March 1901, 172–173; Col. C. Selden Smart, Application for Cremation, January 12, 1901, courtesy of Fresh Pond Crematory; HHG, "Two Views," *The Truth Seeker*, August 18, 1888, 520–521.

54. Wills described, Mary Phillips to Mr. Milnor, June 17, 1903, Adelaide Johnson Collection, LOC.

55. "Little One" to "Little Phil," August 11, 1901. There are no probate records for Smart in New York, where they lived, or in Connecticut, where he died.

56. Last Will and Testament Charles S. Smart, June 30, 1893, Charleston, WV, Kanawha County Clerk of Court.

57. Garfield Safe Deposit Company claim receipt, April 12, 1897.

58. Smart obituary, *Free Thought*, March 1901, 172–173; "Wee wifee," T. H. Mac-Queary to Rena B. Smith, November 16, 1926, in Smith unpublished biography, Stantial Collection, SLRI.

11. Around the World with the Sun

1. First sitting August 7, 1902, Adelaide Johnson Sitting Notes, LOC.

2. "Little One" [HHG] to "Little Phil," [Mary A. Phillips], August 11, 1901, Adelaide Johnson Collection, box 66, LOC.

3. "Little One" to "Little Phil," August 11, 1901. The 1900 census enumerates a servant named Maud Baldin living with Gardener and Smart in New York. It is possible that she was "Mrs. B."

4. HHG to Stanton, May 7, 1901, reprinted in the *Boston Investigator*, May 25, 1901, *The Papers of Elizabeth Cady Stanton and Susan B. Anthony*, ed. Patricia Holland and Ann D. Gordon (Wilmington, DE: Scholarly Resources, 1991), reel 42.

5. "Little One" to "Little Phil," August 11, 1901.

6. Summary of Day's biography and military career in Lawrence Wilson, *Itinerary of the Seventh Ohio Volunteer Infantry, 1861–1864* (New York: Neale, 1907), 416–419; Selden Day pension file, NARA.

7. Diary entry of Dr. Craven, the chief medical officer of Fort Monroe, quoted in Varina Davis, *Jefferson Davis, Ex-President of the Confederate States of America, A Memoir* (New York: Belford's, 1890), 694; eighteenth sitting, Friday, September 3, 1902, Adelaide Johnson Sitting Notes.

8. Day obituary, *Army and Navy Register*, undated clipping, Day's Pension File, NARA.

9. Day's 1903 passport application describes face, features, and height, available via ancestry.com.

10. Photo lot 97, National Anthropological Archives, Smithsonian Institution (NAA).

11. HHG to Stanton, May 7, 1901, *The Papers of Elizabeth Cady Stanton and Susan B. Anthony*, reel 42.

12. "Little One" to "Little Phil," August 11, 1901; HHG Last Will and Testament (1923) and Probate Inventory, HHG Papers, SLRI and as filed in Washington, D.C.

13. "Little One" to "Little Phil," August 11, 1901.

14. "Little One" to "Little Phil," November 1, 1901, Adelaide Johnson Collection, LOC.

15. Leslie J. Gordon, "LaSalle Corbell Pickett," *Encyclopedia Virginia*. Virginia Foundation for the Humanities, October 27, 2015; website access April 5, 2019.

16. Pen Women Yearbooks and promotional material, National League of American Pen Women Archives, 1300 17th Street NW, Washington, DC.

17. Story of horses in "Helen Gardener in this City," *San Francisco Chronicle*, February 27, 1903, 8. Horse names appear in the list of slide names, Gardener Collection, Photo lot 98, National Anthropological Archives (NAA), Smithsonian Institution; Society, *Town Topics*, undated clipping, April 1902, 6.

18. Frances E. Willard, *A Wheel within a Wheel: How I Learned to Ride the Bicycle with Some Reflections by the Way* (New York: Fleming H. Revell, 1895).

19. Twentieth sitting of Helen Gardener, September 7, 1902, Adelaide Johnson Sitting Notes, LOC.

20. Clipping, *Town Topics*; "The World of Society," *Evening Star* (Washington), April 9, 1902, 5; "Society and the Clubs," *Sandusky Daily Register*, April 2, 1902, 2; "Helen H. Gardener Wed," *United Service: A Quarterly Review of Military and Naval Affairs*, May 1902, 543; "Col. Day and His Wife, Helen Gardener," *Free Thought*, July 1902, 427–429.

21. "Authoress at White House," *The Times* (Washington), June 11, 1902, 2.

22. Sandra Weber, *The Woman Suffrage Statue: A History of Adelaide Johnson's Portrait Monument at the United States Capitol* (Jefferson, NC: McFarland and Company, 2016), 9–11; "Mrs. Adelaide Johnson Is the Sculptor of Suffrage," *Washington Post*, April 4, 1909, 9.

23. HHG to AJ, April 1, 1902, Adelaide Johnson Collection, LOC.

24. Weber, *The Woman Suffrage Statue*, 11–12.

25. Eighteenth sitting, September 3, 1902; first sitting, August 7, 1902; seventeenth sitting, August 31, 1902, Adelaide Johnson Collection, box 71, LOC.

26. Tenth sitting, August 18, 1902.

27. Twelfth sitting, August 19, 1902. This is the only place I have found this book mentioned. I have not been able to locate a draft.

28. Tenth sitting, August 18, 1902; sixteenth sitting, August 29, 1902; third sitting, August 9, 1902.

29. "Revisiting Battlefields," *Harrisonburg Evening News*, September 30, 1902, 1; "Distinguished Visitors in Town," *Harrisonburg Rockingham Register*, October 3, 1902, 3; horses mentioned in "Helen Gardener in this City," 8.

30. HHG to Dr. Spitzka, Nov. 15, 1902, SLRI; "Tributes to Mrs. Stanton . . . Miss Helen Gardener Absent," *New York Times*, November 20, 1902, 9.

31. "Tributes to Mrs. Stanton . . . Miss Helen Gardener Absent," 9; "No, Not Mrs. Stanton's Brain," unidentified clipping, November 1902, Susan B. Anthony Papers, LOC, quoted in Ellen Carol Dubois, *Harriot Stanton Blatch and the Winning of Woman Suffrage* (New Haven, CT: Yale University Press, 1997), 86, note 112. Blatch denial also reported in *Democrat and Chronicle* (Rochester, NY), November 18, 1902, 6. Additional coverage of the brain bequest kerfuffle: "Brains: Wanted by this Trust," *Cincinnati Enquirer*, November 27, 1902, 6. Reprinted from New York *Sun*.

32. HHG to Burt Wilder, October 27, 1915, Burt Green Wilder Papers, Division of Rare and Manuscript Collections, Cornell University Library; twenty-third sitting, Adelaide Johnson Sitting Notes, October 30, 1902.

33. HHG "Elizabeth Cady Stanton," *Woman's Tribune*, November 21, 1902, 1; reprinted in *Free Thought*, January 1903, 3–10.

34. HHG to Dr. Edward A. Spitzka, December 30, 1902, SLRI.

35. HHG to Dr. E. A. Spitzka, December 30, 1902; "Helen Gardener in this City," 8.

36. Mary Phillips to Mr. Milnor (her lawyer), March 7, 1903. Adelaide Johnson Collection, box 66, LOC. Mary Phillips owned a large boarding house at 120 W. 72nd Street (address on her letterhead, confirmed in *Evening World* (New York), November 23, 1911, 2). There are other Mary A. Phillips letters in the Adelaide Johnson Collection that suggest she served as a sort of fixer for other people in addition to Gardener.

37. MP to Milnor, March 15, 1903, Adelaide Johnson Collection, box 66, LOC.

38. MP to Milnor, June 17, 1903, Adelaide Johnson Collection, box 66, LOC.

39. MP to Milnor, March 16, 1903, Adelaide Johnson Collection, box 66, LOC.

40. MP to Milnor, March 16, 1903.

41. MP to Milnor, May 21, 1903, Adelaide Johnson Collection, box 66, LOC.

42. "A Good Woman Gone," *Weekly Register* (WV), September 2, 1903, 1.

43. HHG to Dr. Spitzka, March 20, 1903, 218 B, SLRI.

44. "Maru Has Few Passengers," *Honolulu Advertiser*, June 18, 1903, 7; "Distinguished Authoress Here," *Hawaiian Star*, June 19, 1903, 6; "Helen Gardner Will Write of Hawaii," *Pacific Commercial Advertiser*, June 24, 1903, 5.

45. "Little One" to "Little Phil," August 14, 1903, Adelaide Johnson Collection, box 18, LOC. Gardener's fascination with Japan was part of a larger

trend; see Christopher Benfey, *The Great Wave: Gilded Age Misfits, Japanese Eccentrics, and the Opening of Old Japan* (New York: Random House, 2003).

46. "Ran Away on Tantalus: Col. and Mrs. Day Have Narrow Escape," *Pacific Commercial Advertiser,* June 26, 1903, 7.

47. HHG 1919 will (she updated it in 1923), 3, HHG Papers, SLRI.

48. "Little One" to "Little Phil," August 14, 1903.

49. Thursbys mentioned in HHG to MP August 14, 1903, LOC, and in HHG to Spitzka, April 13, 1904, SLRI.

50. Gardener collection, photo lot 98, NAA.

51. HHG to Spitzka, December 1, 1903, SLRI; Duane E. Haines, "Edward Anthony Spitzka," American National Biography Online 2000.

52. HHG, "Japan: Our Little Friend to the East," *The Arena,* January 1895, 178.

53. HHG to Spitzka, April 27, 1904, SLRI; HHG to Spitzka, December 1, 1903, SLRI; HHG to Spitzka, February 17, 1904, SLRI. Using the information HHG provided, Spitzka published several articles on the brains of Japanese people.

54. "Little One" to "Little Phil," August 14, 1903.

55. HHG, "China as I Saw It: Outside the Home" and "China as I Saw It: Inside the Home," lectures in her series *Ourselves and Other People,* brochure, Day's Pension File, NARA; lantern slide note cards, lists of slides, and slides, lot 98, NAA.

56. HHG, notecard 35, "Photo lot 98 cards with descriptions," NAA, SI.

57. HHG to Spitzka, November 24, 1904; HHG to Spitzka, February 9, 1905, SLRI.

58. HHG, Egypt notes, "Photo lot 98 cards with descriptions," lot 98, NAA, SI.

59. HHG to Spitzka, April 15, 1905, SLRI.

60. HHG to Spitzka, May 20, 1905, 218, SLRI.

61. Rosalind Rosenberg, *Beyond Separate Spheres: Intellectual Roots of Modern Feminism* (New Haven, CT: Yale University Press, 1982); Rosalind Rosenberg, *Changing the Subject: How the Women of Columbia Shaped the Way We Think about Sex and Politics* (New York: Columbia University Press, 2004); Carl N. Degler, *In Search of Human Nature: The Decline and Revival of Darwinism in American Social Thought* (New York: Oxford University Press, 1991).

62. HHG to Spitzka, April 15, 1905, SLRI.

63. HHG to Spitzka, May 20, 1905, SLRI.

64. Edith Wharton, *A Motor Flight Through France* (New York: Scribner's, 1908), reprinted and with an introduction by Mary Suzanne Schriber, Northern Illinois University Press, 1991, 1.

65. HHG to Spitzka, July 8, 1905, SLRI.

66. Notes taken by Edna Stantial when Maud Wood Park was interviewed by Sue Ainsley Clark of the *Boston Post.* Stantial Collection, 5.15, SLRI.

67. HHG diary entry, Sunday, January 20, 1907, Helen Hamilton Gardener Papers, SLRI.
68. HHG diary entry, Monday, January 21, 1907, SLRI.
69. HHG diary entry, Sunday, February 24, 1907, SLRI.
70. HHG diary entry, Wednesday, February 27, 1907, SLRI.
71. HHG diary entry, Monday, April 1, 1907, SLRI.
72. HHG diary entry, March 28, 1907, SLRI.
73. HHG diary entry, June 19, 1907, SLRI.
74. HHG to Spitzka, May 23, 1907, SLRI.
75. Undated reminiscence, Maud Wood Park, HHG folder, box 5, folder 15, Edna Lamprey Stantial Collection, SLRI.
76. Weight recorded in diary as 121.5 pounds, October 5, 1907, SLRI; from Japan, she wrote Spitzka that she weighed 106 pounds, HHG to Spitzka, December 1, 1903, SLRI.
77. "A Truly Noble Woman," *Morning Telegram* (Eau Claire, WI), November 2, 1895, 3, widely reprinted.

12. Mrs. Day Comes to Washington

1. HHG to Mrs. Edith Wilson, November 26, 1921, SLRI.
2. Maud Wood Park, undated reminiscence, HHG folder, box 5, folder 15, Edna Lamprey Stantial Collection, SLRI.
3. Promotional brochures for "Ourselves and Other Peoples," copy residing in Day's pension file, NARA, and in HHG papers, SLRI (there were a couple of different versions of the brochure).
4. HHG to Spitzka, January 29 and February 6, 1909, SLRI.
5. HHG to Spitzka, March 9, 1908, SLRI.
6. HHG last will and testament, May 26, 1925, as filed in the District of Columbia on August 3, 1925; other descriptions based on author visits to 1838 Lamont Street.
7. Margaret B. Downing, "Mrs. Selden Day, Wife of Col. Day, Tells of Japanese Home Life," *Evening Star*, July 23, 1911, 45.
8. Carrie Chapman Catt, Organization Committee Report, NAWSA Convention of 1898, *HOWS*, vol. 4, 289.
9. Trisha Franzen, *Anna Howard Shaw: The Work of Woman Suffrage* (Urbana: University of Illinois Press, 2014).
10. Carrie Chapman Catt and Nettie Rogers Shuler, *Woman Suffrage and Politics: The Inner Story of the Suffrage Movement* (New York: Charles Scribner's Sons, 1923), 235.
11. Aileen Kraditor's count, quoted in Louise Michele Newman, "Reflections on Aileen Kraditor's Legacy: Fifty Years of Woman Suffrage Historiogra-

phy, 1965–2014," *Journal of the Gilded Age and Progressive Era* 14 (July 2015): 293. See also Corinne McConnaughy, *The Woman Suffrage Movement: A Reassessment* (London: Cambridge University Press, 2013).

12. Ida Husted Harper, ed., *HOWS*, vol. 5 (NAWSA, 1922), 253.

13. *HOWS*, vol. 5, 275–276.

14. "Array of Orators to Talk Suffrage," *Washington Herald*, March 24, 1912, 2; "Noted Speakers to Urge Suffrage at Columbia Tonight," *Washington Times*, March 31, 1912, 7.

15. HHG to Martha Wentworth Suffren, January 29, 1913, reel 1; Donald L. Haggerty, *National Woman's Party Papers: The Suffrage Years, 1913–1920* (Sanford, NC: Microfilming Corporation of America, 1981).

16. Mary Ware Dennett, NAWSA Corresponding Secretary, Report, NAWSA Convention 1912, *HOWS*, vol. 5, 336; HHG to AP, November 1, 1913, NWP.

17. *Washington Times*, July 27, 1913.

18. "Society," *Washington Herald*, August 18, 1912.

19. HHG to Paul Kester, August 7, 1912, Paul Kester collection, NYPL.

20. "In the World of Society," *Evening Star*, September 4, 1912, 7; "Society," *Washington Herald*, October 11, 1912, 5; "Reception Tonight," *Washington Times*, November 15, 1912, 9; "Society," *Evening Star*, March 10, 1912; "Society," *Washington Times*, January 16, 1912, 10; "Society," *Washington Herald*, January 16, 1912, 5; and "Society," *Sunday Star*, January 21, 1912, 1.

21. Davis, *Jefferson Davis*; Day's Appointment, Commission, and Personal Branch (ACP) records at NARA; Hooker also visited them in New Jersey in 1907, HHG diary.

22. "One-Armed Gen. Hooker, in Capital, Not Forgotten," *Washington Herald*, June 11, 1911, 3; "In the World of Society," *Evening Star* (Washington, DC), June 10, 1911, 7.

23. David Blight, *Race and Reunion: The Civil War in American Memory* (Cambridge, MA: Harvard University Press, 2002); Nina Silber, *The Romance of Reunion: Northerners and the South, 1865–1900* (Chapel Hill: University of North Carolina Press, 1993).

24. Rosalyn Terborg-Penn, *African American Women in the Struggle for the Vote* (Bloomington: Indiana University Press, 1998), 6; Marjorie Spruill Wheeler, *New Women of the New South: The Leaders of the Woman Suffrage Movement in the Southern States* (New York: Oxford University Press, 1993); Marjorie Julian Spruill, "Race, Reform, and Reaction at the Turn of the Century: Southern Suffragists, the NAWSA, and the 'Southern Strategy' in Context," in *Votes for Women: The Struggle for Suffrage Revisited*, ed. Jean H. Baker (New York: Oxford University Press, 2002). See also Louise Michele Newman, *White Women's Rights: The Racial Origins of Feminism in the United States* (New York: Oxford University Press, 1999).

25. Terborg-Penn, *African American Women in the Struggle for the Vote*; Ann Gordon, editor with Arlene Voski Avakian, Joyce Avrech Berkman, John H.

Bracey, and Bettye Collier-Thomas, *African American Women and the Vote, 1837–1965* (Amherst: University of Massachusetts Press, 1997).

26. *Conversations with Alice Paul: Woman Suffrage and the Equal Rights Amendment*. Interview conducted by Amelia R. Fry. Suffragists Oral History Project (The Regents of the University of California 1976, 2011), 68. For a history of suffrage protest tactics, see Linda J. Lumsden, *Rampant Women: Suffragists and the Right of Assembly* (Knoxville: University of Tennessee Press, 1997).

27. "Chignila" [HHG] to My Dear One [Day], February 16, 1913. NWP reel 1. HHG presents herself as aligned with Paul against NAWSA leadership, who are leery of their big plans.

28. Alice Paul, oral history, 78; J. D. Zahniser and Amelia R. Fry, *Alice Paul: Claiming Power* (New York: Oxford University Press, 2014), 130–132; "May Join in Parade," *Evening Star*, December 5, 1912, 4.

29. HHG to Ira Bennett, editor, *Washington Post*, January 22, 1913, NWP reel 1.

30. AP to Mrs. Lawrence Lewis, January 31, 1913, NWP reel 1.

31. Alice Paul, oral history, 78–79.

32. HHG to Amanda Lauderbach, February 20, 1913, NWP reel 1; HHG to Mary Ware Dennett, February 4, 1913, NWP reel 1.

33. "Mrs. Helen Gardener Is Publicity Agent for the Suffrage Parade on March 3," *Tribune* (Coshocton, OH), February 11, 1913, 4; *Evening Standard* (Ogden, UT), February 18, 1913, 10; "Four Leaders of the Equal Suffrage Movement Who Will Help Make Parade a Success," *Arizona Daily*, February 23, 1913, 2; clippings from NAWSA reel 59.

34. HHG letter to Rudolph, January 5, 1913, inserted along with her Senate Subcommittee testimony, "Suffrage Parade Hearings Before a Subcommittee of the Committee on the District of Columbia United States Senate, Sixty-Third Congress, Special Session of Senate, S. Res. 499," Part 1, March 6–17, 1913 (Washington, DC: Government Printing Office), 441–442.

35. HHG to Hon. Horace Towner, January 29, 1913, NWP reel 1.

36. "Men's League," November 6, 1913, NWP reel 5.

37. AP to Mrs. Lawrence Lewis, January 31, 1913, NWP reel 1.

38. For more on Hazel MacKaye and other lesser-known suffrage activists, see Susan Ware, *Why They Marched: Untold Stories of the Women Who Fought for the Right to Vote* (Cambridge, MA: Harvard University Press, 2019).

39. HHG to Mrs. Tinnin, February 16, 1913, NWP reel 1.

40. As described in Official Program, Woman Suffrage Procession, Washington, DC, March 3, 1913, NAWSA reel 49, and in HHG Senate Subcommittee Testimony, 438–453.

41. Zahniser and Fry, *Alice Paul*, 137–138.

42. HHG, "The Negro in the North," *Atlanta Constitution*, June 16, 1896, 4.

43. HHG to Miss Blackwell [Alice Stone], January 14, 1913, NWP reel 1.

44. Alice Stone Blackwell to AP, January 23, 1913, NWP reel 1; AP to Alice Stone Blackwell, January 26, 1913, NWP reel 1.
45. Mrs. M. D. Butler to Lucy Burns, February 10, 1913, NWP reel 1.
46. Nellie Quander to AP, February 15 and February 17, 1913, NWP reel 1.
47. Zahniser and Fry, *Alice Paul*, 139.
48. MWD to AP, January 14, 1913, NWP reel 1; AP to MWD, January 15, 1913, NWP reel 1.
49. MWD to AP, February 28, 1913, NWP reel 1.
50. Mia Bay, *To Tell the Truth Freely: The Life of Ida B. Wells* (New York: Hill and Wang, 2009), 290.
51. "Suffrage Paraders," *The Crisis* 5, no. 6 (April 1913): 298.
52. "Politics," *The Crisis*, 5, no. 6 (April 1913): 267; AP to Mary Beard, April 18, 1913, NWP reel 3.
53. Maud Wood Park, *Front Door Lobby*, ed. Edna Lamprey Stantial (Boston: Beacon Press, 1960), 28.
54. "Women Suffrage Procession, March 3," NWP reel 1.
55. Zahniser and Fry, *Alice Paul*, 146–147, and Senate Subcommittee testimonies.
56. Clyde H. Tavender, "Treatment of Women Marchers a Disgrace to the Nation," unidentified clipping, March 1913, NWP reel 2.
57. "Suffrage Parade Hearings Before a Subcommittee of the Committee on the District of Columbia United States Senate," 436.
58. HHG testimony, "Suffrage Parade Hearings," 438. AP recalled Sylvester describing the crowd as "riff raff" on p. 132.
59. According to clippings in the "parades and parading/women's suffrage" file, Washingtonia Collection, Washington, DC, Public Library.
60. Clyde H. Tavender, "Treatment of Women Marchers a Disgrace to the Nation."
61. AHS to AP, March 5, 1913, NWP reel 2.

13. Old Fogies

1. "Suffragists at Capital Keep Busy During Hot Months," *Ogden Standard*, August 13, 1913, 1, widely reprinted.
2. AP to MWD, April 14, 1913, NWP reel 3; MWD to AP, April 19, 1913, NWP reel 3; AP form letter "Dear Suffragist," April 15, 1913, NWP reel 3; Harriet Taylor Upton to AP ["I know you do not want it to solicit funds"], April 18, 1913, NWP reel 3; AP to Alice Stone Blackwell, May 7, 1913, NAWSA reel 32, NWP reel 3; Agnes Ryan to AP, May 12, 1913, NWP reel 3.
3. For example, AP memo to NAWSA board, April 16, 1913, NWP reel 3; Anna Howard Shaw to AP, April 16, 1913, NWP reel 3.

4. HHG to MWD, January 3, 1914, NAWSA reel 33.
5. Unsigned (Lucy Burns) to AP, March 28, 1913, NWP reel 2.
6. HHG testimony, Woman Suffrage Hearings before the Senate Committee on Woman Suffrage, April 19, 1913, Sixty-Third Congress (Washington: Government Printing Office, 1913), 83–88.
7. "Women Plead for Ballot in Senate," *Washington Times*, April 26, 1913, 7.
8. AP to MWD, May 15, 1913, NWP reel 3; *HOWS*, vol. 5, 380.
9. AP to Mary Beard, May 22, 1913, NWP reel 3.
10. HHG to Harriet Laidlaw, June 23, 1913, Harriet Laidlaw Collection, SLRI.
11. "Promised Hearing," *Abilene Daily Chronicle*, July 11, 1913, 1, widely reprinted; "Suffragists Eager for Regular Session," *Washington Times*, July 11, 1913, 3.
12. HHG to AP, March 26, 1913, NWP reel 2.
13. For example, MWD to AP, October 30, 1913, NWP reel 5.
14. HHG to Mrs. Lockwood, August 20, 1913, NWP reel 3; Society, *Washington Times*, July 27, 1913; Society, *Washington Times*, August 20, 1913; HHG to AP, Sept 25, 1913, NWP reel 4.
15. HHG to Mrs. McCulloch and Mrs. Stewart, July 1, 1913, Mary Earhart Dillon Papers, Ella Stewart Collection, SLRI.
16. Anna Howard Shaw to AP, no date [Nov. 1913], NWP reel 5.
17. HHG to Harriet Laidlaw, June 23, 1913, Harriet Laidlaw Papers, SLRI.
18. S. A. Day to AP, November 16, 1913, NWP reel 5.
19. "Equal Suffrage Department," *Tuscaloosa News*, December 21, 1913, 10; "Suffragists Meet and Form Southern Body," *Pensacola News*, November 13, 1.
20. HHG to Rep. Edward Pou, November 3, 1917, copy in Woodrow Wilson Papers, LOC.
21. HHG, "Woman Suffrage—Which Way," New York, NAWSA Publishing Company. History of Women Collection, no. 9084, microfilm (Woodbridge, CT: Research Publications, 1977), SLRI.
22. AHS to Lucy Burns, November 19, 1913, NWP reel 5.
23. HHG testimony before the House Rules Committee, December 3, 1913, excerpted in *HOWS*, vol. 5, 384–385.
24. In a strange twist, the report of the committee hearings was stolen; HHG thought that the thief mistook the bundle for a Christmas package. "Suffrage Records Gone," *Washington Star*, 1914 clipping, HHG papers, SLRI; HHG to Blackwell, January 12, 1914, HHG Papers, Woman's Rights Collection, SLRI.
25. Nancy C. Unger, *Belle La Folllette: Progressive Era Reformer* (New York: Routledge, 2015).
26. HHG to Miss [Alice Stone] Blackwell, December 15, 1913, NAWSA reel 8.
27. *HOWS*, vol. 5, 374–376. Press release, signed by M[ary] W[are] D[ennett], "President Wilson and Woman Suffrage," December 1913, NWP reel 6.
28. *HOWS*, vol. 5, 397.

29. Antoinette Funk to Mrs. [Mary Ware] Dennett, January 13, 1914, NAWSA reel 33; Antoinette Funk to AHS, January 21, 1914, NAWSA reel 33.

30. Zahniser and Fry, *Alice Paul,* 133.

31. Terms described in Lucy Burns to AHS, December 17, 1913, NWP reel 6; Lucy Burns to Mary Beard, January 2, 1914, NWP reel 6.

32. Mary Beard to AP, December 2, 1913, NWP reel 6.

33. Doris Stevens to Lucy Burns, December 30, 1913, NWP reel 6.

34. AHS to NAWSA board members, January 2, 1914, Harriet Laidlaw Papers, SLRI.

35. Mrs. [Ruth Hanna] McCormick to AHS, February 3, 1914, NAWSA reel 33; Kristie Miller, *Ruth Hanna McCormick: A Life in Politics, 1880–1944* (Albuquerque: University of New Mexico Press, 1992).

36. HHG to MWD, January 3, 1914, NAWSA reel 33.

37. Lucy Burns to Mary Beard, January 2, 1914, NWP.

38. MWD to HHG, January 9, 1914, NAWSA collection, box 48, LOC.

39. AP to MWD, December 31, 1913, NWP; MWD to AP, February 19, 1914, NWP; Zahniser and Fry, *Alice Paul,* 177–191.

40. Society Page, *Washington Post*, January 22, 1914, 7; "Stops Suffrage Plan," *Washington Post*, January 22, 1914, 5.

41. HHG remarks before the Judiciary Committee, March 3, 1914, reprinted in *HOWS*, vol. 5, 435–436.

42. "Women Answer, 'Why I'm a Suffragist,'" *Washington Herald*, March 1, 1914, 10.

43. *HOWS*, vol. 5, 411; Society, *Washington Times*, February 2, 1914, 4; Sec. to Sen. William Borah to HHG, April 2, 1914, William Borah Collection, LOC.

44. For example, Mary Ware Dennett's protest letters and resignation, MWD to the NAWSA board, April 4, 1914; MWD to NAWSA board, April 18, 1914; Harriet Laidlaw to MWD, April 1914; MWD to AHS, September 1, 1914; MWD to NAWSA Board, October 15, 1914, all MWD folder 214, scrapbook 1, Mary Ware Dennett Collection, SLRI.

45. *HOWS*, vol. 5, 411.

46. "Society," *Washington Herald*, December 27, 1914, 8; Selden Day to Paul Kester, April 15, 1915, Paul Kester collection, NYPL.

47. "Women Prepare for Convention," *Indianapolis Star*, October 24, 1915, 44, widely reprinted; "Suffragists Occupy Joint Headquarters," *Washington Herald*, November 16, 1915, 11; Forty-Seventh Annual Convention, NAWSA Official Program 1915, NAWSA reel 59.

48. *HOWS*, vol. 5, 452–453.

49. Jacqueline Van Voris, *Carrie Chapman Catt: A Public Life* (New York: The Feminist Press, CUNY, 1987), 130.

50. CCC to MWP, January 18, 1916, NAWSA reel 15.

51. CCC to MWP, January 27, 1916, NAWSA reel 32.

14. NAWSA's "Diplomatic Corps"

1. Kathi Kern, *Mrs. Stanton's Bible*, 184; *HOWS*, vol. 4, 263–264.
2. HHG report to NAWSA, inserted in larger file, "Congressional Union: Anti-Democratic Party Policy of Congressional Union," NAWSA reel 33, LOC; see also "Attacks Congressional Union for Threatening Democrats," *Washington Herald*, November 28, 1915, 3. Nancy Cott analyzes this strategy in *The Grounding of Modern Feminism* (New Haven, CT: Yale University Press, 1987).
3. Society, *Washington Times*, June 15, 1916, 11; "Society," *Washington Herald*, June 19, 1916, 5.
4. HHG to Joseph P. Tumlty, July 5, 1916, Woodrow Wilson Papers, Case File 89, Manuscript Division, LOC.
5. A. Scott Berg, *Wilson* (New York: G. P. Putnam's Sons, 2013), 356; Kristie Miller, *Ellen and Edith: Woodrow Wilson's First Ladies* (Lawrence: University of Kansas Press, 2010).
6. "States Rights Suffrage Plank Called Victory," *Chicago Tribune*, June 6, 1916, NAWSA reel 59; CCC to WW, June 16, 1916, WW Papers, LOC; WW to CCC, June 19, 1916, NAWSA; "Says Wilson Will Be for Amendment," clipping including Catt's statement after her 8/1/16 meeting, Woodrow Wilson Papers, reel 209, LOC.
7. Memo to the President, July 27, 1916, re: Mrs. Frank Roessing and CCC request meeting with the President; WW handwrites question on memo, Woodrow Wilson Papers, LOC.
8. Memo attached to the July 27, 1916, request; Sen. Charles Thomas, chair of Senate Committee on Woman Suffrage, *Congressional Record*, August 21, 1916, 15089.
9. HHG to CCC and Miss Paterson, August, 18, 1916, HHG Papers, Women's Rights Collection, folder 69, SLRI.
10. *HOWS*, vol. 5, 480, 496–500.
11. Wilson's speech, September 8, 1916, NAWSA reel 55, LOC.
12. CCC, "The Crisis," NAWSA reel 59.
13. Robert Booth Fowler, "Carrie Chapman Catt, Strategist," in Marjorie Spruill Wheeler, ed., *One Woman, One Vote: Rediscovering the Woman Suffrage Movement* (Troutdale, OR: New Sage Press, 1995). See also Robert Booth Fowler, *Carrie Catt: Feminist Politician* (Boston: Northeastern University Press, 1986).
14. Maud Wood Park, *Front Door Lobby*, ed. Edna Lamprey Stantial (Boston: Beacon Press, 1960), 16–17; Sara Hunter Graham, *Woman Suffrage and the New Democracy* (New Haven, CT: Yale University Press, 1996), 88 –90; Catt and Shuler, *Woman Suffrage and Politics*, 259–263.
15. Quoted in Christine A. Lunardini and Thomas J. Knock. "Woodrow Wil-

son and Woman Suffrage: A New Look," *Political Science Quarterly* 95 (Winter 1980–1981): 655–671.

16. Marjorie Julian Spruill, "Race, Reform, and Reaction at the Turn of the Century: Southern Suffragists, the NAWSA, and the 'Southern Strategy' in Context," in *Votes for Women: The Struggle for Suffrage Revisited*, ed. Jean H. Baker (New York: Oxford University Press, 2002).

17. HHG to Wilson, October 23, 1916, NAWSA collection, reel 32, LOC.

18. Berg, *Wilson*, 416. Lynda G. Dodd's analysis credits Paul's electoral strategy with putting Wilson and the Democrats "on notice." Dodd, "Parades, Pickets, and Prison: Alice Paul and the Virtues of Unruly Constitutional Citizenship," *Journal of Law and Politics* 24 (2008), 426.

19. "National Suffrage Club, Housewarming Planned," *Evening Star*, December 8, 1916, 27; "Open Suffrage Home," *Washington Post*, December 10, 1916, 22.

20. Park, *Front Door Lobby*, 32.

21. Membership listed in *HOWS*, vol. 5, 515.

22. Park, *Front Door Lobby*, 21–22.

23. Day's Appointment, Commission, and Personal Branch (ACP) Record, NARA.

24. John Sharp Williams, *Congressional Record*, March 13, 1914, 4816.

25. Park, *Front Door Lobby*, 58.

26. JSW to Pomerene, January 16, 1917, Williams Papers, Manuscript Division, LOC.

27. HHG to JSW, January 17, 1917, Williams Papers, LOC.

28. AP to WW, January 1, 1917; WW memo to staff January 4, 1917; AP to Thomas Brahany, January 4, 1917; Memorandum for the President, January 6, 1917; WW memo January 8, 1917, all WW Papers, LOC.

29. Memo re: Abby Scott Baker to Wilson, February 3, 1917, WW Papers, LOC.

30. HHG call record, January 9, 1917, WW Papers, LOC.

31. CCC to Tumulty, January 17 and 19, 1917; HHG to WW, January 25 and 26, 1917; HHG to Tumulty, January 26, 1917, WW Papers, LOC.

32. HHG to CCC, January 25 and 26, 1917, HHG Papers, Woman's Rights Collection, folder 69, SLRI.

33. Park, *Front Door Lobby*, 71.

34. HHG to CCC, January 25, 1917; "Congressional Scheme," spring 1917, NAWSA reel 32.

35. HHG to CCC, January 26, 1917; HHG to CCC, January 31, 1917, HHG Papers (WRC), folder 69, SLRI.

36. HHG to CCC, February 4, 1917, HHG Papers (WRC), folder 69, SLRI; Society, *Washington Times*, February 10, 1917, 7.

37. HHG to JSW, February 9, 1917, JSW Papers, LOC.

38. Caroline Noble to CCC, [Feb. 1917], HHG Papers (WRC), SLRI.

39. JSW to HHG, February 8, 1917; HHG to JSW, February 20, 1917; JSW to HHG, March 17, 1917, all JSW Papers, LOC.

40. "Suffs to Adopt Their Congressmen," *Evening Sun* (Baltimore), August 8, 1917, 3.

41. MWP to Ruth White, March 27, 1917, NAWSA reel 32; "Cheers Greet Advent of Congresswoman," *Washington Herald*, April 3, 1917, 14; Mary Gray Peck, *Carrie Chapman Catt: A Biography* (New York: H. W. Wilson Company, 1944), 270.

42. Day to Secretary of War Newton Baker, April 13, 1917, Day Pension File, NARA.

43. HHG to JSW, April 4, 1917, JSW Papers, LOC.

44. Anna Howard Shaw to WW, March 26, 1917, WW Papers, LOC.

45. Congressional Committee, meeting minutes, April 12, 1917, NAWSA reel 32, LOC. Kate Clarke Lemay, "'Où sont les dames?': Suffragists and the American Women's Oversea Hospitals Unit in France during World War I," in Lemay, ed. *Votes for Women! A Portrait of Persistence* (Princeton, NJ: Princeton University Press, 2019), 69–87.

46. "Women Name Leaders," *San Antonio Light*, February 27, 1917, 1, widely reprinted; "Women Prepare for War Service If Needed," *Buffalo Commercial*, February 27, 1917, 8.

47. CCC, "Ready for Citizenship," *The Public*, August 24, 1917, clipping, NAWSA reel 59.

48. HHG to CCC, March 14, 1917, HHG Papers (WRC), SLRI.

49. Address confirmed in Rena B. Smith, unpublished bio, SLRI.

50. Park, *Front Door Lobby*, 88–89.

51. Maud Wood Park, "Supplementary Notes about Helen Hamilton Gardener," NAWSA collection, LOC.

52. HHG to Wilson, May 10, 1917, WW Papers, LOC.

53. WW to HHG, May 14, 1917, WW Papers, LOC.

54. Wilson to Pou, May 14, 1917, WW Papers, LOC; "Suffs Encouraged," *The Sun* (New York), May 17, 1917, 6; "Wilson Aids Suffrage Cause," *Washington Post*, May 17, 1917, 8.

55. Zahniser and Fry, *Alice Paul*, 256, 260–261, 264. See also Jean H. Baker, "Endgame: Alice Paul and Woodrow Wilson," in *Sisters: The Lives of America's Suffragists* (New York: Hill and Wang, 2005), and Mary Chapman, *Making Noise, Making News: Suffrage Print Culture and U.S. Modernism* (New York: Oxford University Press, 2014).

56. Quoted in Berg, *Wilson*, 489.

57. HHG to WW, May 25, 1917, WW Papers, LOC.

58. Maud Wood Park memo to state congressional chairmen, May 24, 1917, NAWSA reel 32.

59. CCC to AP, May 24, 1917, NAWSA reel 8.

60. HHG to WW, May 25, 1917, with enclosure CCC to AP, May 24, 1917, WW Papers, LOC.

61. HHG to WW, June 10, 1917; WW to Heflin, June 13, 1917; Heflin to Wilson, June 28, 1917, WW Papers, LOC.

62. AP fundraising letter, June 14, 1917, copy in WW, LOC.
63. HOWS, vol. 5, 526–527; Graham, *Woman Suffrage and the New Democracy*, 93. See also Joan Marie Johnson, *Funding Feminism: Monied Women, Philanthropy, and the Women's Movement, 1870–1967* (Chapel Hill: University of North Carolina Press, 2017).
64. "Report of Special Interviews," June 23, 1917, NAWSA reel 32.
65. "Report of Special Interviews," June 28, 1917, NAWSA reel 32.
66. Park, *Front Door Lobby*, 96.
67. Maud Wood Park, "Report on the Press Situation," July 5, 1917, NAWSA reel 60; Zahniser and Fry, *Alice Paul*, 273.
68. HHG to Wilson, July 19, 1917, WW Papers, LOC; Wilson memo, circa July 20, 1917, WW Papers, LOC; HHG to CCC, July 20, 1917, HHG Papers (WRC), SLRI.
69. Ruth White to Mrs. C. W. McClure, August 27, 1917, NAWSA reel 32.
70. Ruth White to Mrs. Charles McClure, September 7, 1917, NAWSA reel 32.
71. HHG to Tumulty, September 20, 1917, WW Papers, LOC.
72. "House Committee on Woman Suffrage Established," NAWSA press release, September 24, 1917, NAWSA reel 60; "House Moves for Woman Suffrage," *New York Times*, September 25, 1917, 11.
73. Park, *Front Door Lobby*, 117.
74. Ethel Smith to Maud Wood Park, October 3, 1917, Maud Wood Park Papers, Women's Rights Collection, folder 196, SLRI.
75. HHG to Pou, November 3, 1917, copy in WW Papers, LOC.
76. HHG, Fifth Vice President and Vice Chairman of Congressional Committee Report, April 13, 1919, HHG Papers (WRC), SLRI and NAWSA reel 37.
77. MWP, Additional Congressional Summary (written to Inez Hayes Irwin), April 28, 1933, NAWSA reel 32.
78. Park, *Front Door Lobby*, 89.
79. MWP, Additional Congressional Summary, April 28, 1933, written to Inez Haynes Irwin, NAWSA reel 32.
80. AP, NWP mass mailing, October 16, 1917, copy NAWSA reel 24.
81. Zahniser and Fry, chapters 13, 14.
82. CCC to HHG, October 11, 1917, NAWSA reel 8.
83. Tumulty to HHG, October 16, 1917, NAWSA reel 8.
84. WW to CCC, October 13, 1917, NAWSA reel 8; "President Wilson Again Urges Woman Suffrage," NAWSA press release, October 18, 1917, NAWSA reel 8.
85. Park, *Front Door Lobby*, 121; Johanna Neuman, *Gilded Suffragists: The New York Socialites Who Fought for Women's Right to Vote* (New York: New York University Press, 2017).
86. CCC, "Address to the Legislatures of the United States," 1919, Dillon Collection, SLRI; Quoted in Graham, *Woman Suffrage and the New Democracy*, 113.

87. "National Victory Next," *Belvidere Daily Republican* (IL), November 7, 1917, 1.
88. Memorandum for the President, November 6, 1917, WW Papers, LOC. Meeting set up via phone with HHG.
89. HHG to Tumulty, November 9, 1917, WW Papers, LOC enclosure with handwritten note on top of NAWSA press release; CCC statement, *New York Times*, November 10, 1917; "Women Already Wielding Power," *Dayton* (OH) *Daily News*, November 9, 1917, 20; "Suffragists Call on Wilson Today," *Washington Post*, November 9, 1917, 7.
90. "Suffrage Leaders Have Conference with President," *Austin* (TX) *American Statesman*, November 10, 1917, 1, 3.
91. HHG to Pou, November 3, 1917, copy in WW Papers, LOC.
92. "National Suffrage Association Renews Federal Amendment Campaign at Washington," November 19, 1917, NAWSA press release, NAWSA reel 32; "National Association Calls National Convention in Washington to Push Federal Amendment," NAWSA press release, October 13, 1917, NAWSA reel 60.
93. *HOWS*, vol. 5, 525.
94. *HOWS*, vol. 5, 541.
95. Tumulty to WW with enclosure Senate Poll, December 12, 1917; MWP to HHG, November 24, 1917, WW Papers LOC; WW to MWP, November 27, 1917, NAWSA reel 15; Tumulty to WW, December 15, 1917, with enclosure House Poll, WW Papers, LOC.
96. Club membership estimate from Graham, *Woman Suffrage and the New Democracy*, 23. For black women's suffrage activities, see Rosalyn Terborg-Penn, introduction to the document collection "The Writings of Black Women Suffragists" in the Women and Social Movements Database, plus the hundreds of linked primary sources in Kathryn Kish Sklar and Thomas Dublin, eds., *The Black Woman Suffragists Collection* (Alexandria, VA: Alexander Street, 2016). See also Martha S. Jones, *All Bound Up Together: The Woman Question in African American Public Culture, 1830–1900* (Chapel Hill: University of North Carolina Press, 2007); Terborg-Penn, *African American Women in the Struggle for the Vote*; and Ann Gordon, ed., *African American Women and the Vote*.
97. NAWSA executive council minutes, Dec. 19, 1917, NAWSA reel 60, LOC.

15. Twenty-Two Favors

1. Liette Gidlow, "The Sequel: The Fifteenth Amendment, the Nineteenth Amendment, and Southern Black Women's Struggle to Vote," *Journal of the Gilded Age and Progressive Era* 17 (July 2018): 436.
2. Maud Wood Park, *Front Door Lobby*, ed. Edna Lamprey Stantial (Boston:

Beacon Press, 1960), 177; House Woman Suffrage Committee Report, Sixty-Fifth Congress, report no. 234, January 8, 1918, copy WW Papers, LOC.

3. Gidlow, 438.

4. Mary Church Terrell, "Woman Suffrage and the Fifteenth Amendment," *The Crisis* 10 (August 1915): 191.

5. For example, CCC testimony, Committee on Woman Suffrage, U.S. Senate, April 20, 1917, Washington Government Printing Office, NAWSA reel 60. Catt's book, *Woman Suffrage by Federal Constitutional Amendment* (New York: National Woman Suffrage Publishing Company, 1917), includes statistics in chap. VI showing that white majorities would be increased by women voting. This is also the strategy that helped build the Southern suffrage movement in the 1890s: see Marjorie Spruill Wheeler, *New Women of the New South: The Leaders of the Woman Suffrage Movement in the Southern States* (New York: Oxford University Press, 1993).

6. Spruill Wheeler, *New Women of the New South*, 120–132.

7. Notes taken by Edna Stantial when Mrs. Park was talking to Sue Ainslee Clark for *Boston Post* article, Edna Stantial Collection, box 5, folder 15, SLRI.

8. HHG to Tumulty, November 14, 1917, WW Papers, LOC.

9. Thomas Jablonsky, "Female Opposition: The Anti-Suffrage Campaign," in Jean H. Baker, ed., *Votes for Women: The Struggle for Suffrage Revisited* (New York: Oxford University Press, 2002); Manuela Turner, "'Better Citizens without the Ballot': American Anti-Suffrage women and their Rationale during the Progressive Era," in Marjorie Spruill Wheeler, ed., *One Woman, One Vote: Rediscovering the Woman Suffrage Movement* (Troutdale, OR: New Sage Press, 1995).

10. Catt, "States Rights or Justice," testimony, House Committee on Woman Suffrage, January 3, 1918, NAWSA pamphlet, copy in Borah Collection, LOC.

11. Park, *Front Door Lobby*, 125, 130.

12. Quoted in John Milton Cooper, Jr., *Woodrow Wilson: A Biography* (New York: Vintage Books, 2011), 413.

13. Tumulty to WW, January 9, 1918, WW Papers, LOC. "Suffrage" Handwritten note, box 50, folder 14, Tumulty Papers, LOC.

14. HHG to Tumulty, January 10, 1918, WW Papers, LOC.

15. Described in Park, *Front Door Lobby*, 137–151.

16. HOWS, vol. 5, 635–637; Park, *Front Door Lobby*, 151; Zahniser and Fry [*Alice Paul: Claiming Power* (New York: Oxford University Press, 2014), 302–303] credit Paul's campaign against Democrats for increasing the number of "yes" votes.

17. HHG to John Sharp Williams, January 20, 1918, John Sharp Williams Papers, LOC.

18. John Sharp Williams to HHG, January 21, 1918, JSW Papers, LOC.

19. HHG to Tumulty, January 20, 1918, plus enclosure, WW Papers, LOC.

20. For example, HHG to Pou, November 3, 1917, copy WW Papers, LOC.
21. HHG to "My Dear Judge" [Walter M. Clarke], January 1, 1918, WW Papers, LOC.
22. For an analysis of the party affiliations of suffragists, see Rebecca Edwards, chapter 2, "Suffragists, Prohibitionists, and Republicans," in *Angels in the Machinery: Gender in American Party Politics from the Civil War to the Progressive Era* (New York: Oxford University Press, 1997).
23. Zahniser and Fry, *Alice Paul*, 192–195.
24. CCC to MWP, June 20, 1919, NAWSA reel 15.
25. Rena B. Smith, unpublished biography of HHG, 67, Stantial Collection, SLRI.
26. For example, HHG brought NAWSA polls to White House twice in December; Tumulty to WW, December 15, 1917, WW reel 93, LOC; Tumulty to WW, enclosure, December 17, 1917, WW Papers, reel 93, LOC.
27. Regarding the meeting with Senators Fletcher and Trammel, The secretary to WW, March 12, 1918, Tumulty Papers, box 48, folder 10, LOC; WW to Tumulty, no date, WW Papers, reel 210, LOC; Tumulty to WW, March 14, 1918, Tumulty Papers, box 48, folder 10, LOC.
28. HHG call record, April 30, 1918; WW to HHG, May 2, 1918; HHG call record, May 3, 1918; HHG to Brahany, no date, attachment to May 3, 1918, letter, WW Papers, LOC.
29. CCC to Tumulty, May 14, 1918, WW Papers, LOC; WW to CCC, June 7, 1918, WW Papers, LOC; Memorandum for the President, June 10, 1918, WW Papers, LOC; CCC to WW, June 11, 1918, NAWSA reel 21, LOC; WW to CCC, June 13, 1918 [revised], NAWSA reel 8, LOC; Tumulty to HHG, June 14, 1918, NAWSA reel 8, enclosed the revised copy of WW letter to CCC; NAWSA press release, June 13, 1918, WW Papers, LOC; HHG to WW, June 17, 1918, WW Papers, LOC; MWP recollection, December 1944, NAWSA reel 8, LOC. For a comparative study, see Dawn Langan Teele, *Forging the Franchise: The Political Origins of the Women's Vote* (Princeton, NJ: Princeton University Press, 2018).
30. HHG to Tumulty, June 17, 1918, WW Papers.
31. Tumulty to HHG, November 25, 1918, HHG Papers (WRC), folder 71, SLRI.
32. CCC to MWP, Sunday a.m., November 1918. MWP, CCC folder, LOC.
33. Park, *Front Door Lobby*, 92–93.
34. HHG, Fifth Vice President and Vice Chairman of Congressional Committee Report, April 13, 1919, HHG Papers (WRC), SLRI.
35. Isabella Aniba to WW, May 24, 1918; Memorandum to WW, May 24, 1918; WW to Tumulty in reply, WW Papers, LOC.
36. WW to HHG, June 24, 1918, WW Papers, LOC; For example, WW to Sen. John Shields, June 26, 1918; WW to Sen. Ollie James, June 24, 1918, WW Papers, LOC. Copies of other WW letters to senators are in NAWSA reels 8 and 21—Tumulty gave copies to HHG.

37. HHG to Forster, July 9, 1918, WW Papers, LOC.
38. HHG to Forster, July 4, 1918, WW Papers, LOC.
39. HHG to WW, June 23, 1918, WW Papers, LOC.
40. HHG to Forster, July 30, 1918; Tumulty to WW, July 31, 1918; HHG to Forster, August 2, 1918; HHG to Tumulty, August 3, 1918, all WW Papers, LOC; HHG to MWP, July 23, 1918, HHG Papers (WRC), SLRI; HHG to MWP, July 30, 1918, HHG Papers (WRC), SLRI. Press coverage of these letters "The War and Votes for Women," *New Republic*, August 10, 1918.
41. HHG to WW, August 16, 1918, WW Papers, LOC; WW to HHG, August 21, 1918, WW Papers, LOC.
42. HHG to Carrie Chapman Catt, August 24, 1918, HHG Papers (WRC), SLRI; HHG thanks Tumulty for flowers, August 24, 1918, WW Papers, LOC.
43. CCC to MWP, September 4, 1918, MWP, CCC folder, LOC; Christine Smith to CCC, September 7, 1918, WW Papers, reel 210, LOC.
44. MWP to Mary Garrett Hay, September 6, 1918, Mary Garrett Hay Series, WRC, SRLI.
45. CCC to WW, September 29, 1918, copy NAWSA reel 21, LOC.
46. WW to CCC, September 30, 1918, NAWSA reel 21, LOC.
47. WW Address to the Senate on the Nineteenth Amendment, September 30, 1918, digital copy at www.presidency.ucsb.edu.
48. Park, *Front Door Lobby*, 212.
49. MWP to Congressional Chairmen, October 5, 1918, NAWSA reel 49.
50. Blanche Ames, "The Congressional Situation," clipping; Non-Partisan Suffrage Committee mass mailing, October 21, 1918, WW Papers, LOC.
51. CCC statement on federal amendment, 1919, NAWSA reel 32.
52. Zahniser and Fry, *Alice Paul*, 309.
53. HHG to WW, November 13, 1918, WW Papers, LOC.
54. WW to HHG, November 18, 1918, WW Papers, LOC.
55. HHG to WW, November 27, 1918, Ray Stannard Baker Papers, Manuscript Division, LOC.
56. HHG to Tumulty, November 26, 1918, WW Papers, LOC.
57. Tumulty to HHG, November 29, 1918, Ray Stannard Baker Papers, LOC; WW to Tumulty, November 27, 1918, WW Papers, LOC.
58. Selden Allen Day Pension File, NARA.
59. HHG to Paul Kester, January 2, 1919, Paul Kester Papers, NYPL.
60. HHG to Commissioner, U.S. Bureau of Pensions, March 24, 1919, Selden Allen Day Pension File, NARA.
61. CCC to MWP, Sunday a.m., November 1918, MWP Papers, CCC folder, LOC.
62. CCC to MWP, no date, handwritten, NAWSA reel 55.
63. CCC to MWP, February 9, 1919, MWP Papers, LOC.
64. CCC to MWP, November 18, 1918, NAWSA reel 15.

65. Tumulty to WW in Paris, January 10, 1919, and again Jan. 23, Tumulty Papers, LOC.

66. WW telegram to JSW, no date [in pencil says January 19?], JSW Papers, Special Correspondence, LOC.

67. Zahniser and Fry, *Alice Paul*, 307–308.

68. HHG to JSW, February 9, 1919, JSW Papers, LOC.

69. HHG to Paul Kester, January 3, 1920, Paul Kester Papers, NYPL.

70. CCC to Mrs. H.W. Stone, January 22, 1918, Borah Papers, LOC.

71. CCC to Borah, January 15, 1918; Borah to CCC, February 23, 1918, Borah Papers, LOC.

72. CCC to MWP, November 1918, MWP Papers, LOC.

73. Roosevelt to Borah, April 26, 1918, Borah Collection, LOC; Stacy A. Cordery, *Alice: Alice Roosevelt Longworth, from White House Princess to Washington Power Broker* (New York: Penguin, 2007).

74. "Thousands and thousands," Borah to S. D. Taylor, May 27, 1918; "Thousands," Borah to Mrs. Turner, February 7, 1918, Borah Papers LOC.

75. Borah to Callaway, December 4, 1917, Borah Papers, LOC.

76. Mrs. J. B. Evans to Borah, December 9, 1917, Borah Papers, LOC.

77. Borah to S. D. Taylor, May 27 and 29, 1918, Borah Papers, LOC; "Senator Borah's Letter," Georgia Association Opposed to Woman Suffrage, NARA RG 46, box 128.

78. Tumulty cablegram to Wilson, April 30, 1919, Tumulty box 49, folder 6, LOC; Tumulty cablegram to Wilson, May 2, 1919, Tumulty box 49, folder 6, LOC.

79. WW to Tumulty, May 13, 1919, Tumulty box 49, folder 7, LOC; Tumulty to WW, in code, May 9, 1919, Tumulty box 49, folder 10, LOC; Cooper, *Wilson*, 499.

80. MWP to CCC, May 11, 1919, copy NAWSA reel 32; Park, *Front Door Lobby*, 242–245.

81. Jeannette Rankin did not run for the House in 1918, so the chamber was again all male.

82. Tumlty to Wilson, May 2, 1919, Tumulty Papers, LOC; Cooper, *Wilson*, 414; MWP to congressional chairmen, May 23, 1919, NAWSA reel 32; Park, *Front Door Lobby*, 244–257.

83. "Women Who Figure in the Day's News," *Pittsburg Press*, May 27, 1919, 1, widely reprinted; MWP scrapbook 1 SLRI.

84. Descriptions and quotes from Park, *Front Door Lobby*, 259–263.

85. "Ratification by 36 States Now Needed," *New York Tribune*, June 5, 1919, 1, 11.

86. "Suffrage Passes Senate 56 to 25, Goes to States," *News Journal* (Wilmington, DE), June 5, 1919, 2.

87. "Ratification by 36 States Now Needed," 1, 11.

88. "Women Who Engineered Suffrage Congress Victory," *Washington Times*, June 5, 1919, 2; "Story of the Signing of the Amendment," *Woman Citizen*,

clipping, Stantial Collection, SLRI; Caroline Reilly to Dear Ladee [Anna Howard Shaw], June 11, 1919, copy MWP Papers, LOC; "victory pen," clippings, *Rochester Herald*, June 8 and *Woman Citizen*, June 14, MWP scrapbook 1, SLRI.

89. HHG, Fifth Vice President and Vice Chairman of Congressional Committee Report, April 13, 1919, HHG Papers (WRC), SLRI.

90. HHG, Fifth Vice President and Vice Chairman of Congressional Committee Report, April 13, 1919.

91. Park, *Front Door Lobby*, 269; see also MWP, Supplementary Notes about Helen Gardener, HHG Papers, WRC, SLRI.

92. MWP, "Remember the Ladies," 78, MWP Papers, box 15, LOC; MWP, notes for more "Rampant Women," 13, NAWSA, reel 37. See also Park eulogy, HHG funeral booklet, 16–17, SLRI; "Four Factors" in Maud Wood Park, "Hasty Summary of Congressional Work written in reply to Mrs. Inez Hayes Irwin's inquiry," copy, NAWSA reel 37, LOC.

93. Alice Paul, Transcript of Oral History with Amelia Fry, 82–83, 132.

16. Our Heroic Dead

1. Party description from Caroline Reilly to Dear Ladee [Anna Howard Shaw], June 11, 1919, MWP Papers, LOC; *Washington Post*, June 8, 1919, 9.

2. CCC to MWP, June 20, 1919, NAWSA reel 15.

3. Theodore Belote to William Holmes, February 9, 1918, accession file 64601, Smithsonian Institution (SI).

4. William Holmes to William Ravenel, June 12, 1919, accession file 64601, SI. Rudolph Forster called Ravenel and sent along a card introducing HHG.

5. Their relationship is described in Trisha Franzen, *Anna Howard Shaw: The Work of Woman Suffrage* (Urbana: University of Illinois Press, 2014).

6. List of items "Received of Mrs. Helen H. Gardener" and delivered to Theodore Belote, History Curator, June 25, 1919, accession 64601, SI.

7. Lucy Anthony to HHG, June 19, 1919, copy, 64601, SI.

8. Described in Rena B. Smith, unpublished biography of HHG, Stantial Collection, SLRI.

9. HHG, "An Important Epoch in American History," *Woman Citizen*, March 13, 1920, 977.

10. HHG to William Ravenel, July 4, 1919, accession file 64601, SI.

11. HHG to Lucy Anthony, cc to William Ravenel, May 5, 1922, accession file 64601, SI.

12. Lisa Tetrault, *The Myth of Seneca Falls: Memory and the Women's Suffrage Movement, 1848–1898* (Chapel Hill: University of North Carolina Press, 2014).

13. HHG to MWP, October 6, 1919, NAWSA reel 8.

14. *HOWS*, vol. 5, 263. See also Ellen Carol DuBois, "Making Women's History: Historian-Activists of Women's Rights, 1880–1940," in Dubois, *Woman Suffrage and Women's Rights* (New York: New York University Press, 1998).

15. HHG to Lucy Anthony, July 21, 1919, Ida Husted Harper Papers, Manuscripts and Archives Division, New York Public Library. Astor, Lenox, and Tilden Foundations (NYPL).

16. HHG to PK, August 19, 1919, Paul Kester Papers, NYPL.

17. For example, HHG to Forster, August 22, 1919, WW Papers, LOC; telegram to Tumulty re: Oklahoma, September 25, 1919, WW Papers, LOC.

18. HHG to "My Dear Little Boss-Lady" [MWP], September 29, 1919, NAWSA reel 8.

19. HHG to Tumulty, October 22, 1919, WW Papers, reel 375.

20. A. Scott Berg, *Wilson* (New York: G. P. Putnam's Sons, 2013), 643–644; John Milton Cooper, Jr., *Woodrow Wilson: A Biography* (New York: Vintage Books, 2011), 537–560; Kristie Miller, *Ellen and Edith: Woodrow Wilson's First Ladies* (Lawrence: University of Kansas Press, 2010), 188–207.

21. HHG to PK, December 18, 1919, Paul Kester Papers, NYPL.

22. Biographical sketch of HHG, dated June 18, 1923, NAWSA reel 36.

23. HHG, "Miss Anthony—A Historical Recognition," *HOWS*, vol. 5, 616; condensed minutes NAWSA Victory Convention + First Congress League of Women Voters, February 12–18, 1920, Chicago, MWP Papers (WRC), SLRI, 30; HHG, "An Important Epoch in American History," *Woman Citizen*, March 13, 1920.

24. Condensed minutes NAWSA Victory Convention + First Congress League of Women Voters, Feb 12–18, 1920, Chicago.

25. Stoner described, *HOWS*, vol. 5, 672–673. Stoner had been lobbying for the position for several months; for example, Edith Owen Stoner to Tumulty, June 30, 1919, WW Papers, LOC.

26. HHG to Mrs. Wilson, March 27, 1922, WW Papers, LOC.

27. HHG twice telegrammed Tumulty, February 16, 1920, WW Papers, LOC.

28. Berg, *Wilson*, 308–313; Eric S. Yellin, *Racism in the Nation's Service: Government Workers and the Color Line in Woodrow Wilson's America* (Chapel Hill: University of North Carolina Press, 2013).

29. HHG to Tumulty, no date [at her six-month anniversary] 1920, WW Papers, LOC.

30. "The Right Woman Honored," *Woman Citizen*, March 27, 1920, 1038.

31. "Names Woman for Civil Service Board," *New York Times*, March 23, 1920, 1; "Women in Government," *Atlanta Constitution*, March 25, 1920, 8; "First Woman Civil Service Commissioner," *Philadelphia Inquirer*, March 24, 1920, 10; Hannah Mitchell, "A Woman Occupies Col. Roosevelt's Seat," *New York Tribune*, August 1, 1920, E7; "Welcome Lady Commissioner," *The Federal Employee* 5, no. 24 (June 1920): 8.

32. HHG to WW, March 21, 1920, WW Papers, LOC.

33. HHG to Paul Kester, March 26, 1920; HHG to PK, April 3, 1920, Paul Kester Papers, NYPL.

34. HHG to Tumulty, March 24, 1920, copied in Rena B. Smith unpublished biography, 58, Stantial Collection, SLRI.

35. HHG to Forster, July 19 and July 30, 1920, WW Papers, LOC; Edith Wilson to HHG, July 21, 1920, HHG Papers, SLRI; Tumulty to HHG, July 22, 1920, HHG Papers, SLRI; HHG to Forster, July 30, 1920, WW reel 161, LOC.

36. Maud Wood Park, *Front Door Lobby*, ed. Edna Lamprey Stantial (Boston: Beacon Press, 1960), 274–275; "What's the Matter with Tennessee," *Woman Citizen*, July 3, 1920, 1; Cooper, *Wilson*, 414 (though he writes that Catt enlisted Wilson's help).

37. Described in unpublished Rena B. Smith biography of HHG, 54, Stantial Collection, SLRI.

38. Elaine Weiss, *The Woman's Hour: The Great Fight to Win the Vote* (New York: Viking, 2018), 320.

39. HHG to Julia Husbands, July 19, 1920, WW Papers, LOC.

40. Described in Park, *Front Door Lobby*, 276–277; Mary Gray Peck, *Carrie Chapman Catt: A Biography* (New York: H. W. Wilson Company, 1944), 340.

41. HHG profile, June 18, 1923, NAWSA reel 36.

42. HHG to PK, April 16, 1920, Paul Kester Papers, NYPL.

43. HHG to MWP, December 6, 1920, Stantial Collection, box 8, folder 27, SLRI; HHG to Paul Kester, September 2, 1922, Paul Kester Papers, NYPL; Lucille Foster McMillin, *Women in the Federal Service* (Washington, DC: U.S. Civil Service Commission, 1941), 36, copy, HHG Papers (WRC), SLRI.

44. HHG to "My very dearest boss-lady" [MWP], January 19, 1924, Stantial Collection, box 8, folder 27, SLRI.

45. "Women Produce Play; Will Build Capital Theater," *Chicago Tribune*, November 8, 1920, 3. HHG references "Lincoln" in letters to Paul Kester.

46. "Mrs. Gardener Is First Vote League Member," *Washington Times*, May 25, 1921, 13.

47. Address of Helen H. Gardener, "Women in Government Work," before State Federation of Women's Clubs, Raleigh, NC, May 8, 1924, NAWSA box 54, LOC.

48. HHG to Spitzka, February 6, 1909, SLRI.

49. Civil Service Commission, Minutes of Proceedings, 1920–1925, Record Group 146, 3.1, NARA.

50. MWP, Supplementary Notes about HHG, 9, HHG Papers (WRC), SLRI.

51. Significance to HHG described in Rena B. Smith unpublished biography, 72; text of Act, "Proceedings of 67th Congress," March 4, 1923, chapter 265, 1488.

52. "Welcome Lady Commissioner," *Federal Employee*, 22.

53. HHG, "What is the real reason?" NAWSA reel 36; "Woman Commissioner Won Postal Service Rights for Sex," *Durham* (NC) *Morning Herald*,

December 31, 1921, 5; "Square Deal for Fair Sex,"*Nevada State Journal*, January 4, 1922, 4; Rena B. Smith, unpublished bio of HHG, 74–78.

54. Martin Morrison and G. R. Wales to Tumulty, October 13, 1920, NAWSA reel 8; Tumulty sent HHG a copy, HHG Papers (WRC), SLRI; HHG to Tumulty [six-month anniversary], WW Papers, LOC.

55. HHG to WW, April 13, 1923, WW Papers, LOC.

56. Edith Moriarty, "Mrs. Gardener Typifies Women Who Will Hold Political Office," *Sandusky Star-Journal*, December 11, 1920, 8.

57. HHG to Tumulty, December 3 1921, copy Edith Wilson Papers, box 18, LOC.

58. Joseph P. Tumulty, *Woodrow Wilson as I Knew Him* (New York: Doubleday, Page, and Company, 1924).

59. HHG to Ray Stannard Baker, June 11, 1925, NAWSA reel 8.

60. Historians have mainly focused on Wilson's disdain for the NWP and his interactions with Paul. The notable exceptions include: David Morgan, *Suffragists and Democrats: The Politics of Woman Suffrage in America* (E. Lansing: Michigan State University Press, 1972); Christine A. Lunardini and Thomas J. Knock, "Woodrow Wilson and Woman Suffrage: A New Look," *Political Science Quarterly* 95 (Winter 1981): 655–671; Victoria Bissell Brown, "Did Wilson's Gender Politics Matter?" in *Reconsidering Woodrow Wilson: Progressivism, Internationalism, War and Peace*, ed. John Milton Cooper, Jr. (Washington, DC: Woodrow Wilson Center Press, 2008), 125–164. The two most recent biographies of Wilson by Berg and Cooper devote a few pages each to suffrage.

61. Sandra Weber, *The Woman Suffrage Statue: A History of Adelaide Johnson's Portrait Monument at the United States Capitol* (Jefferson, NC: McFarland and Company, 2016).

62. HHG, "Our Heroic Dead," copy in Stantial Collection, 5.15, SLRI; "Looking Backward," *Woman Citizen*, April 19, 1925, 1.

63. HHG to Minnie Fisher Cunningham, July 7, 1925, HHG Papers (WRC), SLRI. She favored Minnie Fisher Cunningham, a NAWSA leader from Texas, but it went to Jessie Dell, an NWP member and War Department employee.

64. Catt remarks, HHG funeral booklet, HHG Papers, SLRI.

65. Quoted in Mary Gray Peck, *Carrie Chapman Catt*, 418.

66. HHG probate record, no. 33, 551, District of Columbia, copy on ancestry.com; HHG will, HHG Papers, SLRI.

67. They are in lots 97 and 98, National Anthropological Archives, Smithsonian Institution. See also Jorge Duany, "Portraying the Other: Puerto Rican Images in Two American Photographic Collections," *Discourse* 23, no. 1 (Winter 2001): 119–153.

68. HHG 1925 will, p. 4, SLRI.

69. Helen Hamilton Gardener, Last Will and Testament, also reprinted in a funeral booklet, 27–28, HHG Collection, SLRI. For another analysis of

Gardener's brain donation, see Kathi Kern "Gray Matters: Brains, Identi-
ties, and Natural Rights," in *The Social and Political Body*, ed. Theodore
R. Schatzki and Wolfgang Natter (New York: The Guilford Press, 1996):
103–122.

70. HHG to Livingston Farrand, February 20, 1923, Farrand Papers, Division
of Rare and Manuscript Collections, Cornell University Library. She had
wanted Edward A. Spitzka or Burt Wilder to remove her brain (1919 will),
but both predeceased her, so the job went to Dr. Robert Young Sullivan.

71. "Woman Wills Brain for Research Work," *New York Times*, August 4, 1925,
1; "Says Brain Bequest Has Been Fulfilled," *New York Times*, August 5, 1925,
3; "Woman's Brain Not Inferior to Men's," *New York Times*, September 29,
1927, 1.

72. James W. Papez, "The Brain of Helen H. Gardener (Alice Chenoweth
Day)," *American Journal of Physical Anthropology* 11 (October 1927): 48.

73. "Woman's Brain Not Inferior to Men's," 1.

74. For counterstudies, see, Rebecca M. Jordan-Young, *Brain Storm: The Flaws
in the Science of Sex Differences* (Cambridge, MA: Harvard University
Press, 2011); Cordelia Fine, *Delusions of Gender: How Our Minds, Society,
and Neurosexism Create Difference* (New York: W. W. Norton, 2011); Anne
Fausto-Sterling, *Myths of Gender: Biological Theories about Women and
Men* (New York: Basic Books, 1985).

75. Maud Wood Park, notes for more "Rampant Women," 13, NAWSA reel
37. Mabel Willard to Edna Stantial regarding Park's interest in Gardener's
legacy, March 1, 1930, HHG papers (WRC), SLRI. Also see various letters
between Rena B. Smith, Maud Wood Park, and Edna Stantial in the 1940s
about the completion of HHG biography, MWP Papers, box 5, LOC. Smith
wrote a complete draft and sent it to Mary Dillon, who apparently lost much
of it. What remains is now in the Edna Lamprey Stantial Collection, SLRI.

Illustration Credits

180 Gardener with Chief Iron Tail, Dr. Leonce Pierre Manouvrier, and others at "Buffalo Bill" Cody's Wild West Show, Paris, 1905. Helen H. Gardener Papers, 1902–1909. A/G218b Schlesinger Library, Radcliffe Institute, Harvard University.

185 Gardener at Joan of Arc statue, Paris, ca. 1906. National Anthropological Archives, Smithsonian Institution, lot 98, F 10.

187 Gardener with parasol, ca. 1907. Schlesinger Library, Radcliffe Institute, Harvard University.

197 Gardener with Alice Paul at NAWSA parade headquarters, 1913. Library of Congress, 90317.

200 Gardener, Alice Paul, and NAWSA parade volunteers at the 1420 F Street headquarters, 1913. National Woman's Party Collection, Belmont-Paul Women's Equality National Monument, Washington, D.C., image number 1921.001.002.1.

205 Crowd at the March 1913 suffrage parade. National Woman's Party Papers, Box 1, 159, Manuscript Division, Library of Congress, Washington, D.C.

231 Interior of NAWSA "Suffrage House," 1626 Rhode Island Avenue NW, Washington, D.C. *History of Woman Suffrage*, Vol. 5.

247 Helen Hamilton Gardener, circa 1919, National American Woman Suffrage Collection, Manuscripts Division, Library of Congress.

261 Gardener with NAWSA officers after meeting with President Wilson, June 1918. National Archives, photo no. 165-WW-600A-3.

263 Gardener and Carrie Chapman Catt leaving the White House, ca. 1920. National Photo Company Collection, Library of Congress, LC-DIG-npcc 02194.

265 Inscribed copy of Carrie Chapman Catt's speech, from Gardener to President Wilson. Woodrow Wilson Papers, Manuscript Division, Library of Congress, Washington, D.C.

271 "The Woman Voter and the Next President of the United States," *Woman Citizen*, March 22, 1919. Courtesy of Persuasive Maps: PJ Mode Collection, Cornell University Library.

276 Gardener (center), NAWSA Congressional Committee members, and congressmen as House Speaker Frederick Gillette signs the Nineteenth Amendment. Library of Congress, 69916.

277 Gardener (right) with Maud Wood Park (left) as Vice President Thomas Marshall signs the Nineteenth Amendment. Schlesinger Library, Radcliffe Institute, Harvard University.

281 Gardener, Carrie Chapman Catt, and Maud Wood Park at Suffrage House, ca. 1919. *History of Woman Suffrage*, vol. 5.

289 Gardener being sworn in as U.S. Civil Service Commissioner, April 13, 1920. Schlesinger Library, Radcliffe Institute, Harvard University.

Index

Note: Page numbers in *italics* indicate figures.